Akira Segami

TRANSLATED BY
Satsuki Yamashita

ADAPTED BY
Nunzio deFilippis & Christina Weir

LETTERING AND RETOUCH BY
North Market Street Graphics

BALLANTINE BOOKS · NEW YORK

Kagetora, volume 9 is a work of fiction. Names, characters, places, and incidents are the products of the author's imagination or are used fictitiously. Any resemblance to actual events, locales, or persons, living or dead, is entirely coincidental.

A Del Rey Manga/Kodansha Trade Paperback Original

Published in the United States by Del Rey Books, an imprint of The Random House Publishing Group, a division of Random House, Inc., New York.

Del Rey is a registered trademark and the Del Rey colophon is a trademark of Random House, Inc.

Publication rights arranged through Kodansha Ltd.

First published in Japan in 2006 by Kodansha Ltd., Tokyo

ISBN 978-0-345-49771-0

Printed in the United States of America

www.delreymanga.com

9 8 7 6 5 4 3 2

Translator—Satsuki Yamashita
Adapters—Nunzio deFillipis and Christina Weir
Lettering and retouch—North Market Street Graphics

Contents

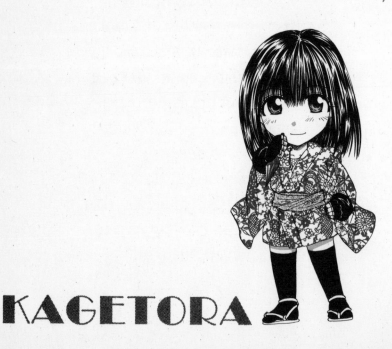

KAGETORA

A Note from the Author

Quick as Lightning
A certain teacher at a ninja
dojo also works at a company.
He says it's because "just being
a ninja in the modern era
is probably not a good idea."
I see.
A businessman but also a ninja.
A manga artist but also a ninja.
...That's an exciting phrase,
isn't it? (laugh)

Segami

Honorifics Explained

Throughout the Del Rey Manga books, you will find Japanese honorifics left intact in the translations. For those not familiar with how the Japanese use honorifics and, more important, how they differ from American honorifics, we present this brief overview.

Politeness has always been a critical facet of Japanese culture. Ever since the feudal era, when Japan was a highly stratified society, use of honorifics—which can be defined as polite speech that indicates relationship or status—has played an essential role in the Japanese language. When addressing someone in Japanese, an honorific usually takes the form of a suffix attached to one's name (example: "Asuna-san"), is used as a title at the end of one's name, or appears in place of the name itself (example: "Negi-sensei," or simply "Sensei!").

Honorifics can be expressions of respect or endearment. In the context of manga and anime, honorifics give insight into the nature of the relationship between characters. Many English translations leave out these important honorifics and therefore distort the feel of the original Japanese. Because Japanese honorifics contain nuances that English honorifics lack, it is our policy at Del Rey not to translate them. Here, instead, is a guide to some of the honorifics you may encounter in Del Rey Manga.

-san: This is the most common honorific and is equivalent to Mr., Miss, Ms., or Mrs. It is the all-purpose honorific and can be used in any situation where politeness is required.

-sama: This is one level higher than "-san" and is used to confer great respect.

-dono: This comes from the word "tono," which means "lord." It is an even higher level than "-sama" and confers utmost respect.

-kun: This suffix is used at the end of boys' names to express familiarity or endearment. It is also sometimes used by men among friends, or when addressing someone younger or of a lower station.

-chan: This is used to express endearment, mostly toward girls. It is also used for little boys, pets, and even among lovers. It gives a sense of childish cuteness.

Bozu: This is an informal way to refer to a boy, similar to the English terms "kid" and "squirt."

Sempai/
Senpai: This title suggests that the addressee is one's senior in a group or organization. It is most often used in a school setting, where underclassmen refer to their upperclassmen as "sempai." It can also be used in the workplace, such as when a newer employee addresses an employee who has seniority in the company.

Kohai: This is the opposite of "sempai" and is used toward underclassmen in school or newcomers in the workplace. It connotes that the addressee is of a lower station.

Sensei: Literally meaning "one who has come before," this title is used for teachers, doctors, or masters of any profession or art.

[blank]: This is usually forgotten in these lists, but it is perhaps the most significant difference between Japanese and English. The lack of honorific means that the speaker has permission to address the person in a very intimate way. Usually, only family, spouses, or very close friends have this kind of permission. Known as *yobisute,* it can be gratifying when someone who has earned the intimacy starts to call one by one's name without an honorific. But when that intimacy hasn't been earned, it can be very insulting.

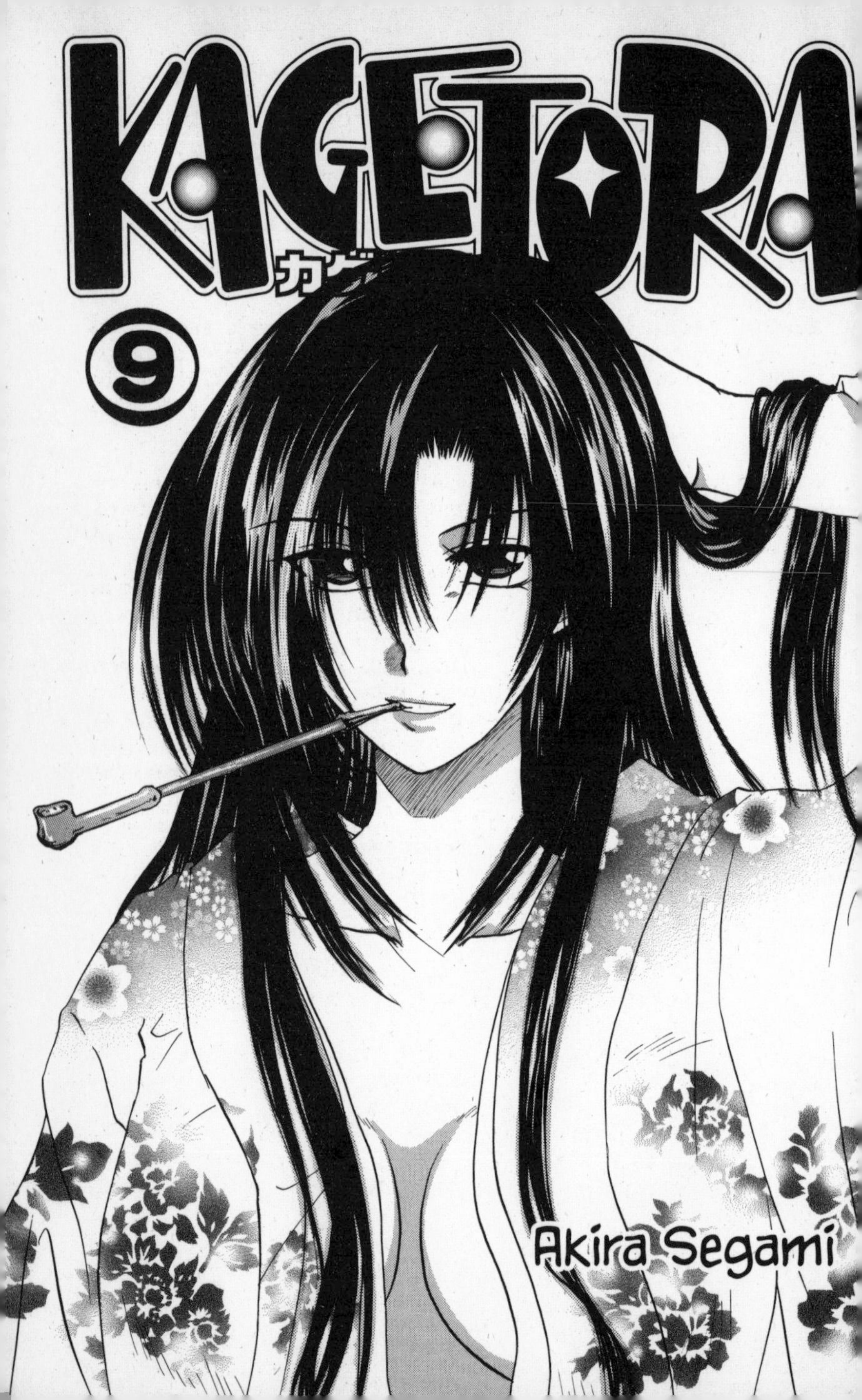
KAGETORA
9
Akira Segami

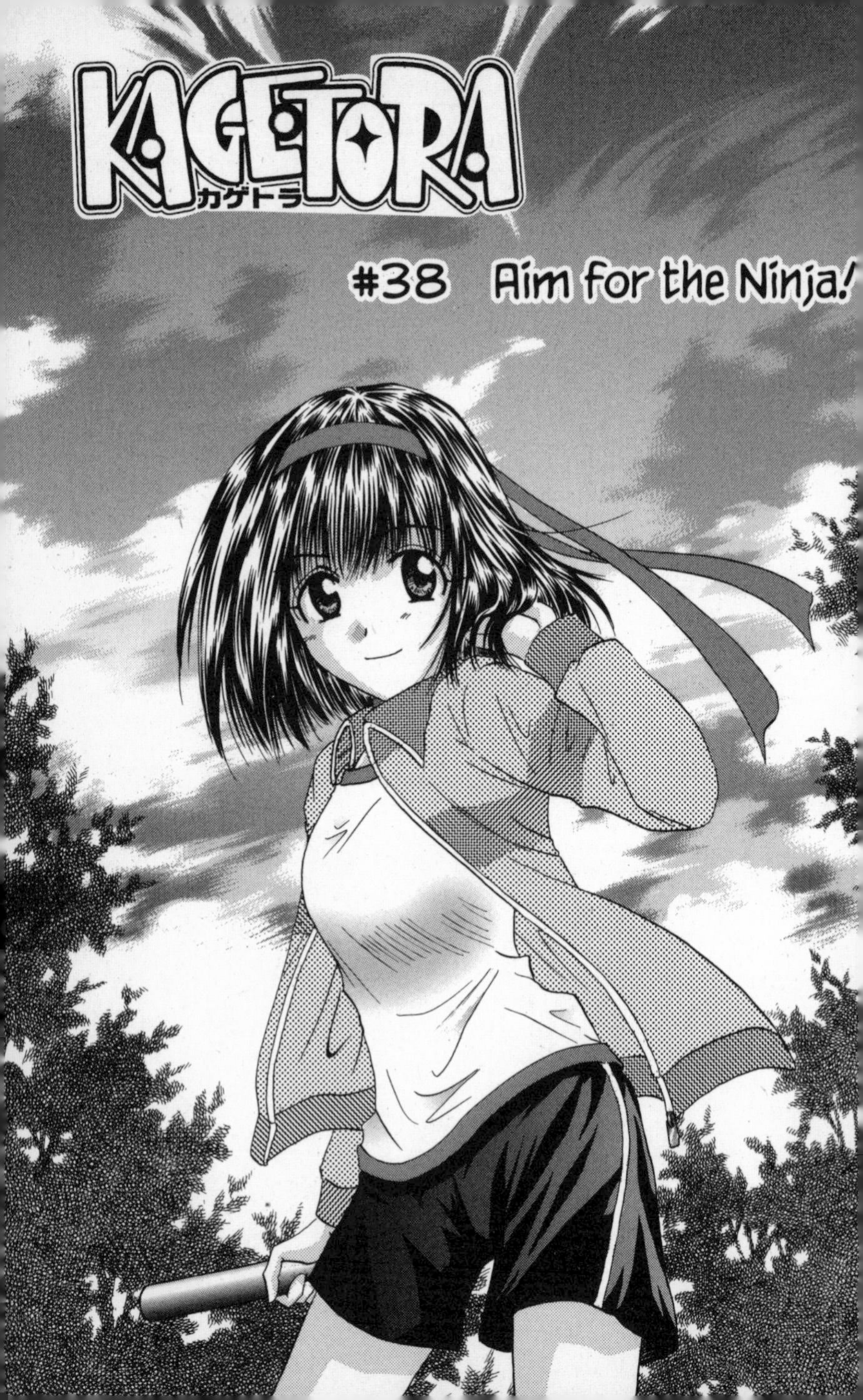
KAGETORA
カゲトラ
#38 Aim for the Ninja!

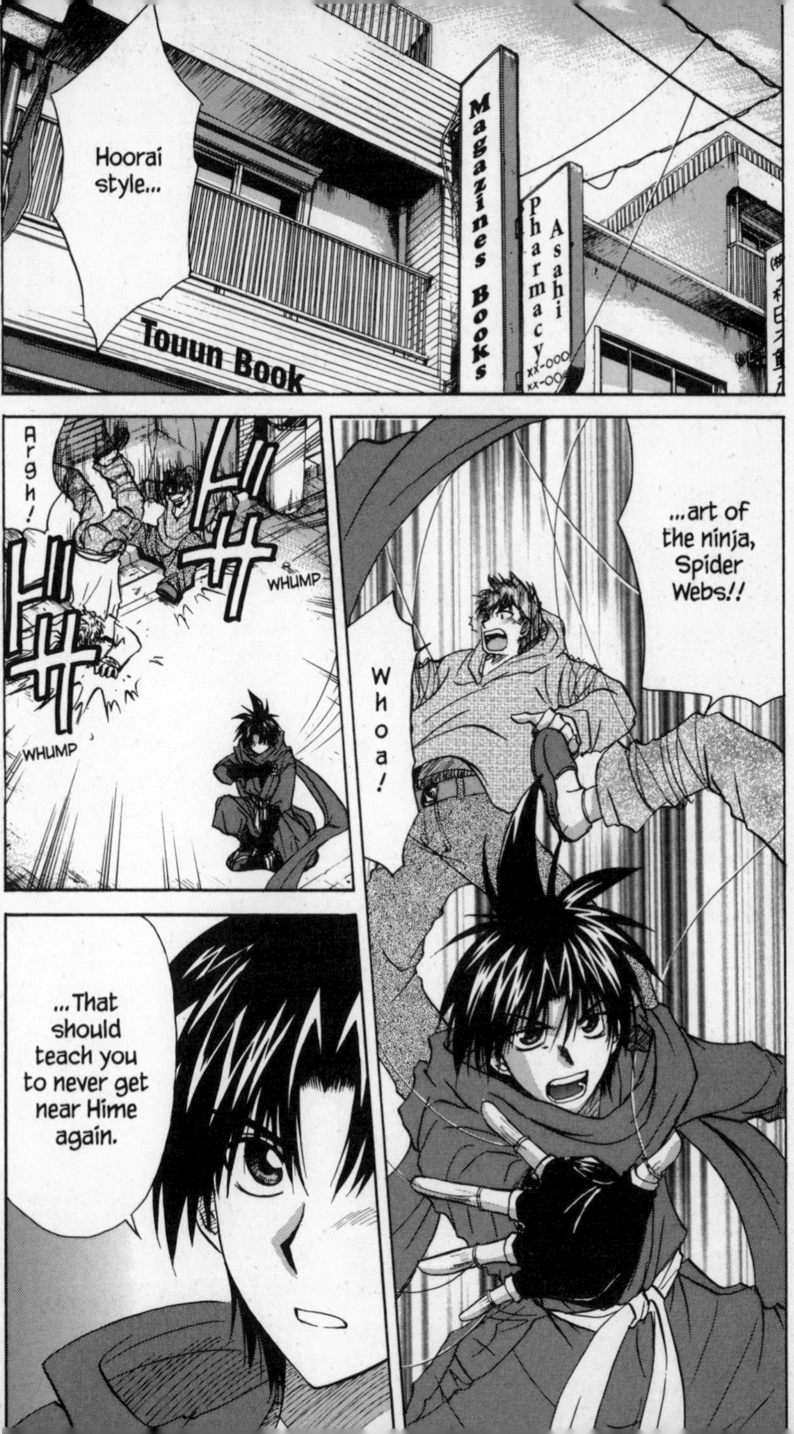
Hoorai style...
Touun Book
Magazines Books
Asahi Pharmacy
...art of the ninja, Spider Webs!!
Whoa!
Argh!
WHUMP
WHUMP
...That should teach you to never get near Hime again.

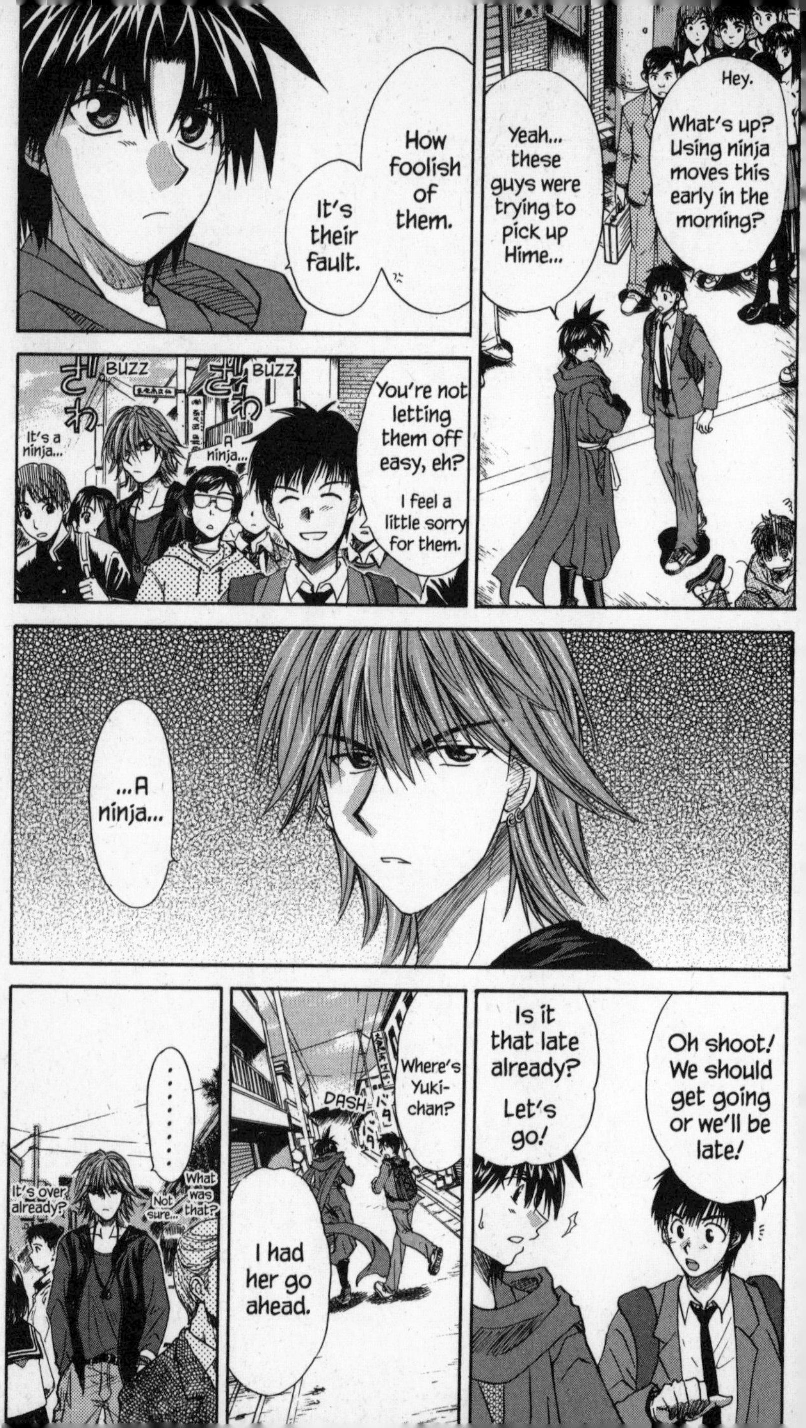
Hey.
What's up? Using ninja moves this early in the morning?
Yeah... these guys were trying to pick up Hime...
How foolish of them.
It's their fault.
You're not letting them off easy, eh?
I feel a little sorry for them.
BUZZ
BUZZ
A ninja...
It's a ninja...
...A ninja...
Oh shoot! We should get going or we'll be late!
Is it that late already?
Let's go!
Where's Yuki-chan?
DASH
I had her go ahead.
......
What was that?
Not sure...
It's over already?

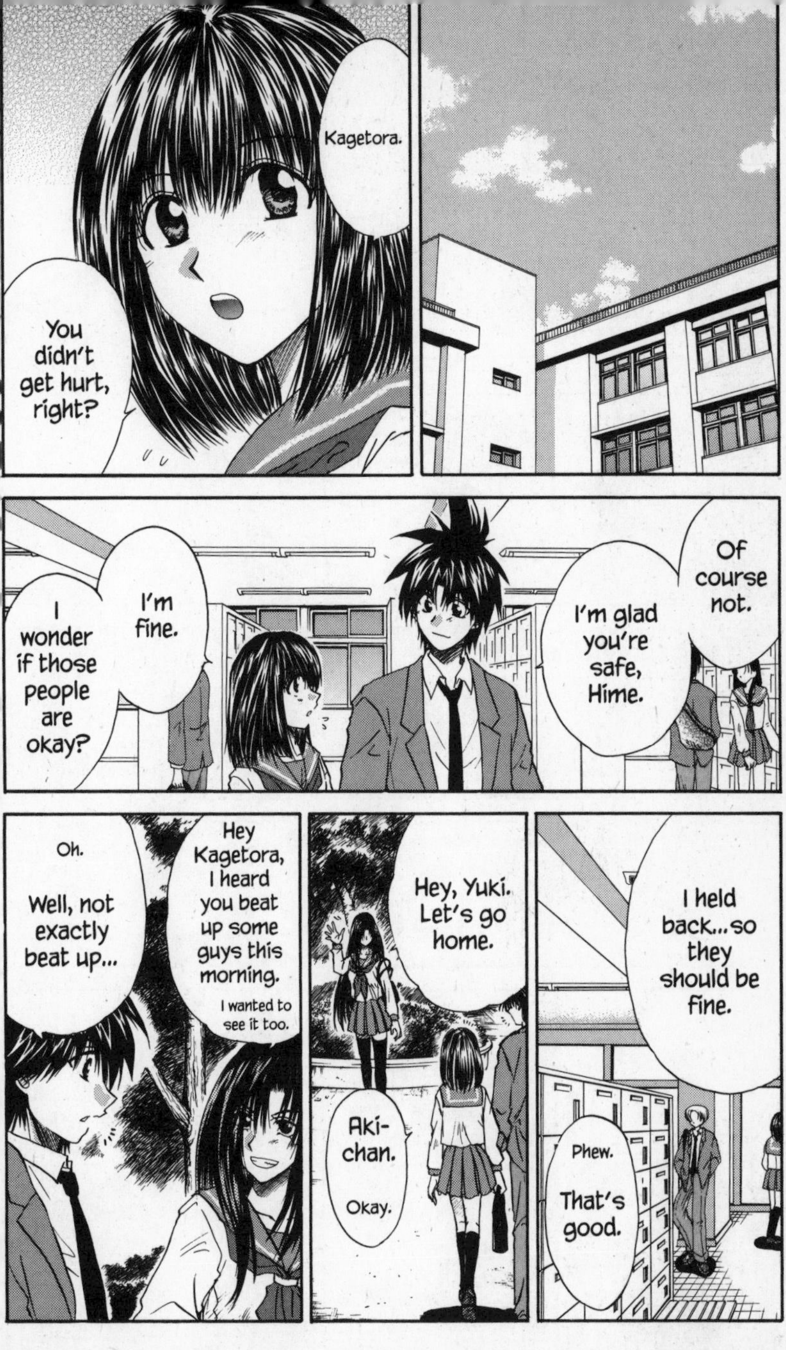
Kagetora.
You didn't get hurt, right?
Of course not.
I'm glad you're safe, Hime.
I'm fine.
I wonder if those people are okay?
I held back...so they should be fine.
Phew.
That's good.
Hey, Yuki. Let's go home.
Aki-chan.
Okay.
Hey Kagetora, I heard you beat up some guys this morning.
I wanted to see it too.
Oh.
Well, not exactly beat up...

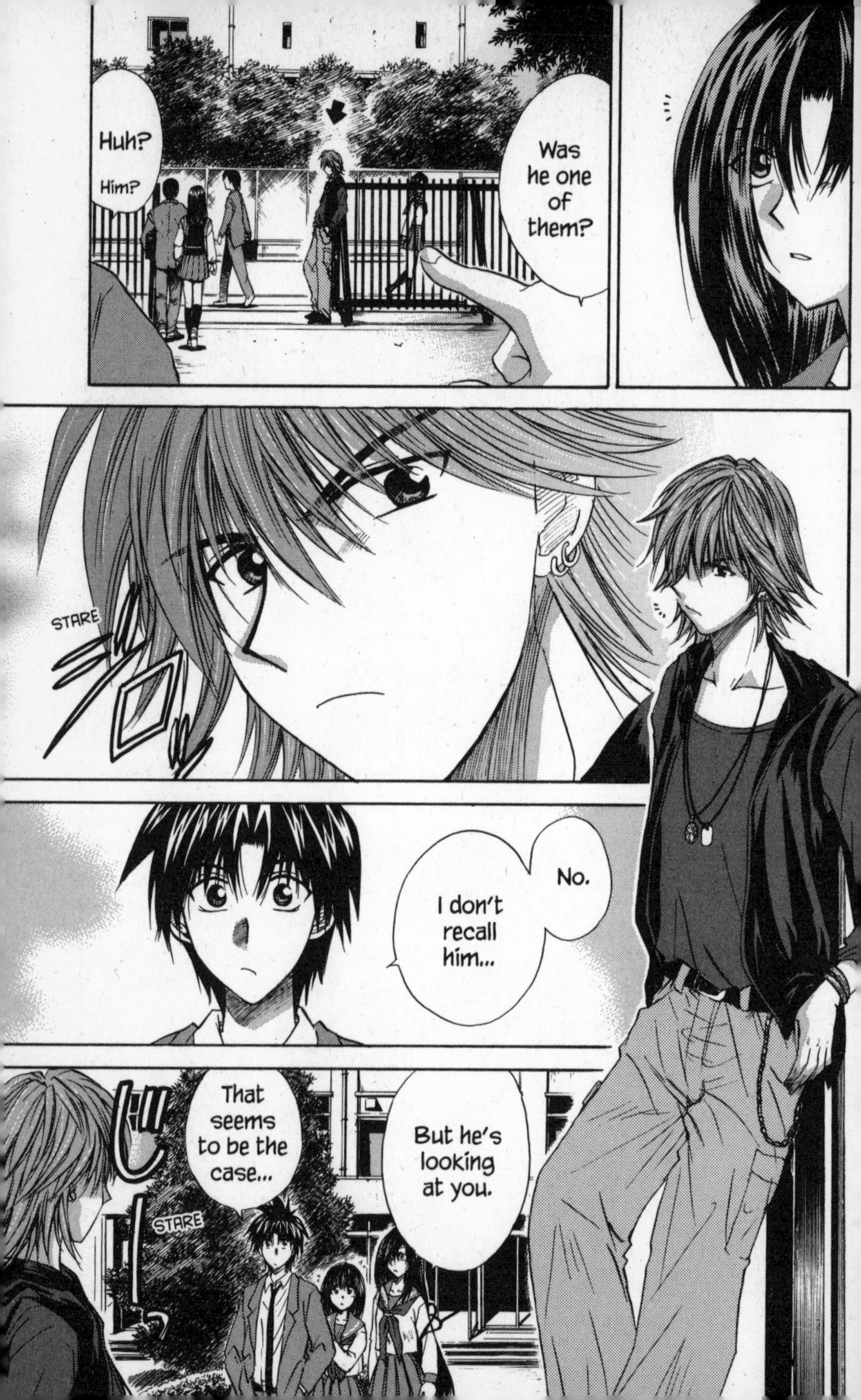

Was he one of them?
Huh?
Him?
STARE
No.
I don't recall him...
But he's looking at you.
That seems to be the case...
STARE

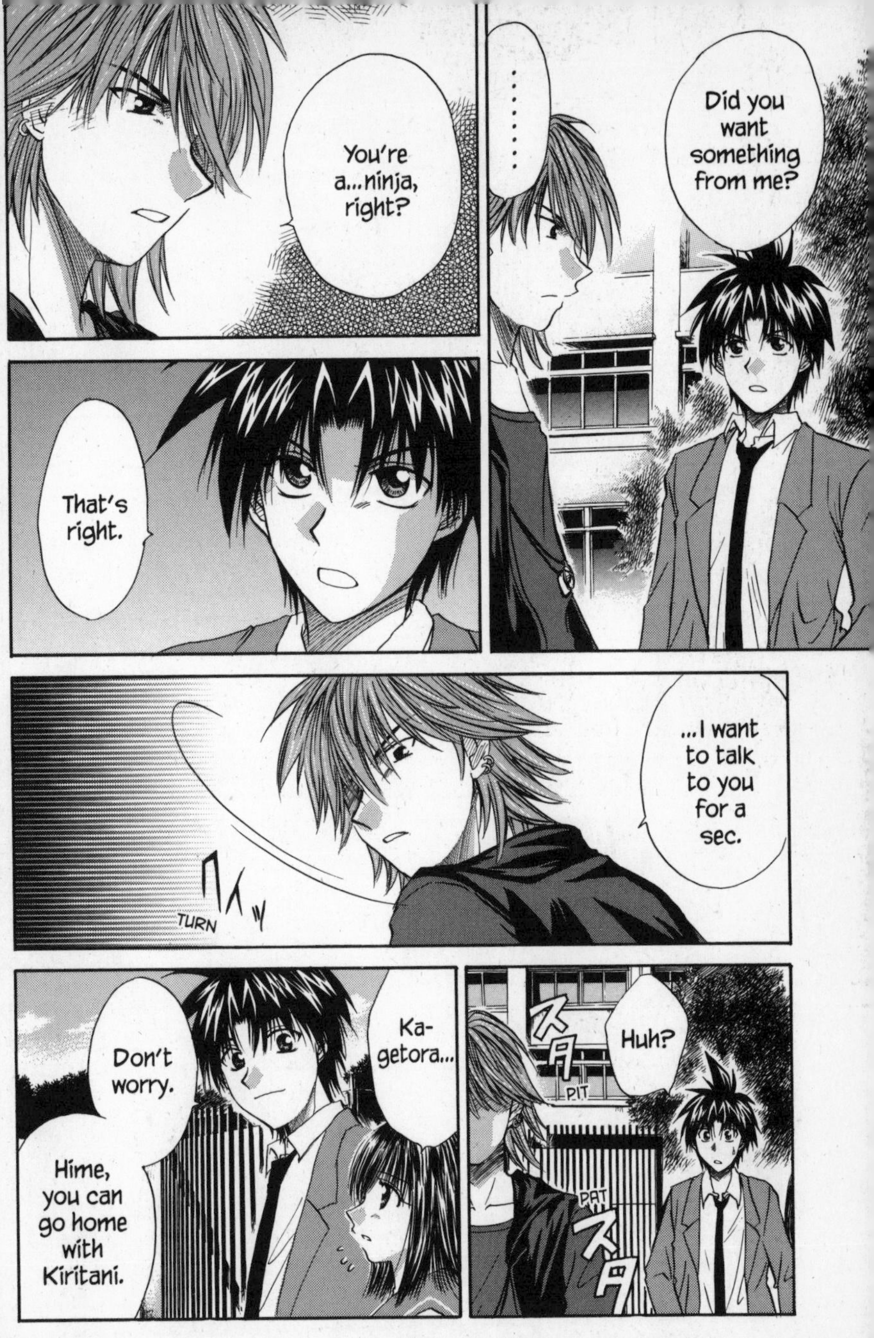
Did you want something from me?
......
You're a...ninja, right?
That's right.
...I want to talk to you for a sec.
TURN
Huh?
PIT
PAT
Ka-getora...
Don't worry.
Hime, you can go home with Kiritani.

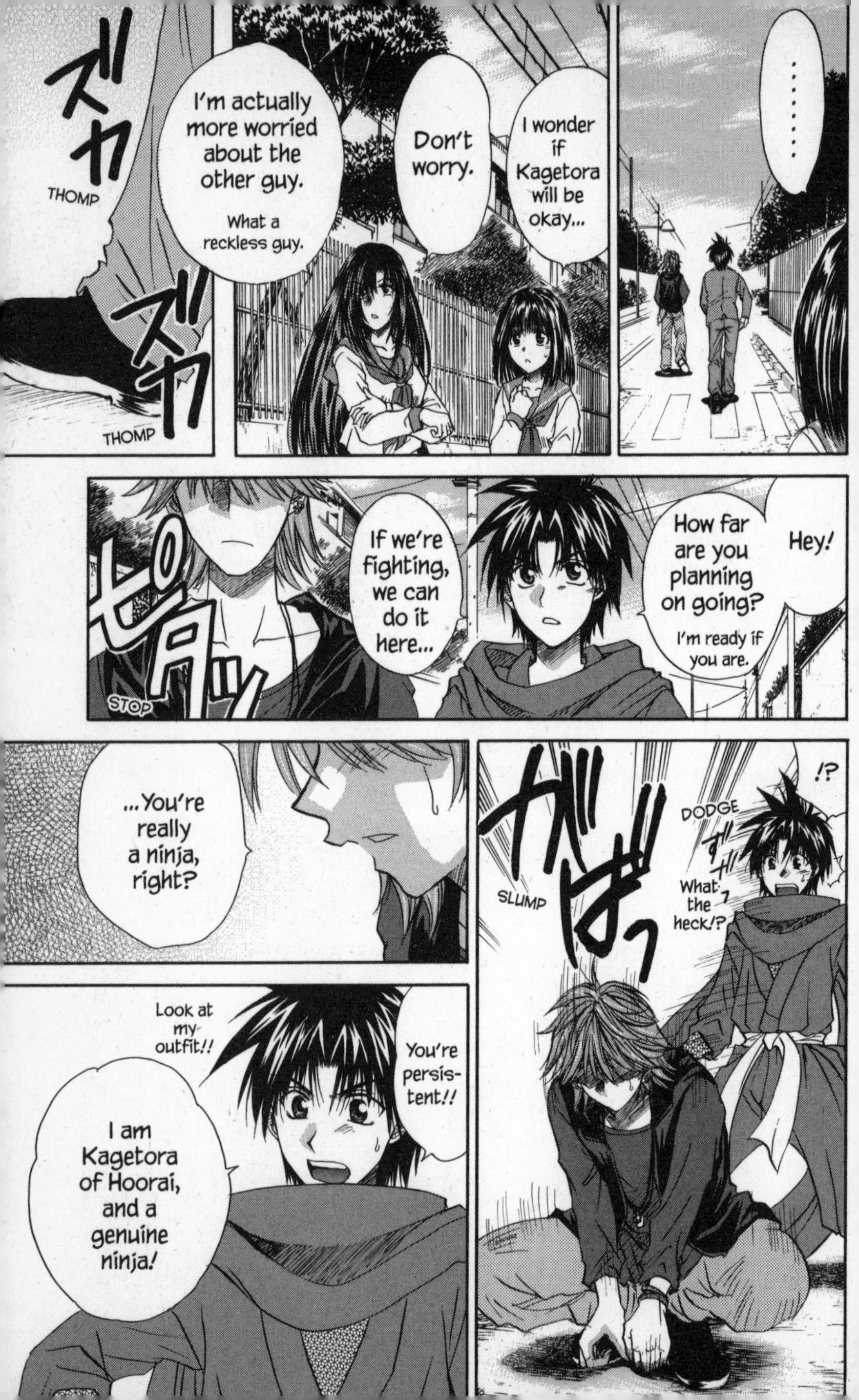
......
I wonder if Kagetora will be okay...
Don't worry.
I'm actually more worried about the other guy.
What a reckless guy.
THOMP
THOMP
Hey!
How far are you planning on going?
I'm ready if you are.
If we're fighting, we can do it here...
STOP
!?
DODGE
What the heck!?
SLUMP
...You're really a ninja, right?
You're persis-tent!!
Look at my outfit!!
I am Kagetora of Hoorai, and a genuine ninja!

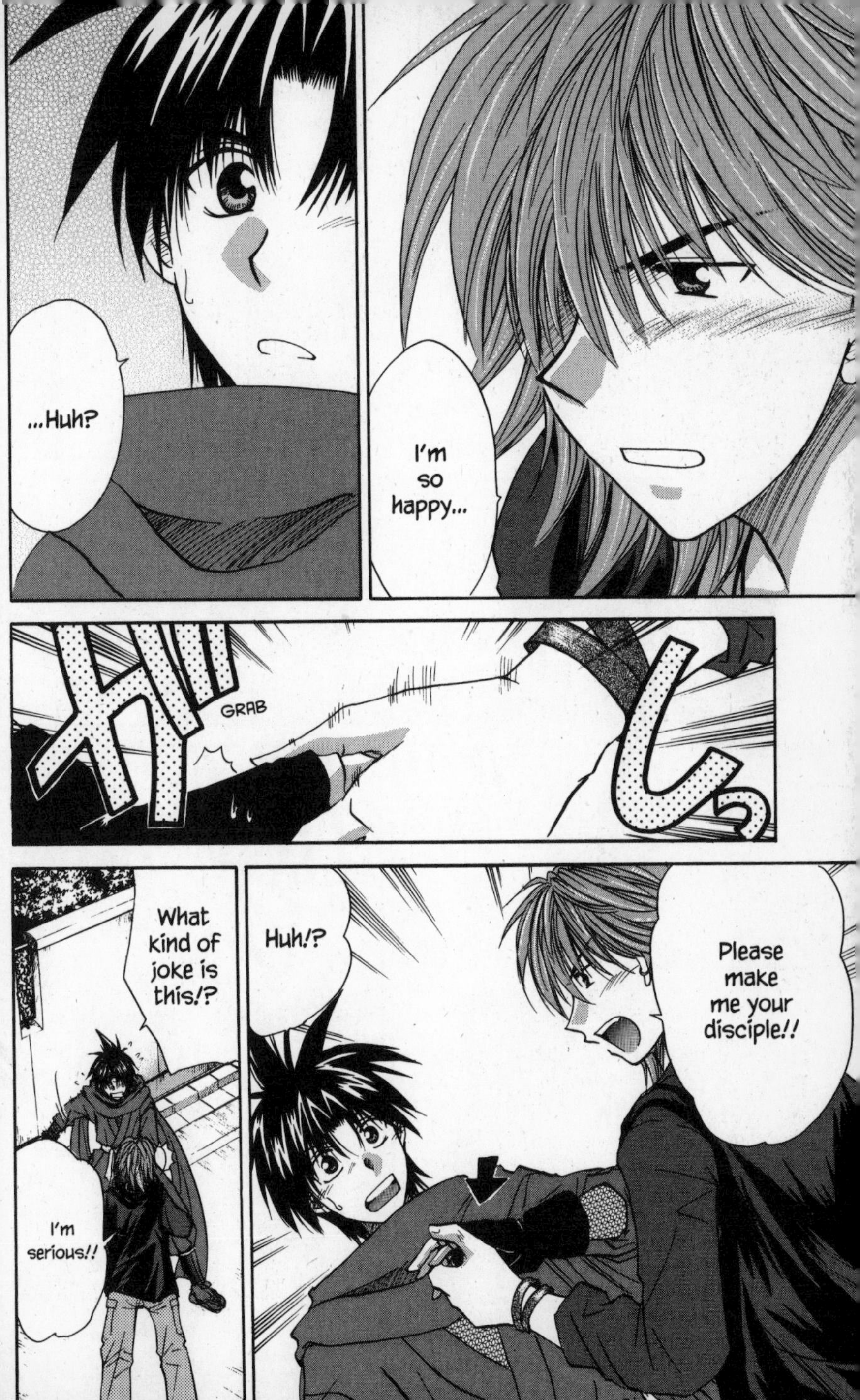
I'm so happy...
...Huh?
GRAB
Please make me your disciple!!
Huh!?
What kind of joke is this!?
I'm serious!!

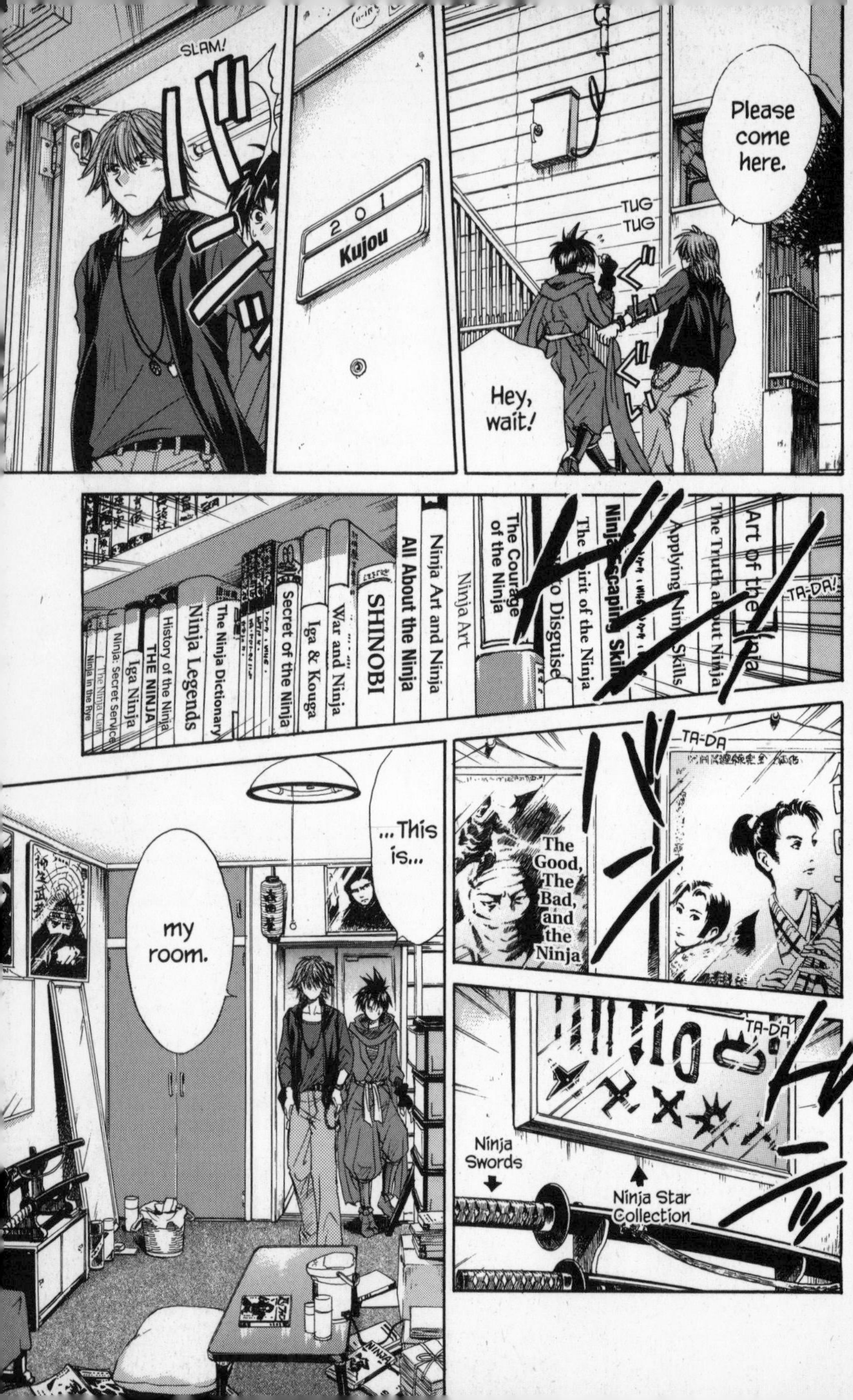
Please come here.
TUG TUG
Hey, wait!
201
Kujou
SLAM!
TA-DA!
Art of the Ninja
The Truth about Ninja
Applying Ninja Skills
The Spirit of the Ninja
The Courage of the Ninja
Ninja Art
Ninja Art and Ninja
All About the Ninja
SHINOBI
War and Ninja
Iga & Kouga
Secret of the Ninja
The Ninja Dictionary
Ninja Legends
History of the Ninja
THE NINJA
Iga Ninja
Ninja: Secret Service
The Ninja Clan
Ninja in the Rye
TA-DA
The Good, The Bad, and the Ninja
TA-DA
Ninja Swords
Ninja Star Collection
...This is...
my room.

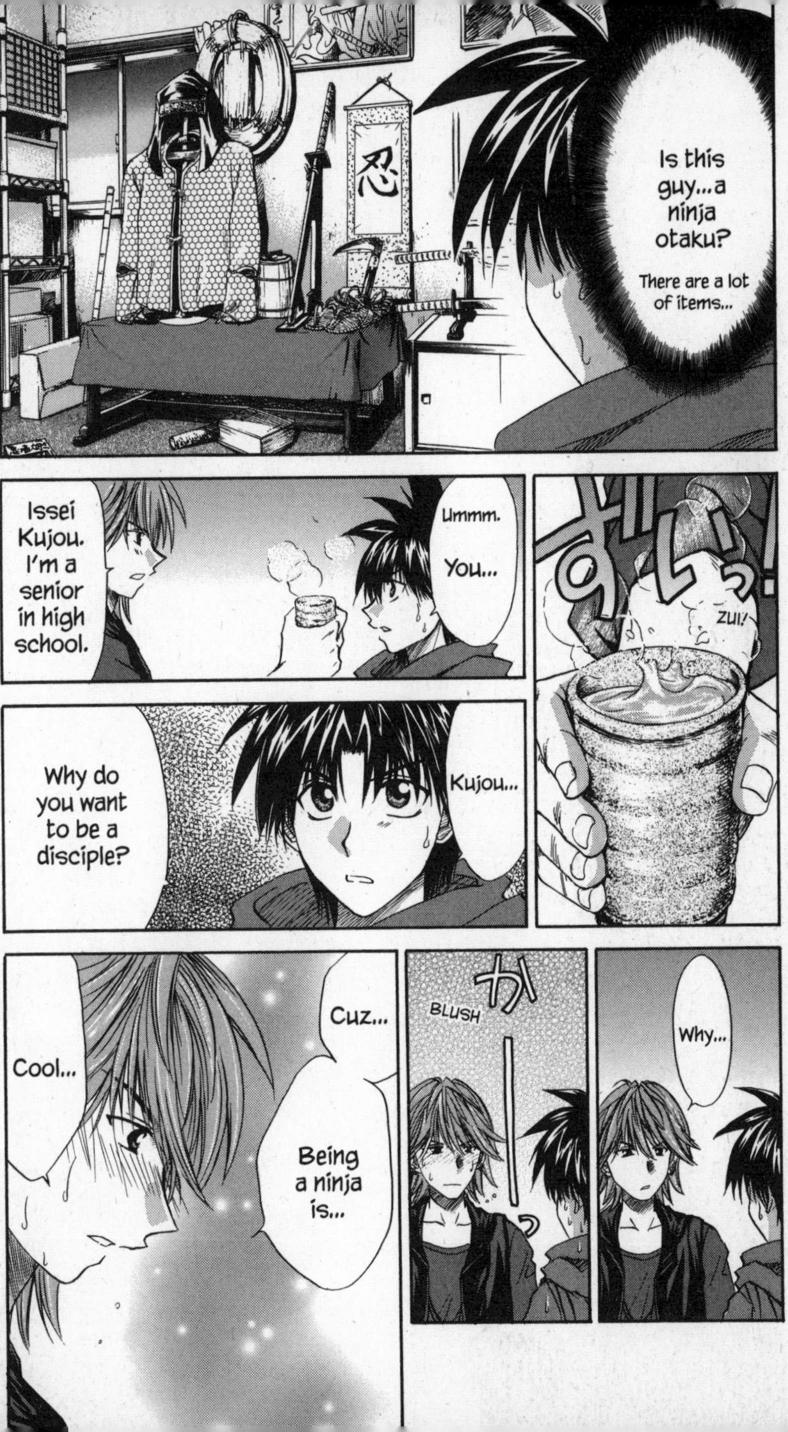
Is this guy...a ninja otaku?
There are a lot of items...
ずいっ!
ZUI!
Ummm.
You...
Issei Kujou. I'm a senior in high school.
Kujou...
Why do you want to be a disciple?
Why...
か
BLUSH
Cuz...
Being a ninja is...
Cool...

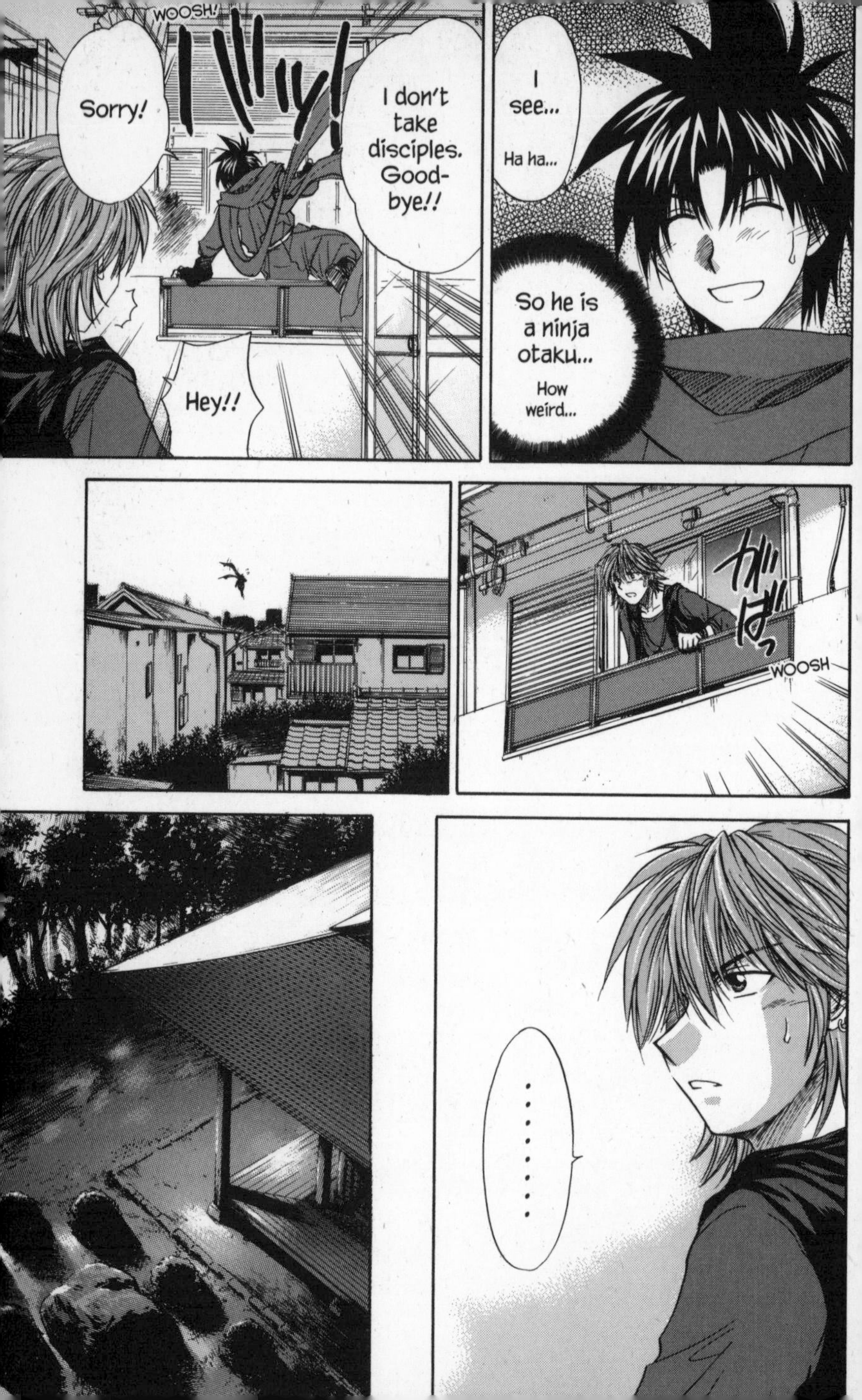
I see...
Ha ha...
So he is a ninja otaku...
How weird...
WOOSH!
I don't take disciples. Good-bye!!
Sorry!
Hey!!
WOOSH
......

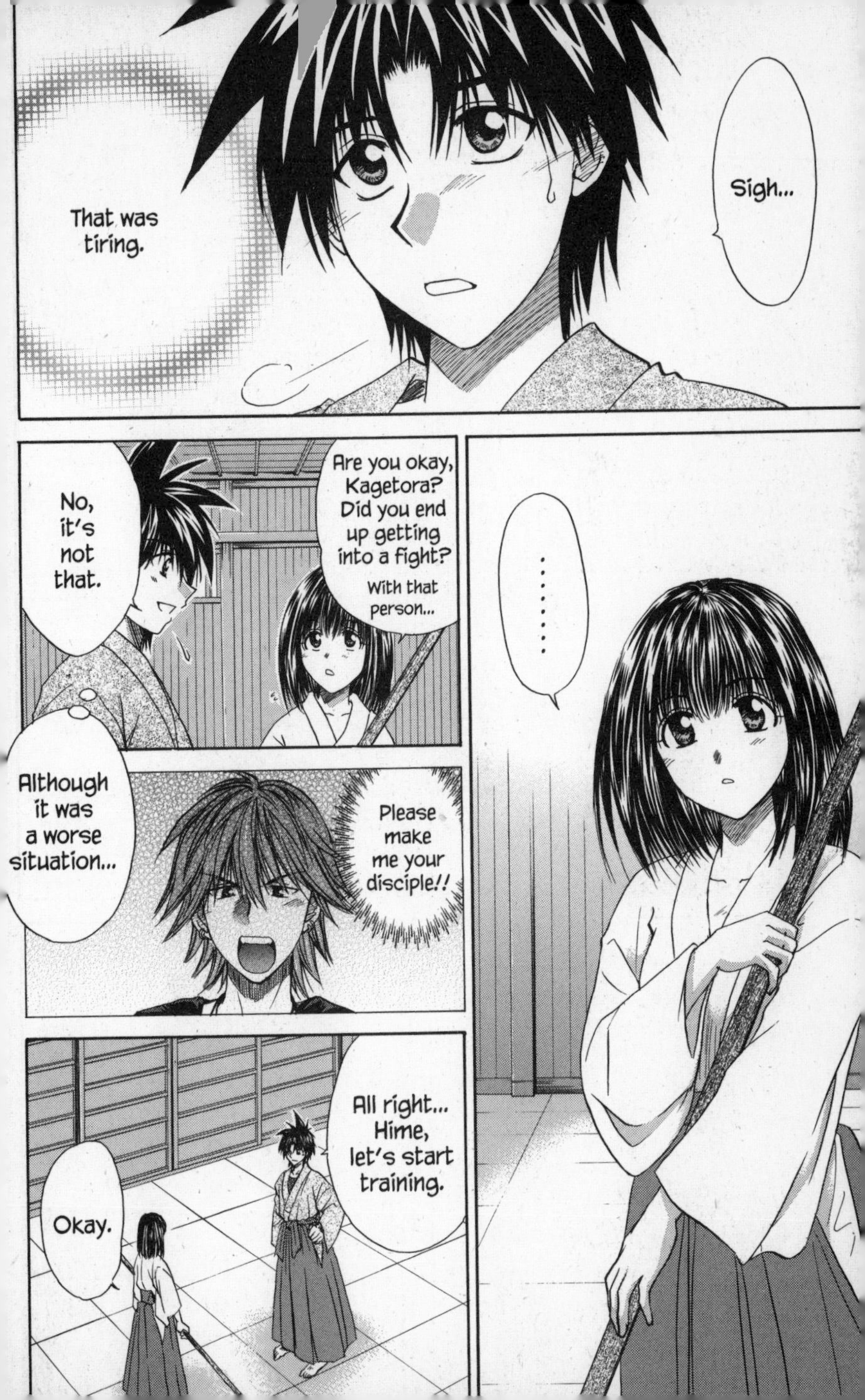
Sigh...
That was tiring.
......
Are you okay, Kagetora? Did you end up getting into a fight? With that person...
No, it's not that.
Although it was a worse situation...
Please make me your disciple!!
All right... Hime, let's start training.
Okay.

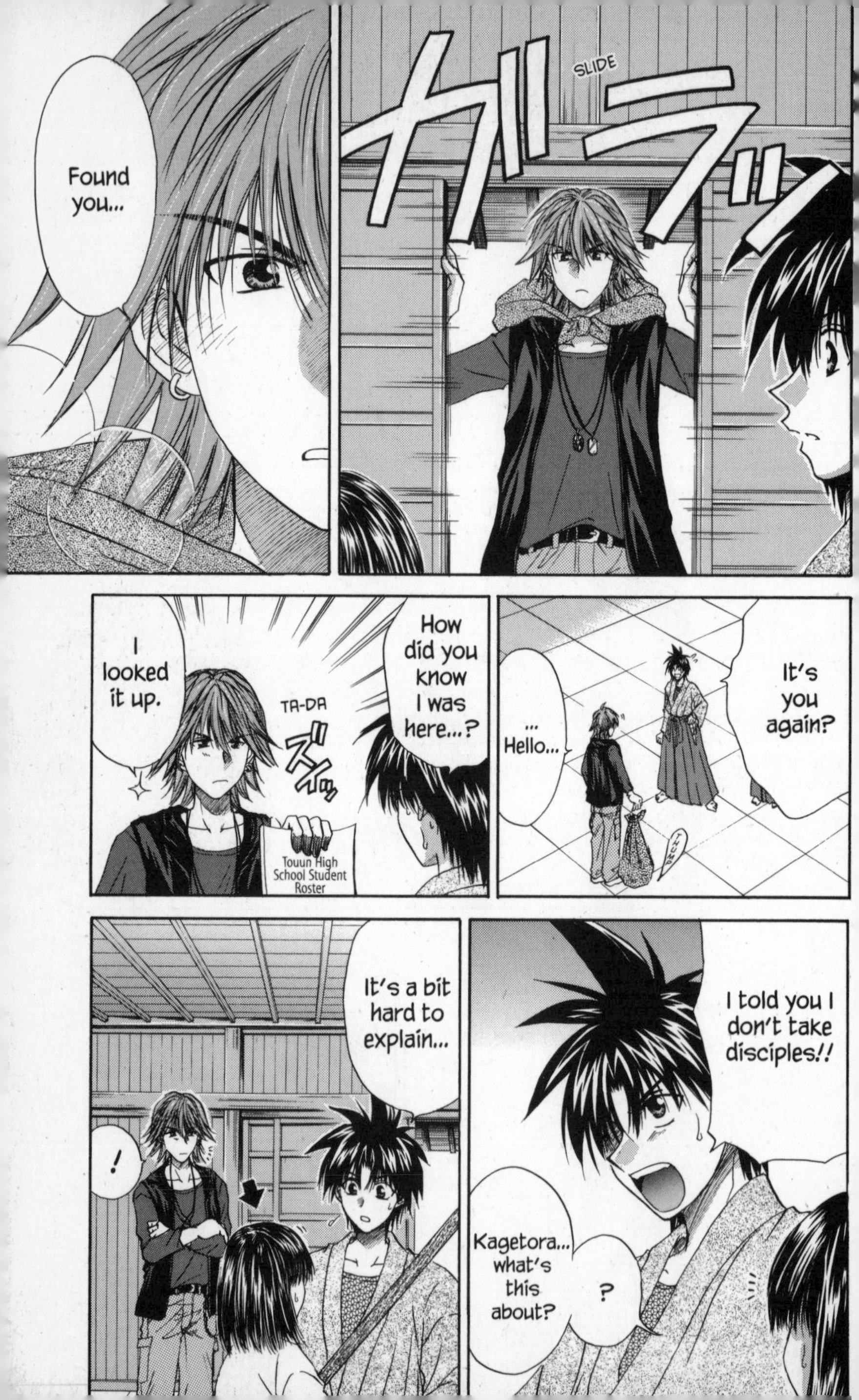
SLIDE
Found you...
It's you again?
... Hello...
THUMP
How did you know I was here...?
I looked it up.
TA-DA
Touun High School Student Roster
I told you I don't take disciples!!
Kagetora... what's this about?
?
It's a bit hard to explain...
!

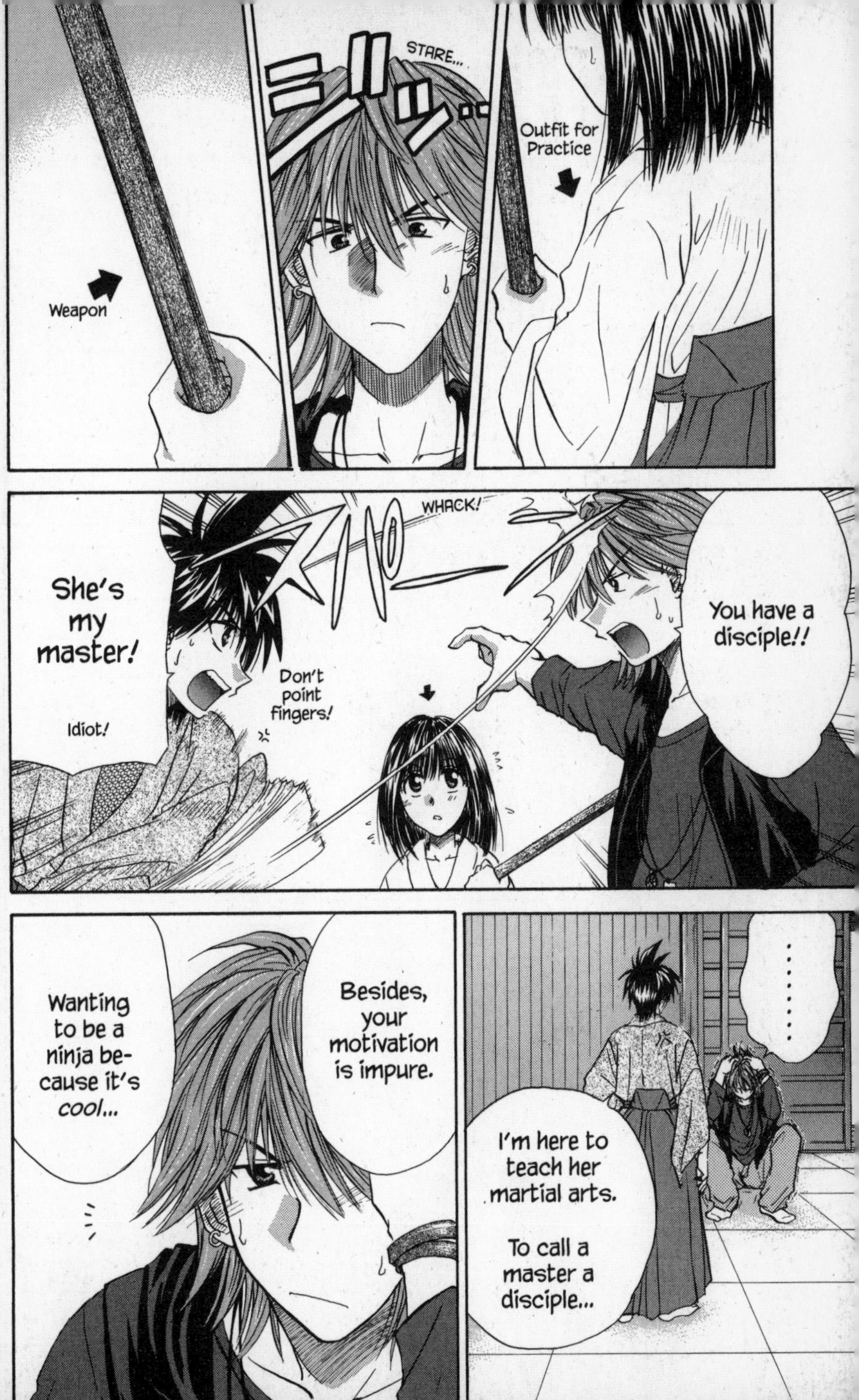
Outfit for Practice
STARE...
Weapon
You have a disciple!!
WHACK!
She's my master!
Don't point fingers!
Idiot!
......
I'm here to teach her martial arts.
To call a master a disciple...
Besides, your motivation is impure.
Wanting to be a ninja be-cause it's *cool*...

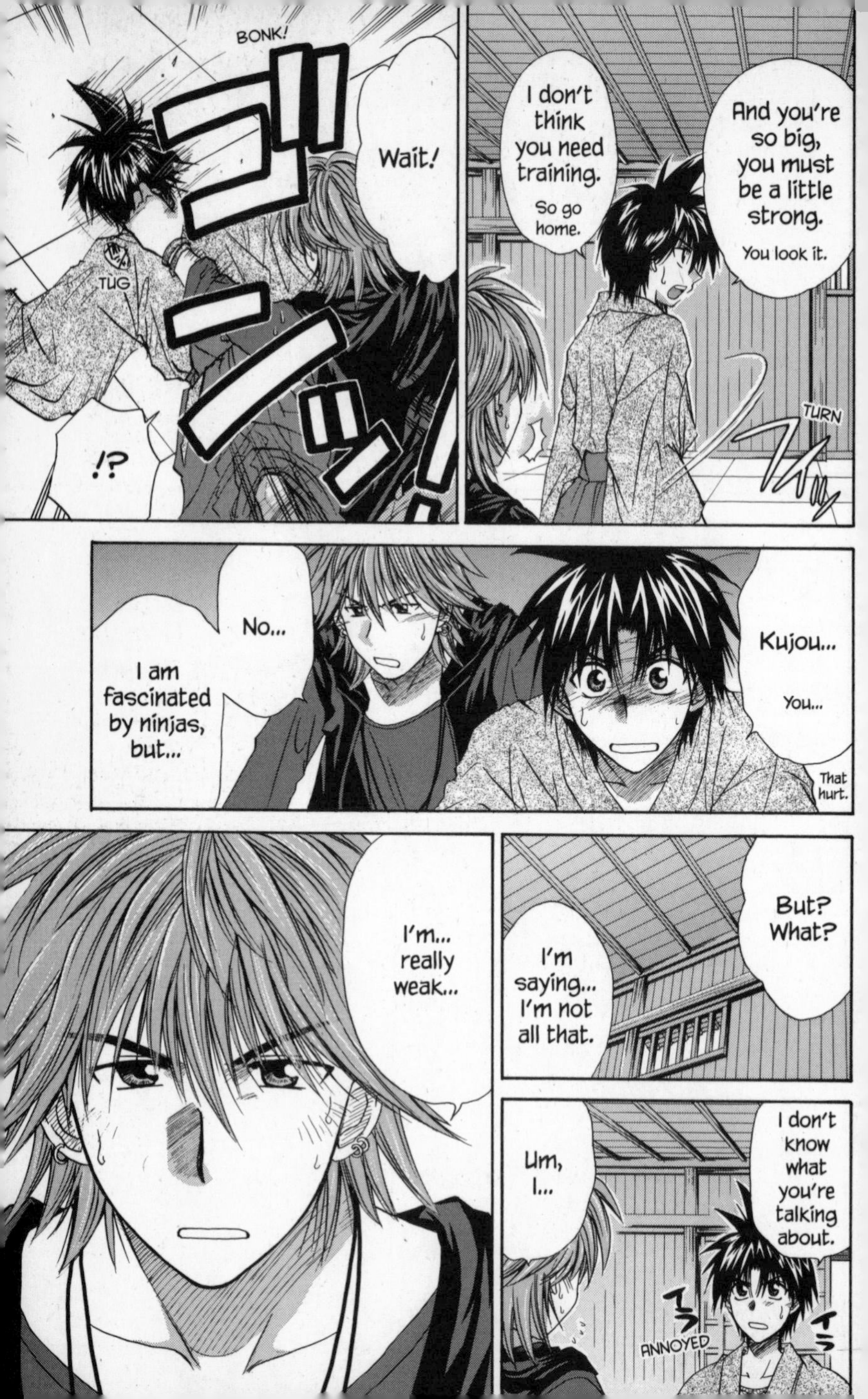
And you're so big, you must be a little strong.
You look it.
I don't think you need training.
So go home.
TURN
Wait!
BONK!
TUG
!?
Kujou...
You...
That hurt.
No...
I am fascinated by ninjas, but...
But? What?
I'm saying... I'm not all that.
I don't know what you're talking about.
ANNOYED
Um, I...
I'm... really weak...

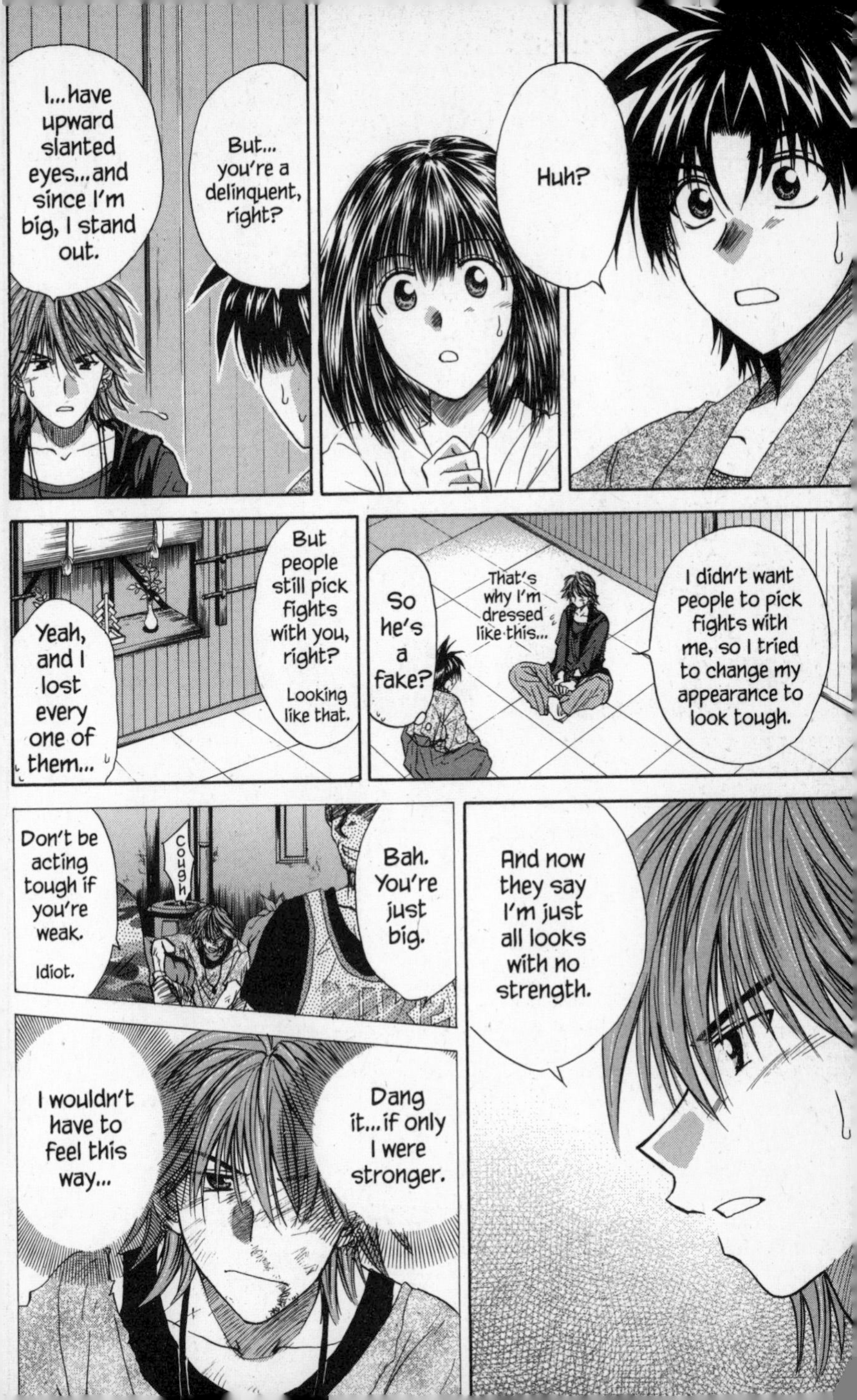
Huh?
But... you're a delinquent, right?
I...have upward slanted eyes...and since I'm big, I stand out.
I didn't want people to pick fights with me, so I tried to change my appearance to look tough.
That's why I'm dressed like this...
So he's a fake?
But people still pick fights with you, right?
Looking like that.
Yeah, and I lost every one of them...
And now they say I'm just all looks with no strength.
Bah. You're just big.
Cough
Don't be acting tough if you're weak.
Idiot.
Dang it...if only I were stronger.
I wouldn't have to feel this way...

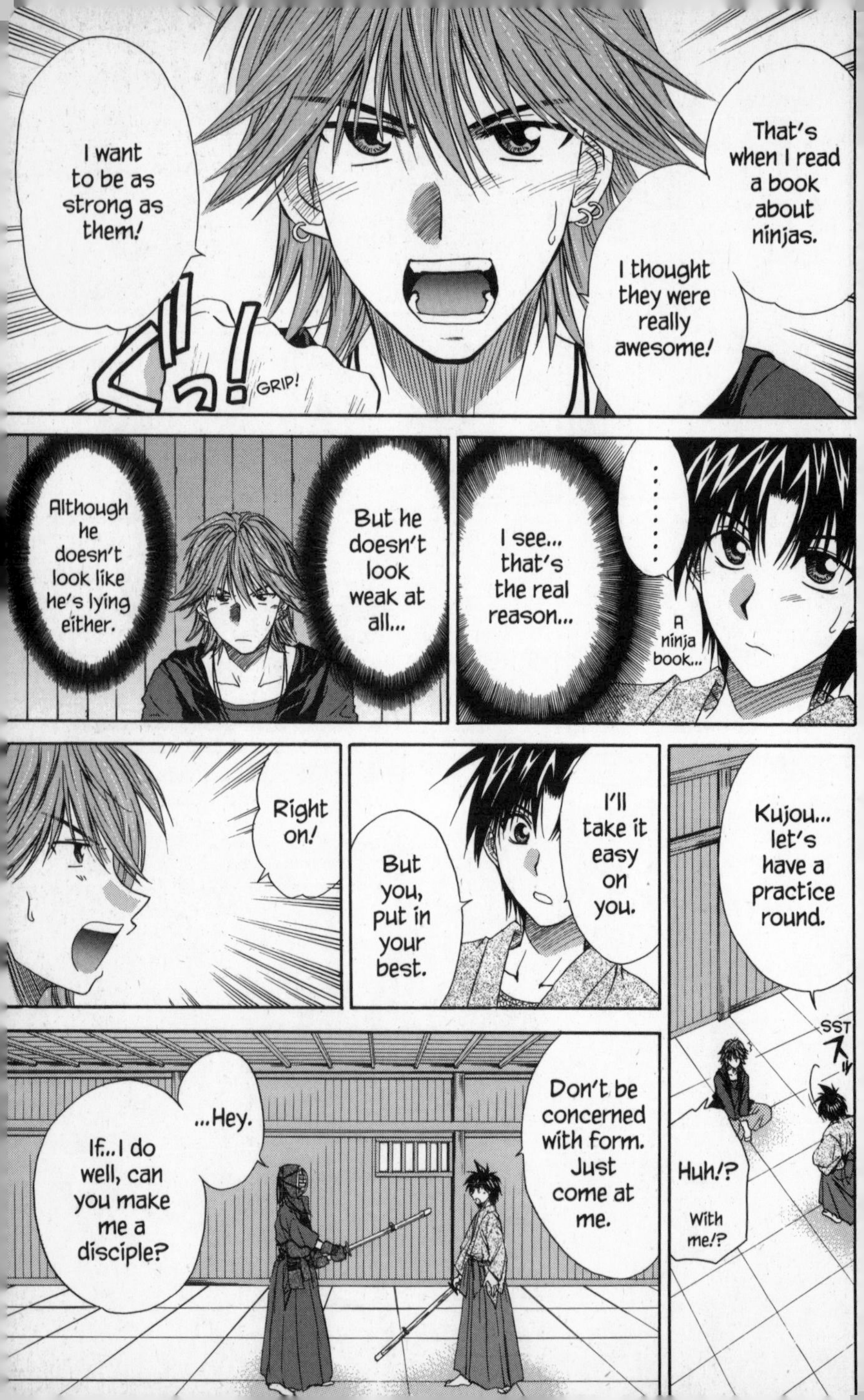
That's when I read a book about ninjas.
I thought they were really awesome!
I want to be as strong as them!
GRIP!
......
A ninja book...
I see... that's the real reason...
But he doesn't look weak at all...
Although he doesn't look like he's lying either.
Kujou... let's have a practice round.
SST
Huh!?
With me!?
I'll take it easy on you.
But you, put in your best.
Right on!
Don't be concerned with form. Just come at me.
...Hey.
If...I do well, can you make me a disciple?

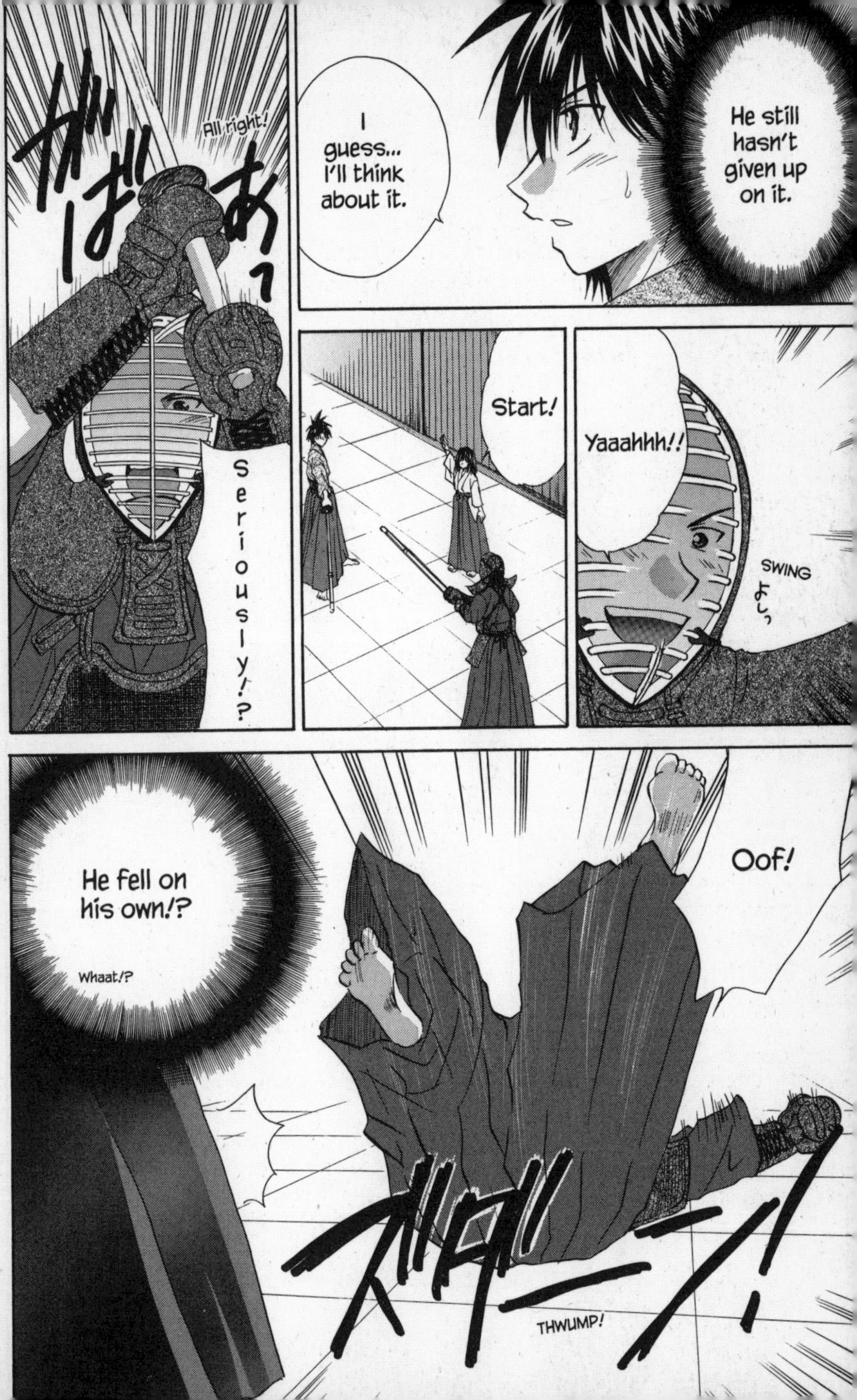
He still hasn't given up on it.
I guess... I'll think about it.
Yaaahhh!!
SWING
よしっ
Start!
All right!
Seriously!?
Oof!
THWUMP!
He fell on his own!?
Whaat!?

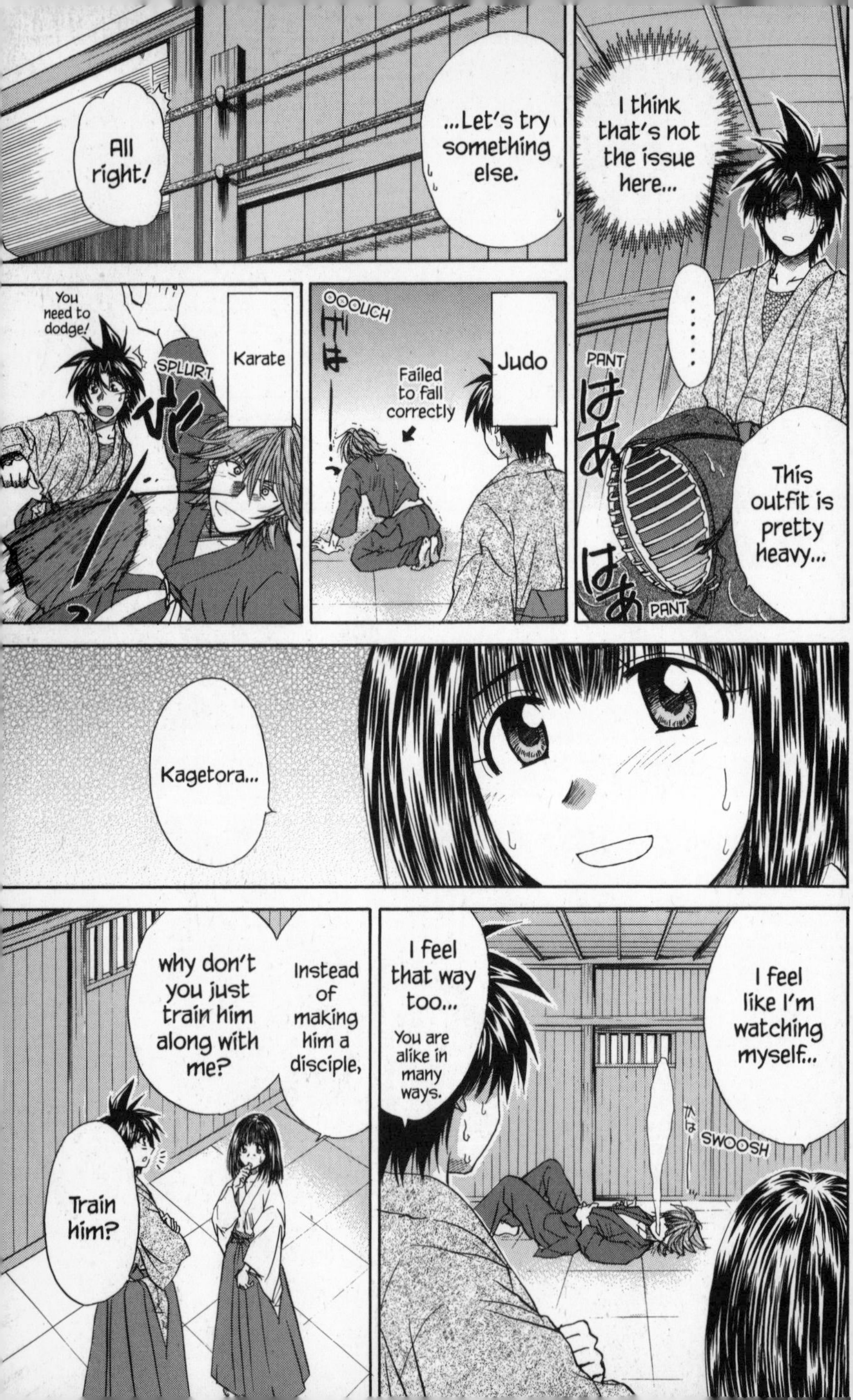
I think that's not the issue here...
...Let's try something else.
All right!
......
PANT
PANT
This outfit is pretty heavy...
Judo
OOOUCH
Failed to fall correctly
Karate
SPLURT
You need to dodge!
Kagetora...
I feel like I'm watching myself...
SWOOSH
I feel that way too...
You are alike in many ways.
Instead of making him a disciple,
why don't you just train him along with me?
Train him?

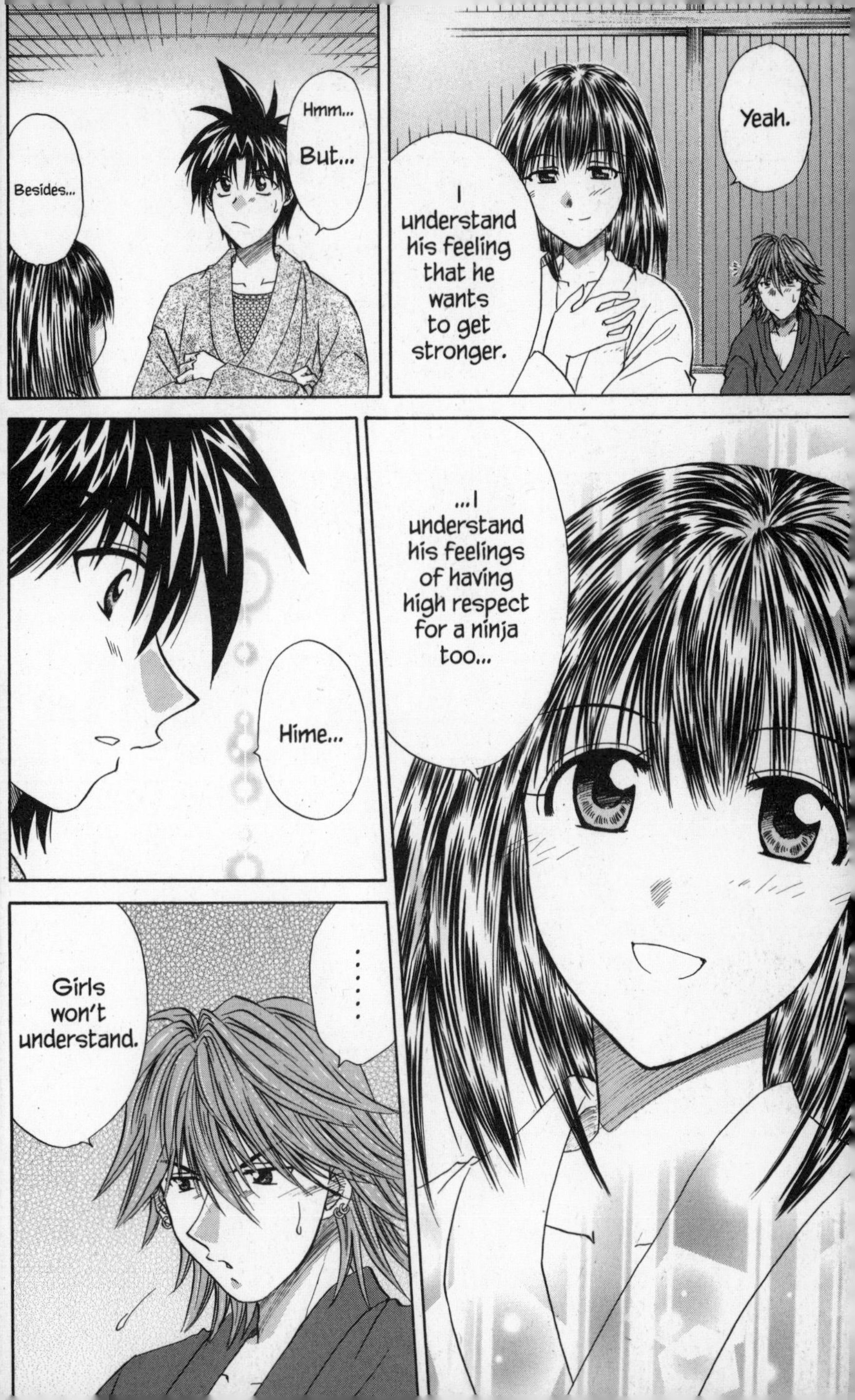
Yeah.
I understand his feeling that he wants to get stronger.
Hmm... But...
Besides...
...I understand his feelings of having high respect for a ninja too...
Hime...
......
Girls won't understand.

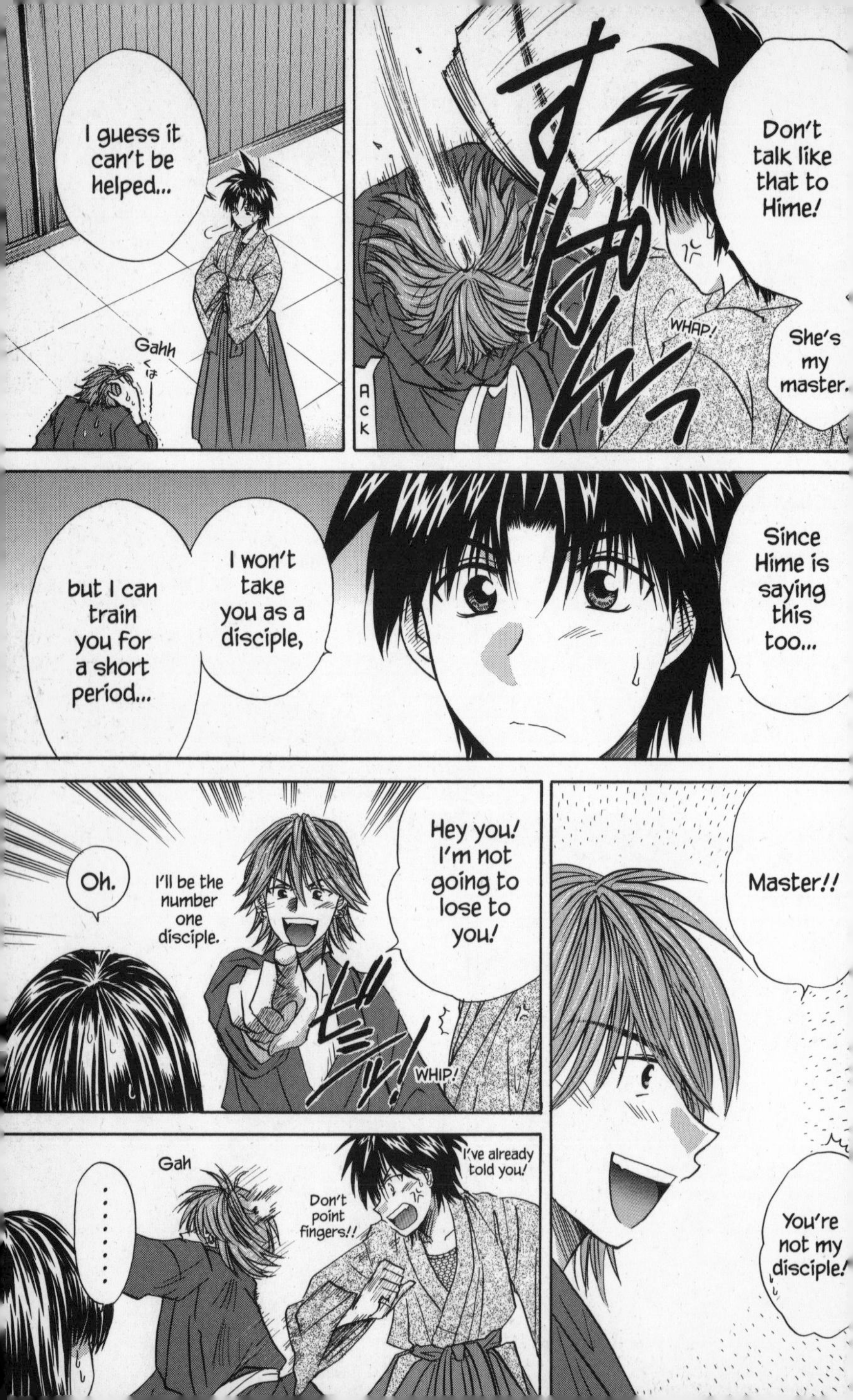
Don't talk like that to Hime!
WHAP!
She's my master.
ACK
I guess it can't be helped...
Gahh
Since Hime is saying this too...
I won't take you as a disciple,
but I can train you for a short period...
Master!!
You're not my disciple!
Hey you! I'm not going to lose to you!
WHIP!
I'll be the number one disciple.
Oh.
I've already told you!
Don't point fingers!!
Gah
....

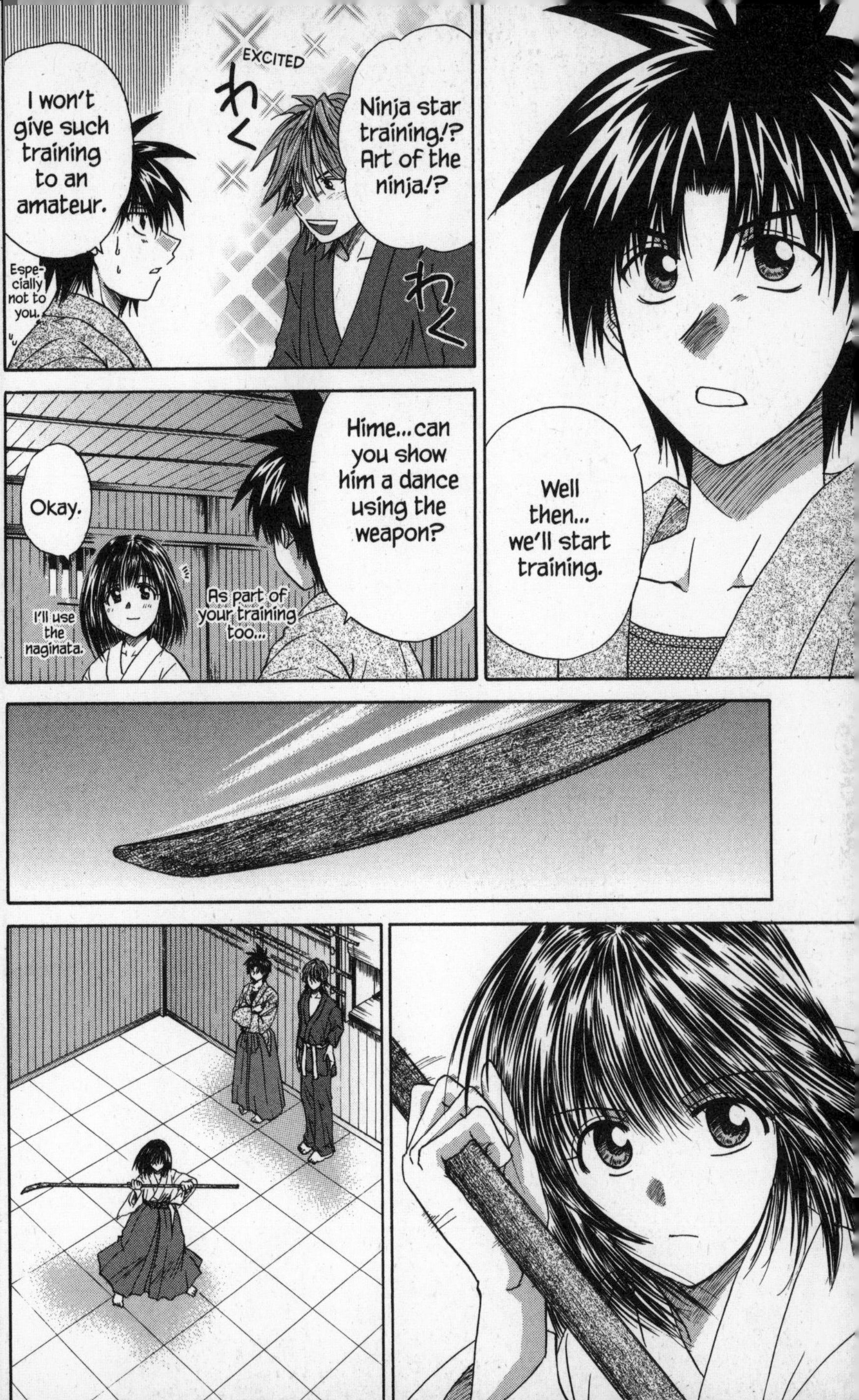
Well then... we'll start training.
Ninja star training!? Art of the ninja!?
EXCITED
わく
わく
I won't give such training to an amateur.
Espe-cially not to you.
Hime...can you show him a dance using the weapon?
As part of your training too...
Okay.
I'll use the naginata.

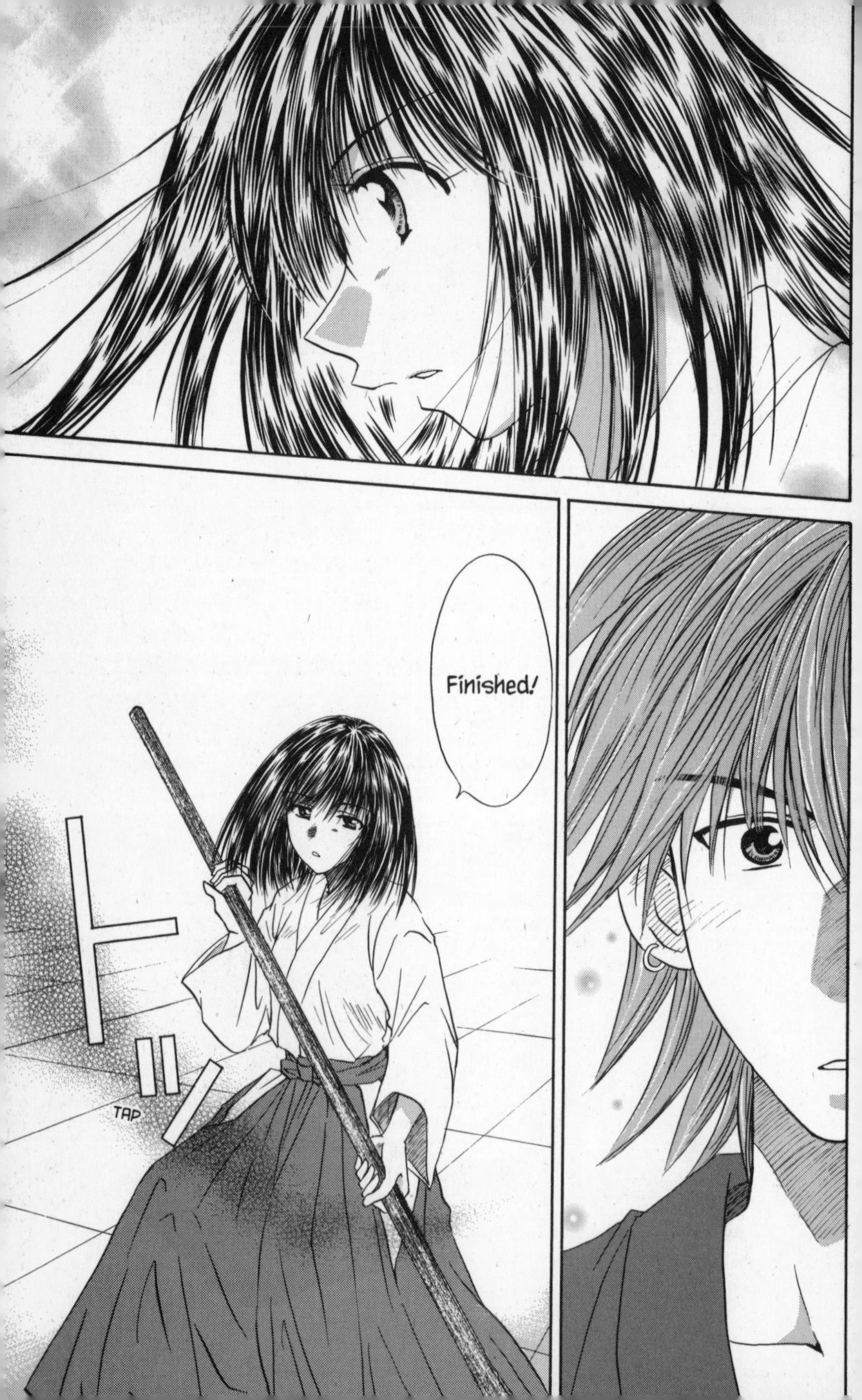
Finished!
TAP

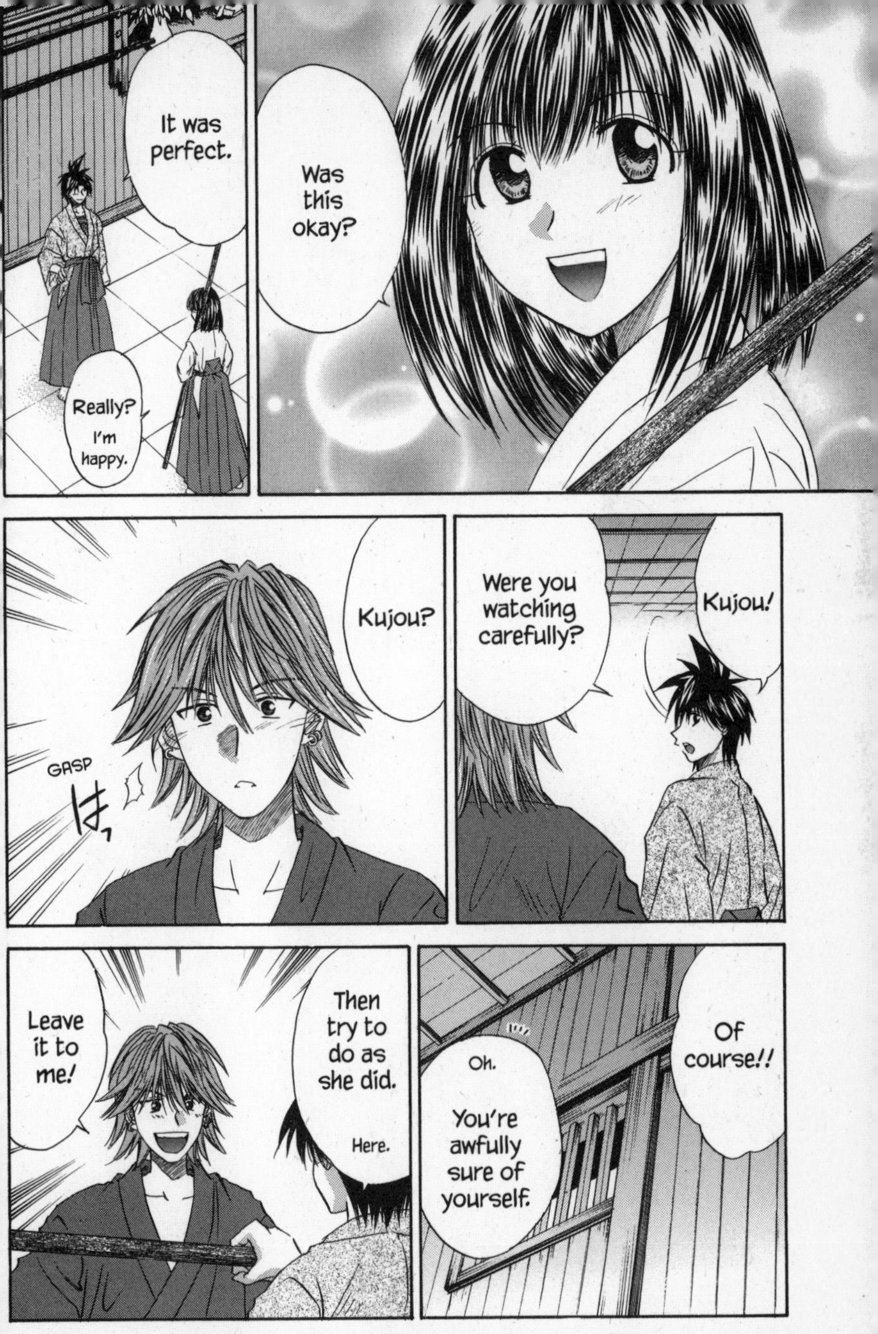
Was this okay?
It was perfect.
Really? I'm happy.
Kujou!
Were you watching carefully?
Kujou?
GASP
は
Of course!!
Oh.
You're awfully sure of yourself.
Then try to do as she did.
Here.
Leave it to me!

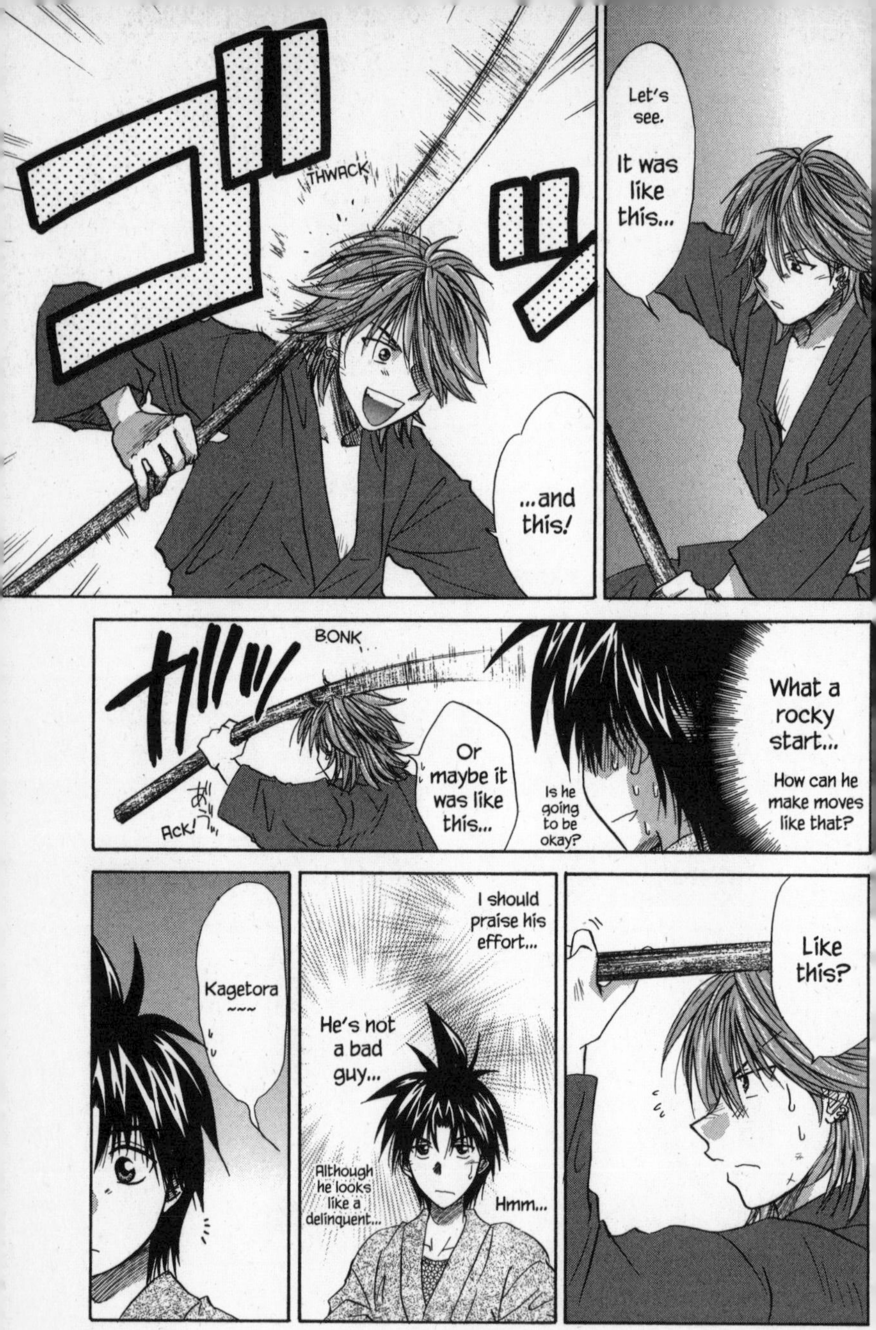
Let's see.
It was like this...
ゴッ
THWACK
...and this!
What a rocky start...
How can he make moves like that?
Is he going to be okay?
Or maybe it was like this...
BONK
Ack!
Like this?
I should praise his effort...
He's not a bad guy...
Hmm...
Although he looks like a delinquent...
Kagetora ~~~

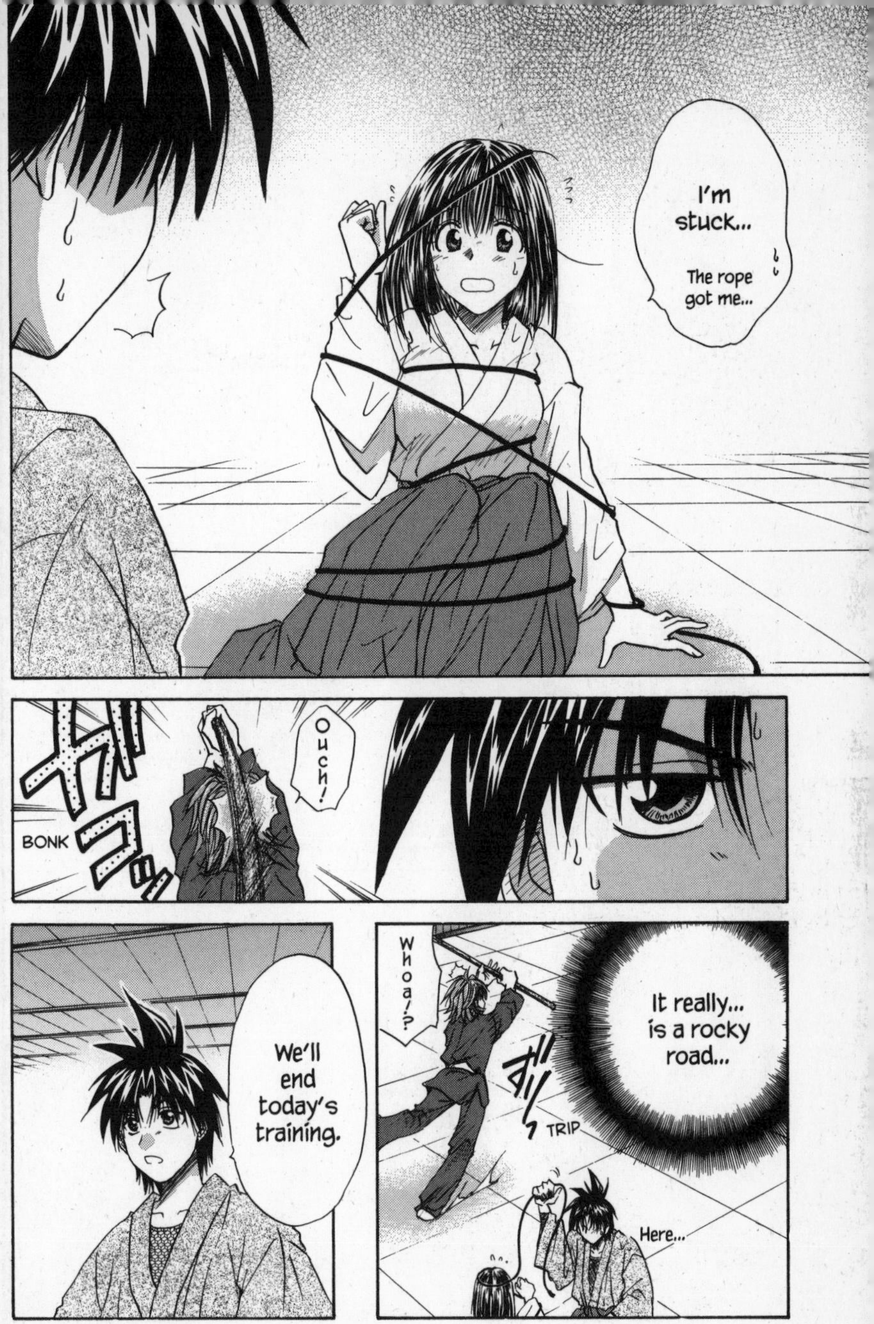
I'm stuck...
The rope got me...
Ouch!
BONK
It really... is a rocky road...
Whoa!?
TRIP
Here...
We'll end today's training.

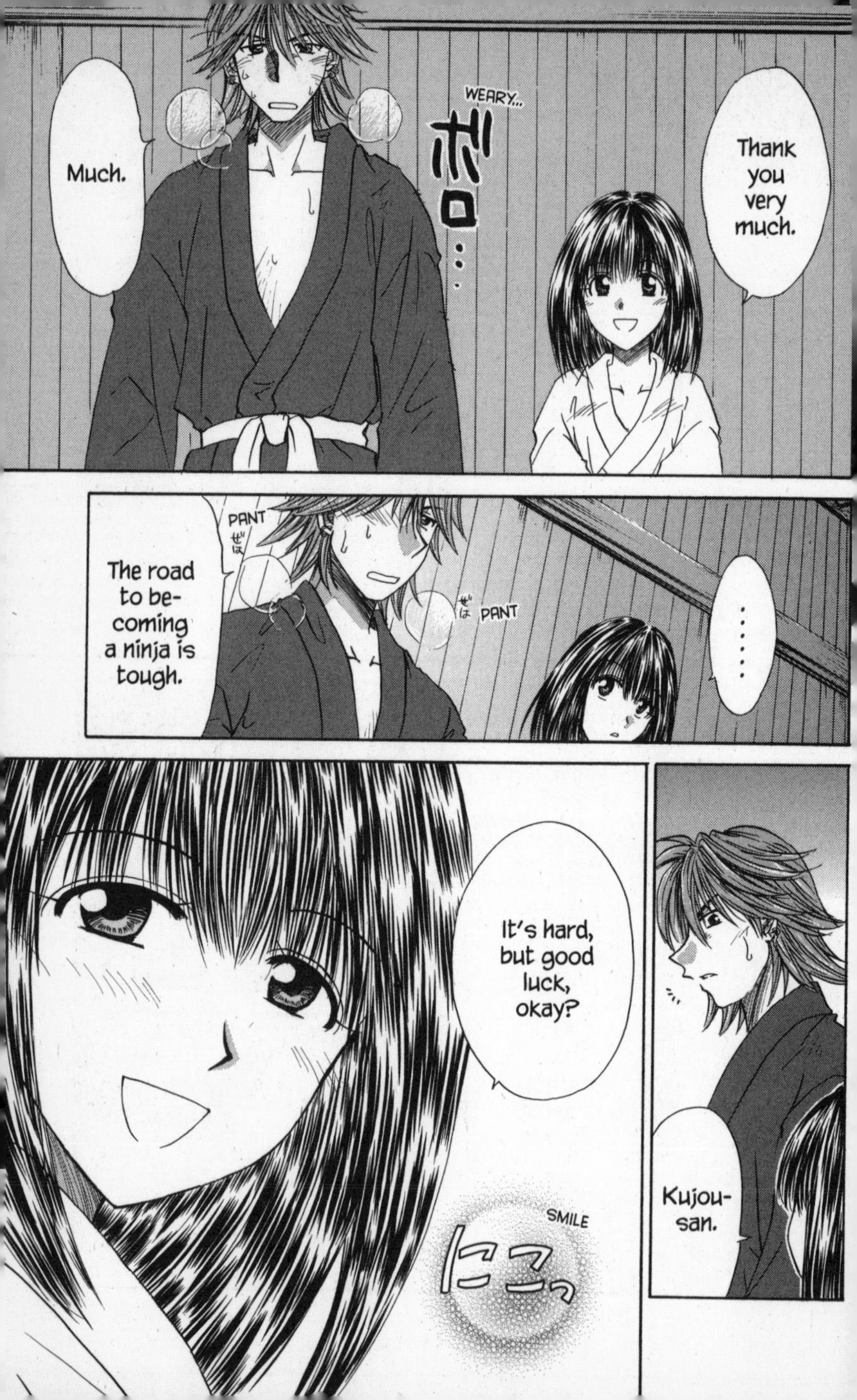
Thank you very much.
WEARY...
ボロ...
Much.
......
ぜは PANT
ぜは PANT
The road to be-coming a ninja is tough.
Kujou-san.
It's hard, but good luck, okay?
SMILE
にこっ

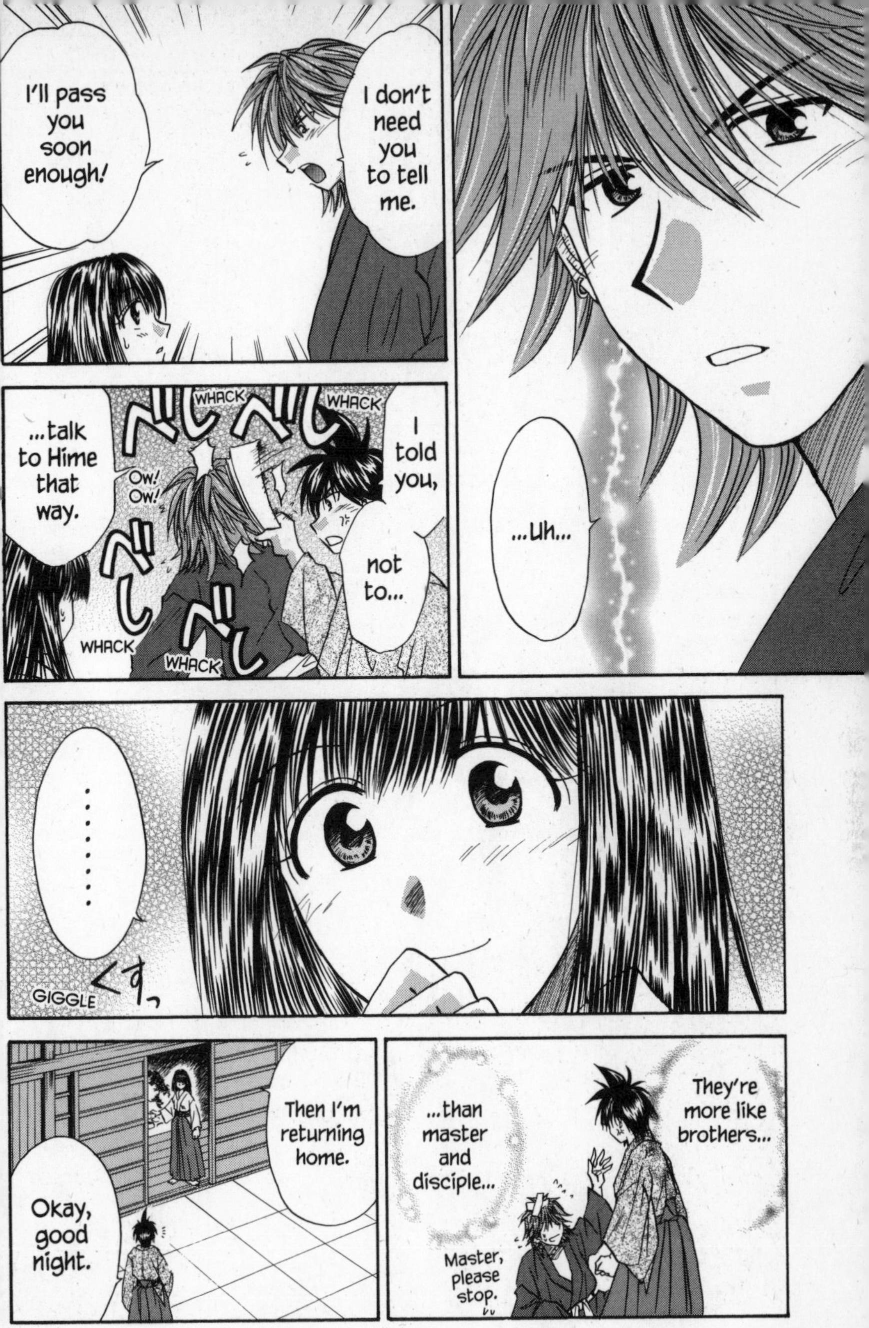
...uh...
I don't need you to tell me.
I'll pass you soon enough!
WHACK
WHACK
I told you,
not to...
...talk to Hime that way.
OW! OW!
WHACK
WHACK
......
GIGGLE
They're more like brothers...
...than master and disciple...
Master, please stop.
Then I'm returning home.
Okay, good night.

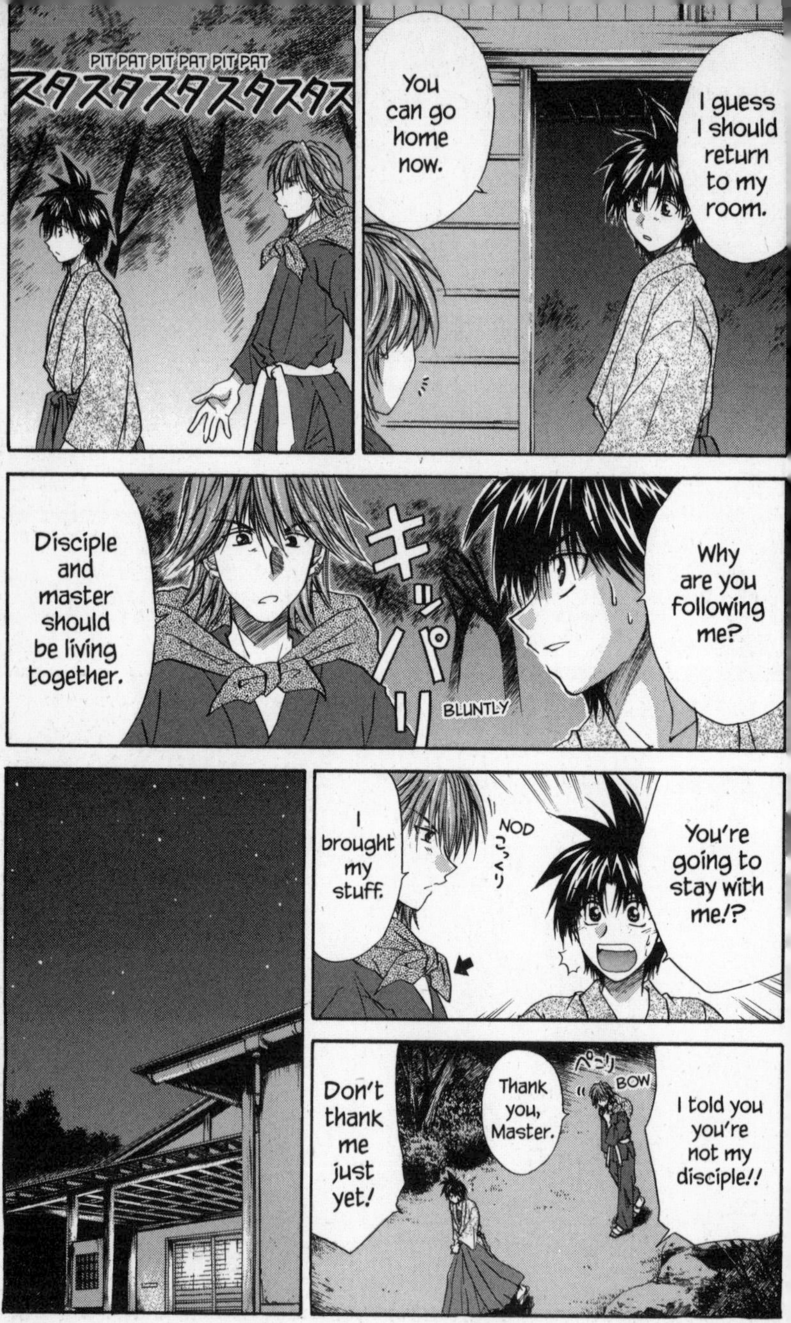

I guess I should return to my room.
You can go home now.
PIT PAT PIT PAT PIT PAT
スタスタスタスタスタス
Why are you following me?
キッパリ
BLUNTLY
Disciple and master should be living together.
You're going to stay with me!?
NOD
こっくり
I brought my stuff.
I told you you're not my disciple!!
ペコリ
BOW
Thank you, Master.
Don't thank me just yet!

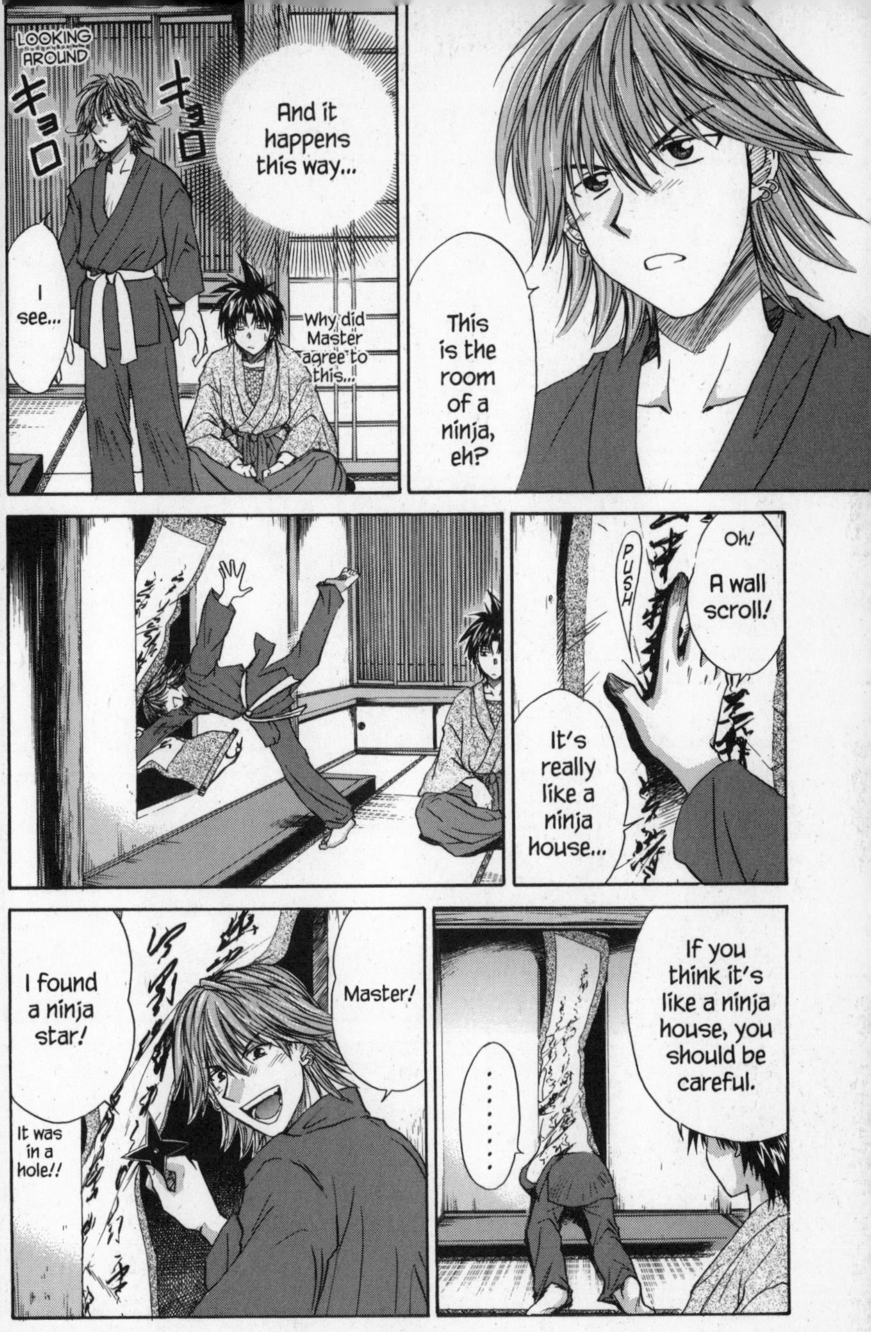
This is the room of a ninja, eh?
キョロ
And it happens this way...
LOOKING AROUND
キョロ
Why did Master agree to this...
I see...
Oh!
A wall scroll!
PUSH
It's really like a ninja house...
If you think it's like a ninja house, you should be careful.
......
Master!
I found a ninja star!
It was in a hole!!

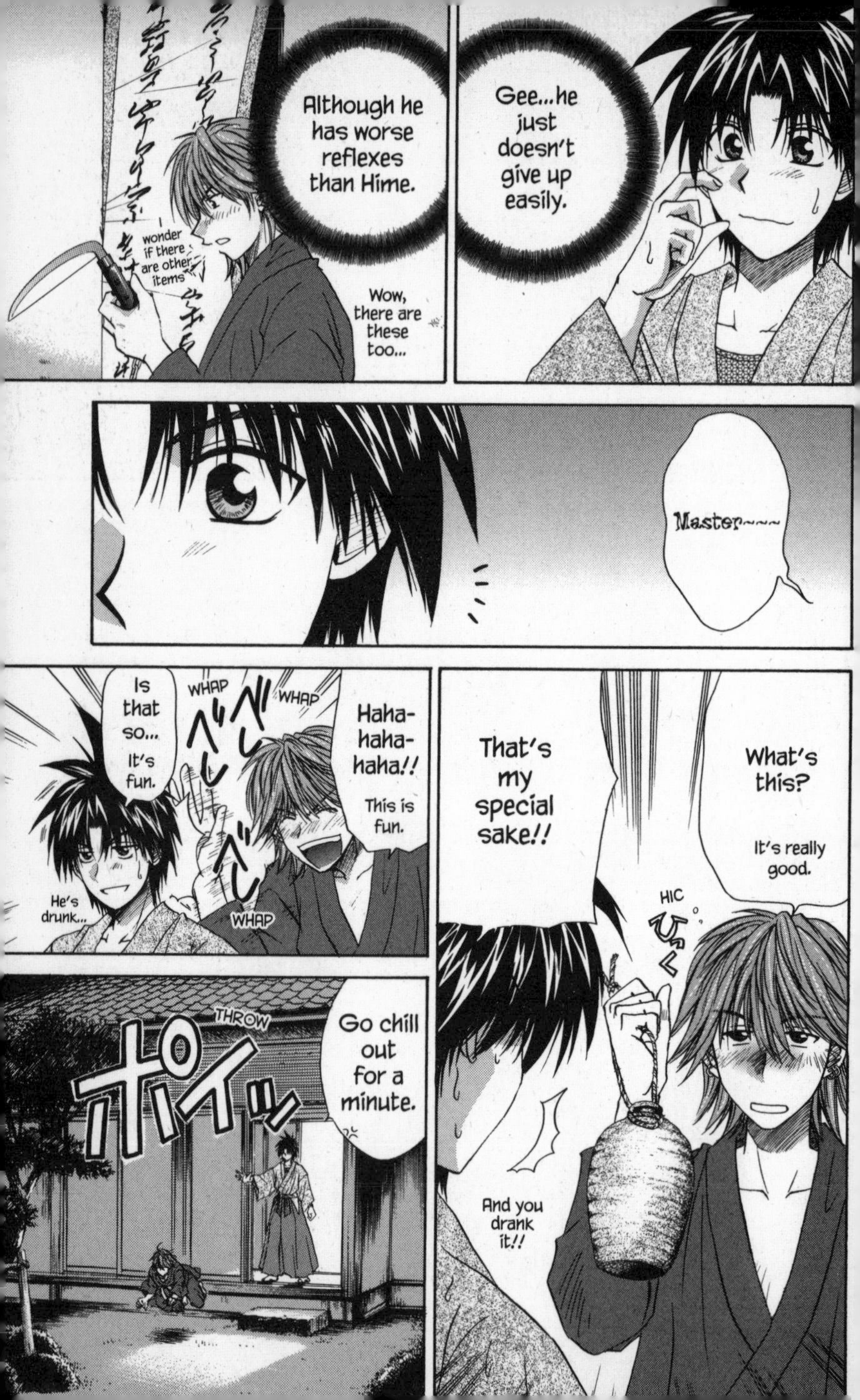
Gee...he just doesn't give up easily.
Although he has worse reflexes than Hime.
I wonder if there are other items
Wow, there are these too...
Master~~~
What's this?
It's really good.
HIC
That's my special sake!!
And you drank it!!
Haha-haha-haha!!
This is fun.
WHAP
WHAP
Is that so...
It's fun.
WHAP
He's drunk...
Go chill out for a minute.
THROW

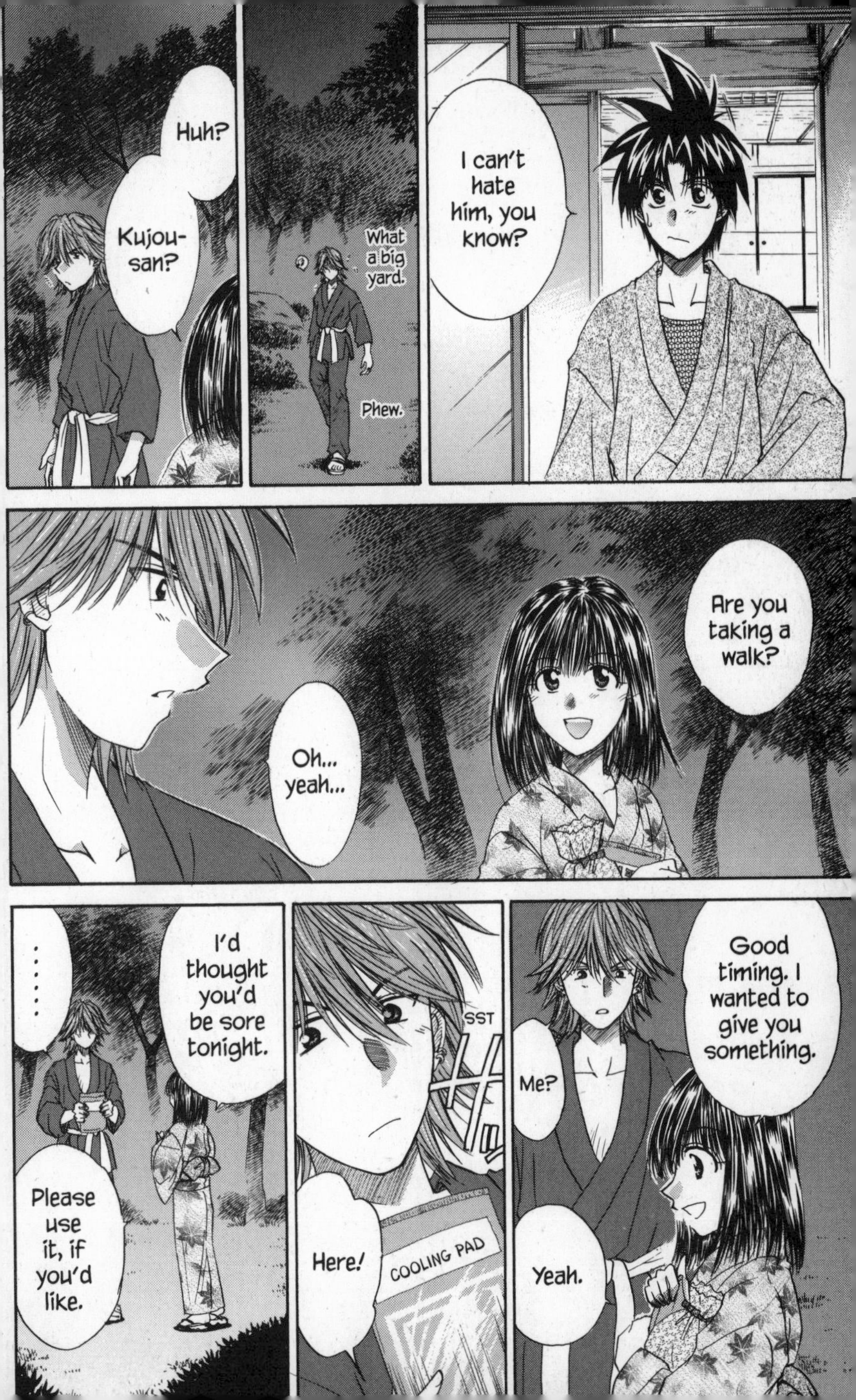

I can't hate him, you know?
What a big yard.
Phew.
Huh?
Kujou-san?
Are you taking a walk?
Oh... yeah...
Good timing. I wanted to give you something.
Me?
Yeah.
SST
Here!
COOLING PAD
I'd thought you'd be sore tonight.
......
Please use it, if you'd like.

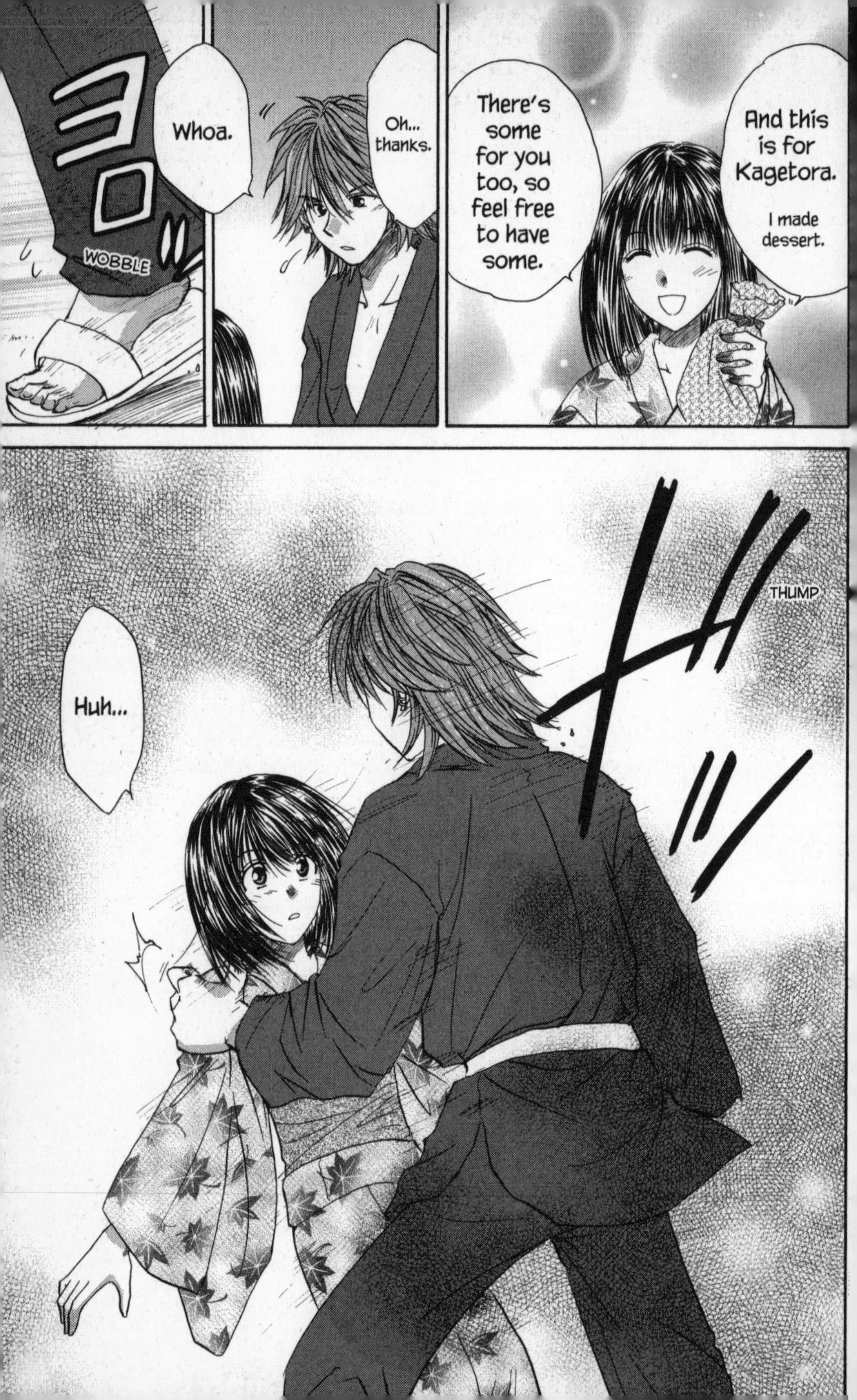
And this is for Kagetora.
I made dessert.
There's some for you too, so feel free to have some.
Oh... thanks.
Whoa.
WOBBLE
THUMP
Huh...

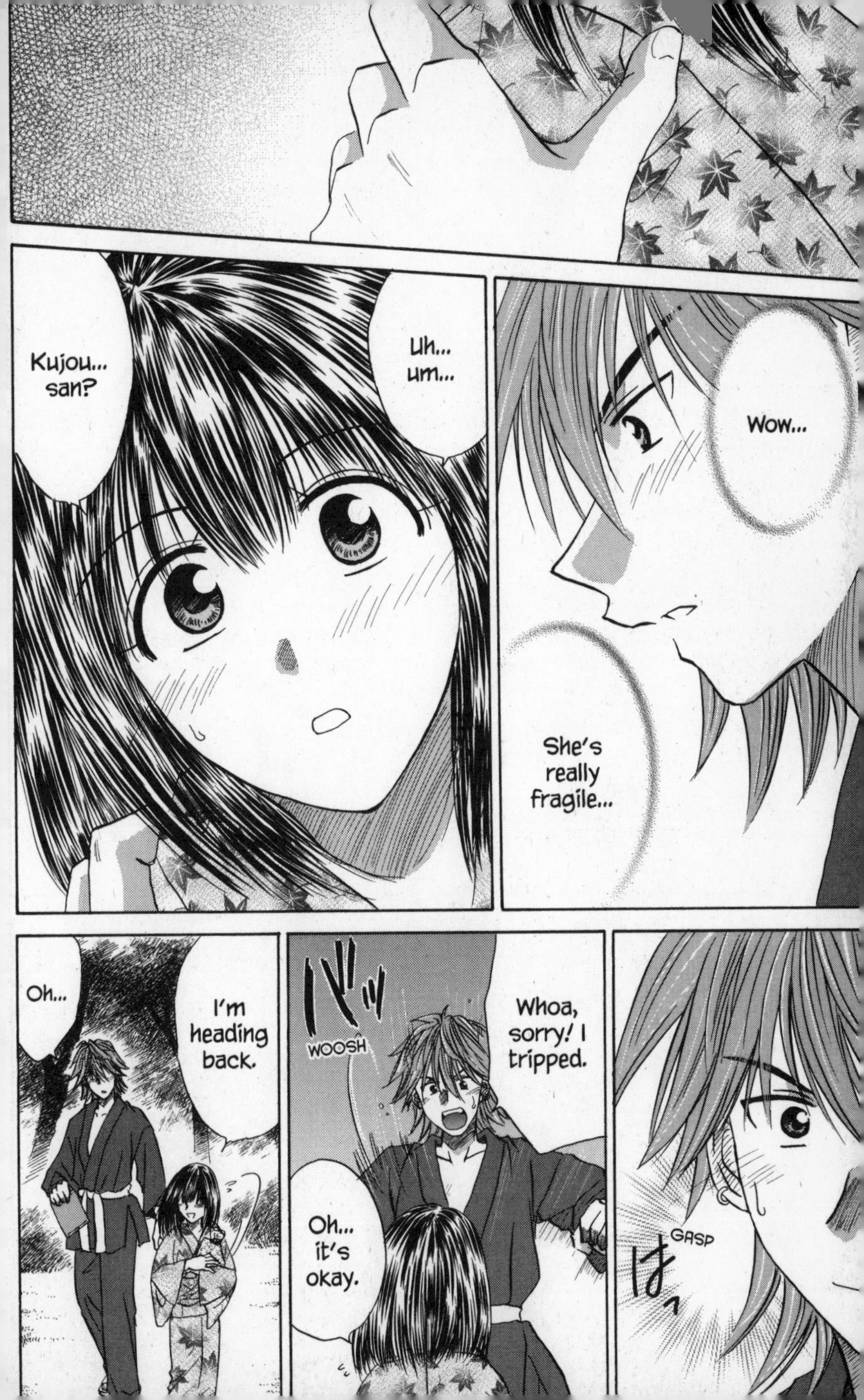
Wow...
She's really fragile...
Uh... um...
Kujou... san?
は
GASP
Whoa, sorry! I tripped.
バッ
WOOSH
Oh... it's okay.
I'm heading back.
Oh...

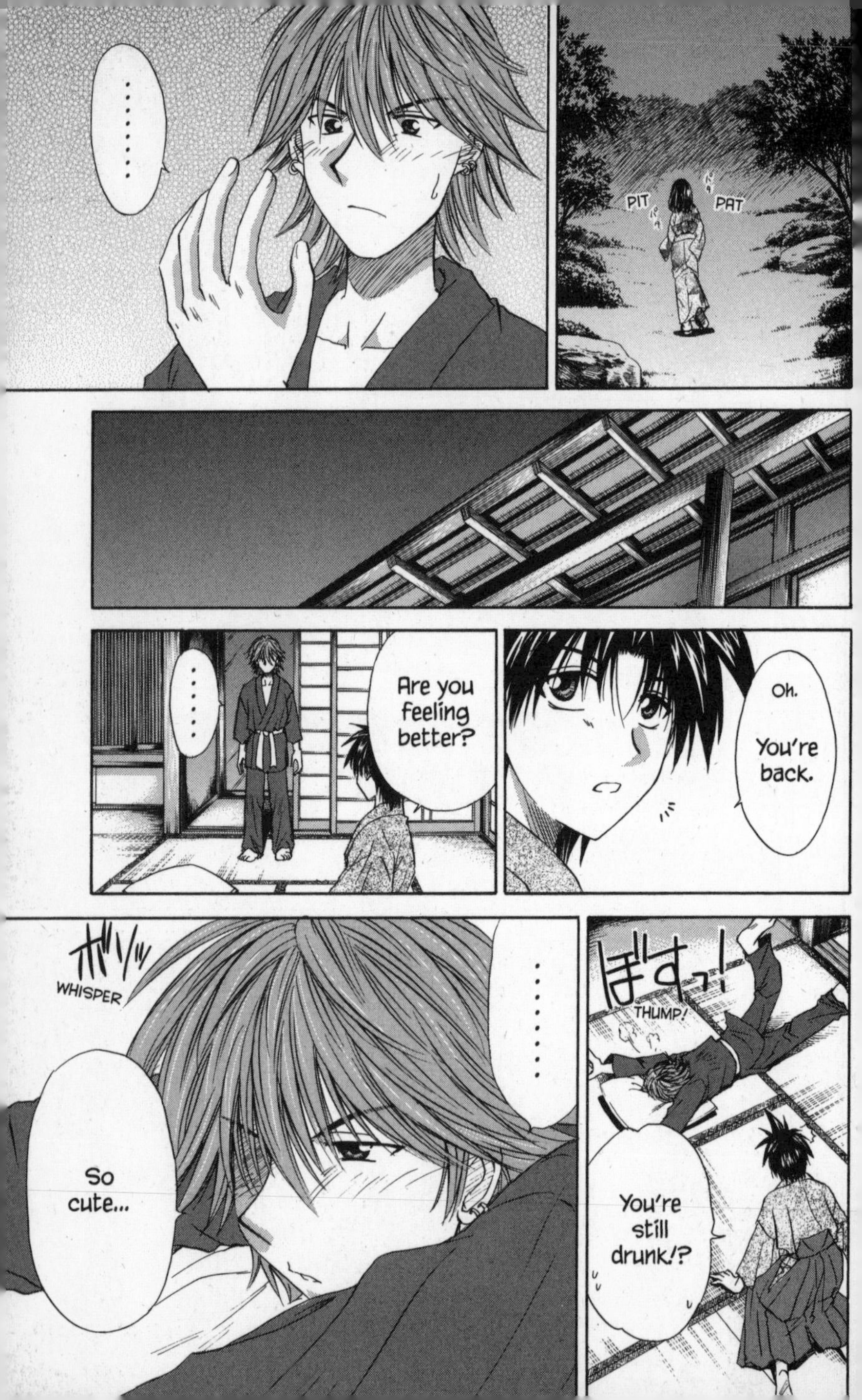
PIT PAT
......
Oh.
You're back.
Are you feeling better?
......
ぼすっ!
THUMP!
You're still drunk!?
......
ボソッ
WHISPER
So cute...

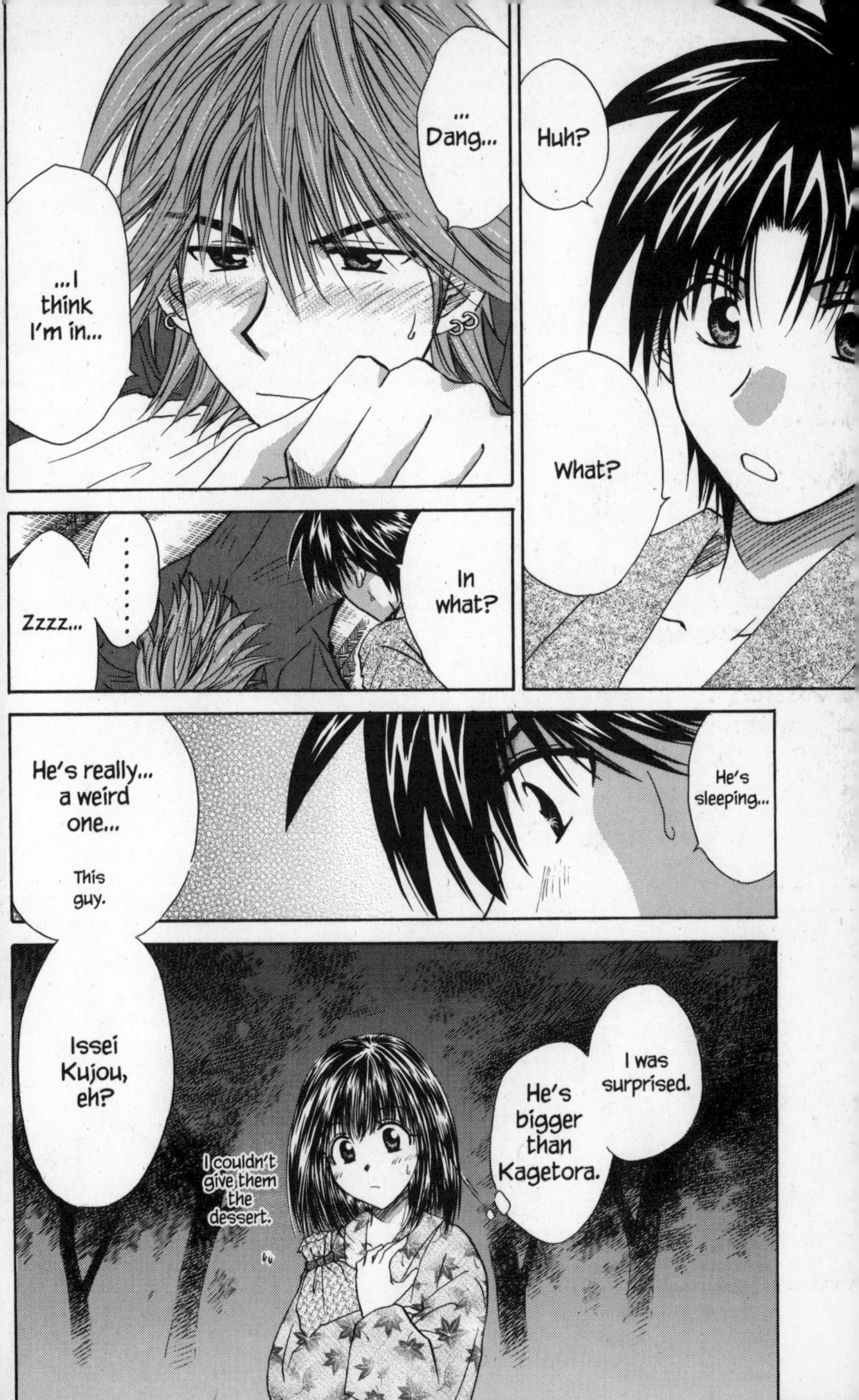
Huh?
What?
... Dang...
...I think I'm in...
In what?
......
Zzzz...
He's sleeping...
He's really... a weird one...
This guy.
I was surprised.
He's bigger than Kagetora.
Issei Kujou, eh?
I couldn't give them the dessert.

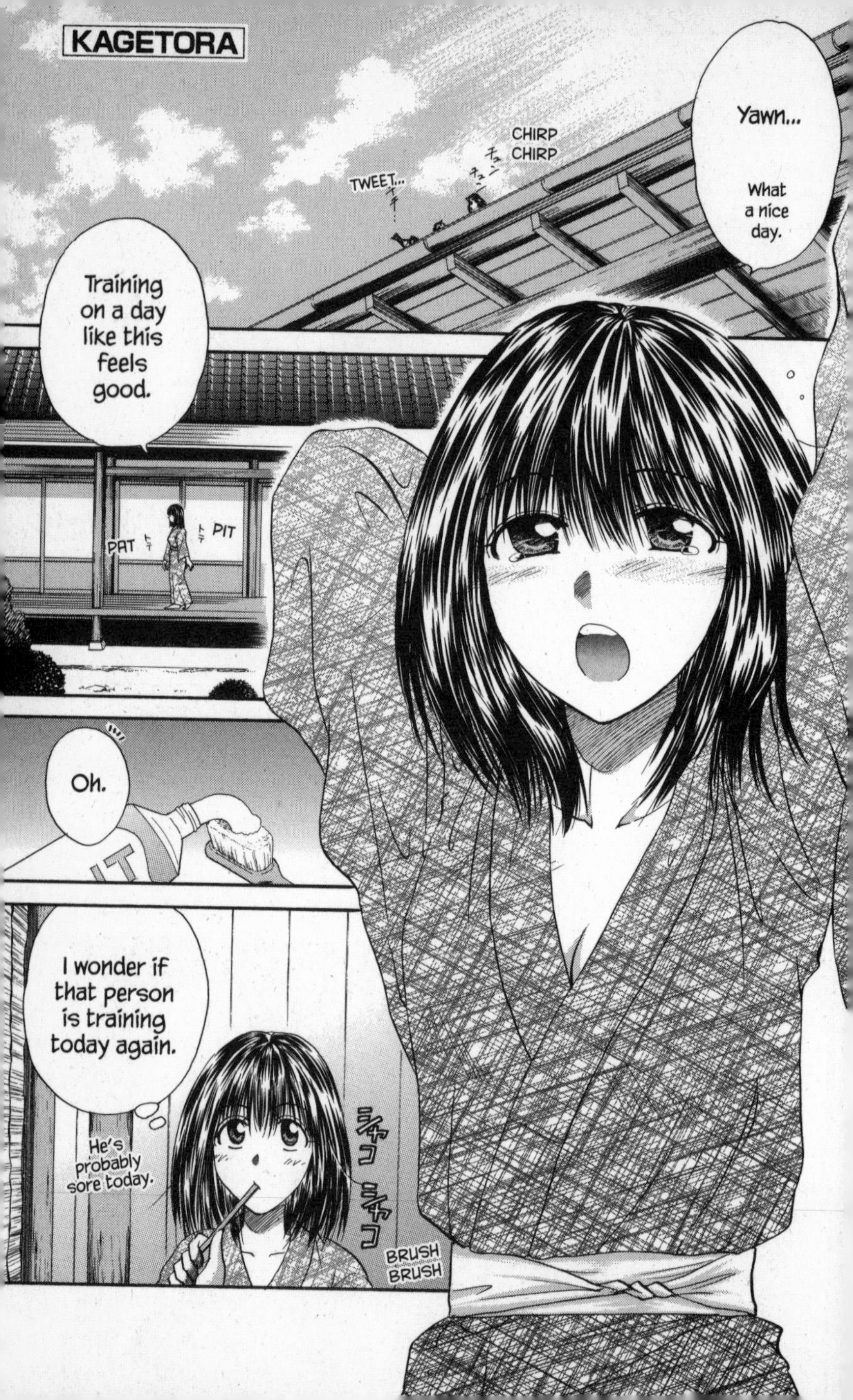

Yawn...
What a nice day.
CHIRP CHIRP
チュン チュン
TWEET...
Training on a day like this feels good.
PAT PIT
Oh.
I wonder if that person is training today again.
He's probably sore today.
シャコ シャコ
BRUSH BRUSH

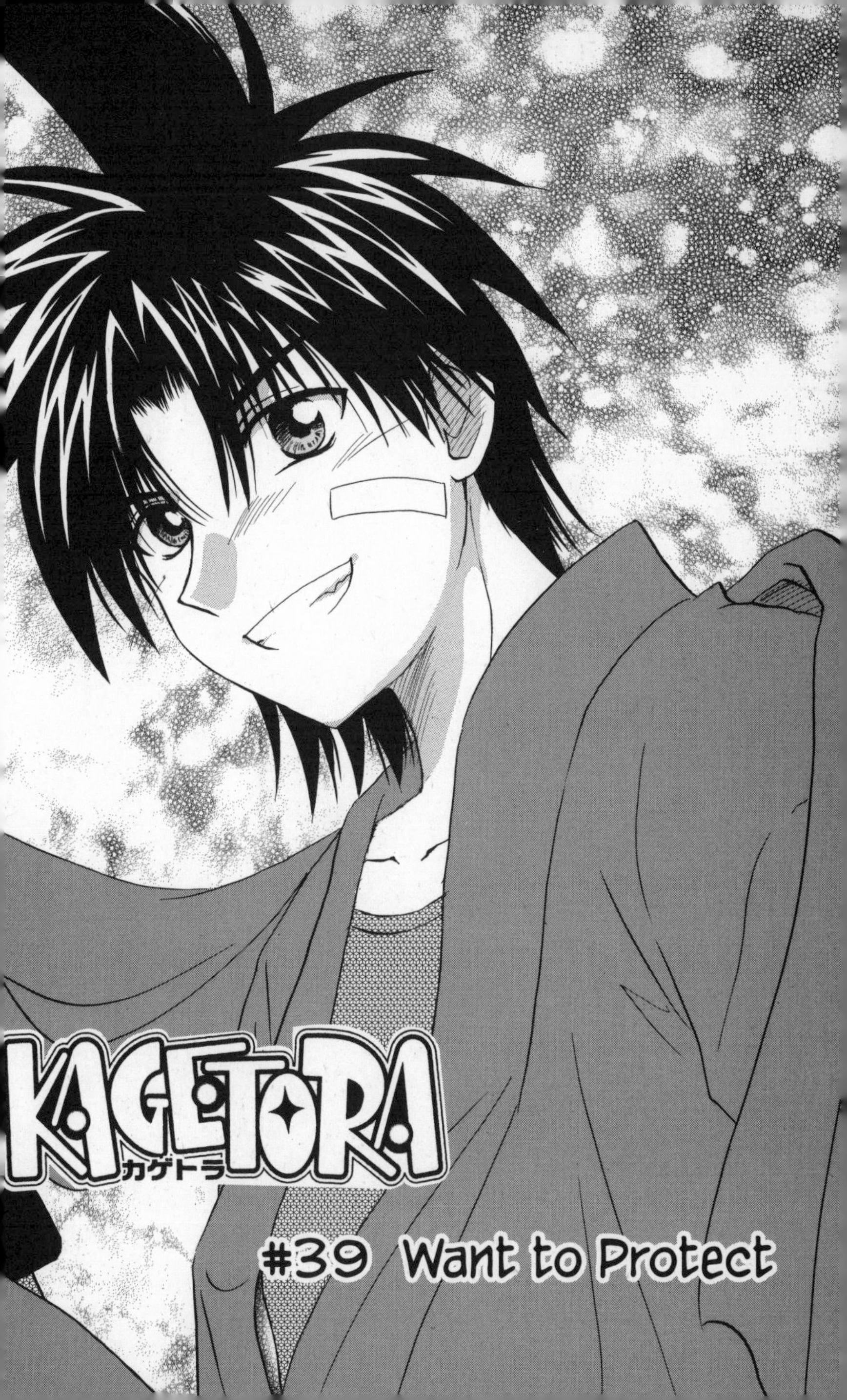
KAGETORA
カゲトラ
#39 Want to Protect

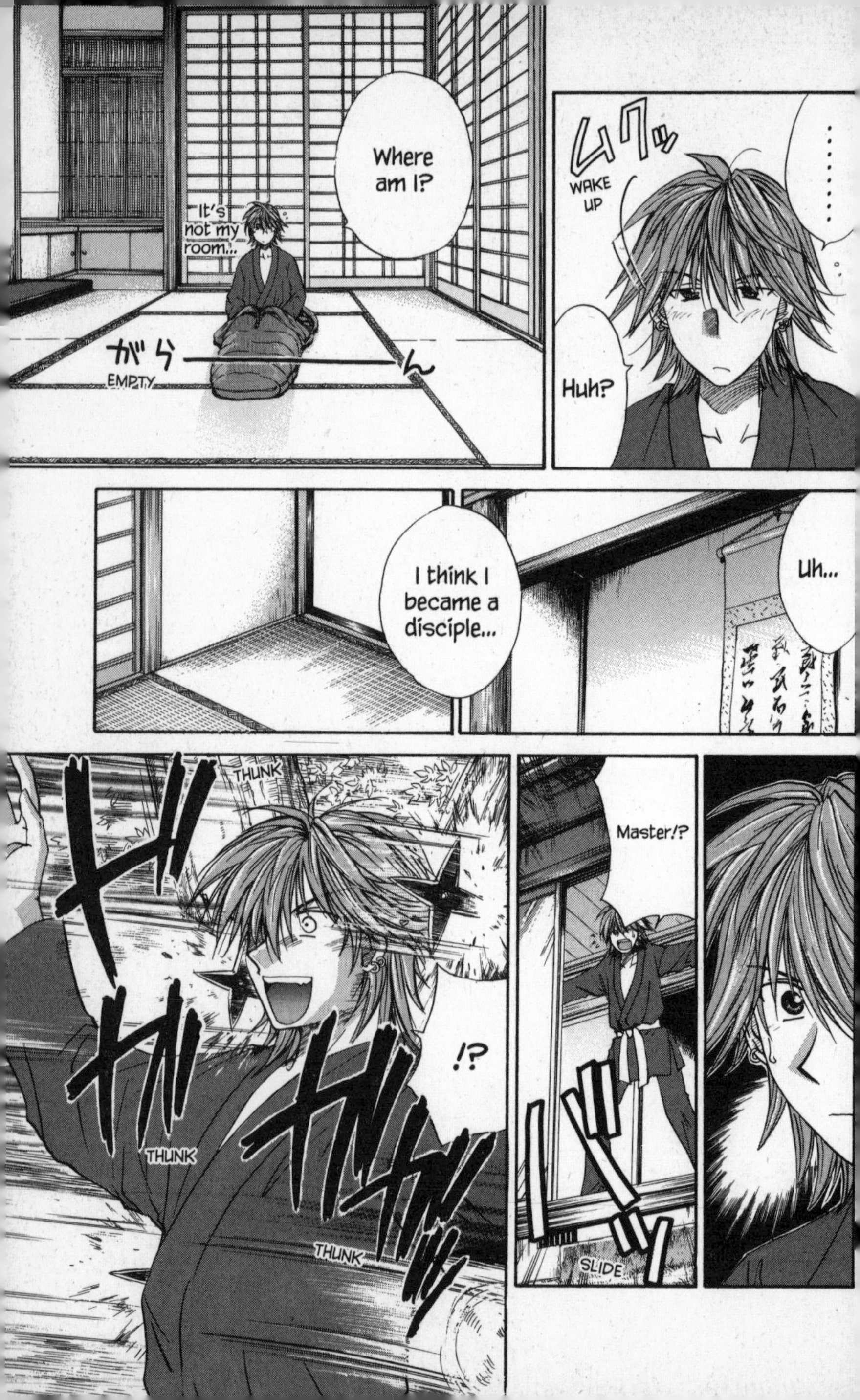

ムクッ
WAKE UP
......
Huh?
Where am I?
It's not my room...
がら——ん
EMPTY
Uh...
I think I became a disciple...
Master!?
SLIDE
THUNK
!?
THUNK
THUNK

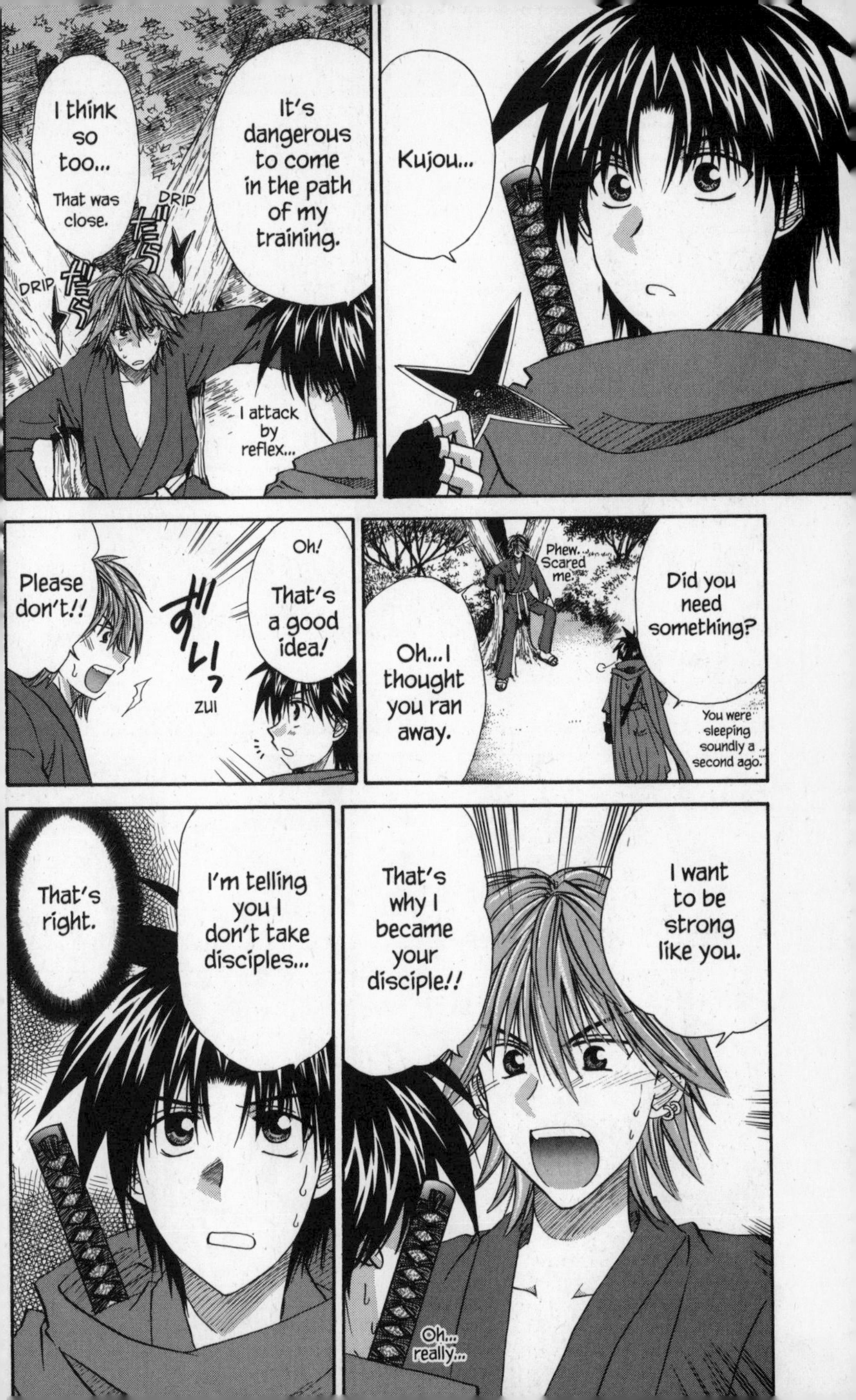
Kujou...
It's dangerous to come in the path of my training.
I think so too...
DRIP
That was close.
DRIP
I attack by reflex...
Did you need something?
Phew... Scared me.
Oh...I thought you ran away.
You were sleeping soundly a second ago.
Oh! That's a good idea!
ZUI
Please don't!!
I want to be strong like you.
That's why I became your disciple!!
Oh... really...
I'm telling you I don't take disciples...
That's right.

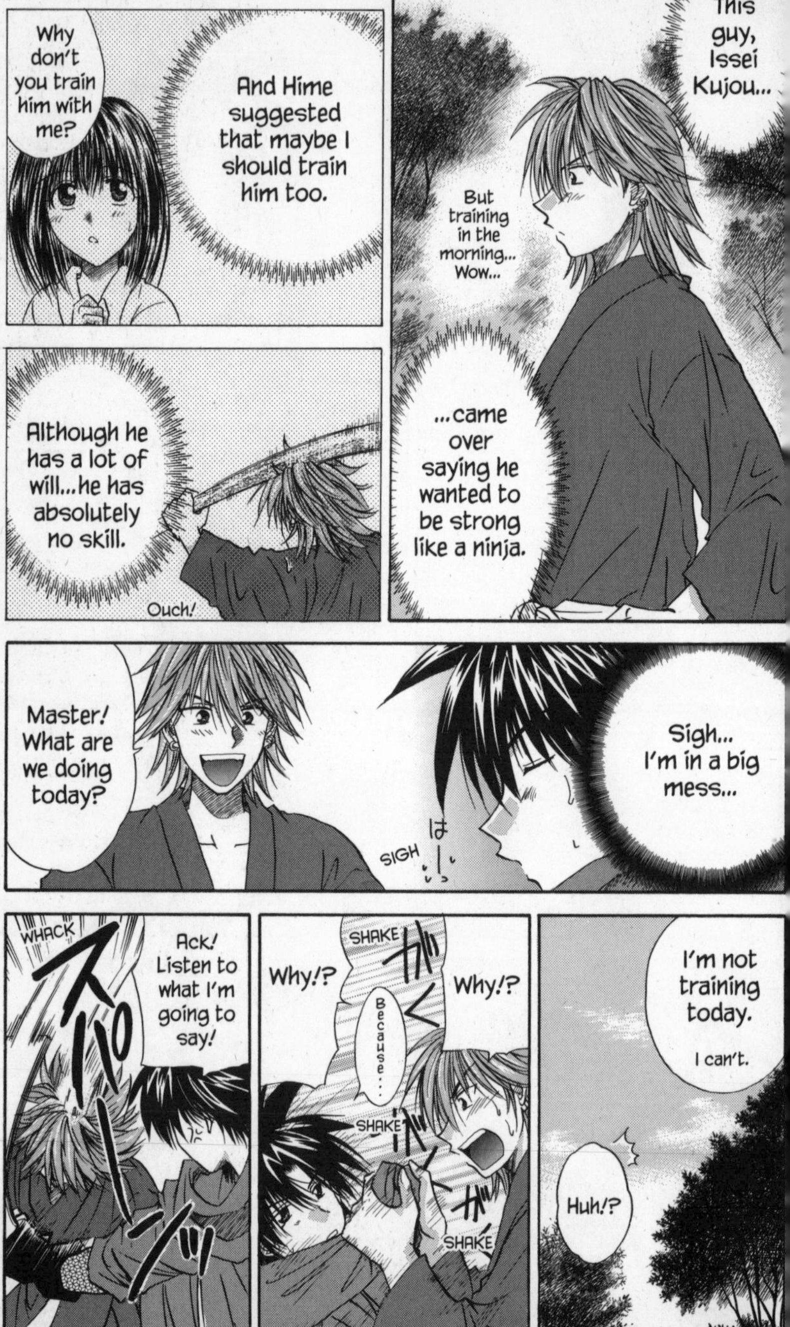
This guy, Issei Kujou...
But training in the morning... Wow...
...came over saying he wanted to be strong like a ninja.
Why don't you train him with me?
And Hime suggested that maybe I should train him too.
Although he has a lot of will...he has absolutely no skill.
Ouch!
Sigh... I'm in a big mess...
Master! What are we doing today?
SIGH
I'm not training today.
I can't.
Huh!?
SHAKE
Why!?
Why!?
Because...
SHAKE
SHAKE
WHACK
Ack! Listen to what I'm going to say!

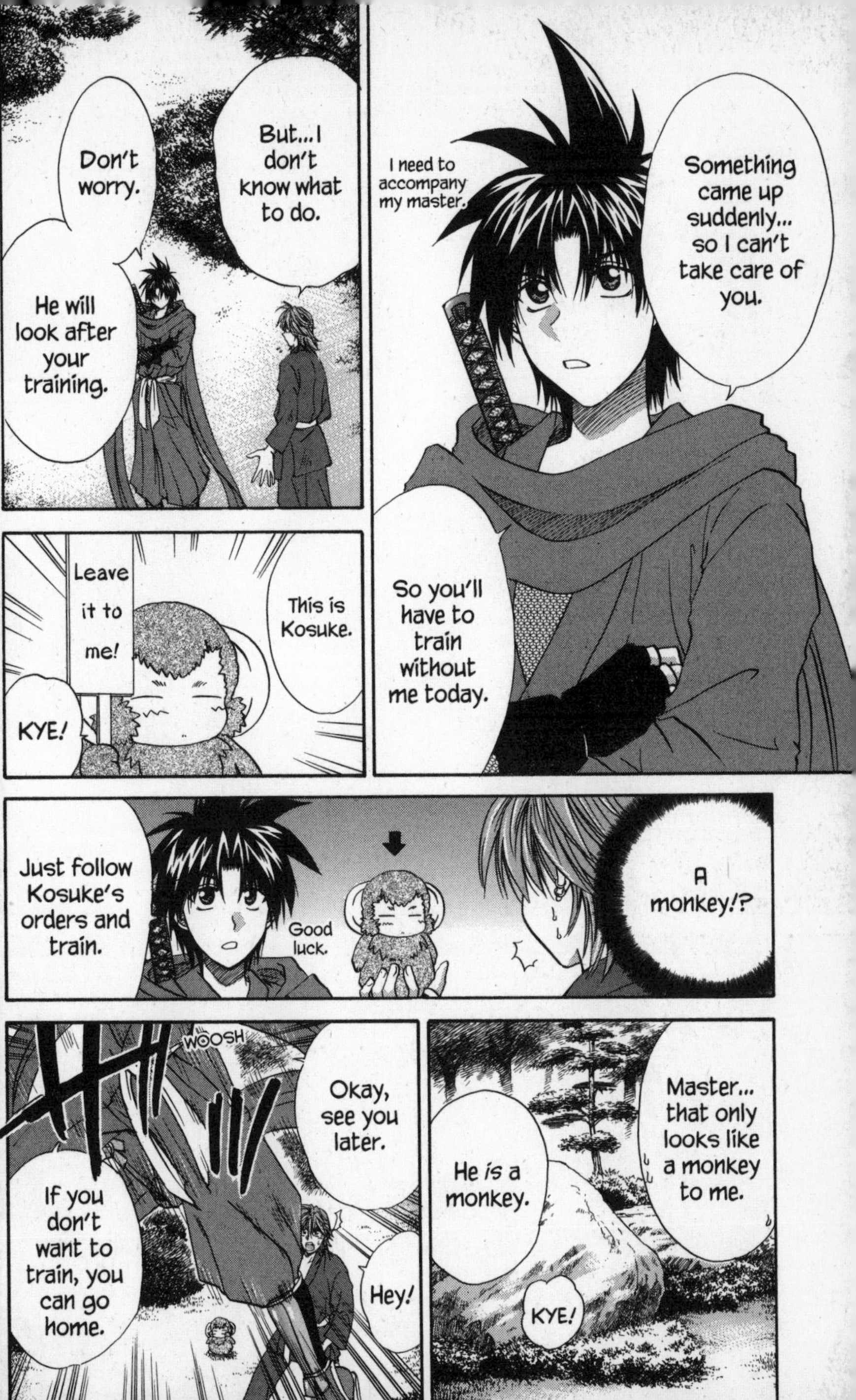
Something came up suddenly... so I can't take care of you.
I need to accompany my master.
So you'll have to train without me today.
But...I don't know what to do.
Don't worry.
He will look after your training.
This is Kosuke.
Leave it to me!
KYE!
A monkey!?
Good luck.
Just follow Kosuke's orders and train.
Master... that only looks like a monkey to me.
He *is* a monkey.
KYE!
Okay, see you later.
WOOSH
Hey!
If you don't want to train, you can go home.

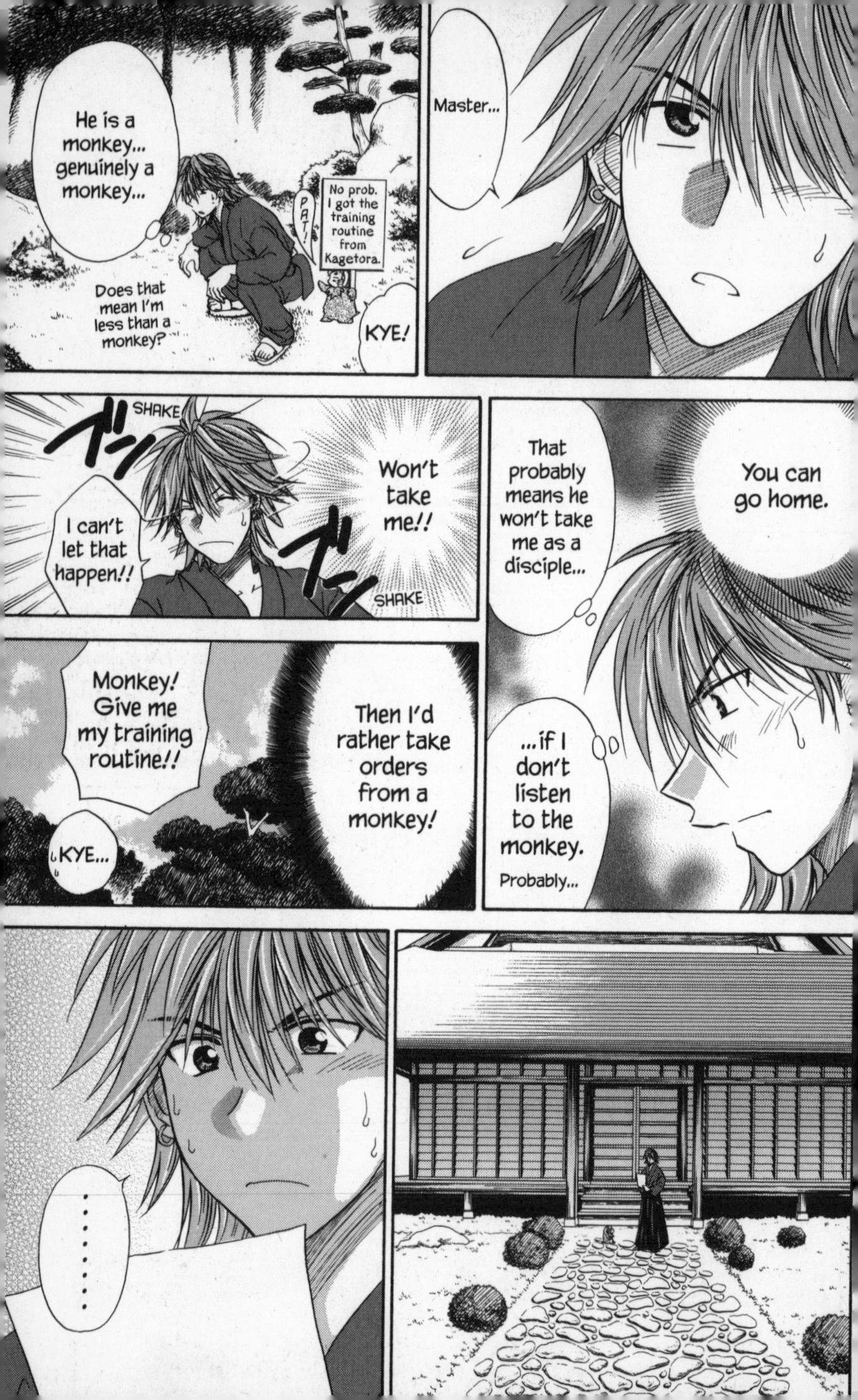

Master...
PAT!
No prob. I got the training routine from Kagetora.
He is a monkey... genuinely a monkey...
KYE!
Does that mean I'm less than a monkey?
You can go home.
That probably means he won't take me as a disciple...
...if I don't listen to the monkey.
Probably...
SHAKE
Won't take me!!
I can't let that happen!!
SHAKE
Then I'd rather take orders from a monkey!
Monkey! Give me my training routine!!
KYE...
......

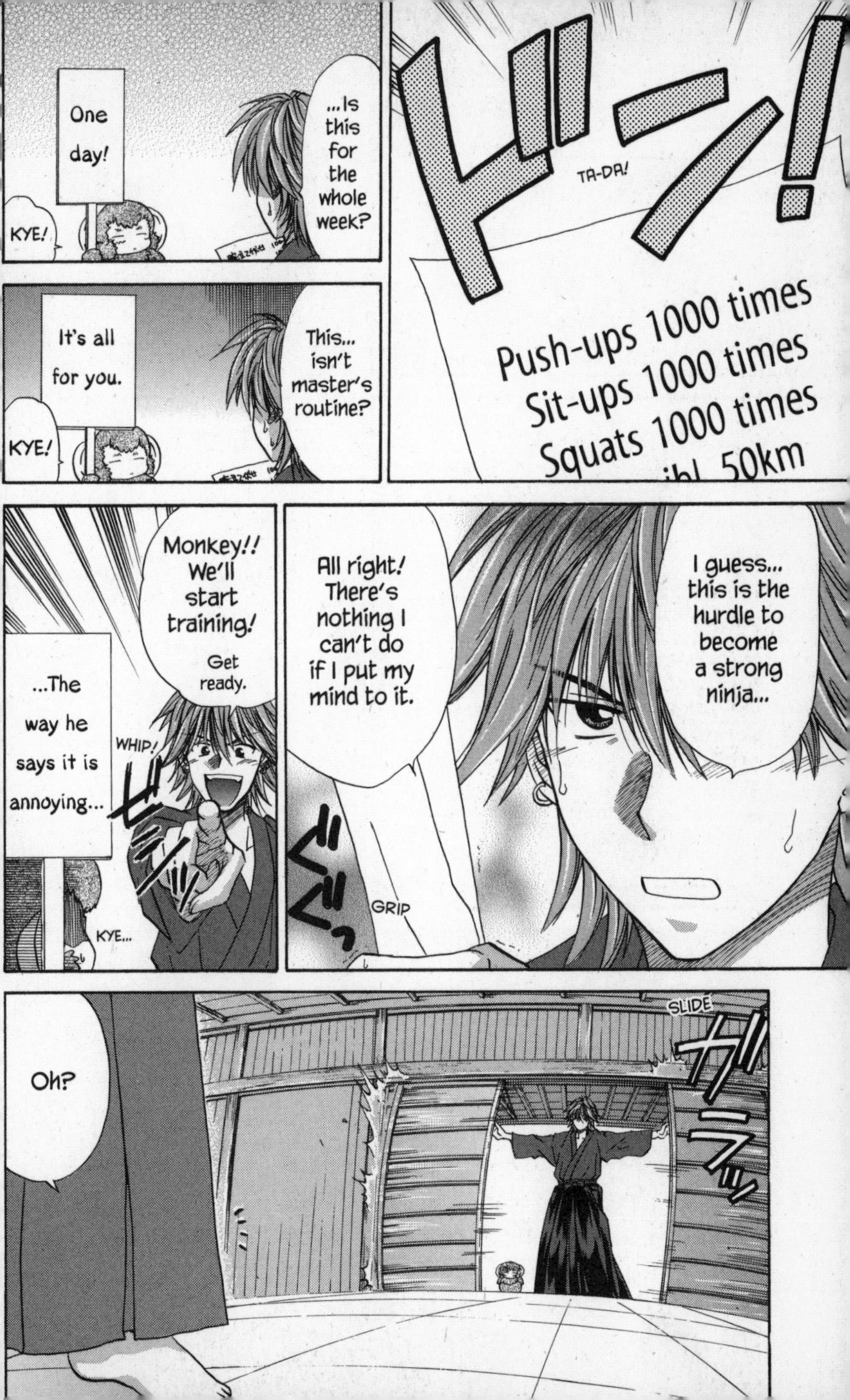
TA-DA!
Push-ups 1000 times
Sit-ups 1000 times
Squats 1000 times
...Is this for the whole week?
One day!
KYE!
This... isn't master's routine?
It's all for you.
KYE!
I guess... this is the hurdle to become a strong ninja...
All right! There's nothing I can't do if I put my mind to it.
GRIP
Monkey!! We'll start training!
Get ready.
WHIP!
...The way he says it is annoying...
KYE...
SLIDE
Oh?

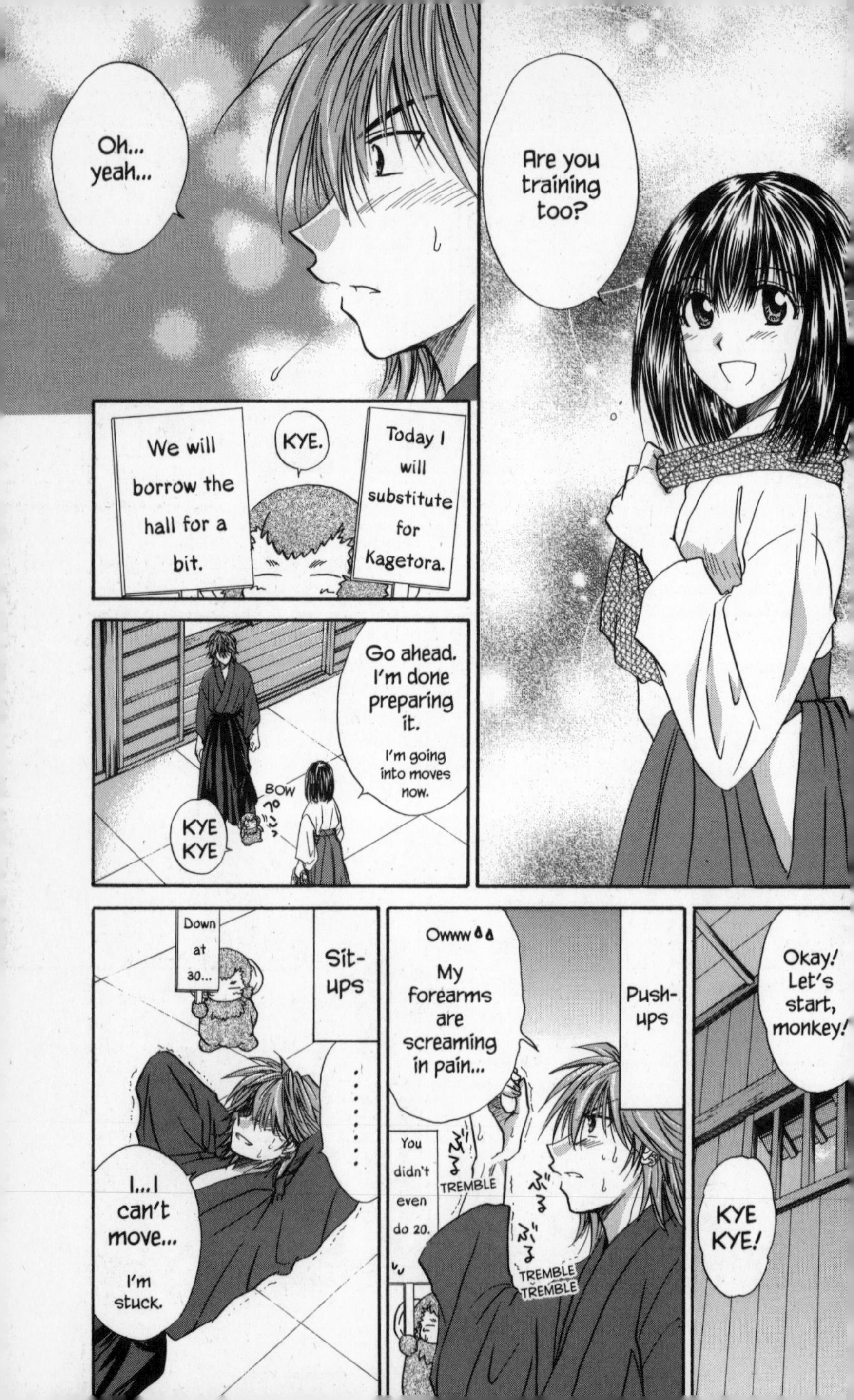

Are you training too?
Oh... yeah...
Today I will substitute for Kagetora.
KYE.
We will borrow the hall for a bit.
Go ahead. I'm done preparing it.
I'm going into moves now.
BOW
KYE KYE
Okay! Let's start, monkey!
KYE KYE!
Push-ups
Owww
My forearms are screaming in pain...
TREMBLE
TREMBLE
TREMBLE
You didn't even do 20.
Sit-ups
Down at 30...
......
I...I can't move...
I'm stuck.

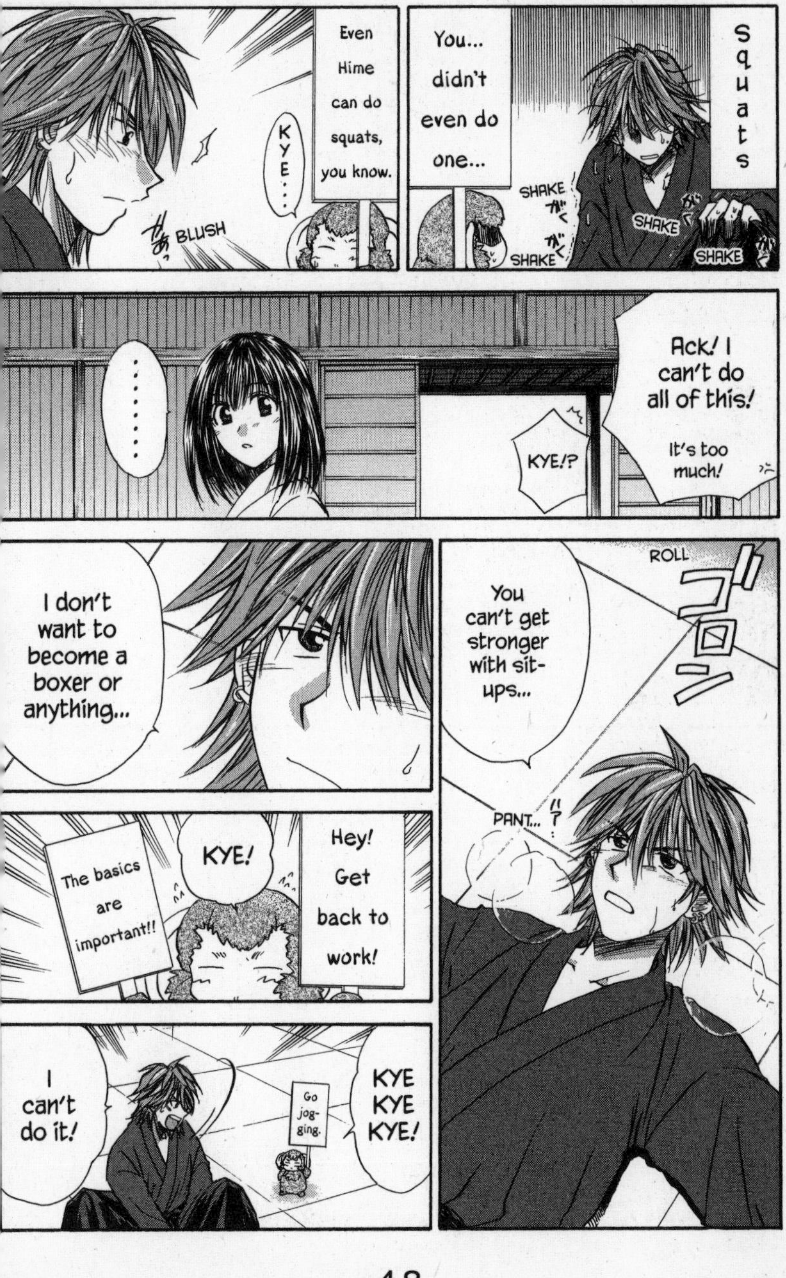
Squats
You... didn't even do one...
SHAKE
SHAKE
SHAKE
SHAKE
Even Hime can do squats, you know.
KYE...
BLUSH
Ack! I can't do all of this!
It's too much!
KYE!?
......
ROLL
You can't get stronger with sit-ups...
PANT...
I don't want to become a boxer or anything...
Hey! Get back to work!
KYE!
The basics are important!!
KYE KYE KYE!
Go jog-ging.
I can't do it!

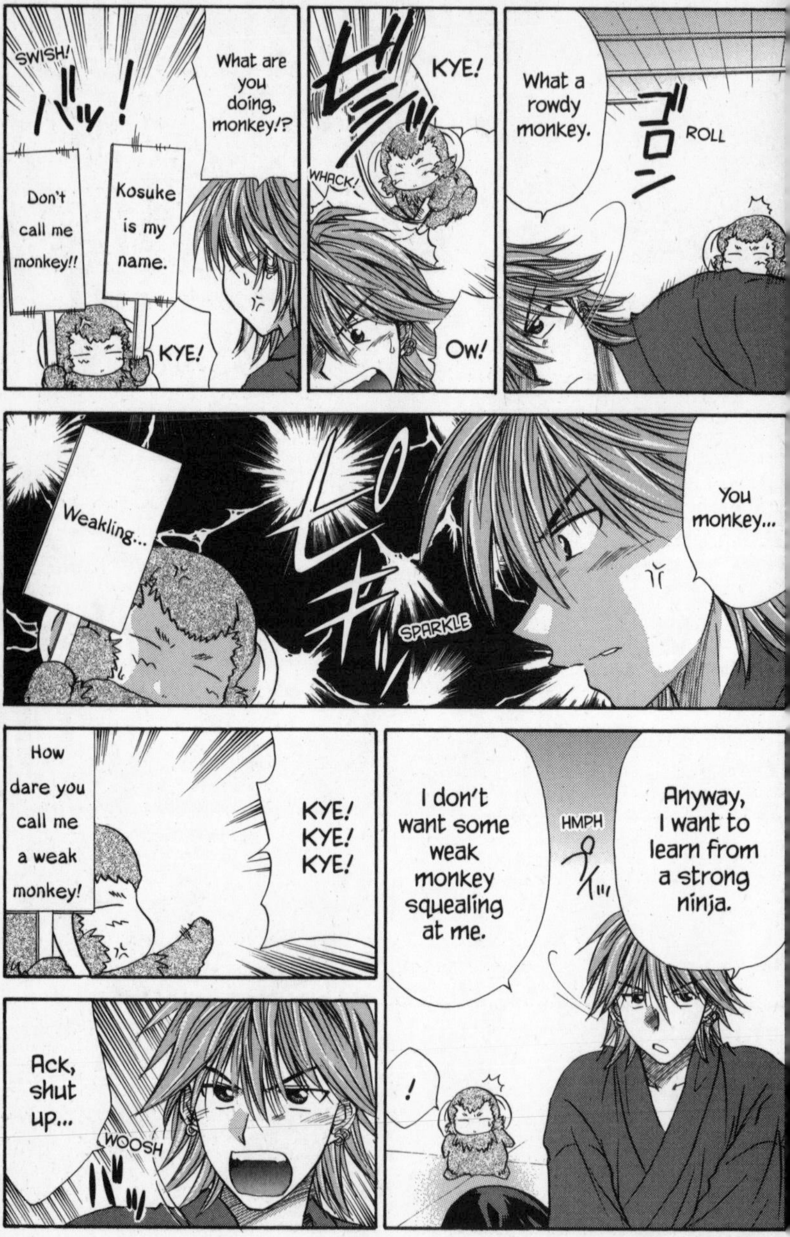
What a rowdy monkey.
ROLL
KYE!
WHACK!
OW!
What are you doing, monkey!?
SWISH!
Kosuke is my name.
Don't call me monkey!!
KYE!
You monkey...
SPARKLE
Weakling...
Anyway, I want to learn from a strong ninja.
HMPH
I don't want some weak monkey squealing at me.
!
KYE! KYE! KYE!
How dare you call me a weak monkey!
Ack, shut up...
WOOSH

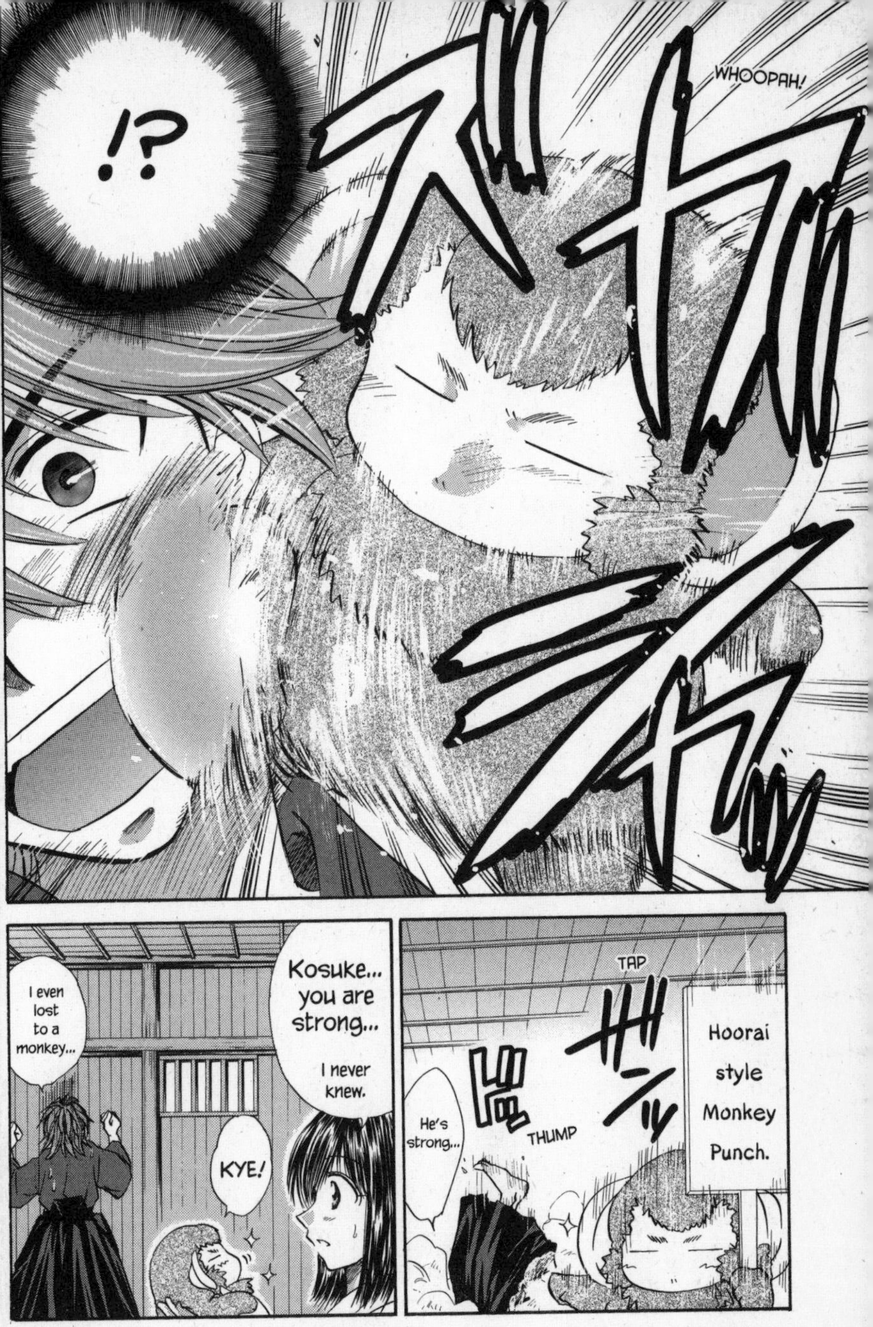
WHOOPAH!
!?
Hoorai style Monkey Punch.
TAP
THUMP
He's strong...
Kosuke... you are strong...
I never knew.
KYE!
I even lost to a monkey...

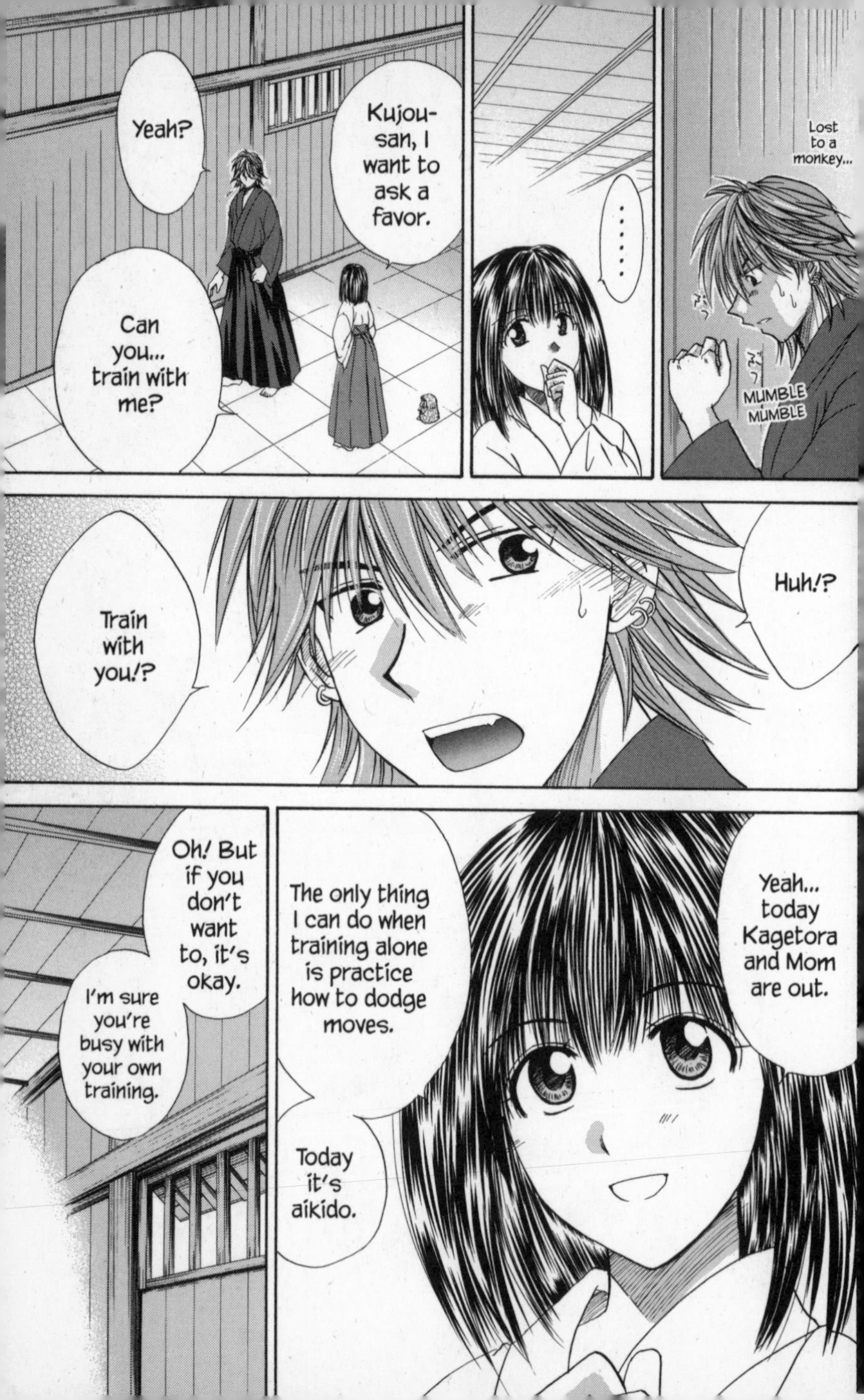
Lost to a monkey...
MUMBLE MUMBLE
......
Kujou-san, I want to ask a favor.
Yeah?
Can you... train with me?
Huh!?
Train with you!?
Yeah... today Kagetora and Mom are out.
The only thing I can do when training alone is practice how to dodge moves.
Today it's aikido.
Oh! But if you don't want to, it's okay.
I'm sure you're busy with your own training.

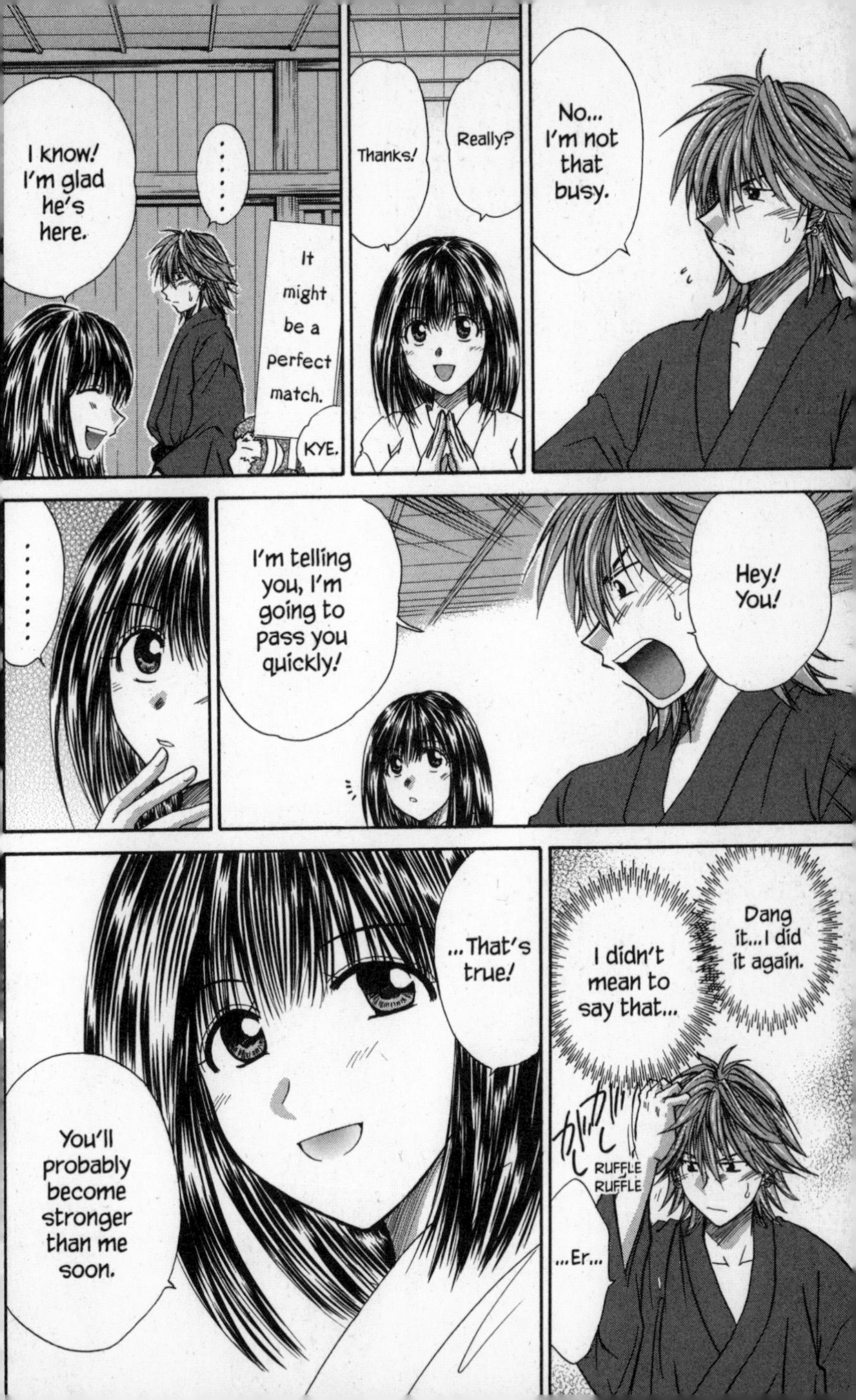
No... I'm not that busy.
Really?
Thanks!
......
I know! I'm glad he's here.
It might be a perfect match.
KYE.
Hey! You!
I'm telling you, I'm going to pass you quickly!
......
Dang it...I did it again.
I didn't mean to say that...
RUFFLE RUFFLE
...Er...
...That's true!
You'll probably become stronger than me soon.

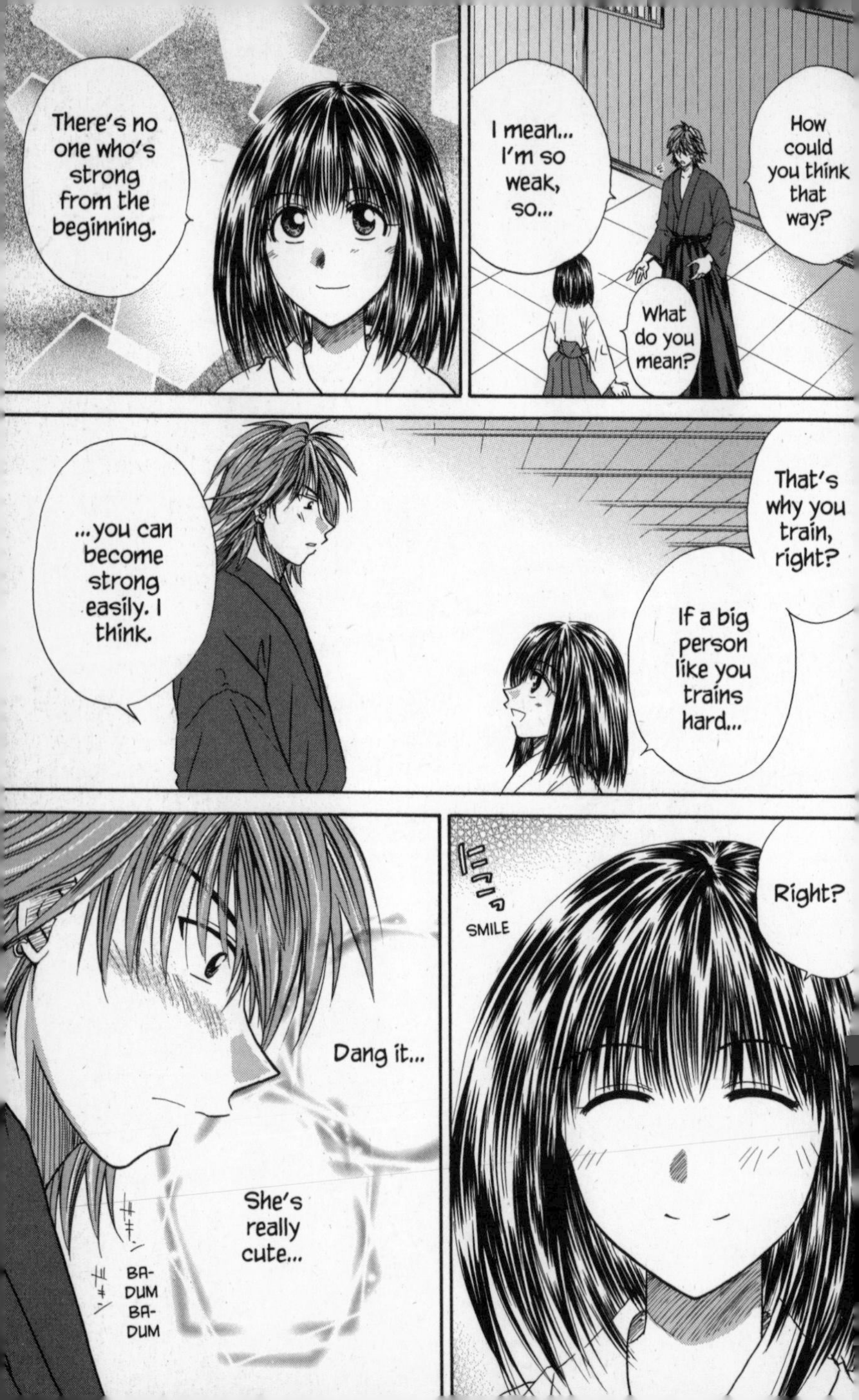
How could you think that way?
I mean... I'm so weak, so...
What do you mean?
There's no one who's strong from the beginning.
That's why you train, right?
If a big person like you trains hard...
...you can become strong easily. I think.
Right?
SMILE
Dang it...
She's really cute...
BA-DUM BA-DUM

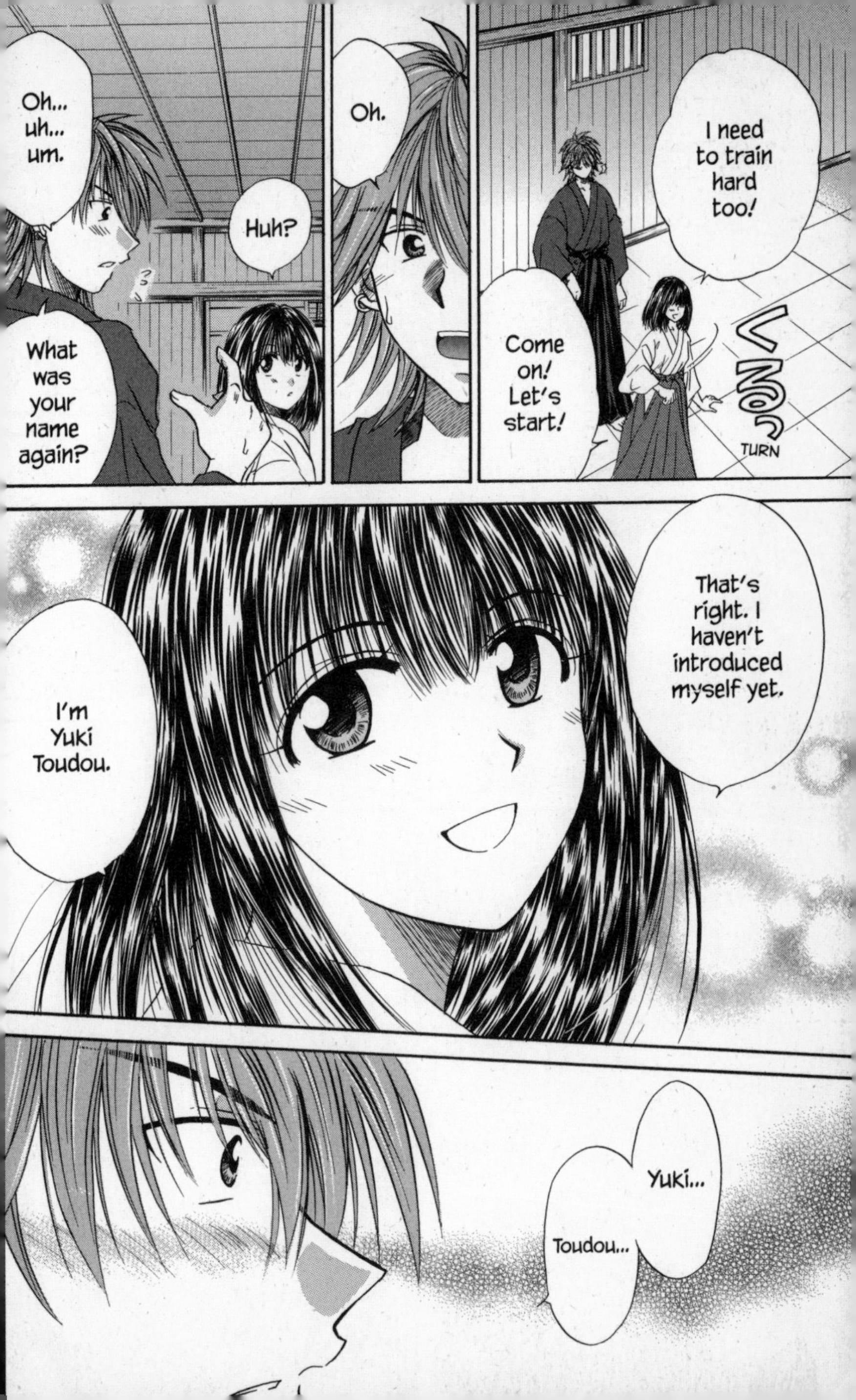

I need to train hard too!
Come on! Let's start!
くるっ
TURN
Oh.
Oh... uh... um.
Huh?
What was your name again?
That's right. I haven't introduced myself yet.
I'm Yuki Toudou.
Yuki...
Toudou...

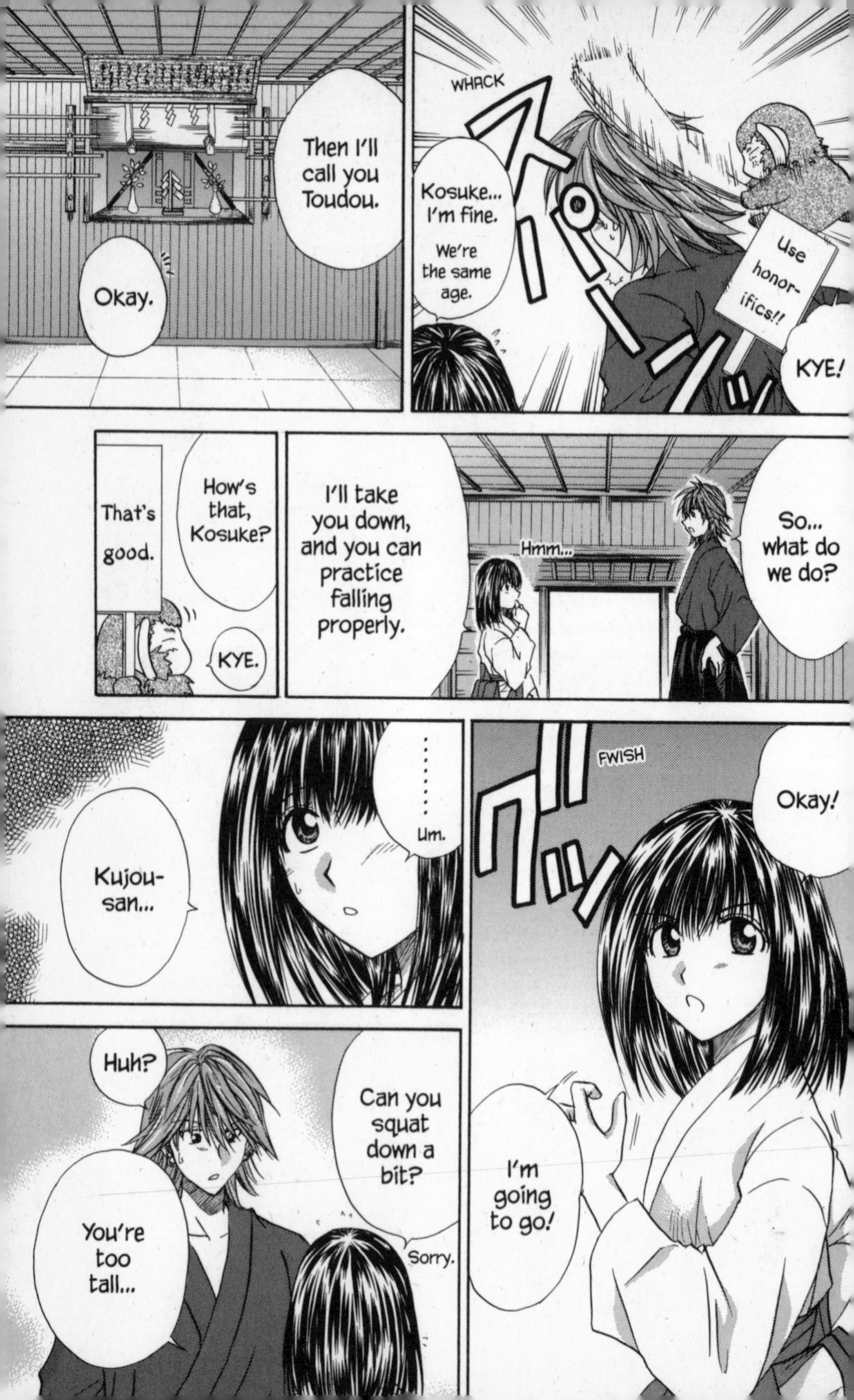
WHACK
Kosuke... I'm fine.
We're the same age.
Use honor-ifics!!
KYE!
Then I'll call you Toudou.
Okay.
So... what do we do?
Hmm...
I'll take you down, and you can practice falling properly.
How's that, Kosuke?
That's good.
KYE.
FWISH
Okay!
I'm going to go!
......
Um.
Kujou-san...
Can you squat down a bit?
Huh?
Sorry.
You're too tall...

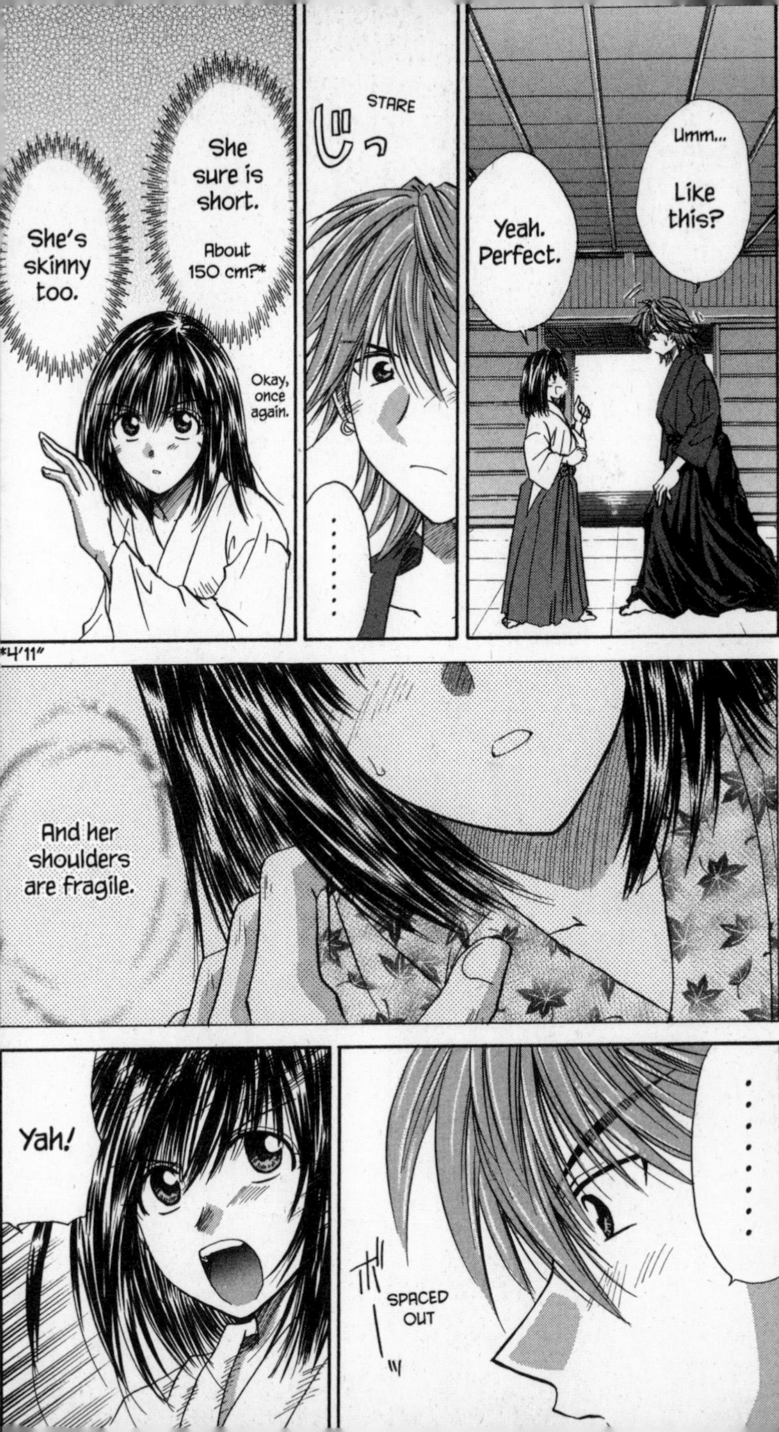
Umm...
Like this?
Yeah. Perfect.
じっ
STARE
......
She sure is short.
About 150 cm?*
She's skinny too.
Okay, once again.
And her shoulders are fragile.
....
ボ
SPACED OUT
Yah!
*4'11"

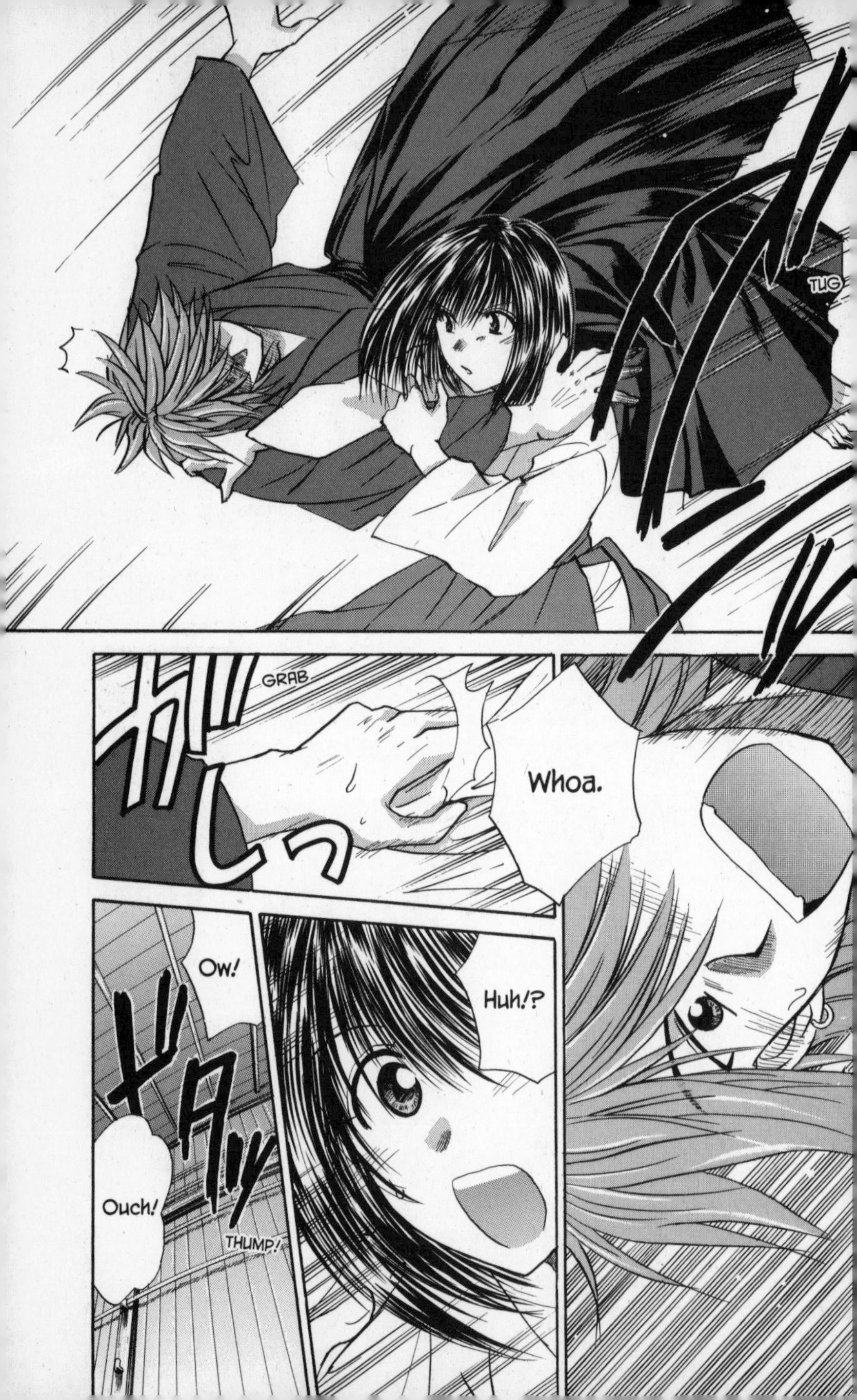
TUG
GRAB
Whoa.
Huh!?
Ow!
Ouch!
THUMP!

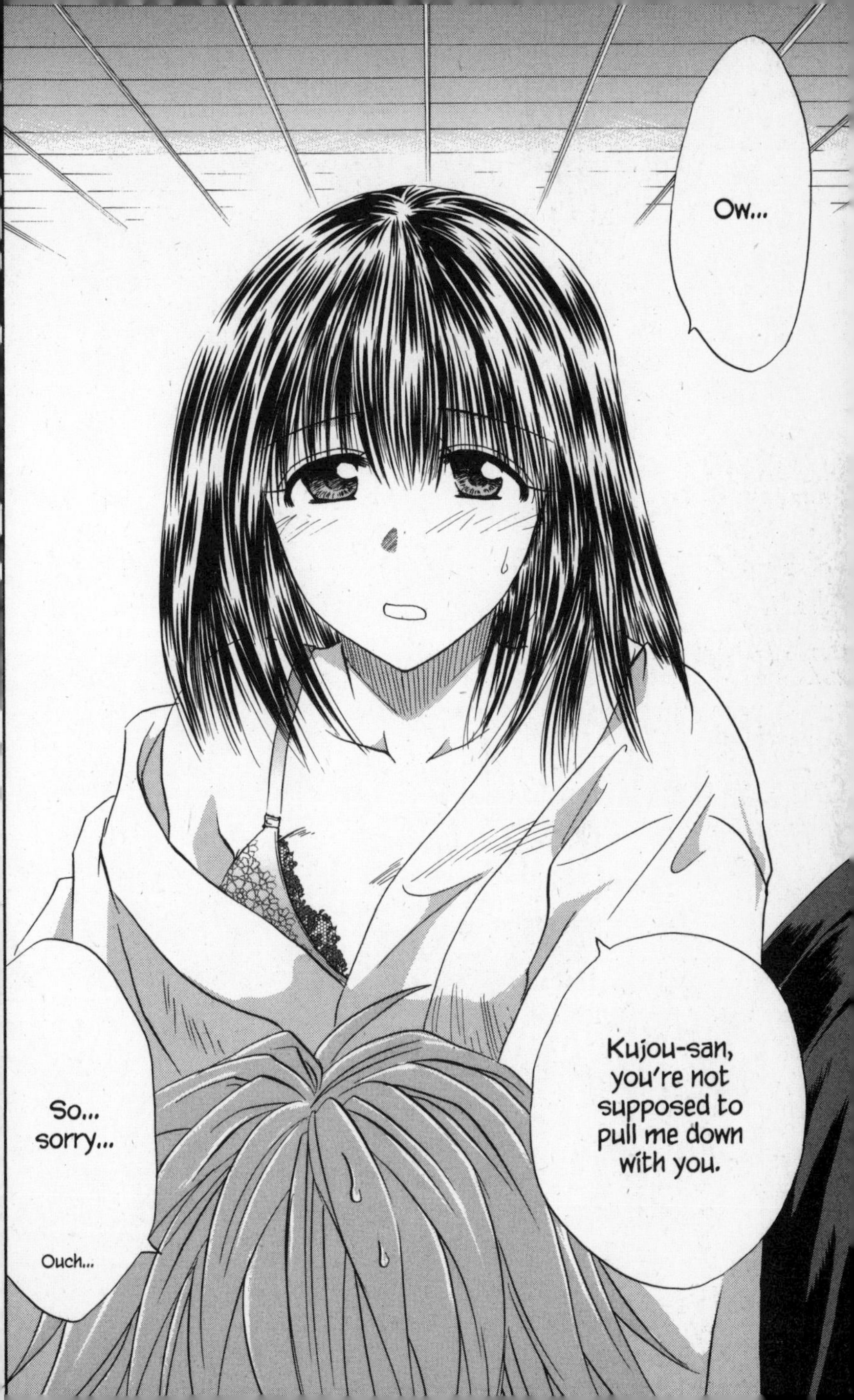
Ow...
Kujou-san, you're not supposed to pull me down with you.
So... sorry...
Ouch...

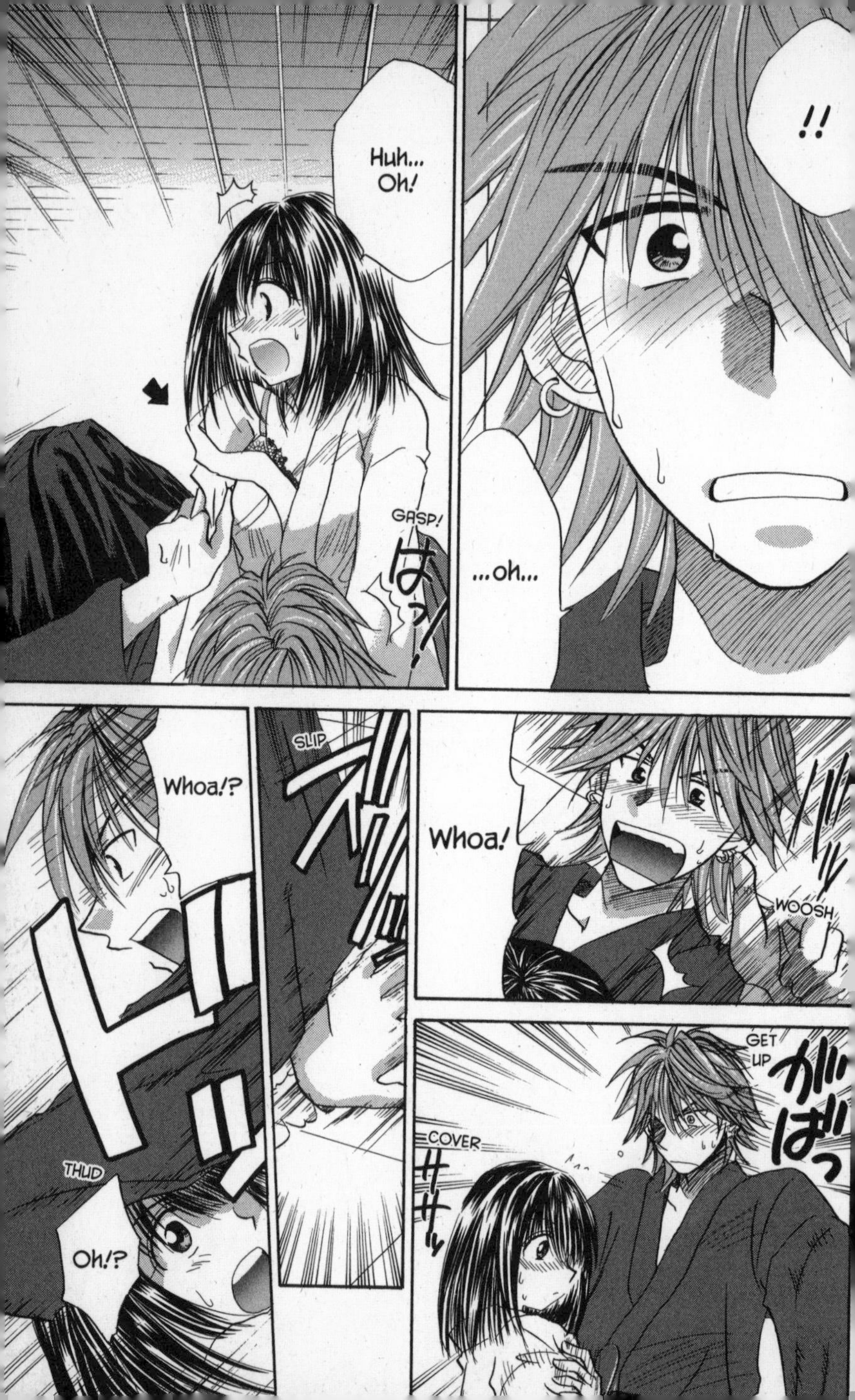
!!
...oh...
Huh... Oh!
GASP!
はっ
Whoa!
WOOSH
GET UP
がばっ
COVER
サッ
SLIP
Whoa!?
THUD
Oh!?

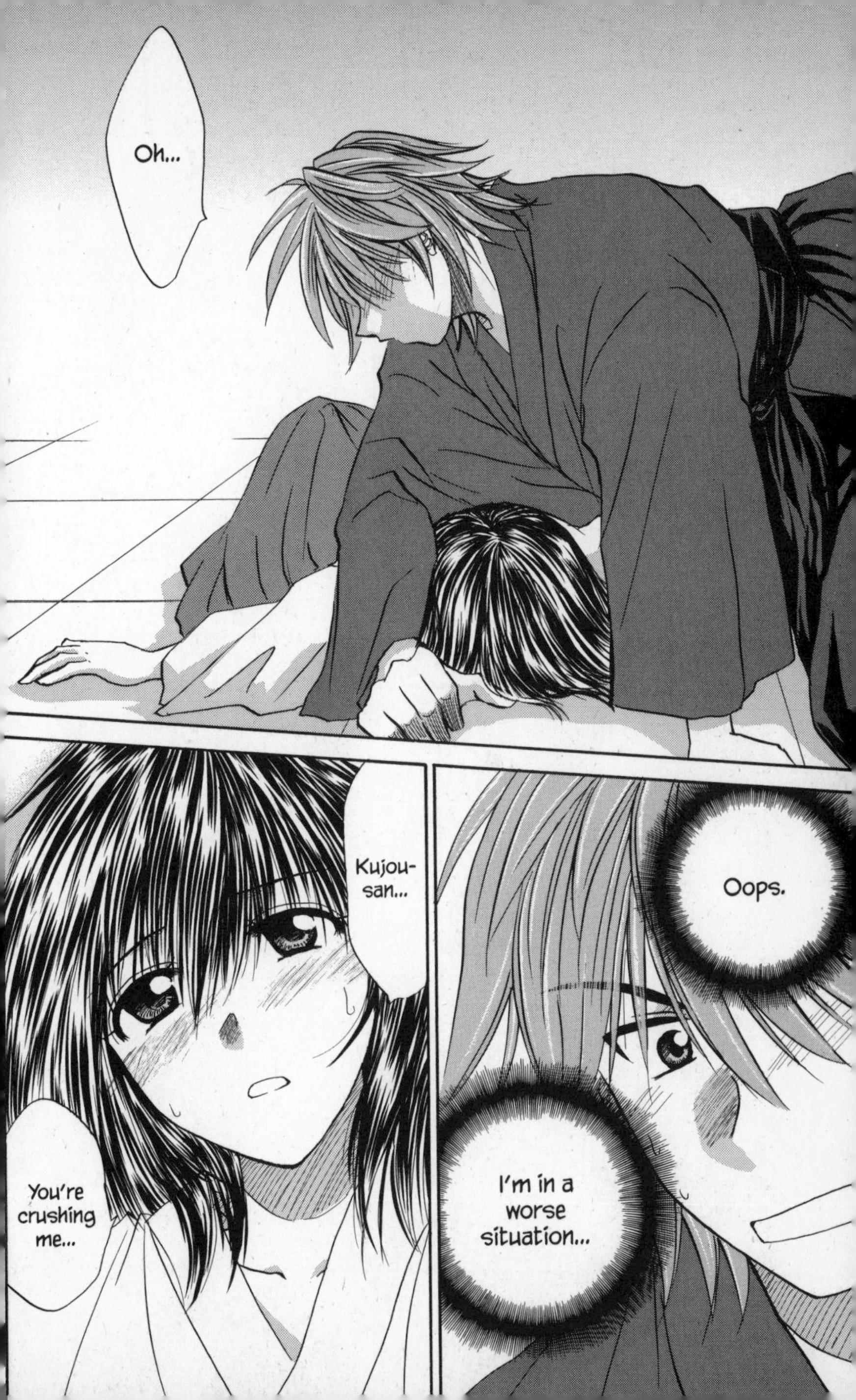
Oh...
Oops.
I'm in a worse situation...
Kujou-san...
You're crushing me...

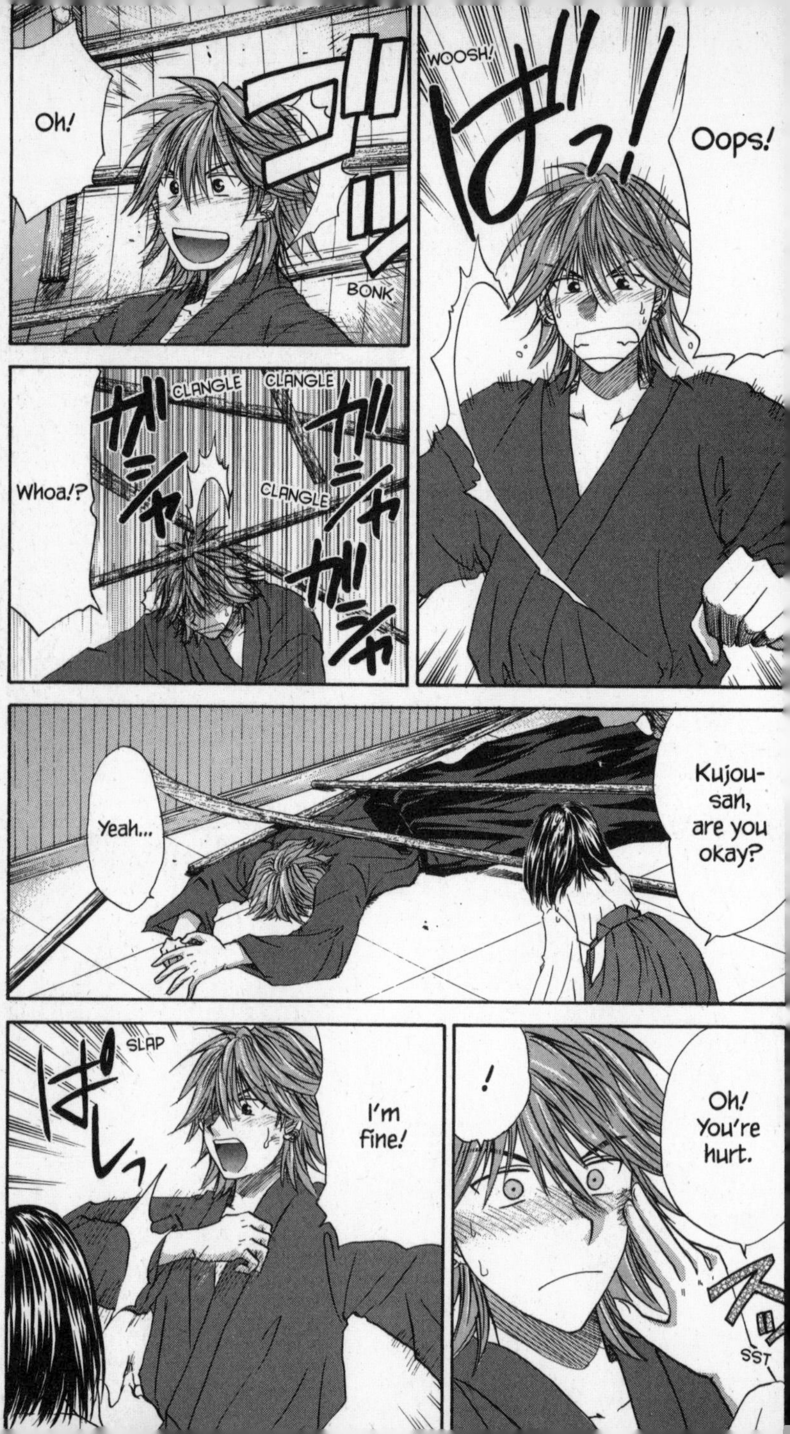

WOOSH!
Oops!
Oh!
BONK
Whoa!?
CLANGLE
CLANGLE
CLANGLE
Kujou-san, are you okay?
Yeah...
!
Oh! You're hurt.
SST
SLAP
I'm fine!

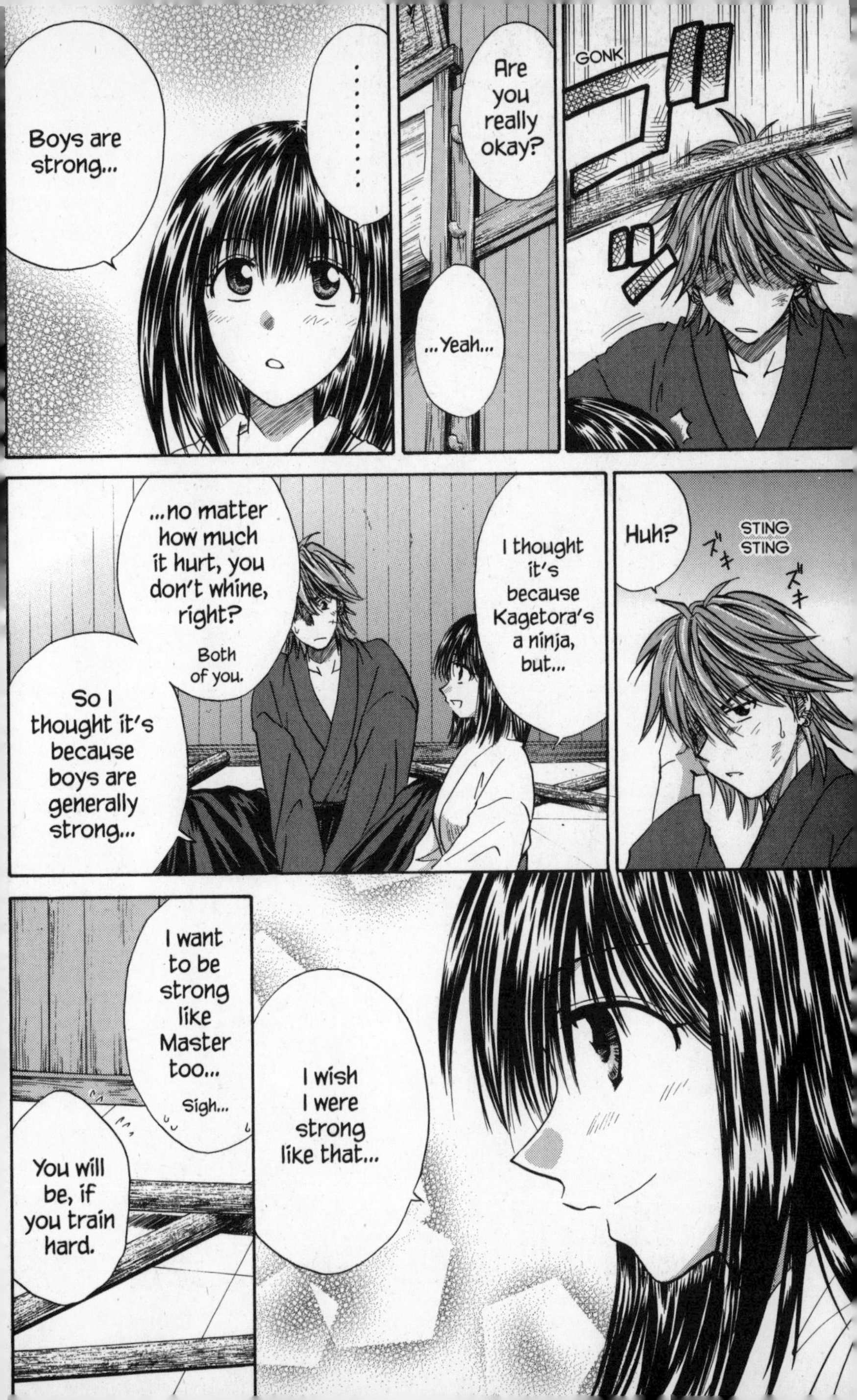
GONK
Are you really okay?
...Yeah...
......
Boys are strong...
Huh?
STING STING
I thought it's because Kagetora's a ninja, but...
...no matter how much it hurt, you don't whine, right?
Both of you.
So I thought it's because boys are generally strong...
I wish I were strong like that...
I want to be strong like Master too...
Sigh...
You will be, if you train hard.

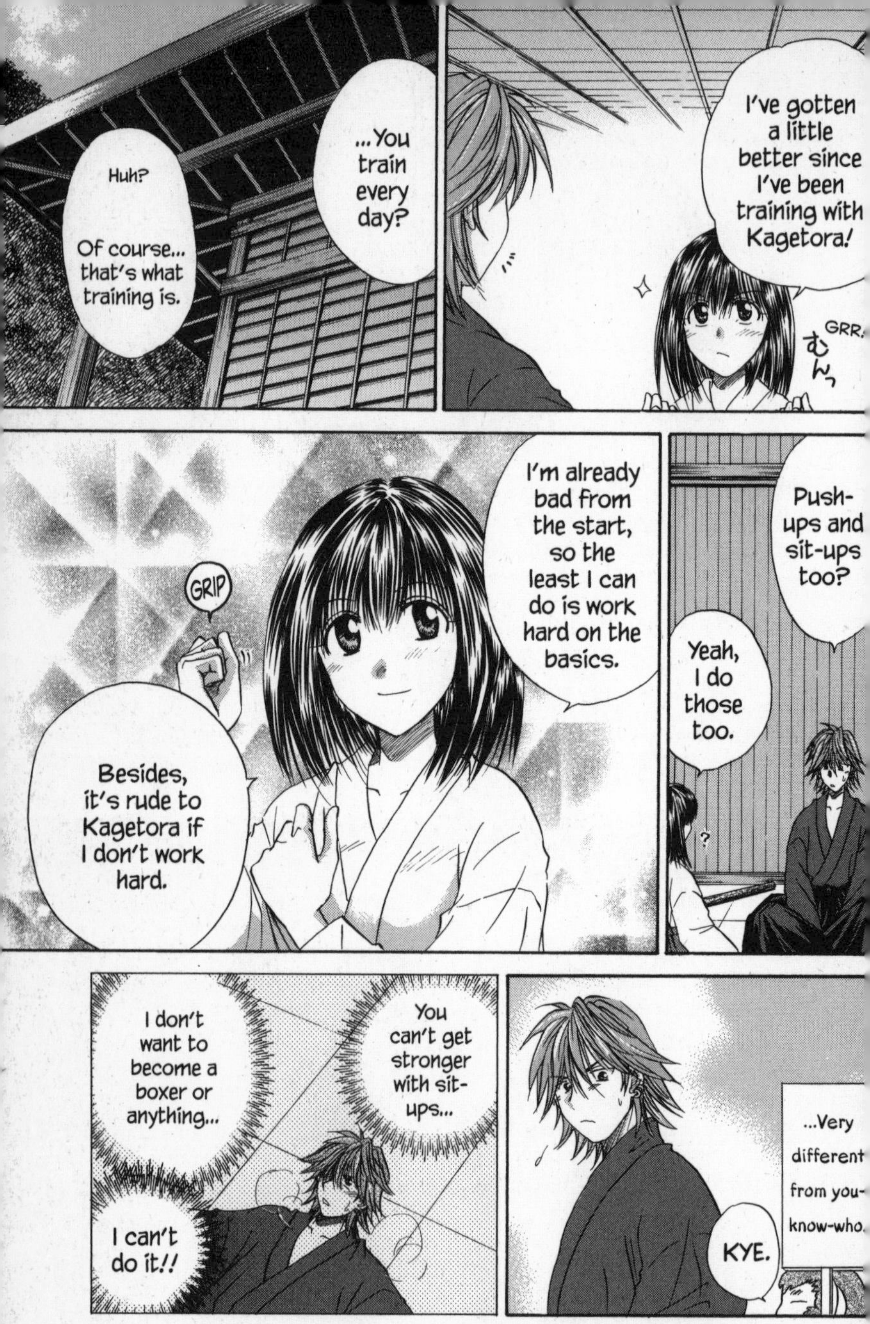
I've gotten a little better since I've been training with Kagetora!
むんっ
GRR.
...You train every day?
Huh?
Of course... that's what training is.
Push-ups and sit-ups too?
Yeah, I do those too.
?
I'm already bad from the start, so the least I can do is work hard on the basics.
GRIP
Besides, it's rude to Kagetora if I don't work hard.
...Very different from you-know-who.
KYE.
You can't get stronger with sit-ups...
I don't want to become a boxer or anything...
I can't do it!!

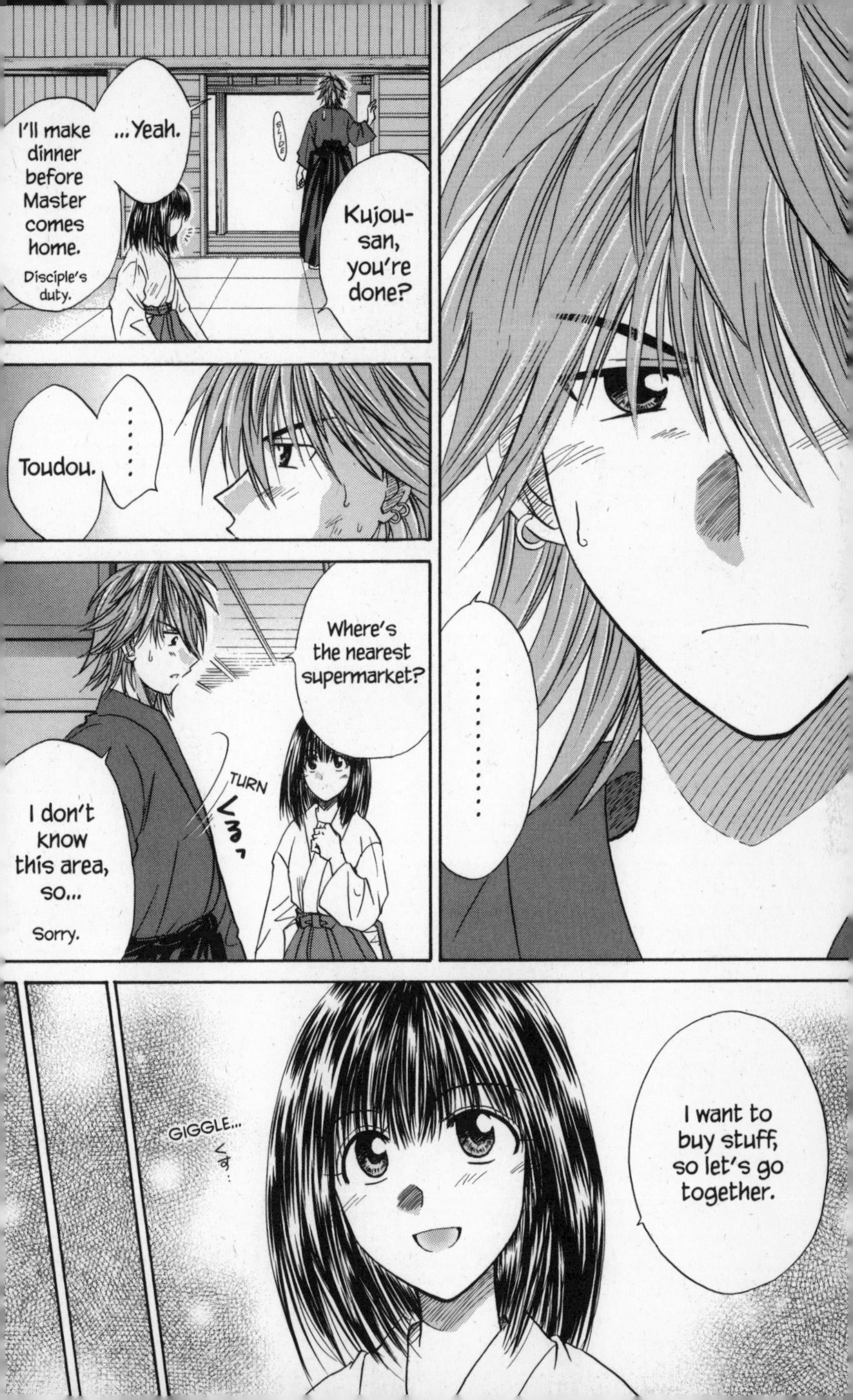
....
Kujou-san, you're done?
SLIDE
...Yeah.
I'll make dinner before Master comes home.
Disciple's duty.
......
Toudou.
Where's the nearest supermarket?
TURN
くる
I don't know this area, so...
Sorry.
I want to buy stuff, so let's go together.
GIGGLE...
くす...

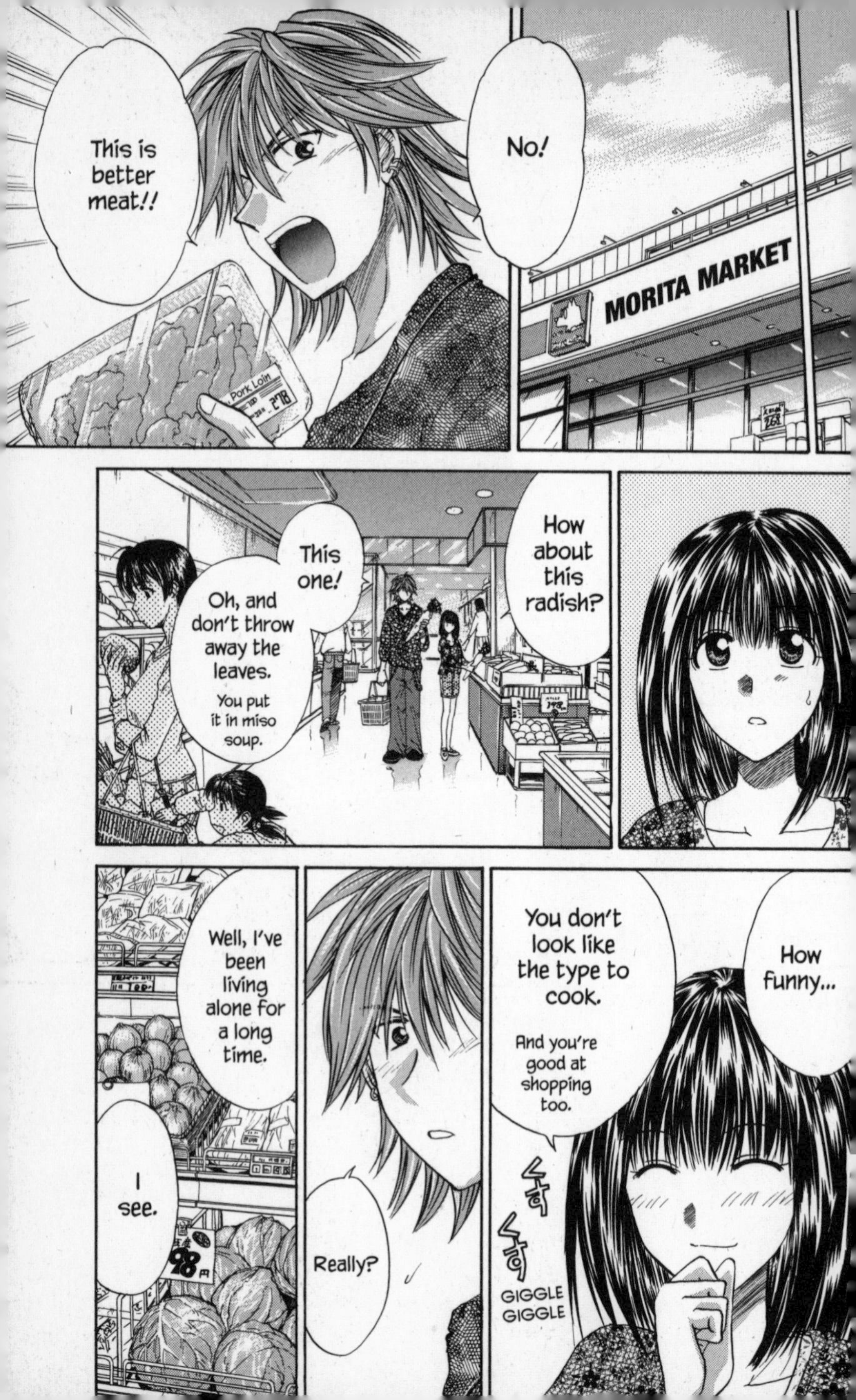
MORITA MARKET
No!
This is better meat!!
Pork Loin
How about this radish?
This one!
Oh, and don't throw away the leaves.
You put it in miso soup.
How funny...
You don't look like the type to cook.
And you're good at shopping too.
くす くす
GIGGLE GIGGLE
Really?
Well, I've been living alone for a long time.
I see.

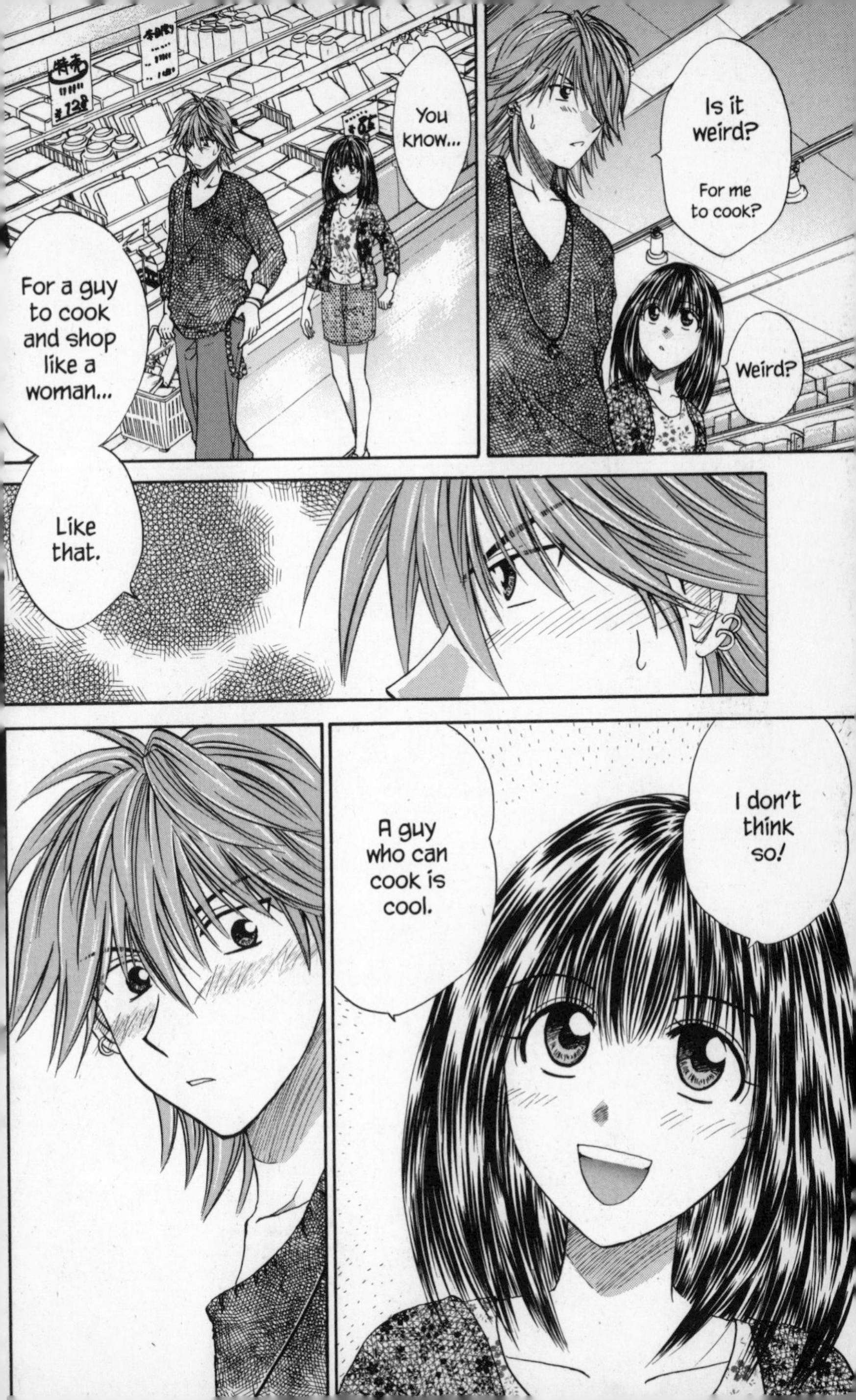
Is it weird?
For me to cook?
Weird?
You know...
For a guy to cook and shop like a woman...
Like that.
I don't think so!
A guy who can cook is cool.

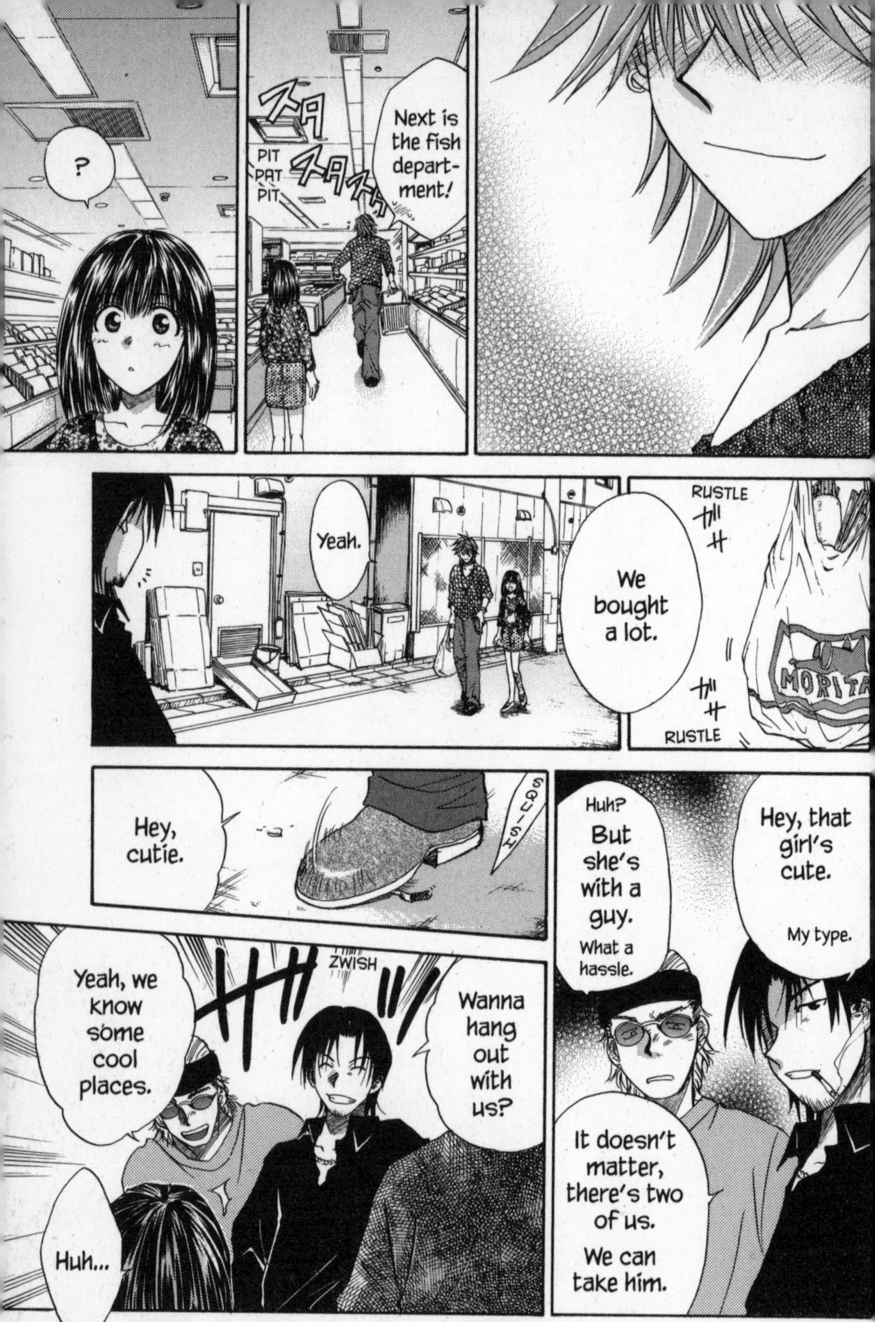
PIT
PAT
PIT
Next is the fish department!
?
RUSTLE
We bought a lot.
RUSTLE
MORITA
Yeah.
Hey, that girl's cute.
My type.
Huh?
But she's with a guy.
What a hassle.
It doesn't matter, there's two of us.
We can take him.
SQUISH
Hey, cutie.
Wanna hang out with us?
ZWISH
Yeah, we know some cool places.
Huh...

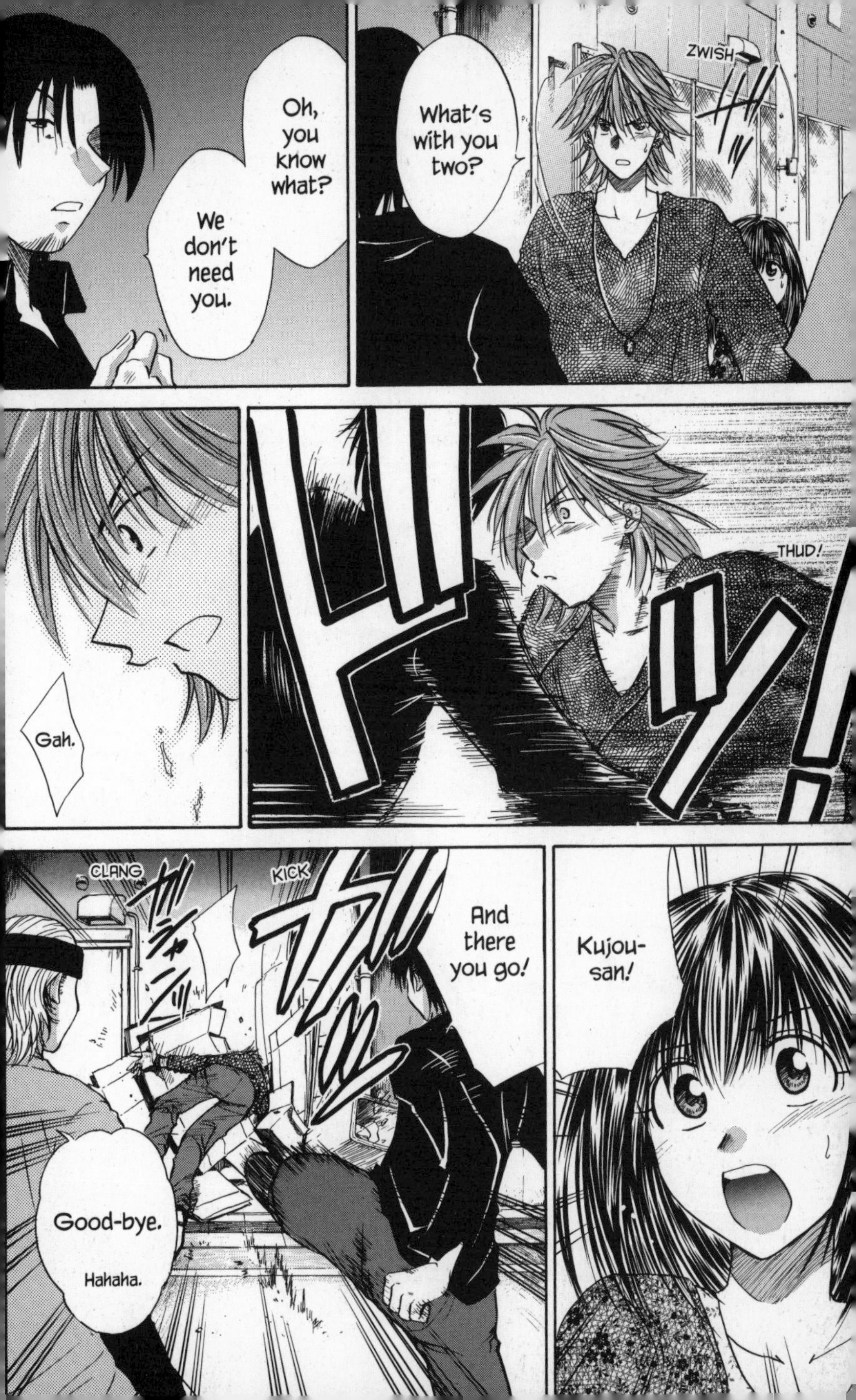
ZWISH
What's with you two?
Oh, you know what?
We don't need you.
THUD!
Gah.
Kujou-san!
And there you go!
KICK
CLANG
Good-bye.
Hahaha.

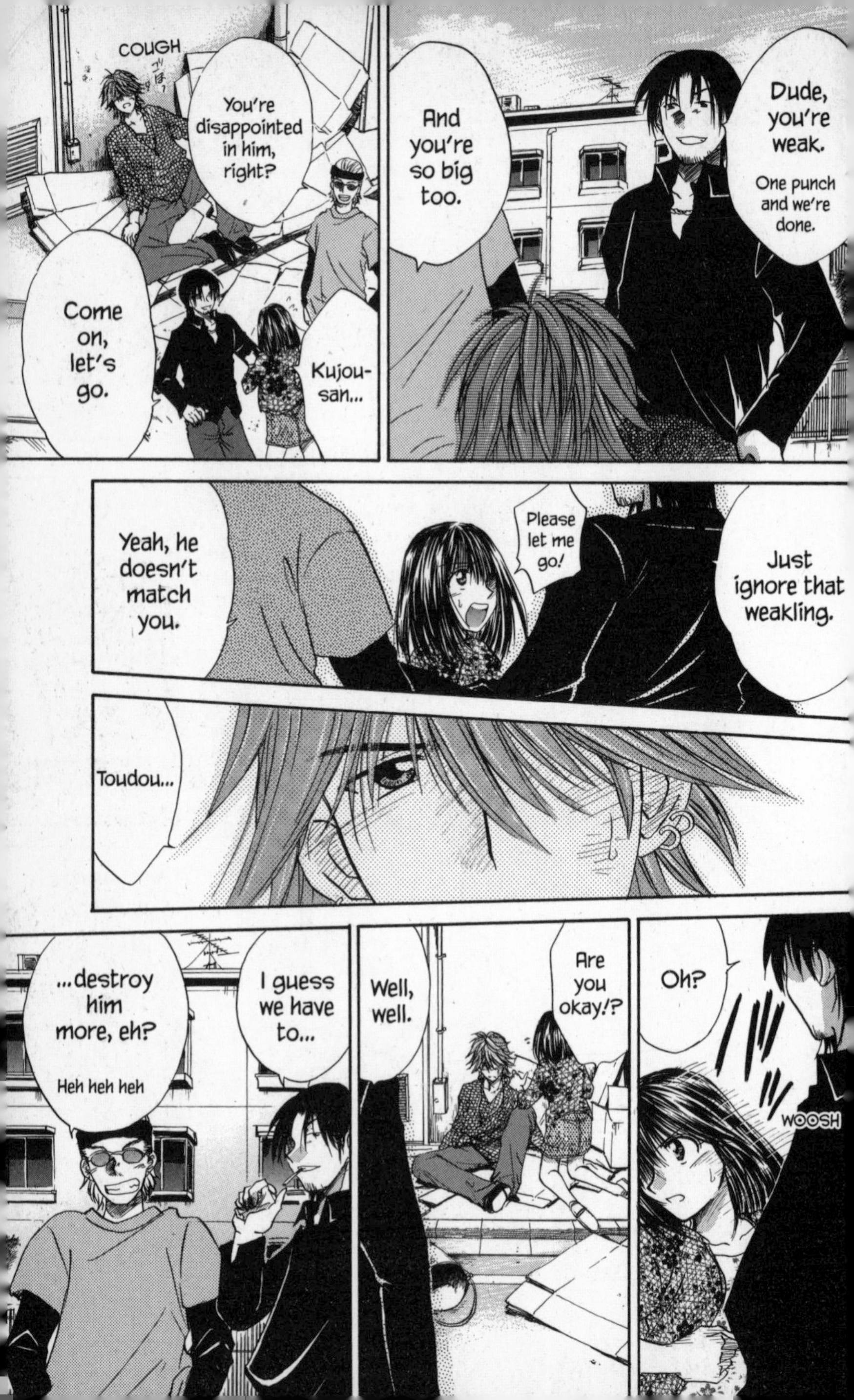
Dude, you're weak.
One punch and we're done.
And you're so big too.
COUGH
You're disappointed in him, right?
Kujou-san...
Come on, let's go.
Just ignore that weakling.
Please let me go!
Yeah, he doesn't match you.
Toudou...
Oh?
WOOSH
Are you okay!?
Well, well.
I guess we have to...
...destroy him more, eh?
Heh heh heh

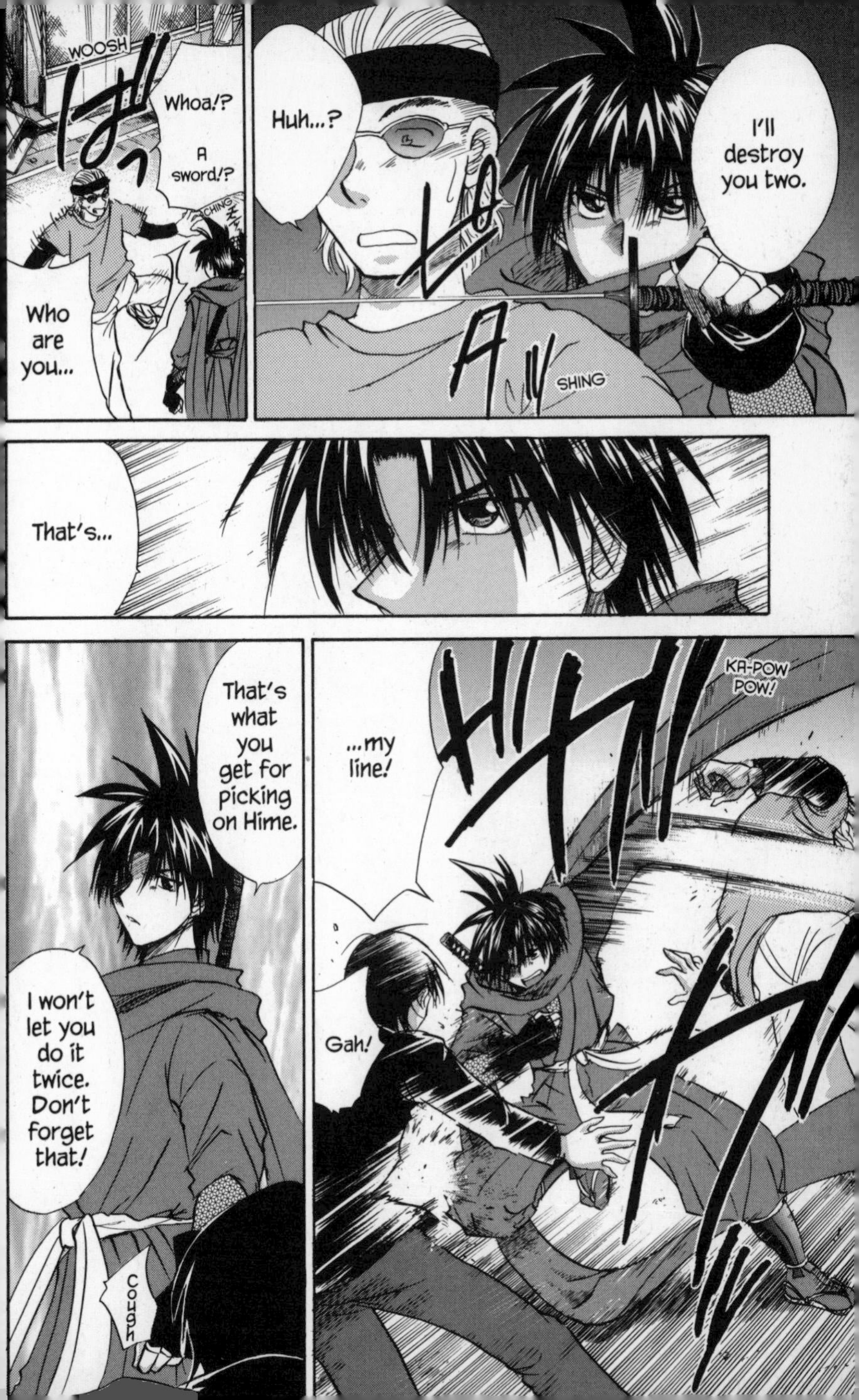
I'll destroy you two.
Huh...?
SHING
WOOSH
Whoa!?
A sword!?
CHING
Who are you...
That's...
KA-POW POW!
...my line!
Gah!
That's what you get for picking on Hime.
I won't let you do it twice. Don't forget that!
Cough

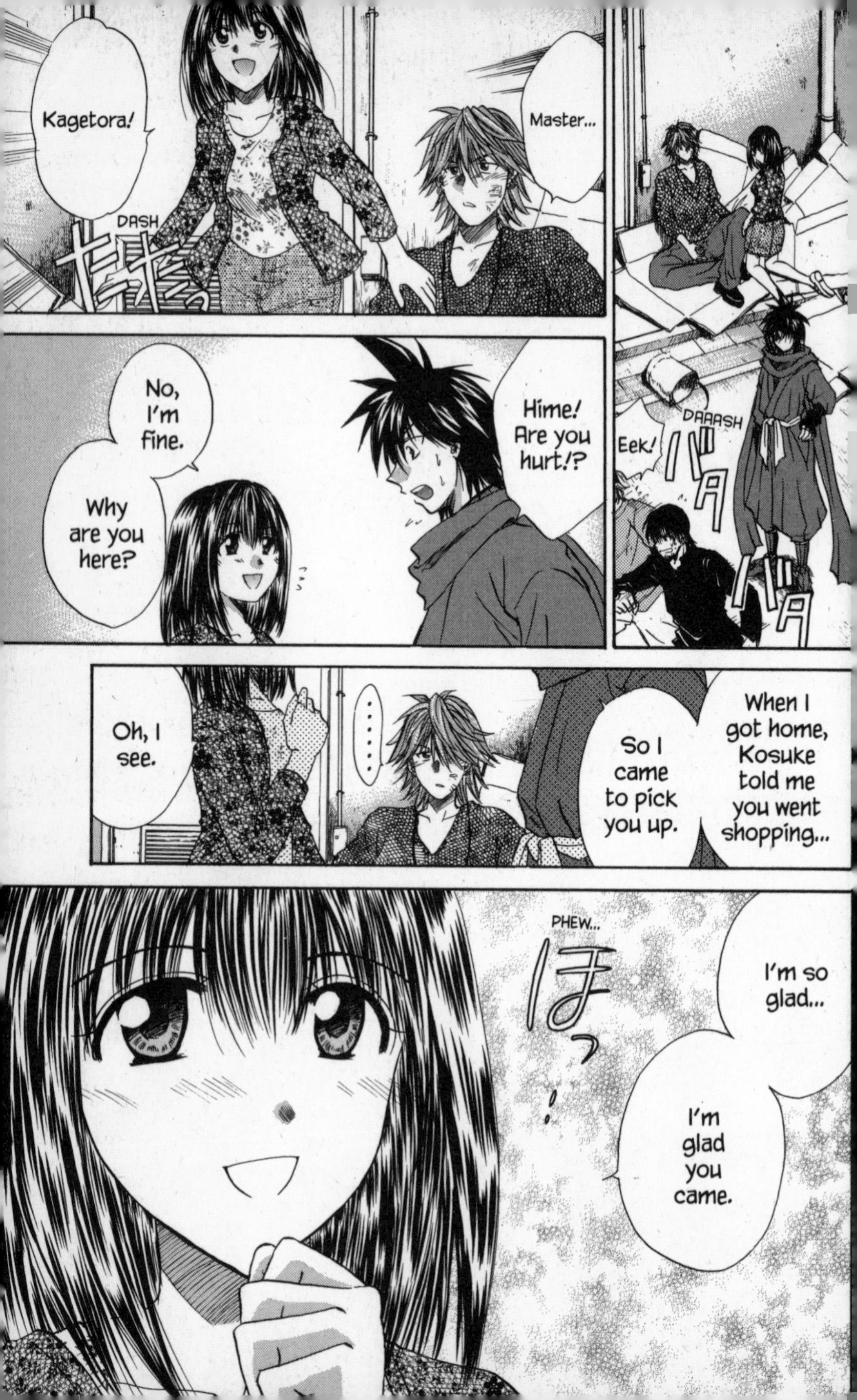
DAAASH
Eek!
Master...
Kagetora!
DASH
Hime! Are you hurt!?
No, I'm fine.
Why are you here?
When I got home, Kosuke told me you went shopping...
So I came to pick you up.
......
Oh, I see.
PHEW...
I'm so glad...
I'm glad you came.

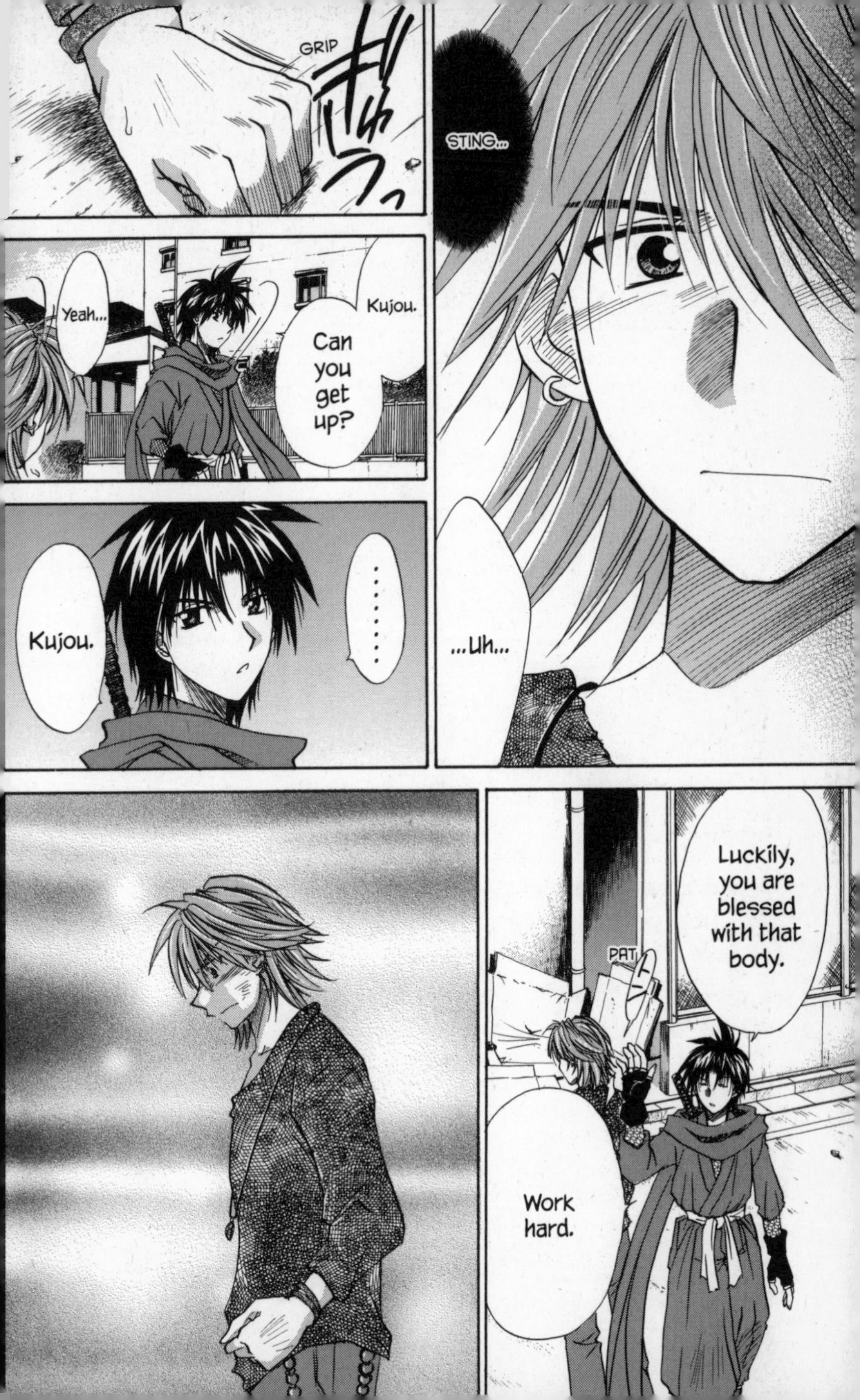
STING...
...uh...
GRIP
Kujou.
Can you get up?
Yeah...
......
Kujou.
Luckily, you are blessed with that body.
PAT
Work hard.

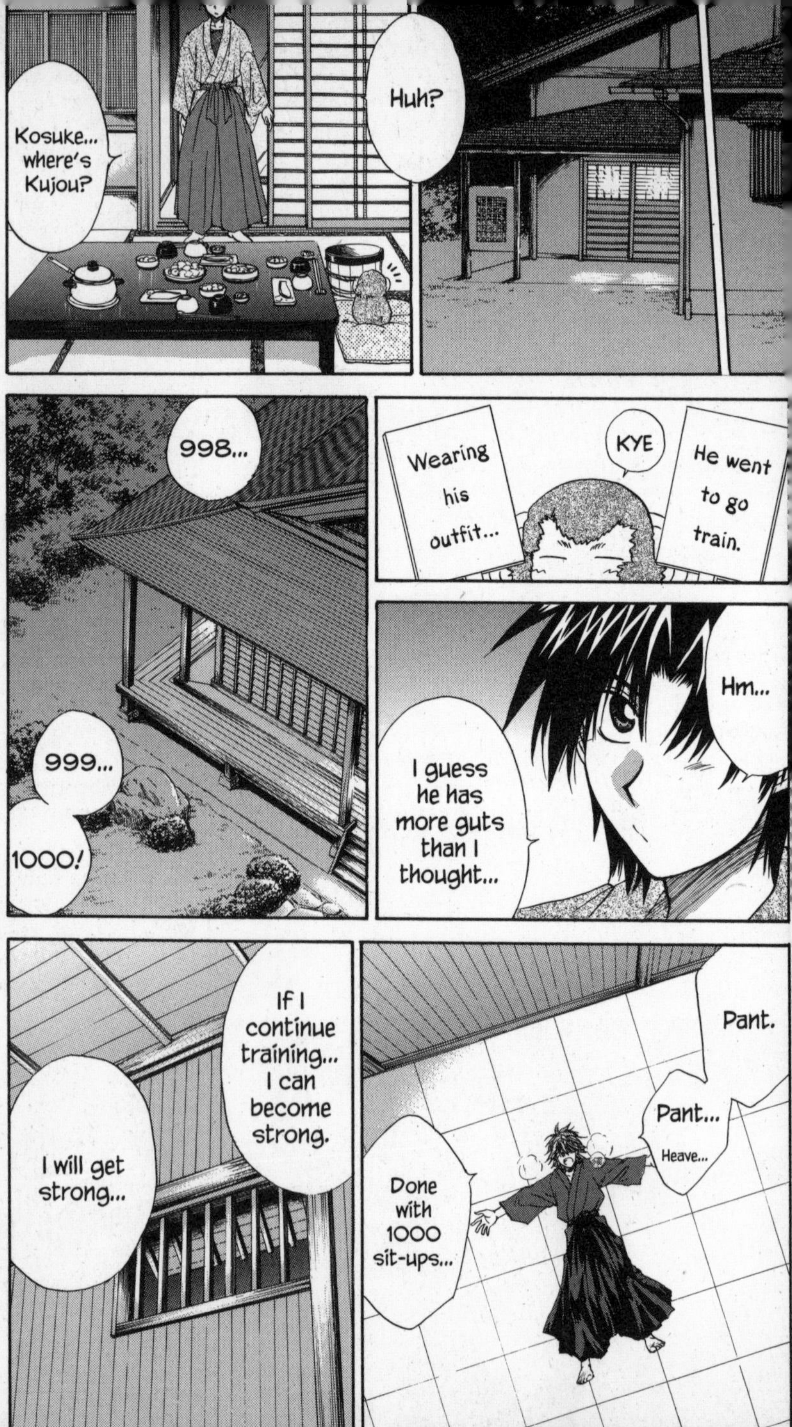
Huh?
Kosuke... where's Kujou?
He went to go train.
KYE
Wearing his outfit...
Hm...
I guess he has more guts than I thought...
998...
999...
1000!
Pant.
Pant...
Heave...
Done with 1000 sit-ups...
If I continue training... I can become strong.
I will get strong...

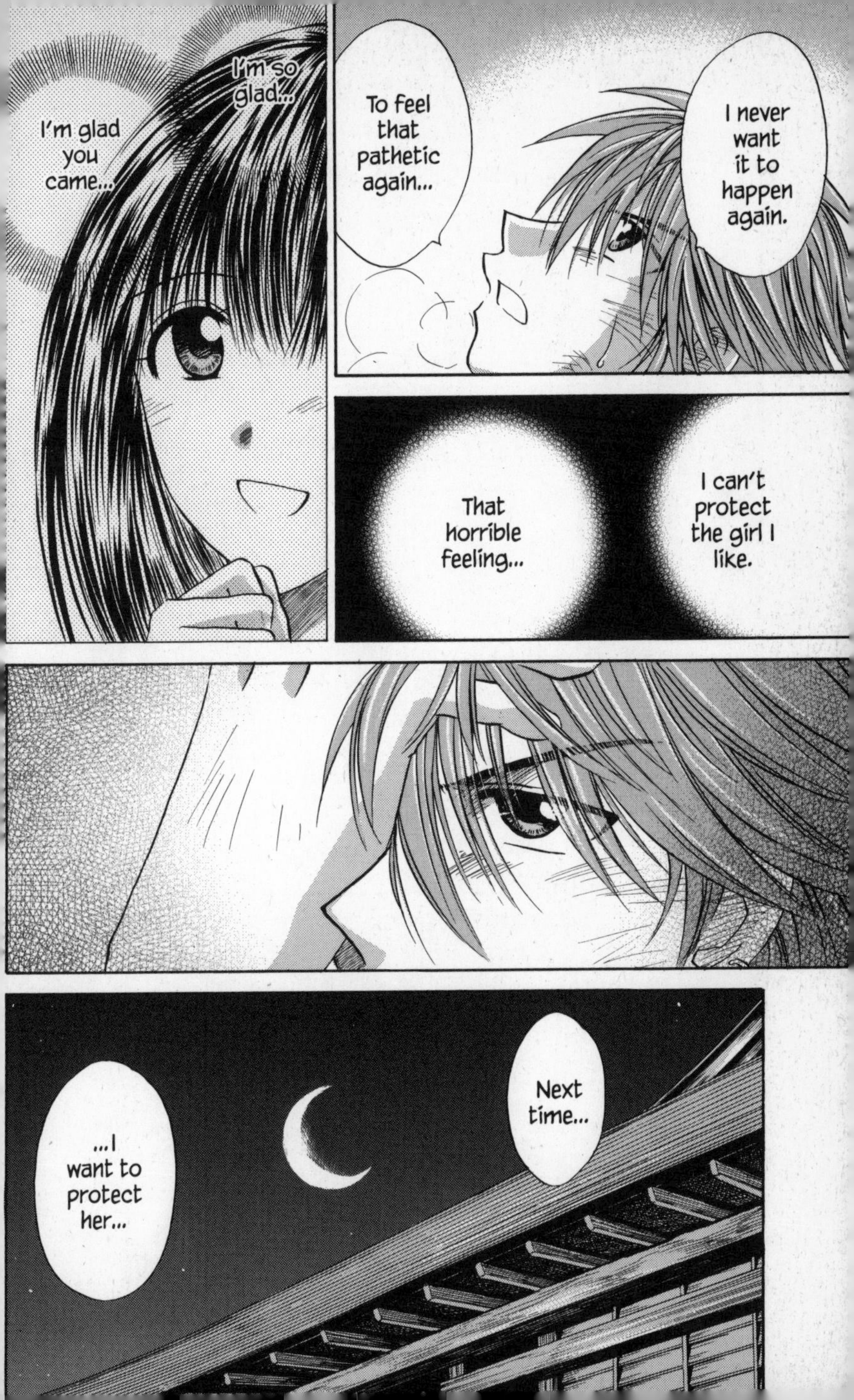
I never want it to happen again.
To feel that pathetic again...
I can't protect the girl I like.
That horrible feeling...
I'm so glad...
I'm glad you came...
Next time...
...I want to protect her...

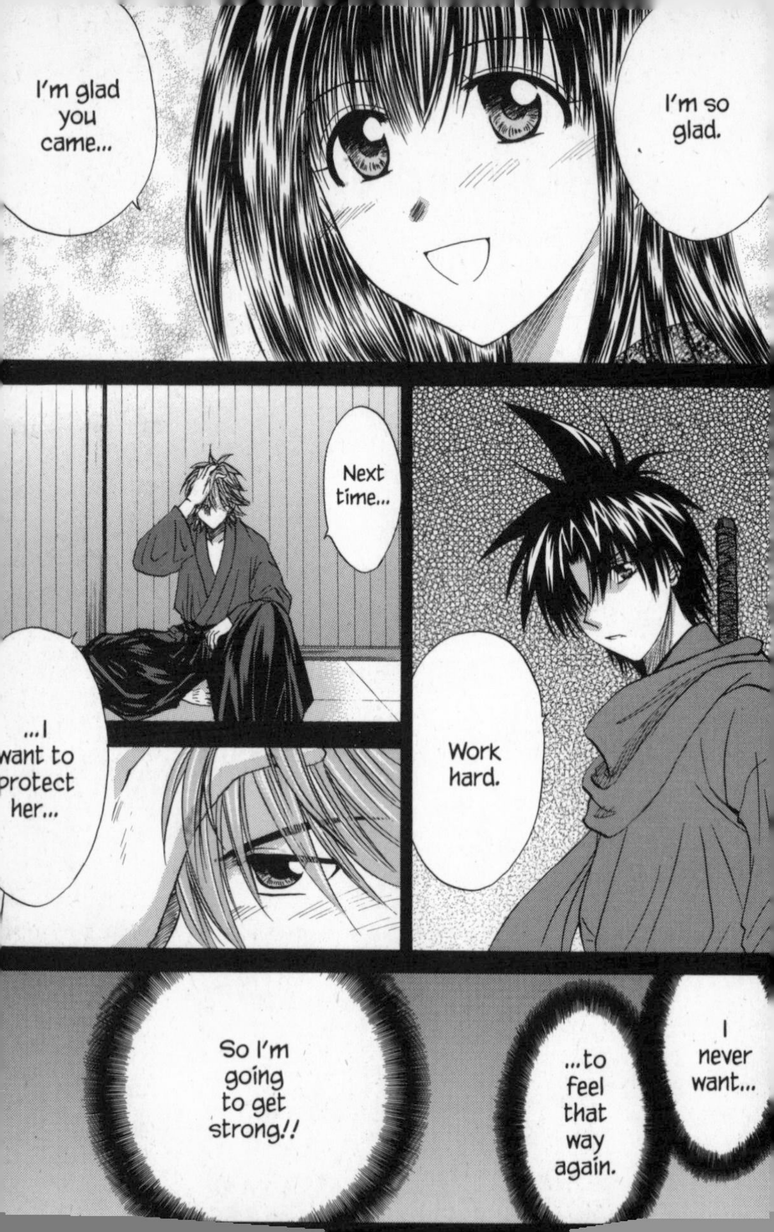
I'm so glad.
I'm glad you came...
Work hard.
Next time...
...I want to protect her...
I never want...
...to feel that way again.
So I'm going to get strong!!

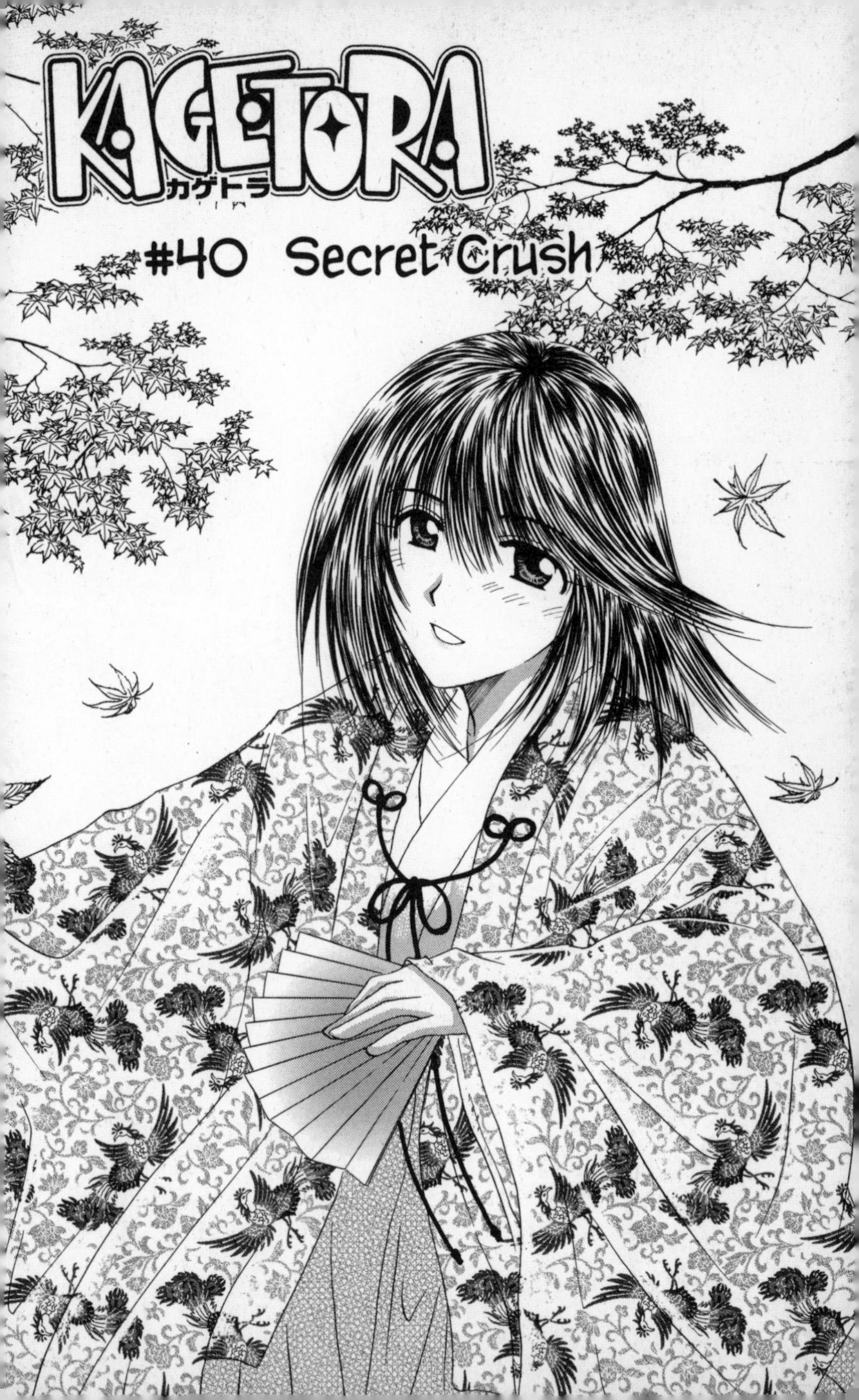
KAGETORA
カゲトラ
#40 Secret Crush

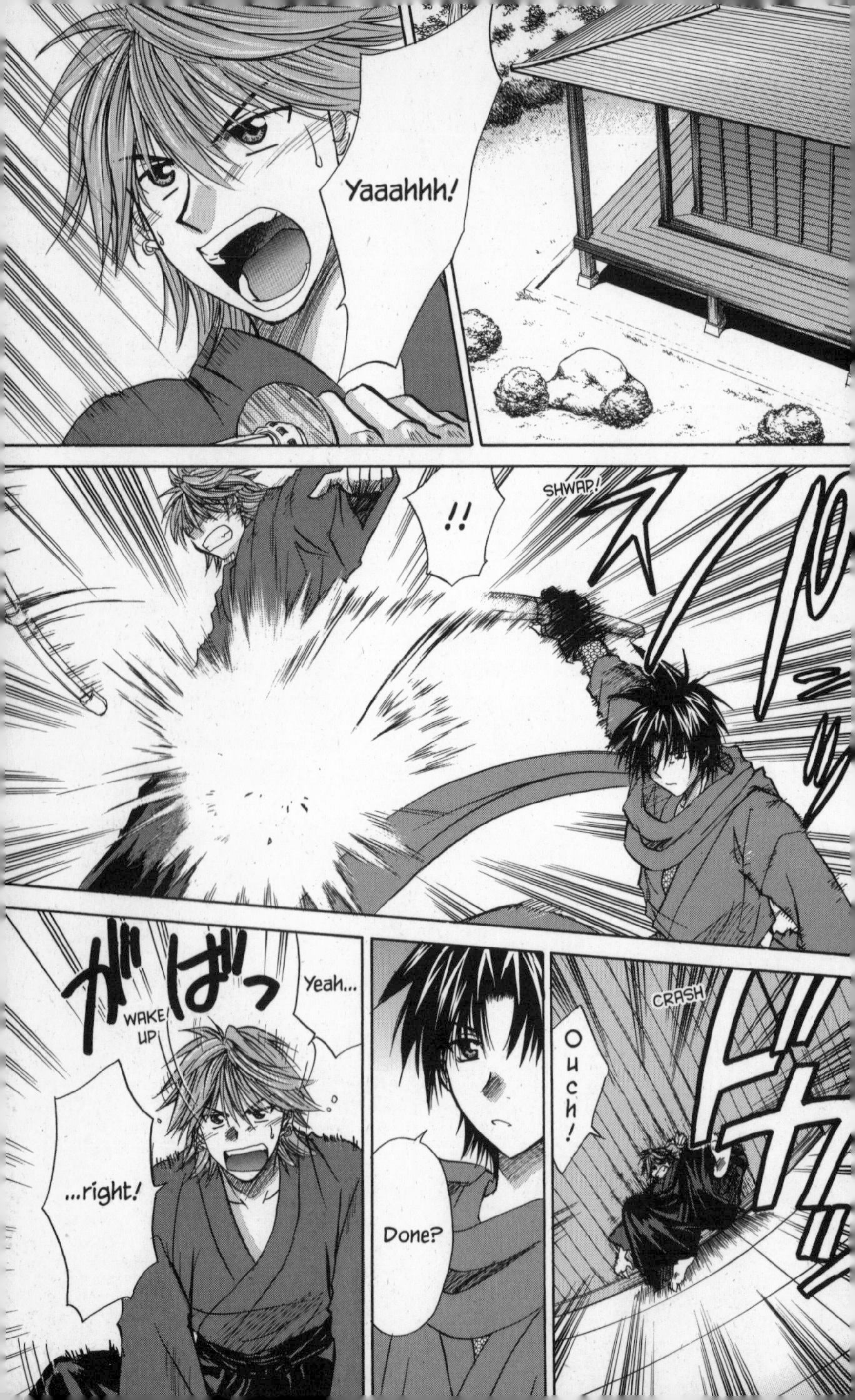

Yaaahhh!
SHWAP!
!!
CRASH
Ouch!
Done?
がばっ
WAKE UP
Yeah...
...right!

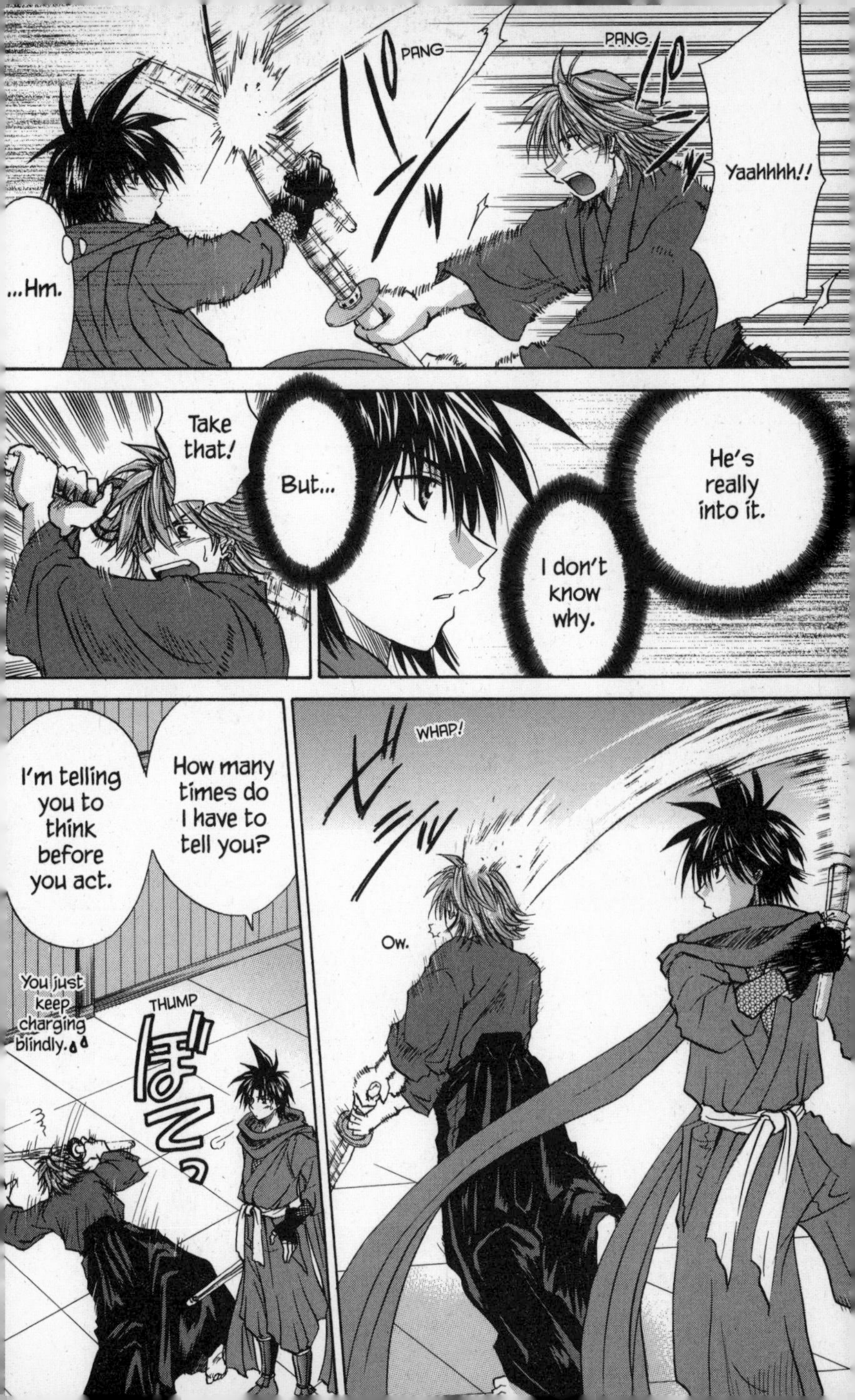
PANG
Yaahhhh!!
PANG
...Hm.
He's really into it.
I don't know why.
But...
Take that!
WHAP!
Ow.
How many times do I have to tell you?
I'm telling you to think before you act.
You just keep charging blindly.
THUMP

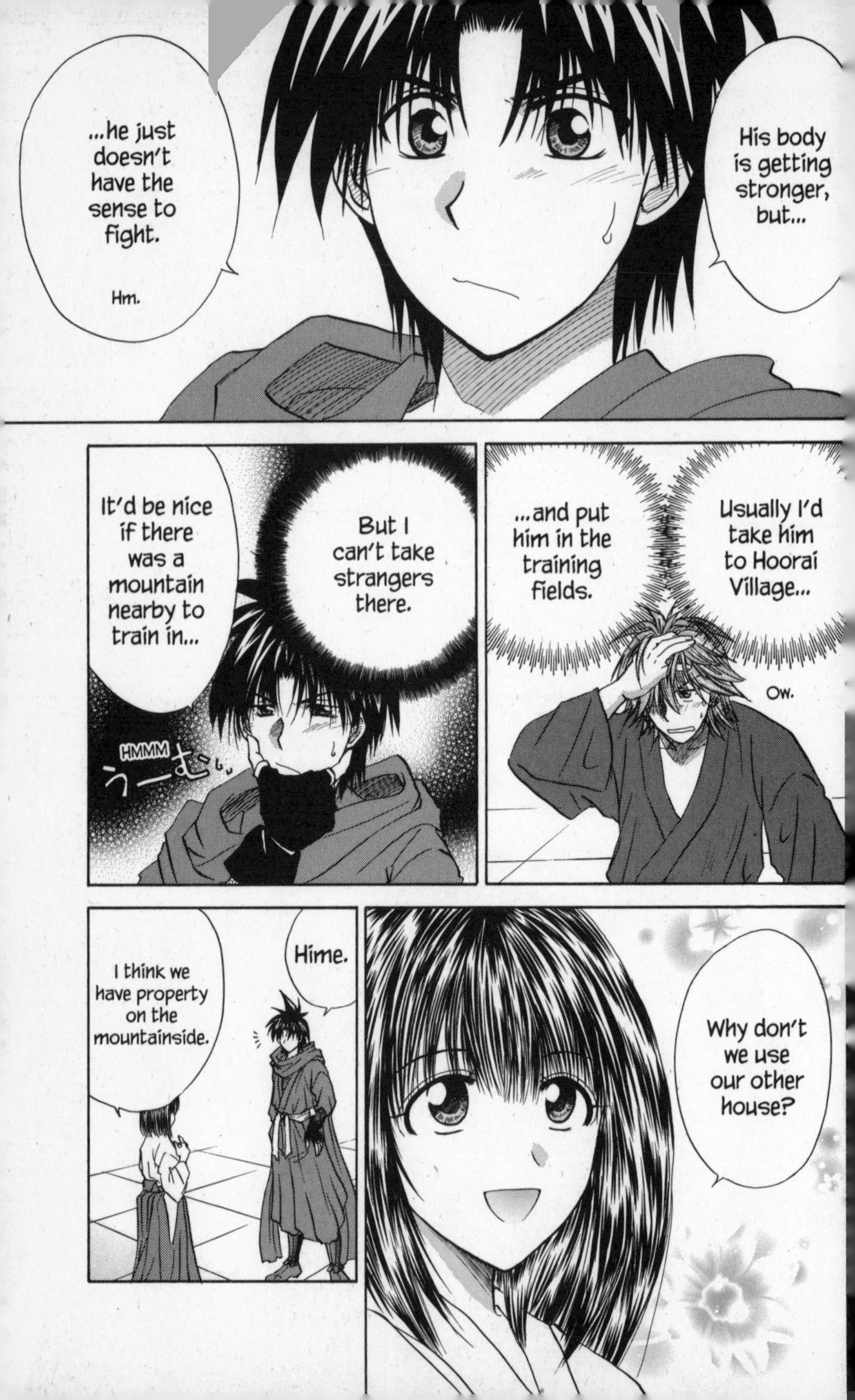
His body is getting stronger, but...
...he just doesn't have the sense to fight.
Hm.
Usually I'd take him to Hoorai Village...
...and put him in the training fields.
Ow.
But I can't take strangers there.
It'd be nice if there was a mountain nearby to train in...
HMMM
Why don't we use our other house?
Hime.
I think we have property on the mountainside.

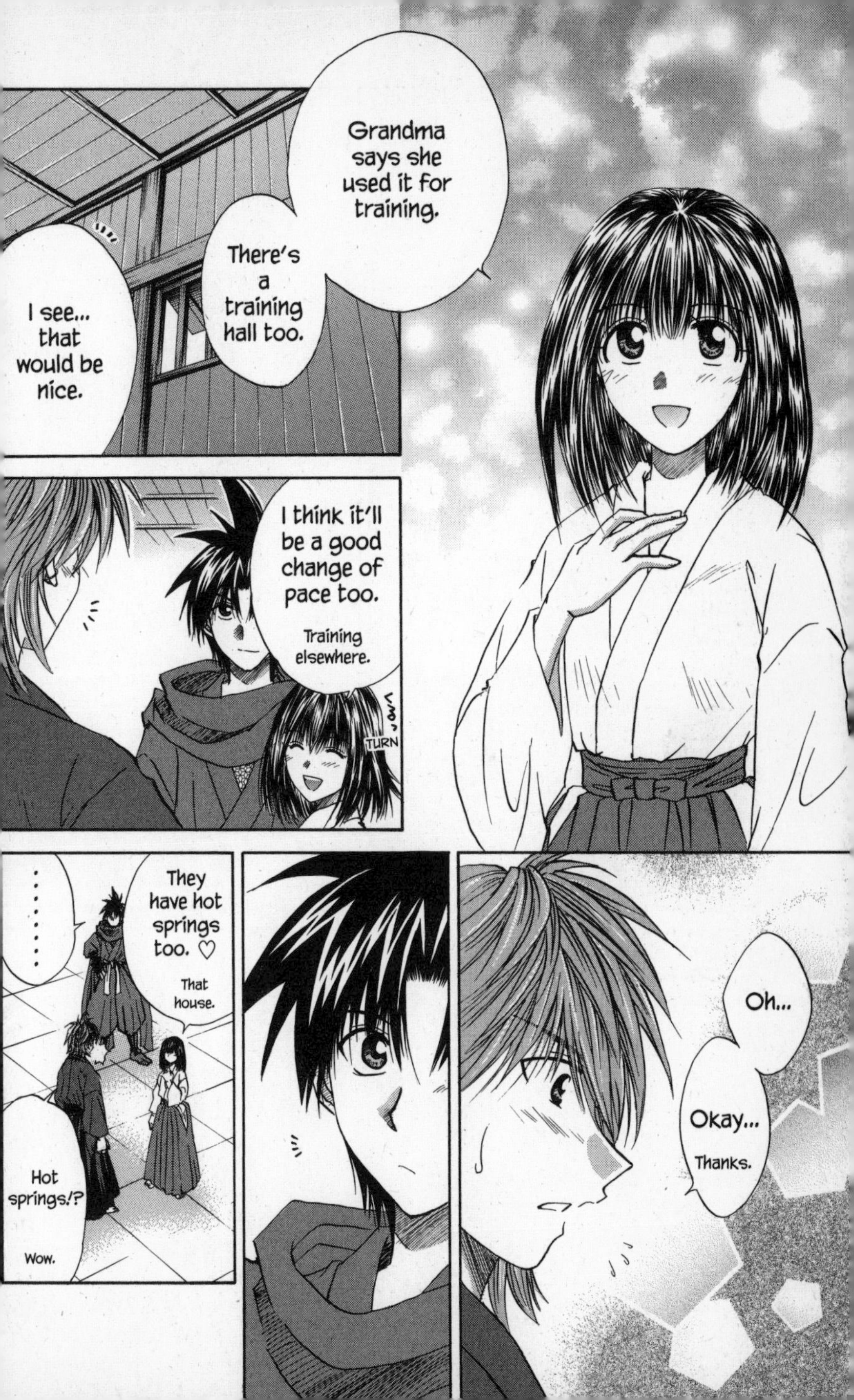

Grandma says she used it for training.
There's a training hall too.
I see... that would be nice.
I think it'll be a good change of pace too.
Training elsewhere.
TURN
Oh...
Okay...
Thanks.
They have hot springs too. ♡
That house.
....
Hot springs!?
Wow.

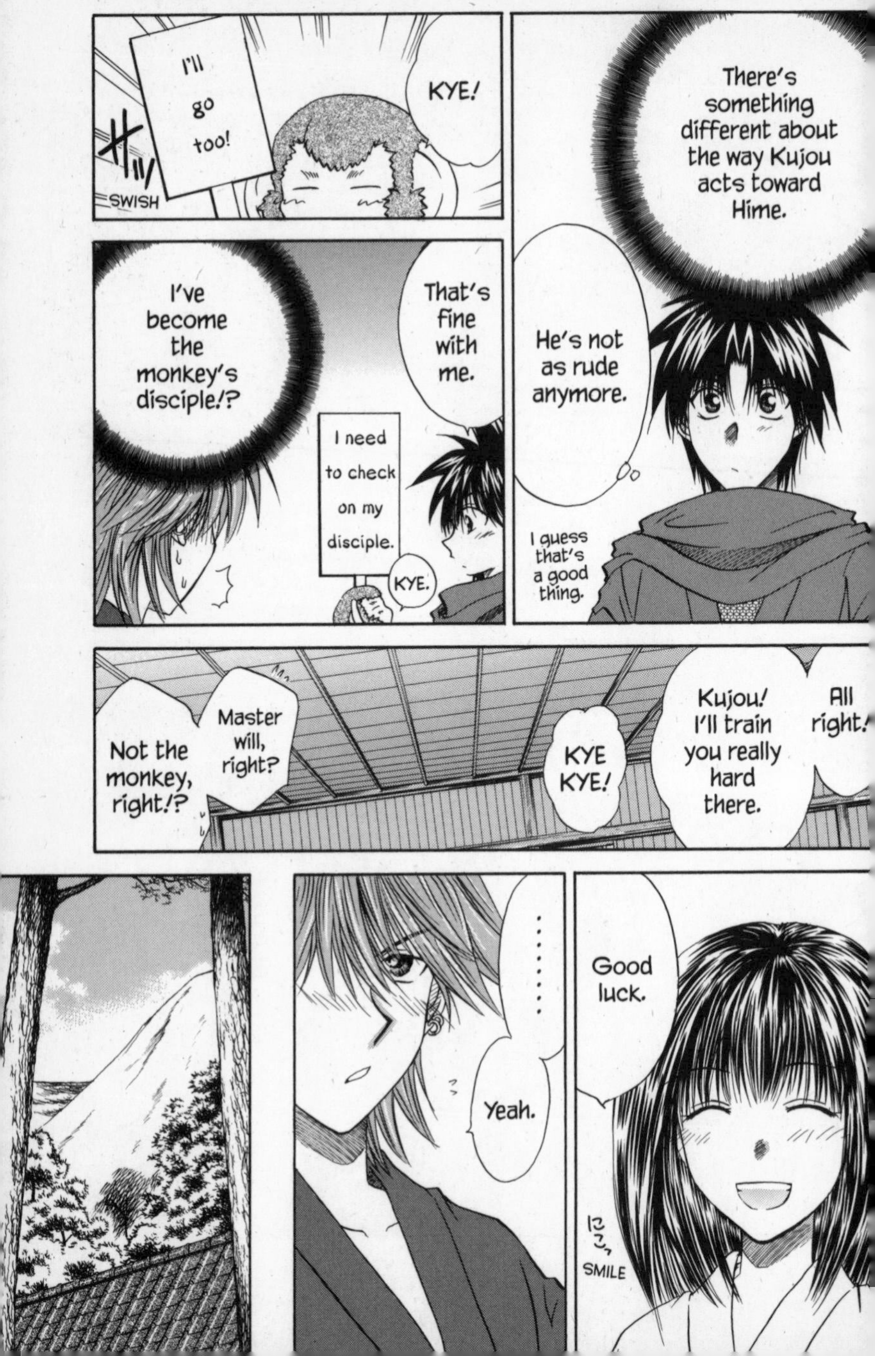
KYE!
I'll go too!
SWISH
There's something different about the way Kujou acts toward Hime.
He's not as rude anymore.
I guess that's a good thing.
That's fine with me.
I need to check on my disciple.
KYE.
I've become the monkey's disciple!?
All right!
Kujou! I'll train you really hard there.
KYE KYE!
Master will, right?
Not the monkey, right!?
Good luck.
SMILE
......
Yeah.

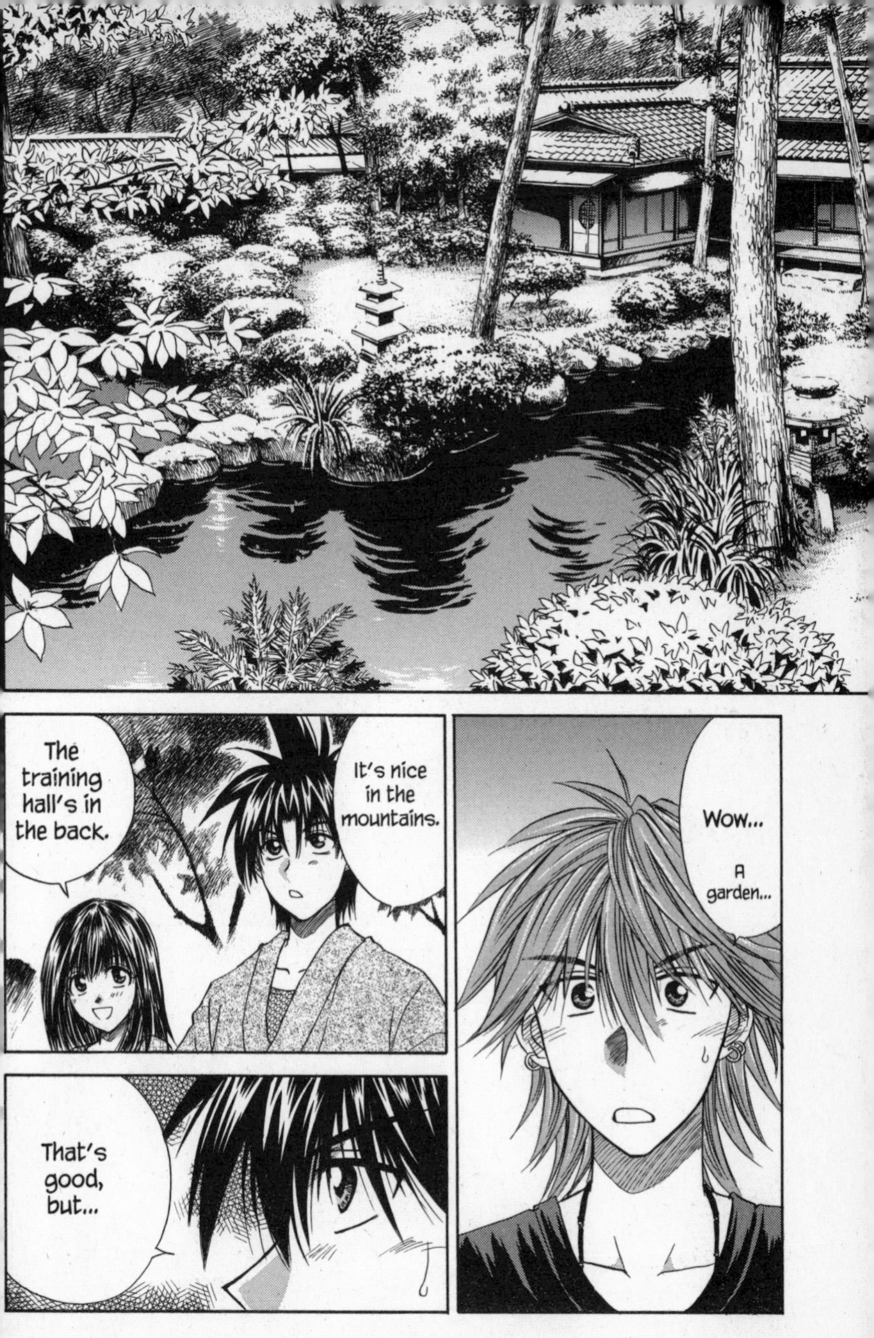
Wow...
A garden...
It's nice in the mountains.
The training hall's in the back.
That's good, but...

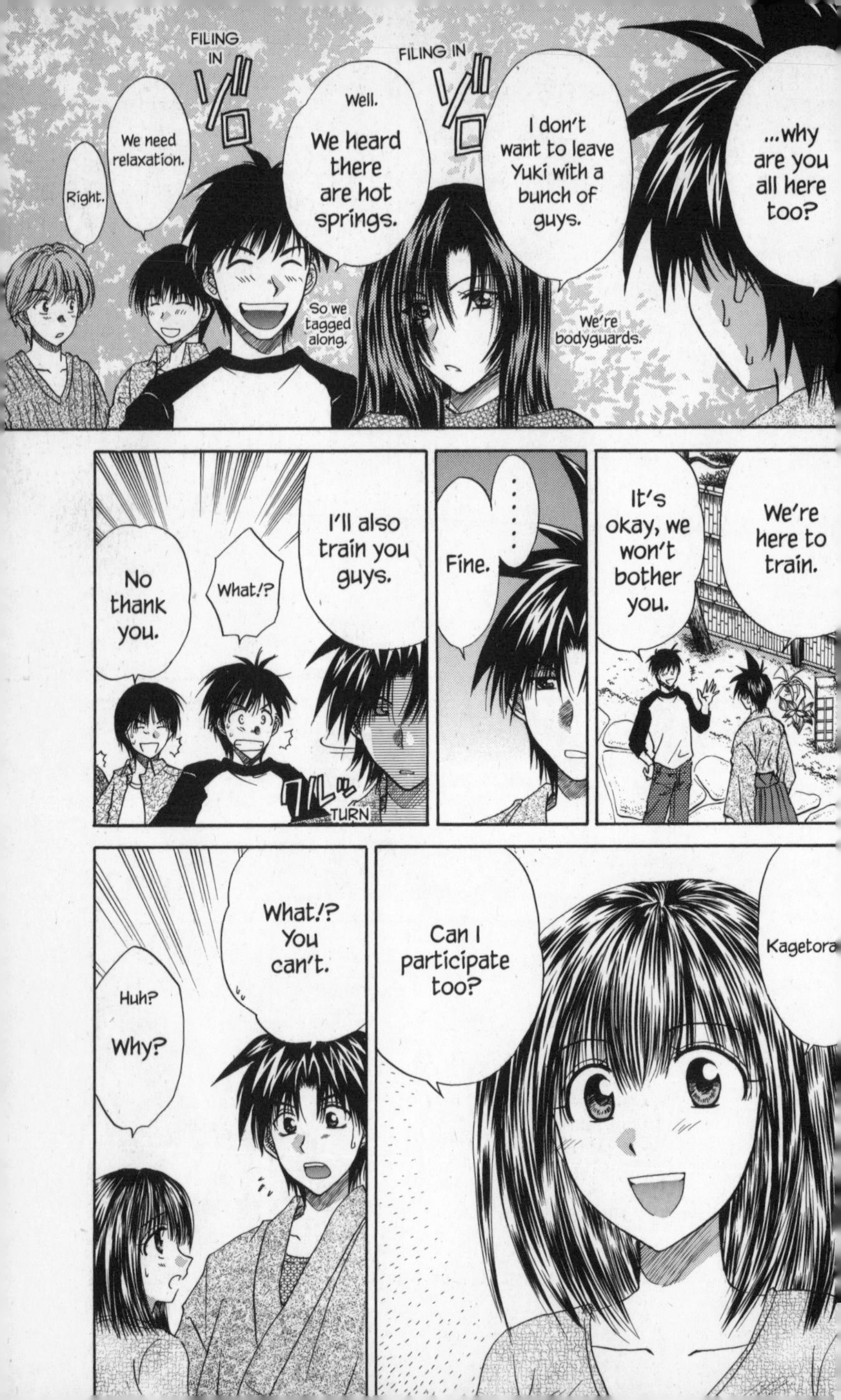

...why are you all here too?
FILING IN
I don't want to leave Yuki with a bunch of guys.
We're bodyguards.
Well.
We heard there are hot springs.
So we tagged along.
FILING IN
We need relaxation.
Right.
We're here to train.
It's okay, we won't bother you.
......
Fine.
I'll also train you guys.
TURN
What!?
No thank you.
Kagetora
Can I participate too?
What!? You can't.
Huh?
Why?

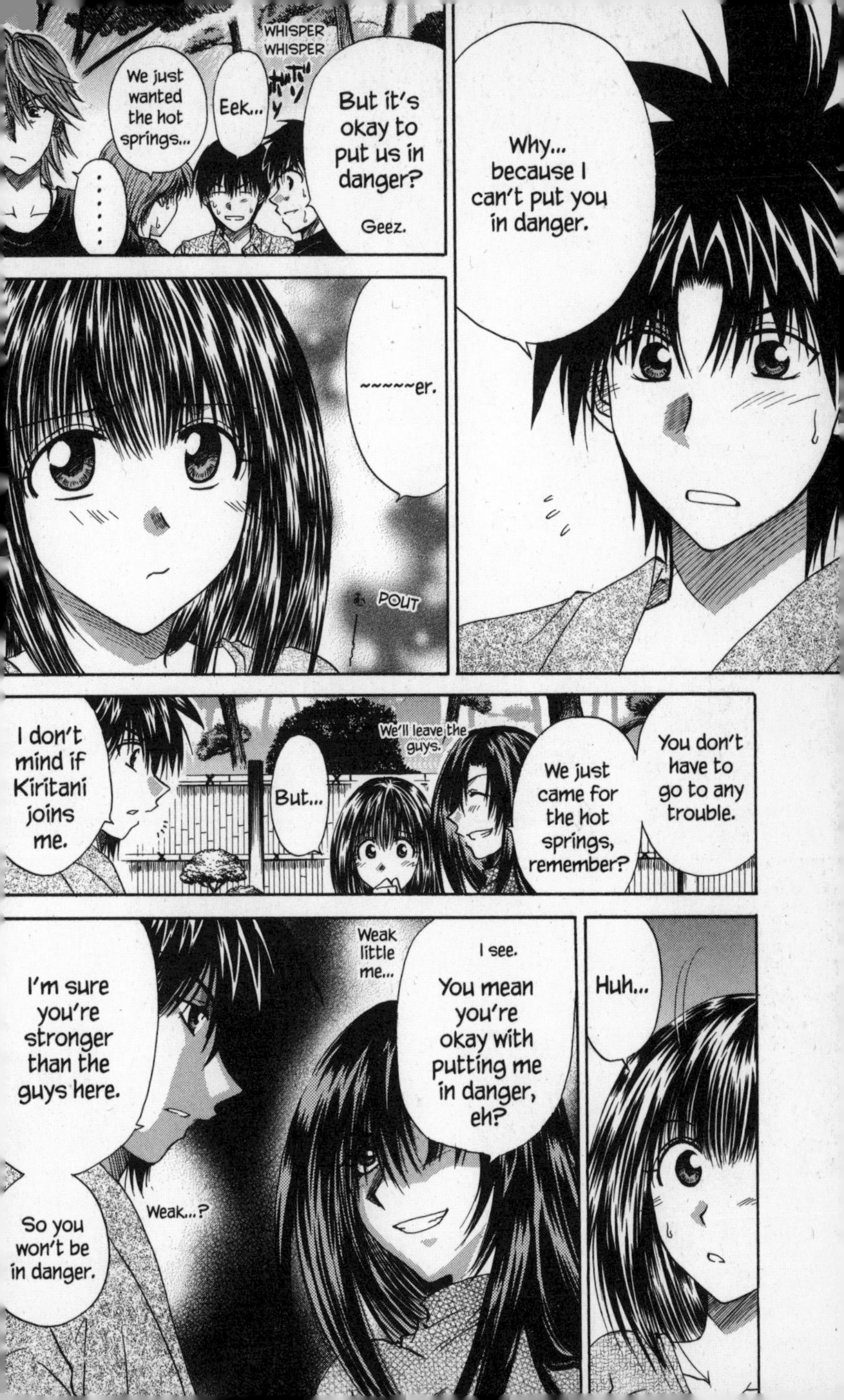
Why... because I can't put you in danger.
But it's okay to put us in danger?
Geez.
WHISPER WHISPER
Eek...
We just wanted the hot springs...
......
~~~~~er.
POUT
You don't have to go to any trouble.
We just came for the hot springs, remember?
We'll leave the guys.
But...
I don't mind if Kiritani joins me.
Huh...
I see.
You mean you're okay with putting me in danger, eh?
Weak little me...
I'm sure you're stronger than the guys here.
Weak...?
So you won't be in danger.
~~~~~

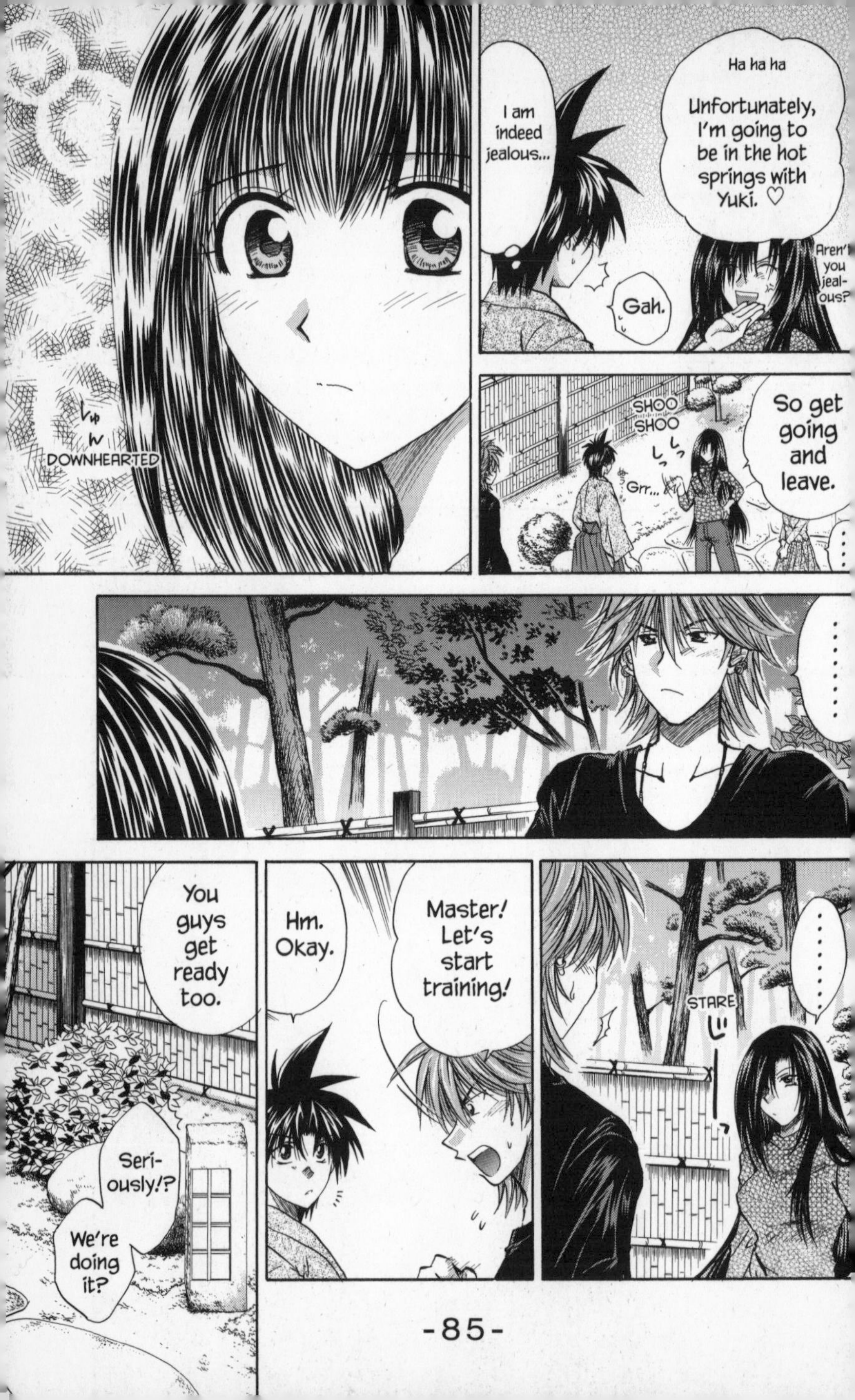
Ha ha ha
Unfortunately, I'm going to be in the hot springs with Yuki. ♡
Aren't you jealous?
I am indeed jealous...
Gah.
So get going and leave.
SHOO SHOO
Grr...
DOWNHEARTED
......
......
STARE
Master! Let's start training!
Hm. Okay.
You guys get ready too.
Seri-ously!?
We're doing it?

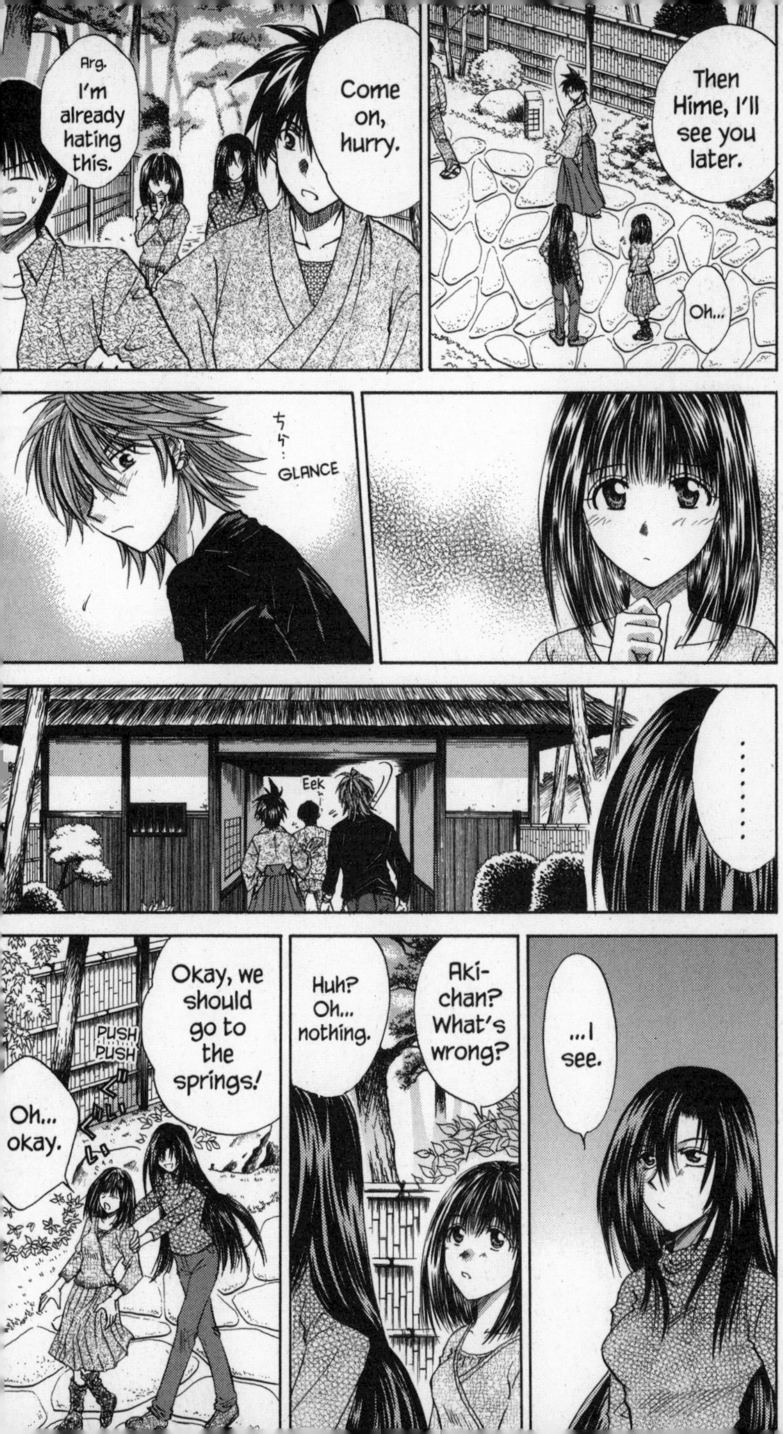
Then Hime, I'll see you later.
Oh...
Come on, hurry.
Arg. I'm already hating this.
ちら
GLANCE
......
Eek
...I see.
Aki-chan? What's wrong?
Huh? Oh... nothing.
Okay, we should go to the springs!
PUSH PUSH
Oh... okay.

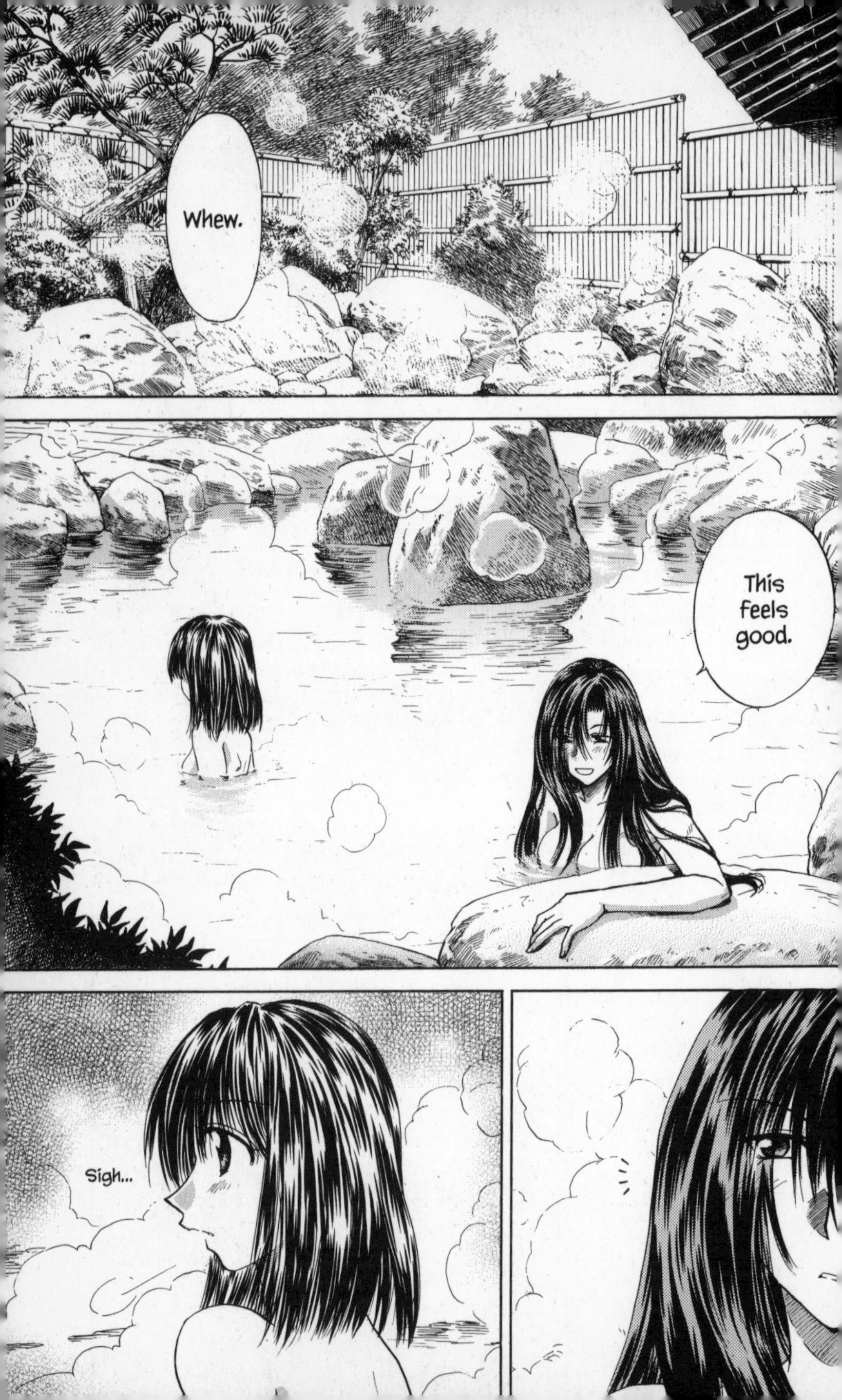
Whew.
This feels good.
Sigh...

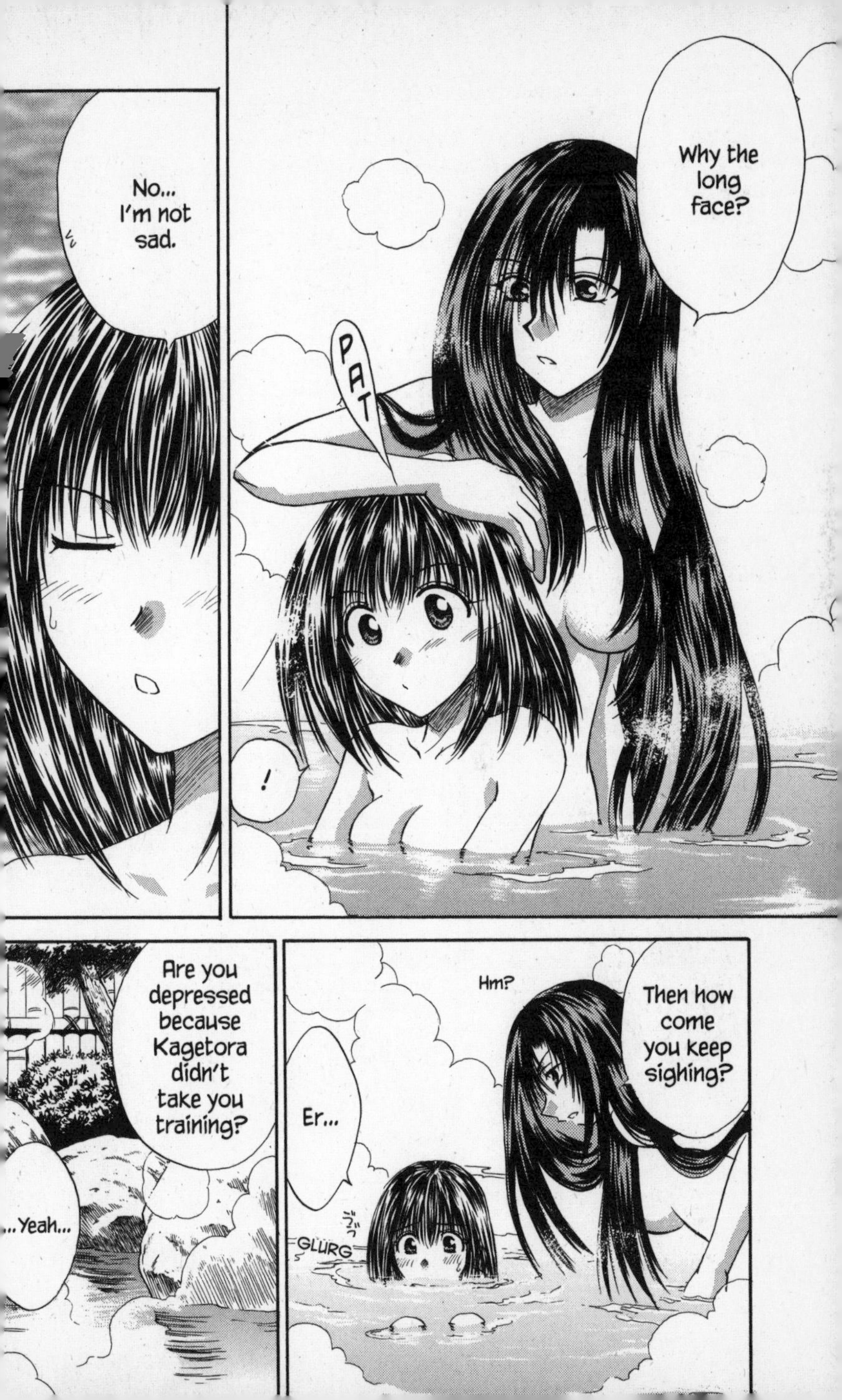
Why the long face?
PAT
!
No... I'm not sad.
Then how come you keep sighing?
Hm?
Er...
GLURG
Are you depressed because Kagetora didn't take you training?
...Yeah...

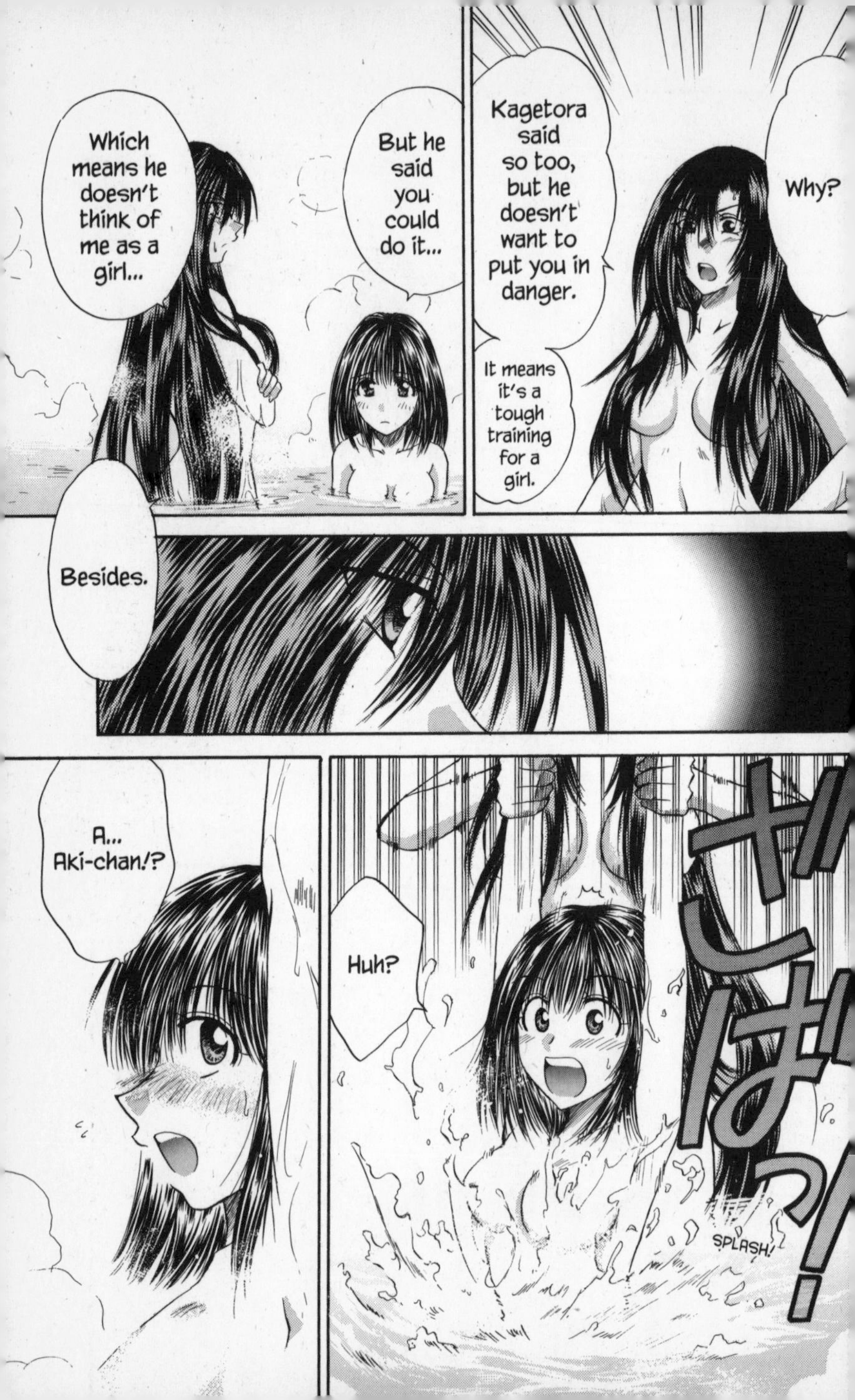
Why?
Kagetora said so too, but he doesn't want to put you in danger.
It means it's a tough training for a girl.
But he said you could do it...
Which means he doesn't think of me as a girl...
Besides.
SPLASH!
Huh?
A... Aki-chan!?

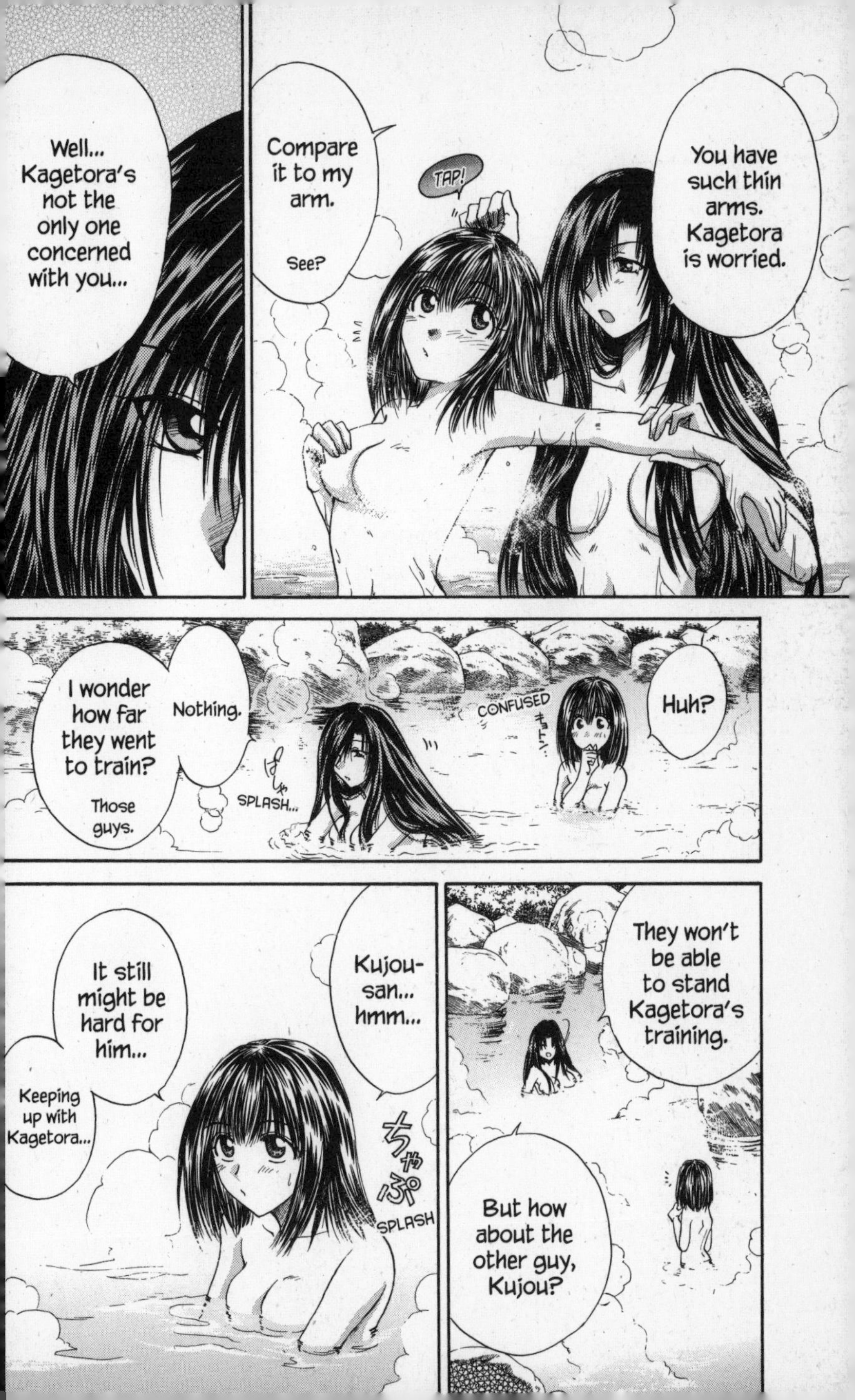
You have such thin arms. Kagetora is worried.
TAP!
Compare it to my arm.
See?
Well... Kagetora's not the only one concerned with you...
Huh?
CONFUSED
キョトン
Nothing.
SPLASH...
ぱしゃ
I wonder how far they went to train?
Those guys.
They won't be able to stand Kagetora's training.
But how about the other guy, Kujou?
Kujou-san... hmm...
ちゃぷ
SPLASH
It still might be hard for him...
Keeping up with Kagetora...

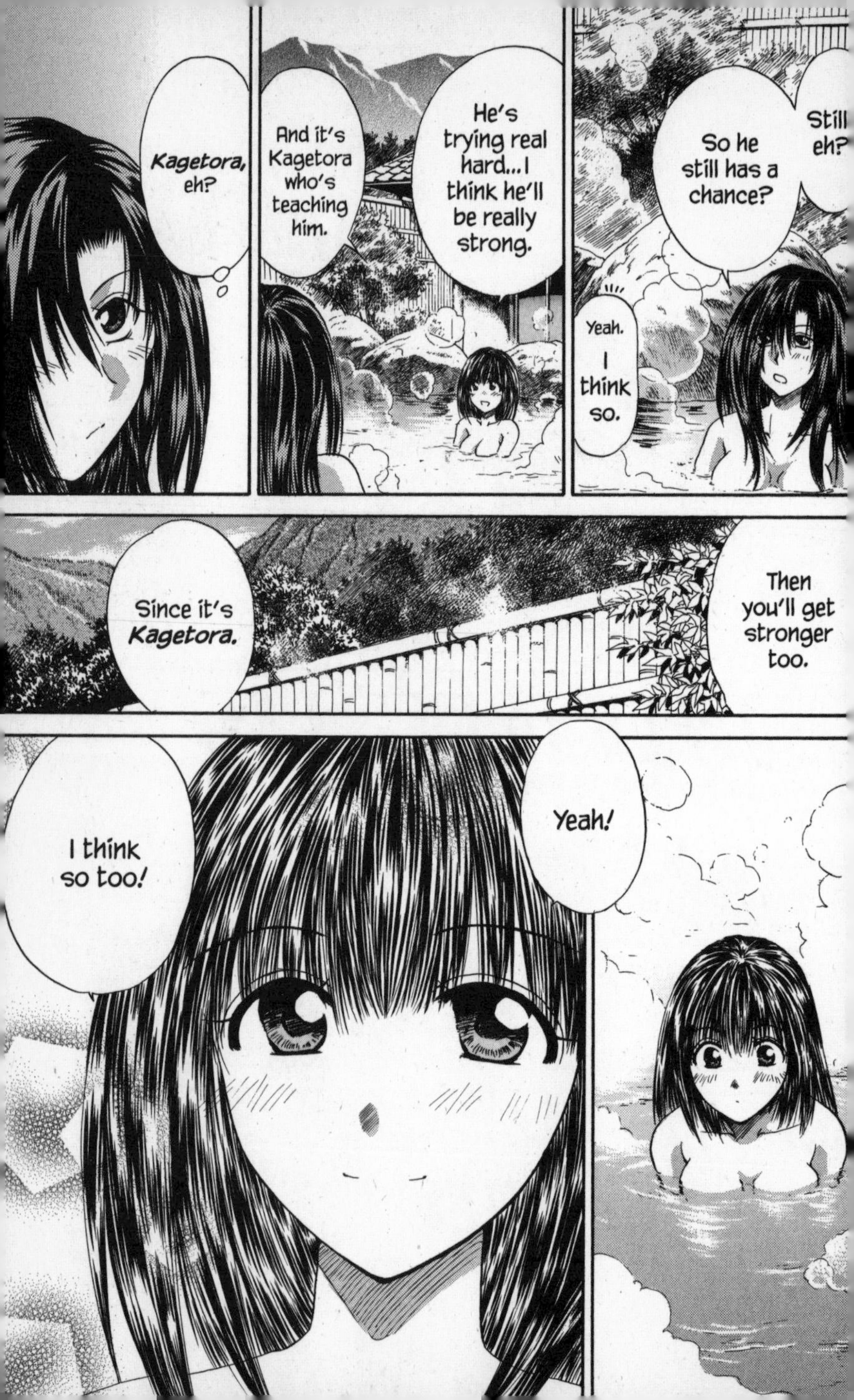
Still eh?
So he still has a chance?
Yeah. I think so.
He's trying real hard...I think he'll be really strong.
And it's Kagetora who's teaching him.
Kagetora, eh?
Then you'll get stronger too.
Since it's *Kagetora.*
Yeah!
I think so too!

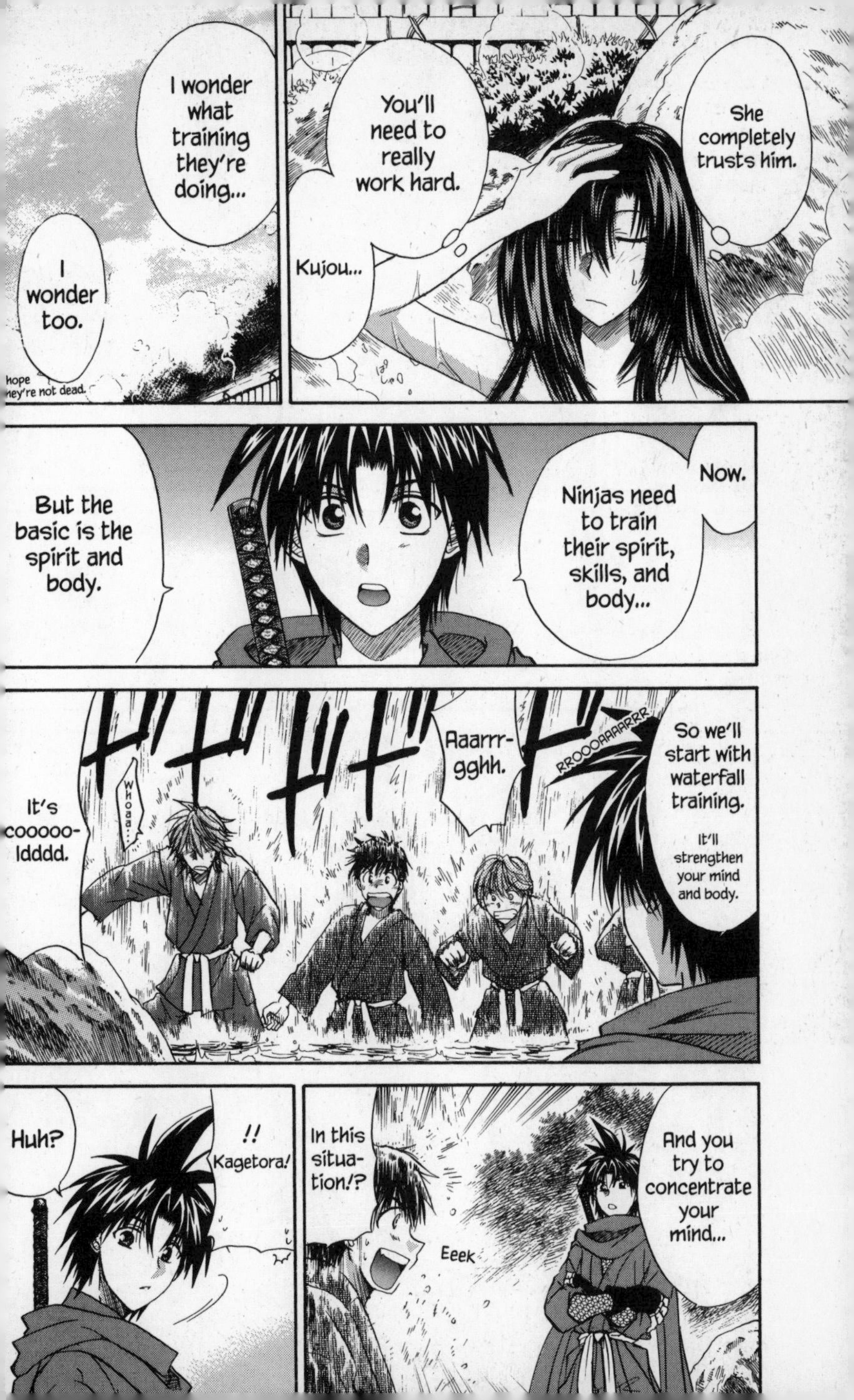

She completely trusts him.
You'll need to really work hard.
Kujou...
I wonder what training they're doing...
I wonder too.
hope
ey're not dead.
Now.
Ninjas need to train their spirit, skills, and body...
But the basic is the spirit and body.
So we'll start with waterfall training.
It'll strengthen your mind and body.
RROOOAAAARRR
Aaarrr-gghh.
Whoaa...
It's cooooo-ldddd.
And you try to concentrate your mind...
In this situa-tion!?
Eeek
!!
Kagetora!
Huh?

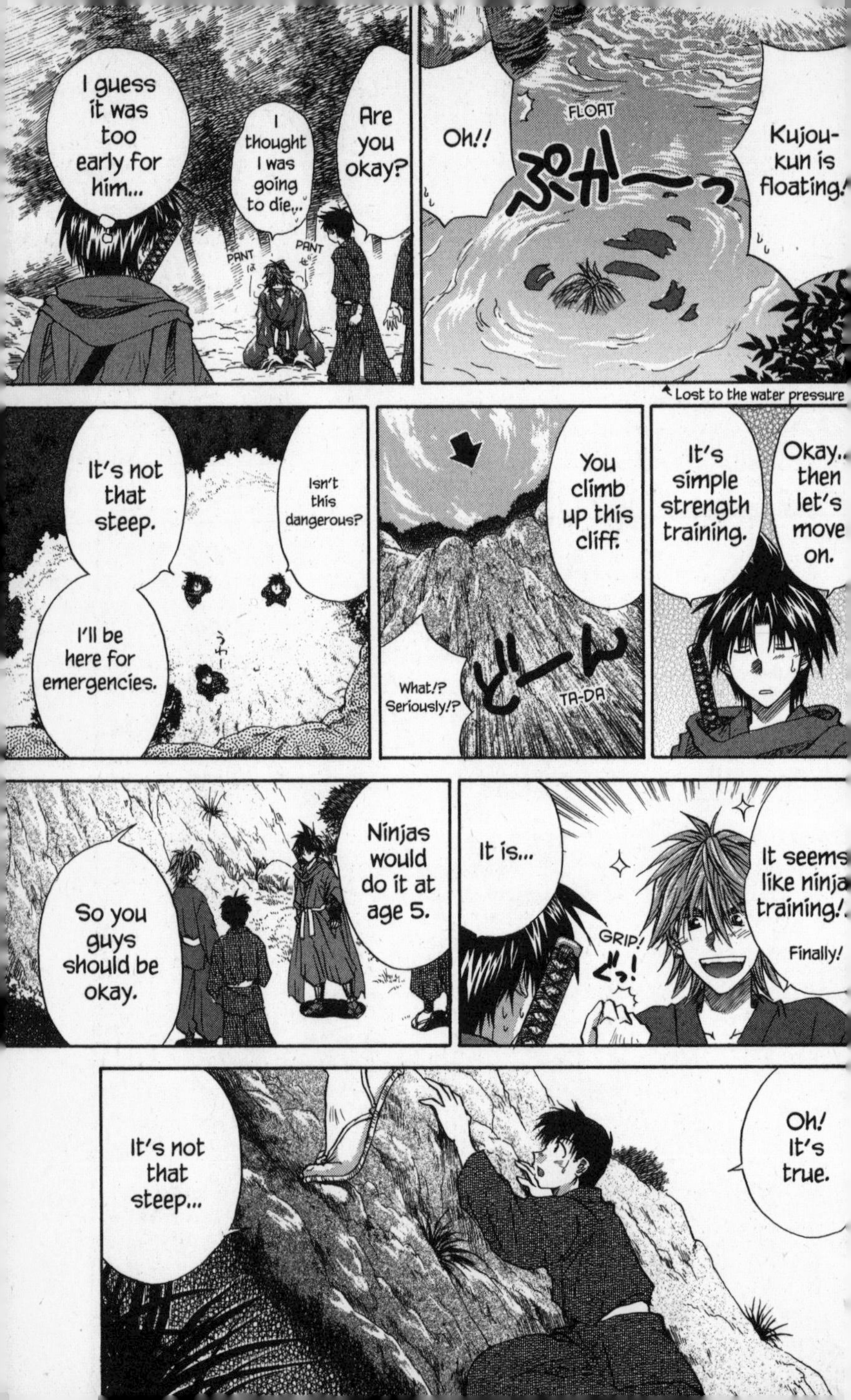
Kujou-kun is floating!
Oh!!
FLOAT
ぷかーっ
Lost to the water pressure
Are you okay?
I thought I was going to die...
PANT
PANT
I guess it was too early for him...
Okay.. then let's move on.
It's simple strength training.
You climb up this cliff.
どーん
TA-DA
What!? Seriously!?
Isn't this dangerous?
It's not that steep.
I'll be here for emergencies.
うわー
It seems like ninja training!
Finally!
It is...
GRIP!
ぐっ!
Ninjas would do it at age 5.
So you guys should be okay.
Oh! It's true.
It's not that steep...

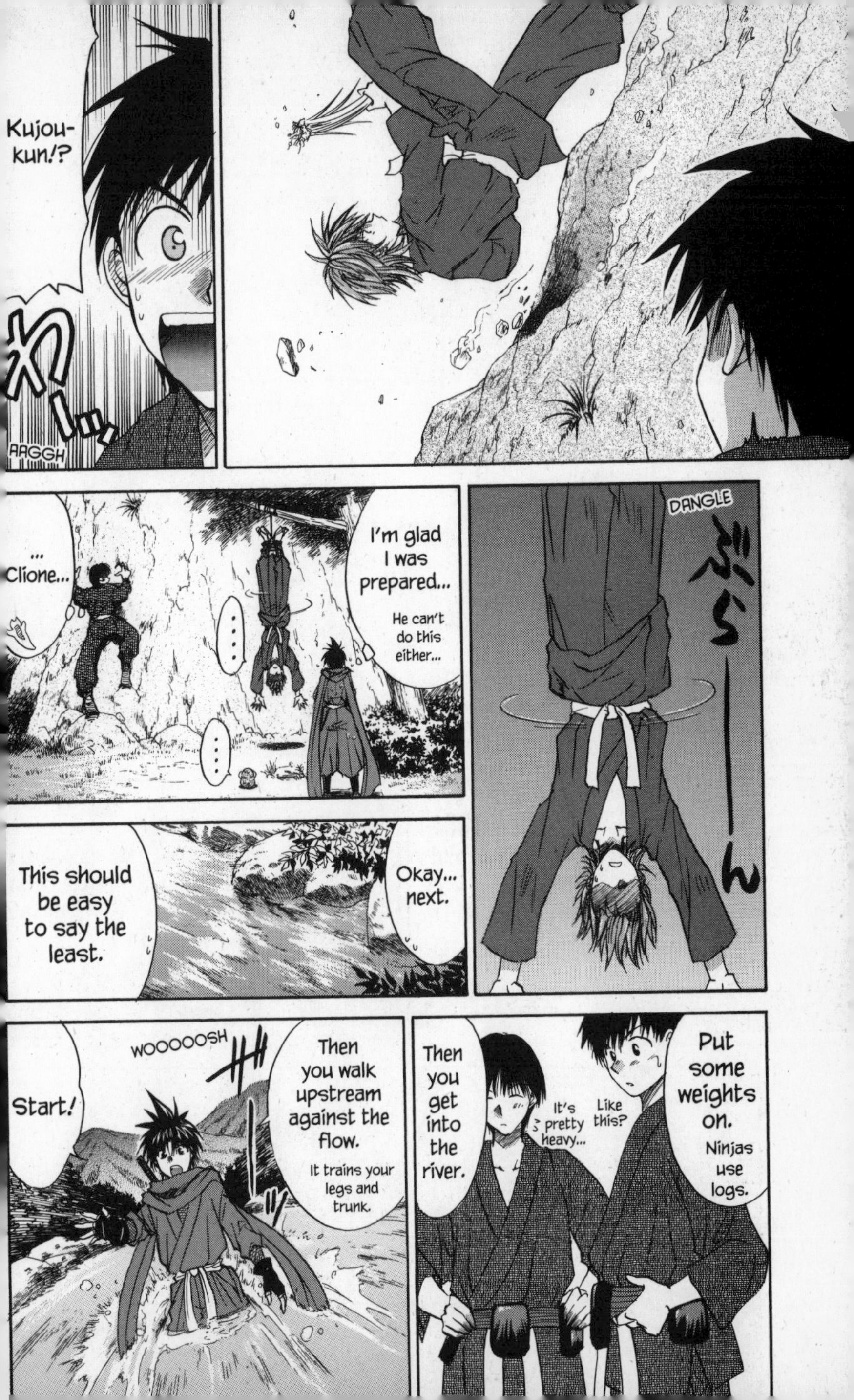
Kujou-kun!?
AAGGH
DANGLE
I'm glad I was prepared...
He can't do this either...
...
...
... Clione...
Okay... next.
This should be easy to say the least.
Put some weights on.
Ninjas use logs.
Like this?
It's pretty heavy...
Then you get into the river.
Then you walk upstream against the flow.
It trains your legs and trunk.
WOOOOOSH
Start!

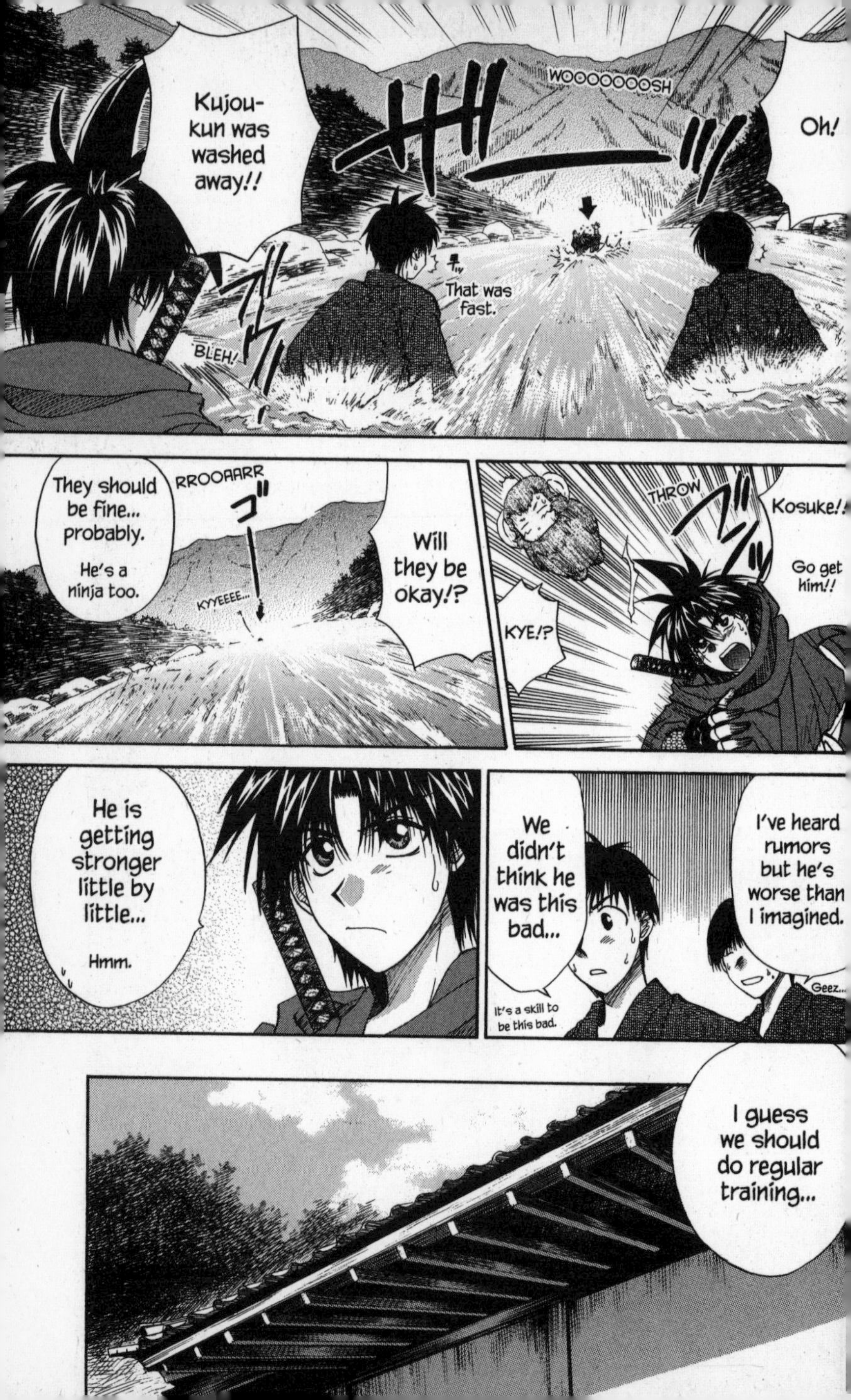

Oh!
WOOOOOOOOSH
Kujou-kun was washed away!!
That was fast.
BLEH!
Kosuke!!
Go get him!!
THROW
KYE!?
Will they be okay!?
RROOAARR
They should be fine... probably.
He's a ninja too.
KYYEEEE...
I've heard rumors but he's worse than I imagined.
Geez...
We didn't think he was this bad...
It's a skill to be this bad.
He is getting stronger little by little...
Hmm.
I guess we should do regular training...

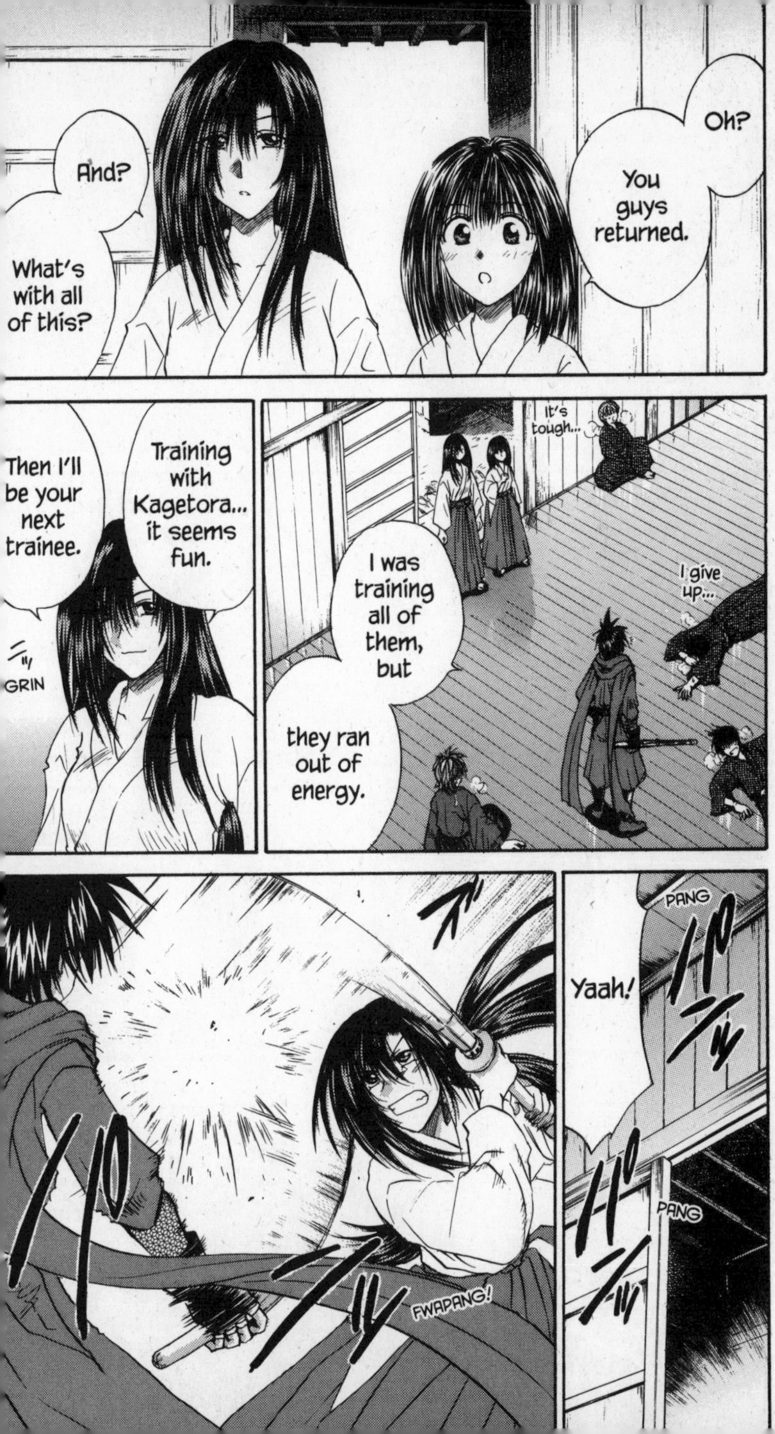
Oh?
You guys returned.
And?
What's with all of this?
It's tough...
I give up...
I was training all of them, but
they ran out of energy.
Training with Kagetora... it seems fun.
Then I'll be your next trainee.
GRIN
PANG
Yaah!
PANG
FWAPANG!

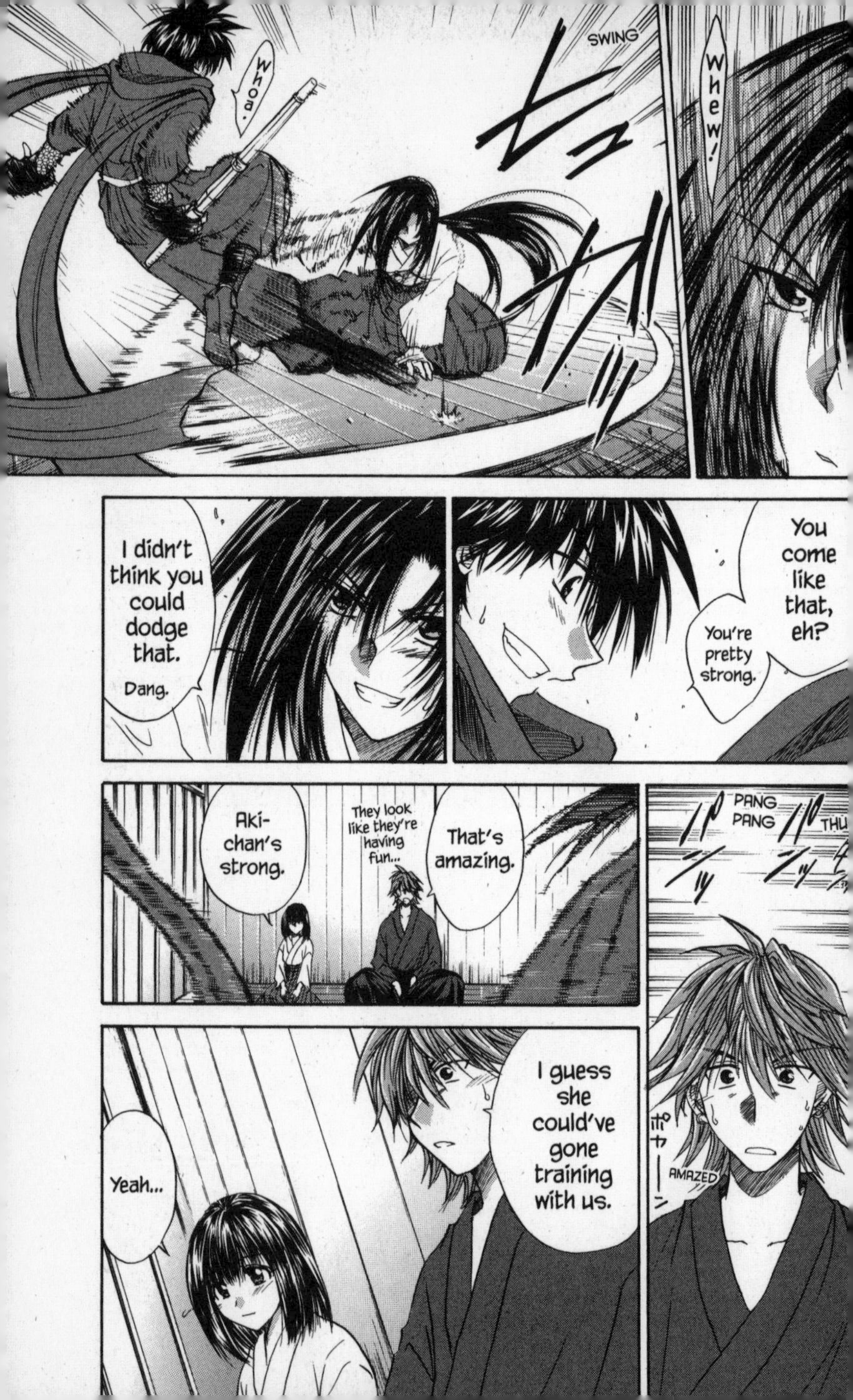

Whew!
SWING
Whoa.
You come like that, eh?
You're pretty strong.
I didn't think you could dodge that.
Dang.
PANG PANG
THU
AMAZED
That's amazing.
They look like they're having fun...
Aki-chan's strong.
I guess she could've gone training with us.
Yeah...

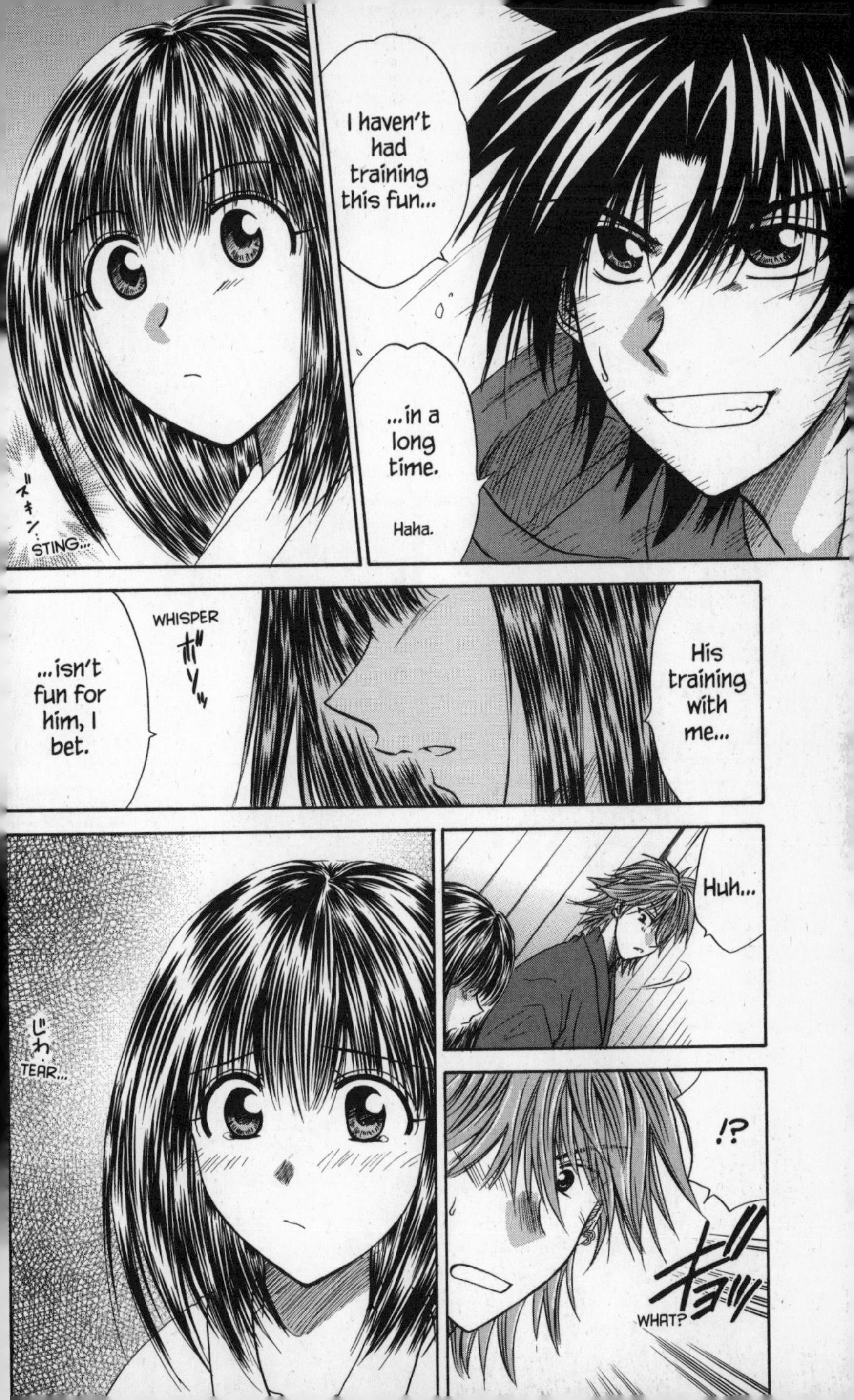
I haven't had training this fun...
...in a long time.
Haha.
ズキン
STING...
His training with me...
...isn't fun for him, I bet.
WHISPER
ボソッ
Huh...
!?
ギョ
WHAT?
じわ
TEAR...

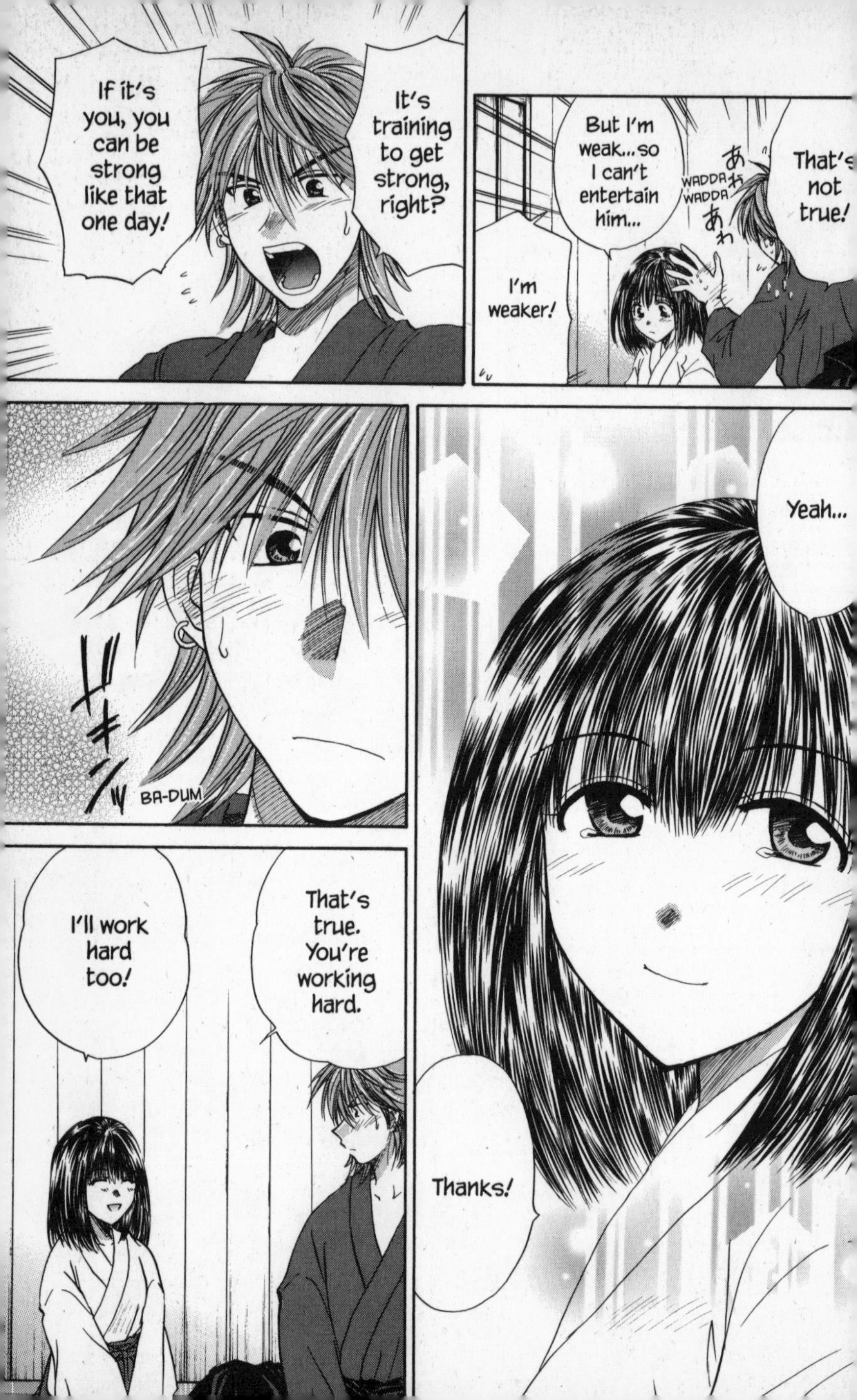
But I'm weak...so I can't entertain him...
WADDA WADDA
That's not true!
I'm weaker!
It's training to get strong, right?
If it's you, you can be strong like that one day!
Yeah...
Thanks!
BA-DUM
That's true. You're working hard.
I'll work hard too!

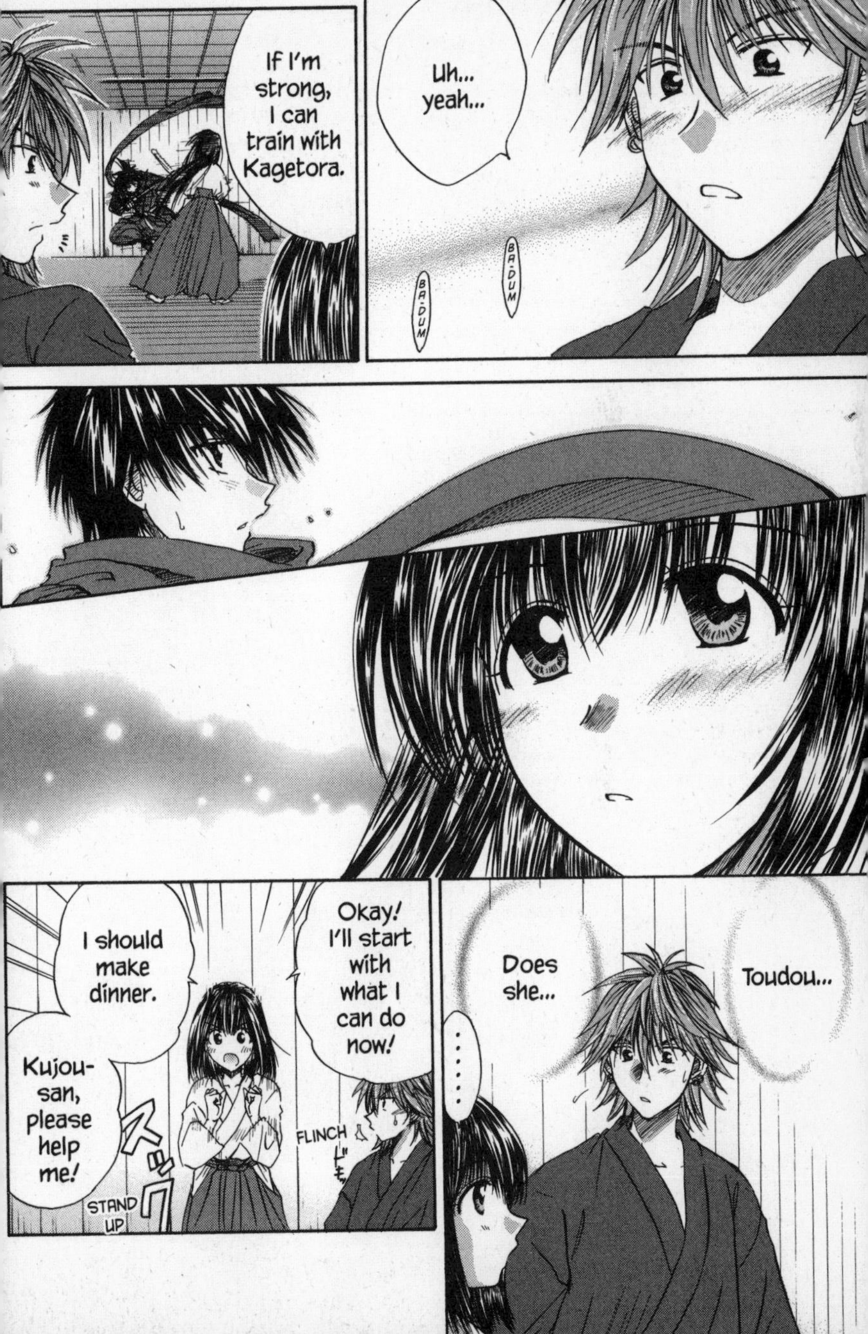
Uh... yeah...
BA-DUM
BA-DUM
If I'm strong, I can train with Kagetora.
Toudou...
Does she...
......
Okay! I'll start with what I can do now!
FLINCH
I should make dinner.
Kujou-san, please help me!
STAND UP

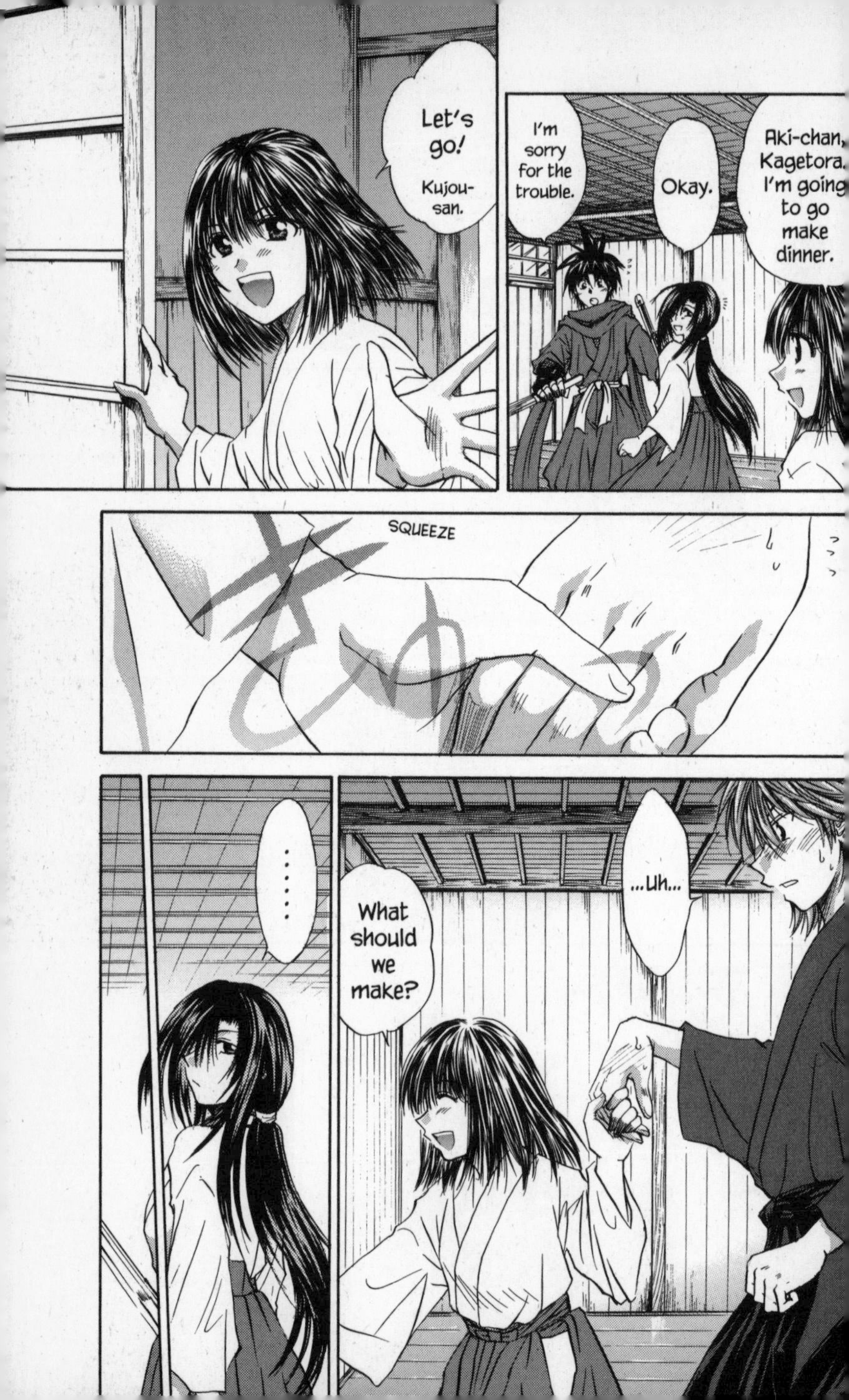
Aki-chan, Kagetora. I'm going to go make dinner.
Okay.
I'm sorry for the trouble.
Let's go!
Kujou-san.
SQUEEZE
...uh...
What should we make?
......

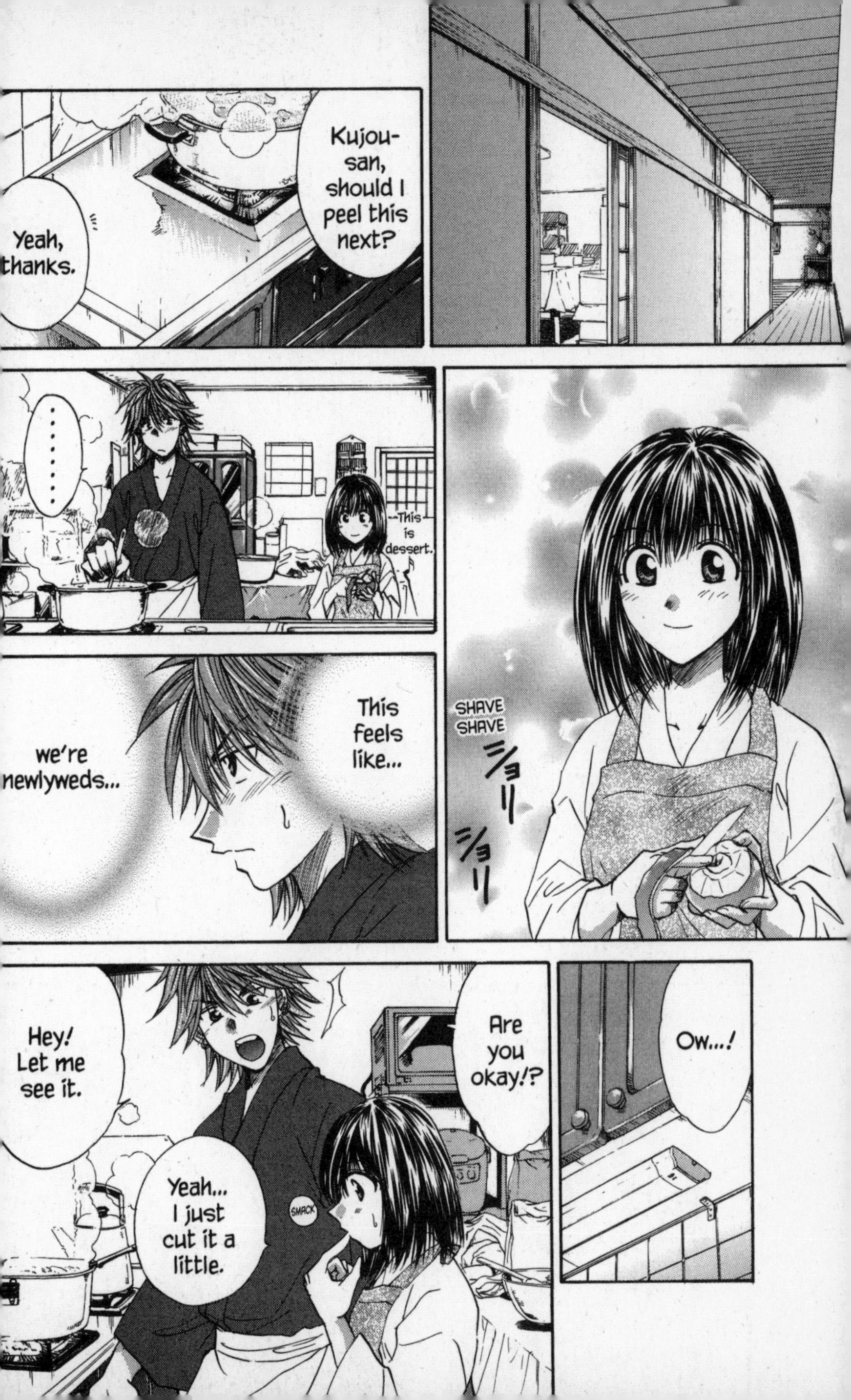
Kujou-san, should I peel this next?
Yeah, thanks.
SHAVE SHAVE
ショリ
ショリ
......
--This is dessert.
This feels like...
we're newlyweds...
Ow...!
Are you okay!?
Hey! Let me see it.
SMACK
Yeah... I just cut it a little.

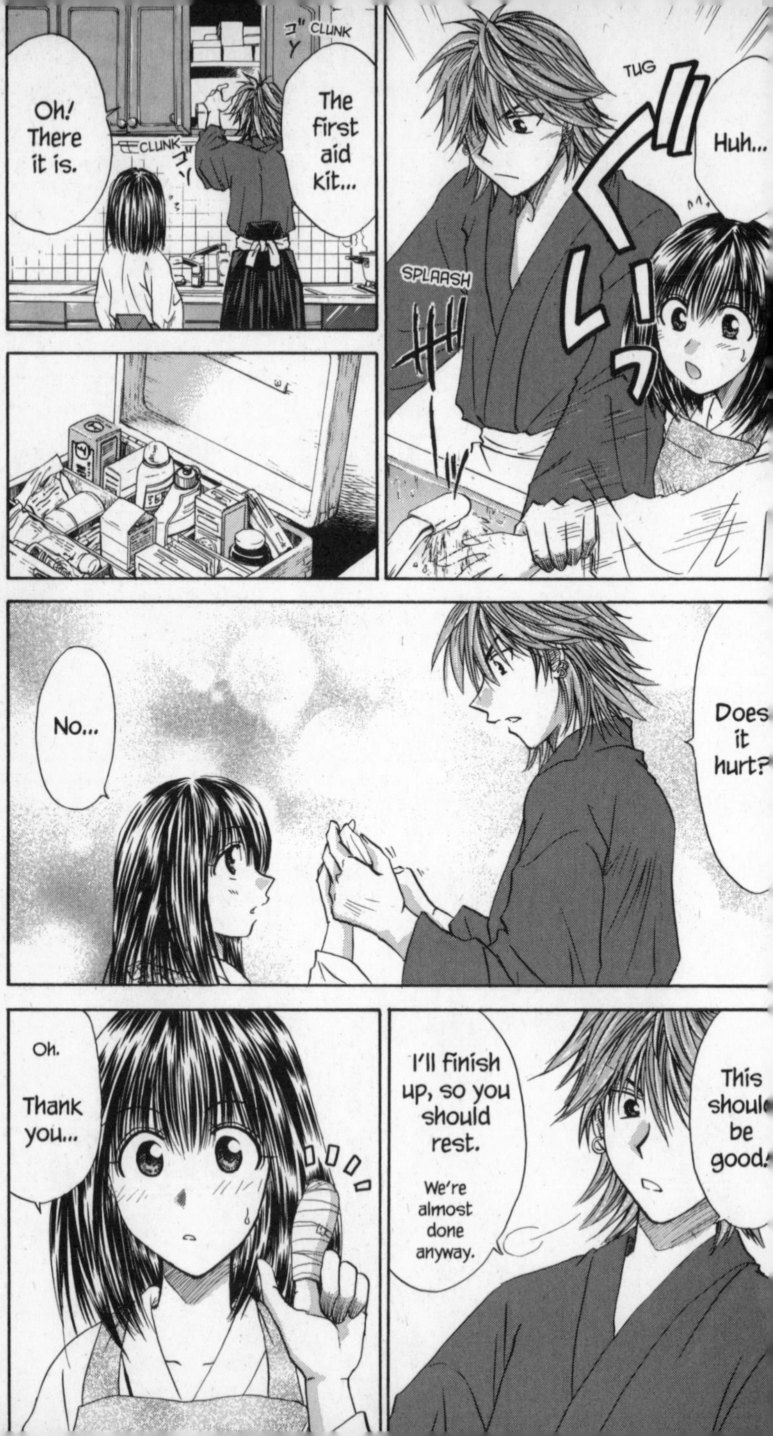
TUG
Huh...
SPLAASH
CLUNK
The first aid kit...
CLUNK
Oh! There it is.
Does it hurt?
No...
This shoul be good
I'll finish up, so you should rest.
We're almost done anyway.
Oh.
Thank you...

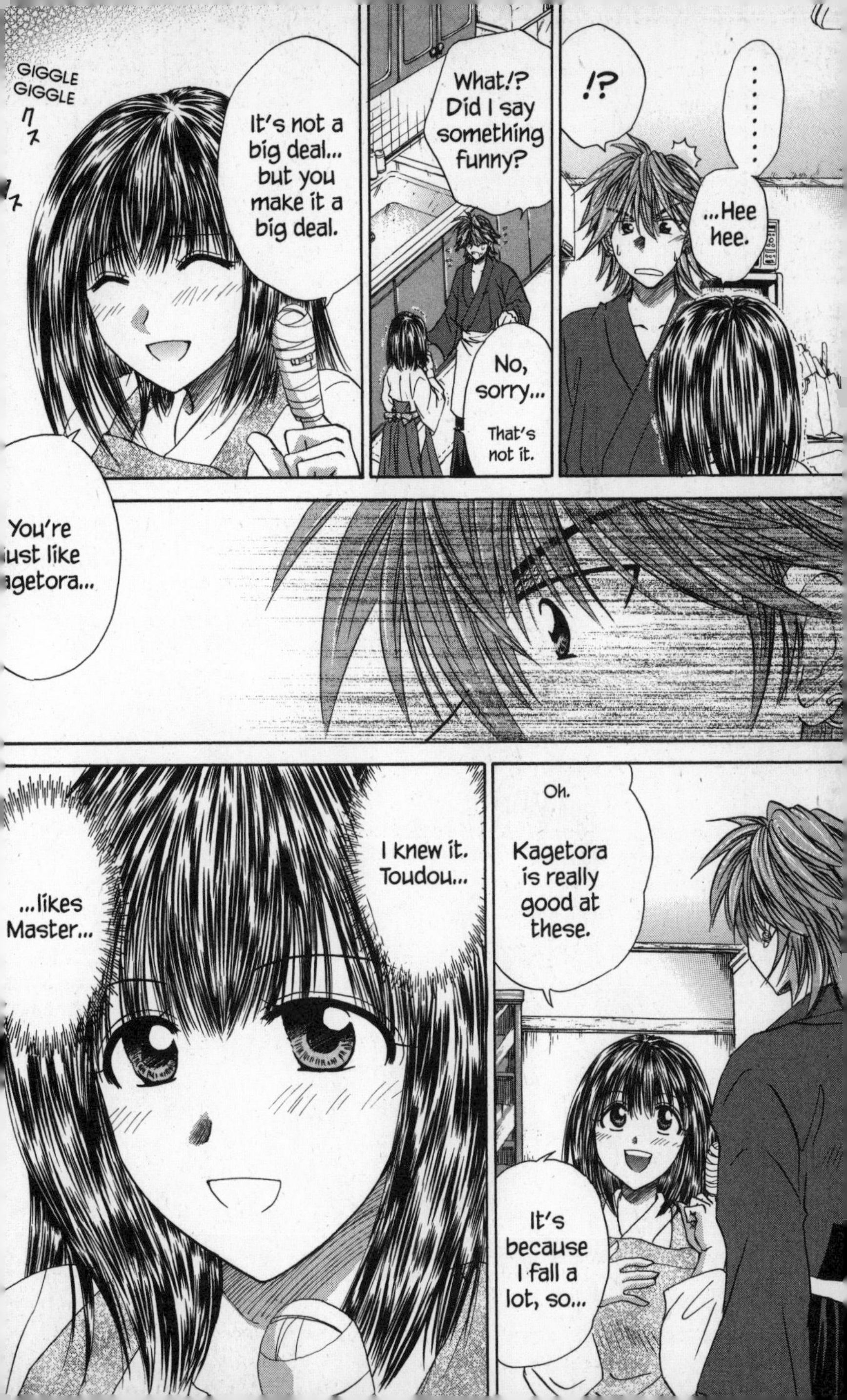
......
!?
...Hee hee.
What!? Did I say something funny?
No, sorry...
That's not it.
GIGGLE GIGGLE
It's not a big deal... but you make it a big deal.
You're ust like agetora...
Oh.
Kagetora is really good at these.
It's because I fall a lot, so...
I knew it. Toudou...
...likes Master...

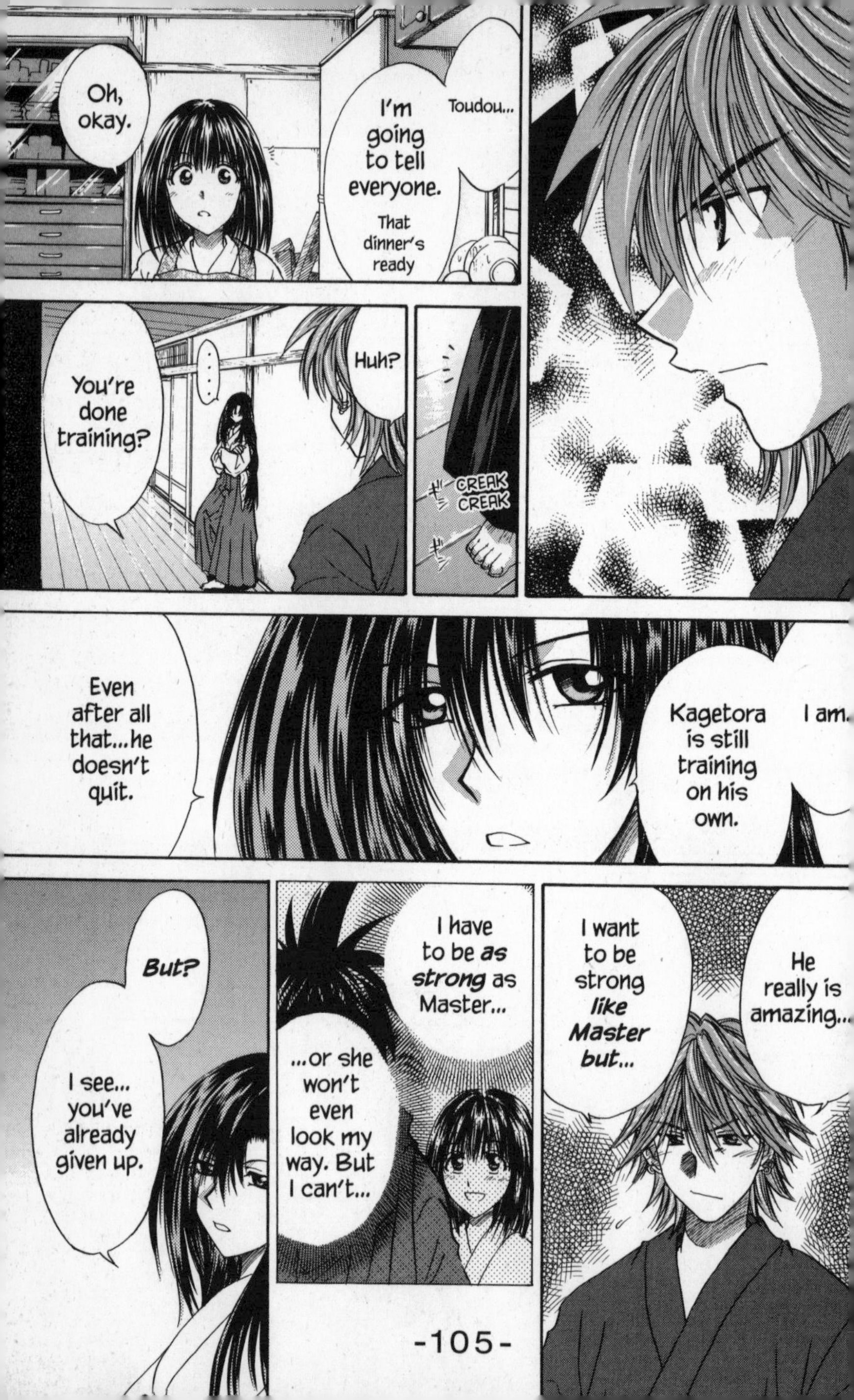
Toudou...
That dinner's ready
I'm going to tell everyone.
Oh, okay.
CREAK CREAK
Huh?
...
You're done training?
I am.
Kagetora is still training on his own.
Even after all that...he doesn't quit.
He really is amazing...
I want to be strong *like Master* but...
I have to be *as strong* as Master...
...or she won't even look my way. But I can't...
But?
I see... you've already given up.

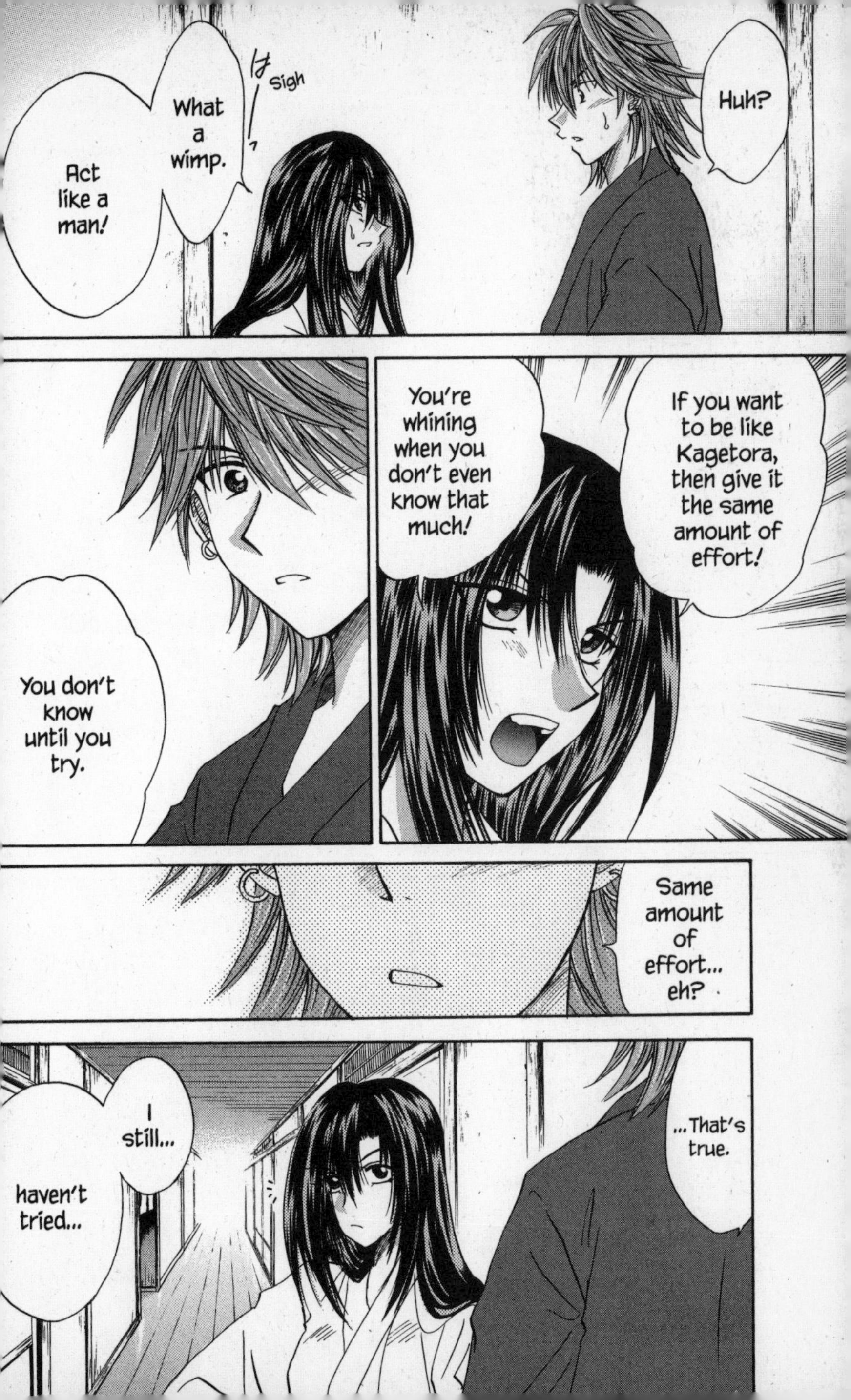
Huh?
は Sigh
What a wimp.
Act like a man!
If you want to be like Kagetora, then give it the same amount of effort!
You're whining when you don't even know that much!
You don't know until you try.
Same amount of effort... eh?
...That's true.
I still...
haven't tried...

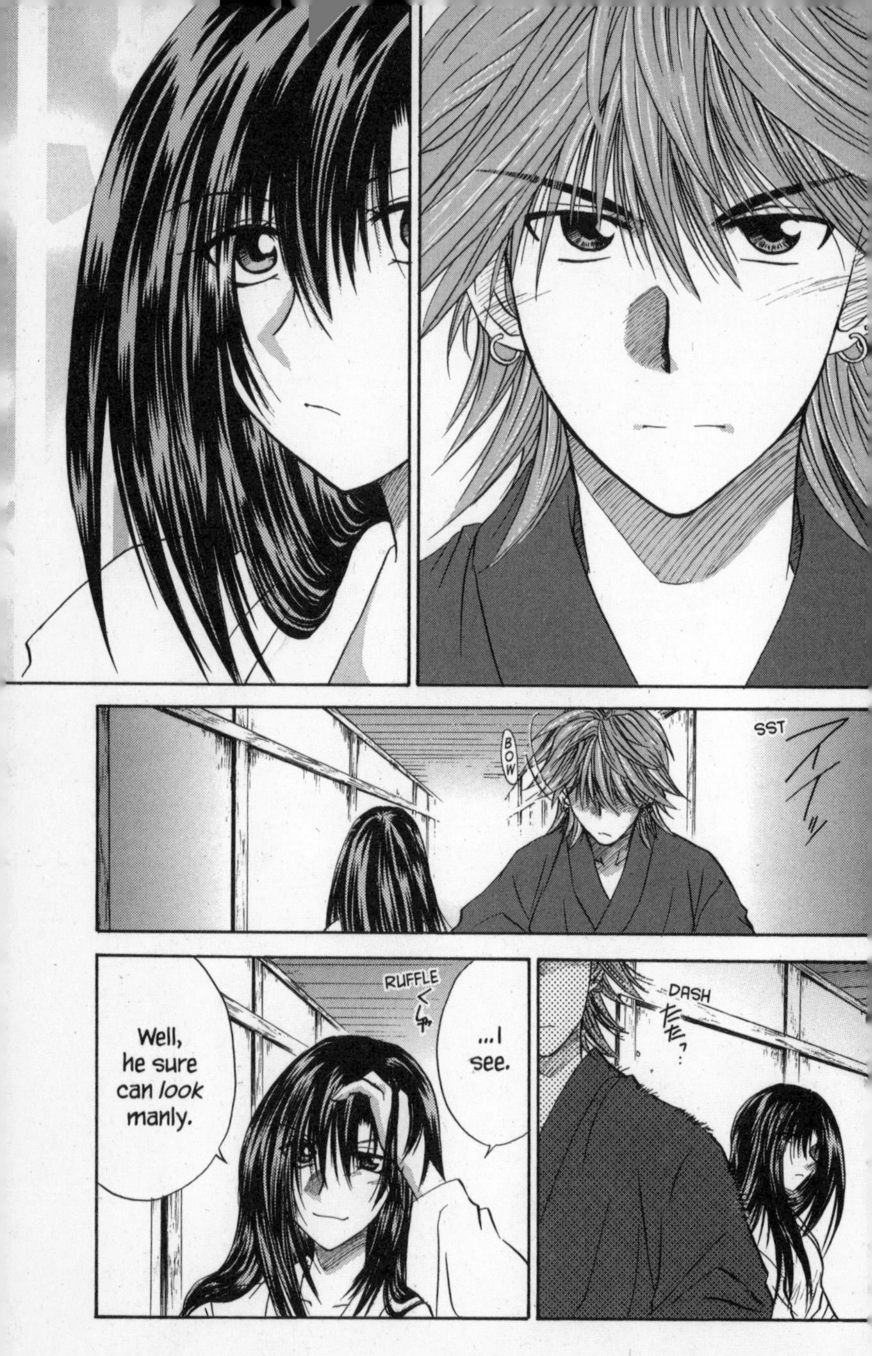
BOW
SST
DASH
RUFFLE
...I see.
Well, he sure can *look* manly.

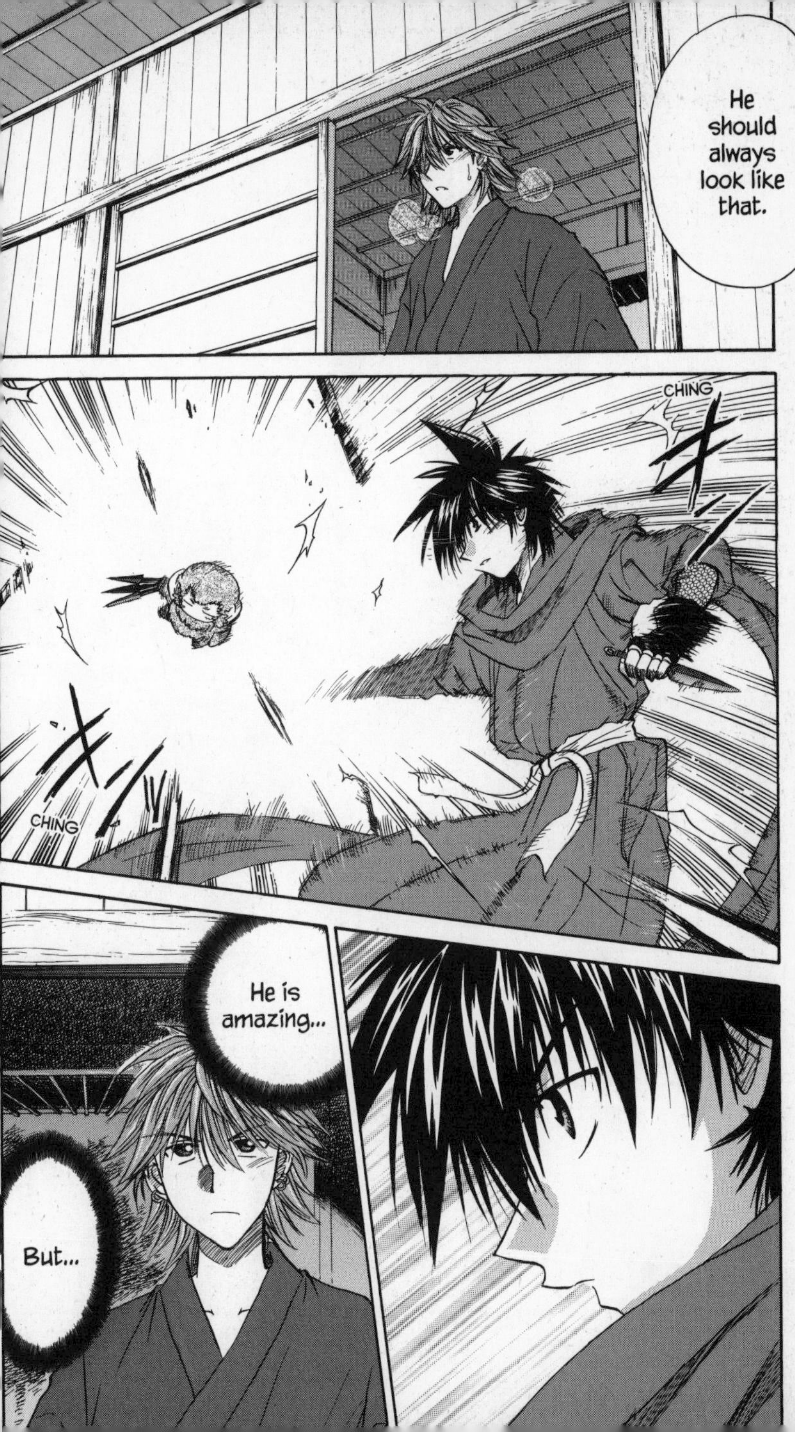
He should always look like that.
CHING
CHING
He is amazing...
But...

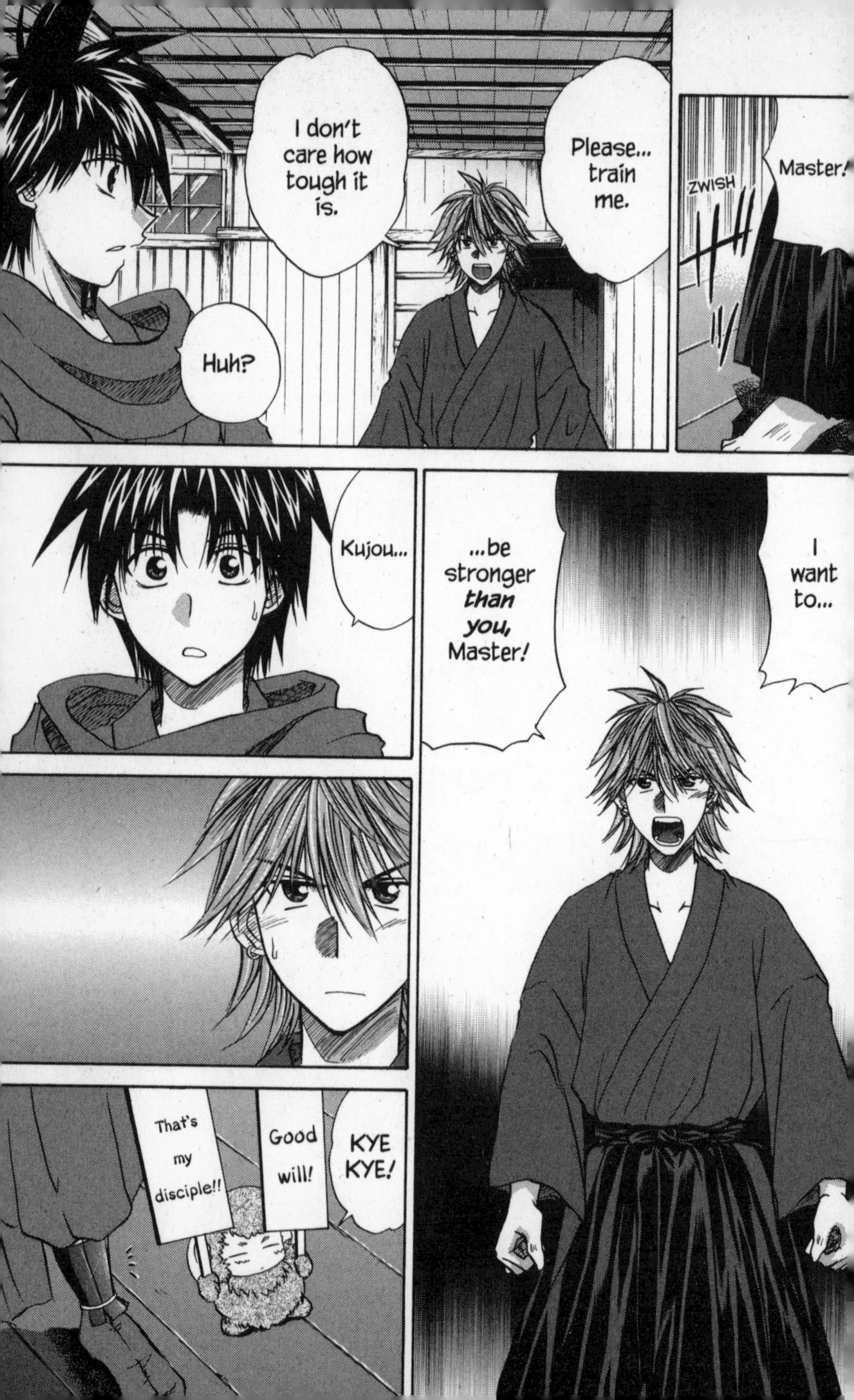
ZWISH
Master!
Please... train me.
I don't care how tough it is.
Huh?
I want to...
...be stronger *than you*, Master!
Kujou...
KYE KYE!
Good will!
That's my disciple!!

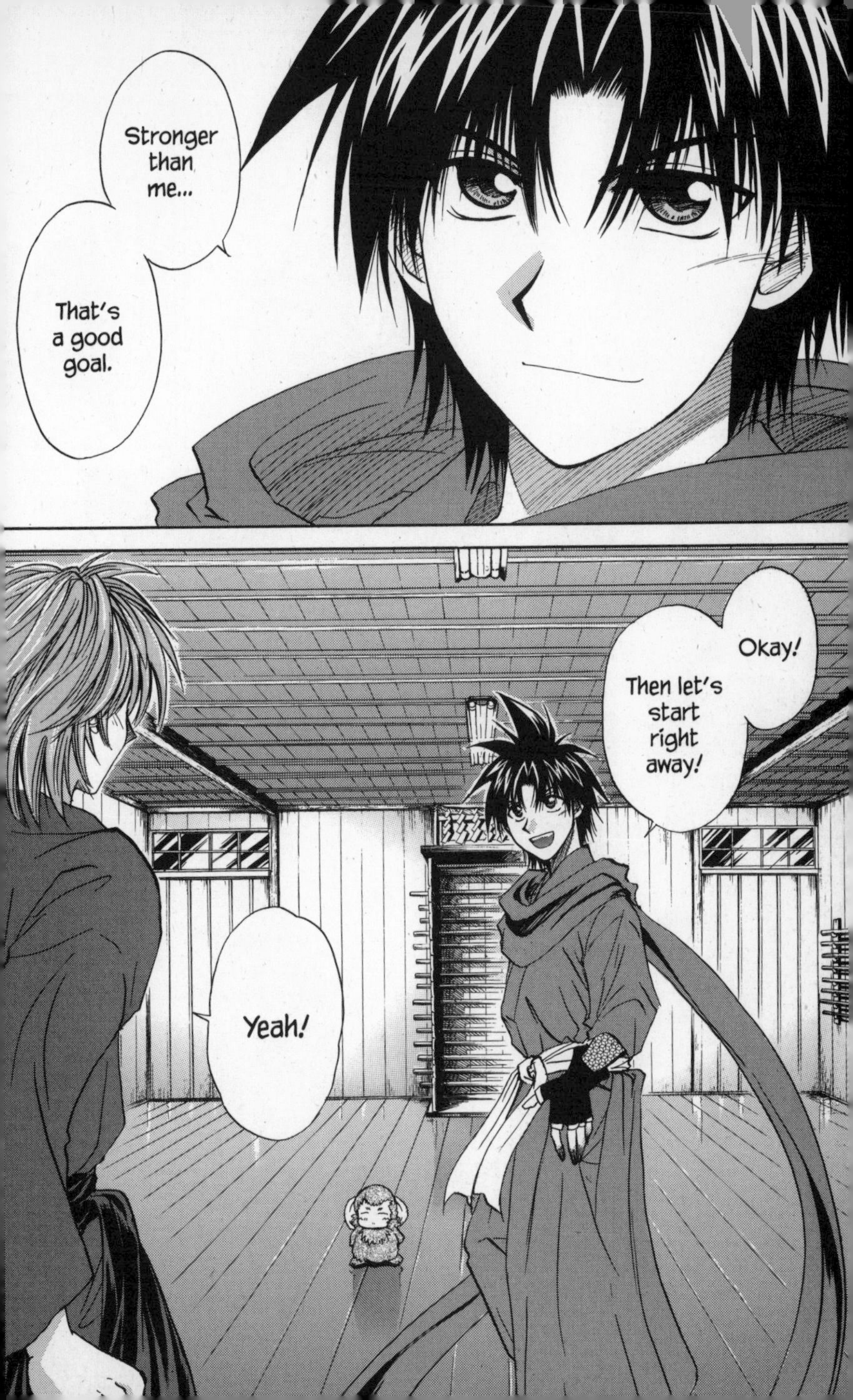
Stronger than me...
That's a good goal.
Okay!
Then let's start right away!
Yeah!

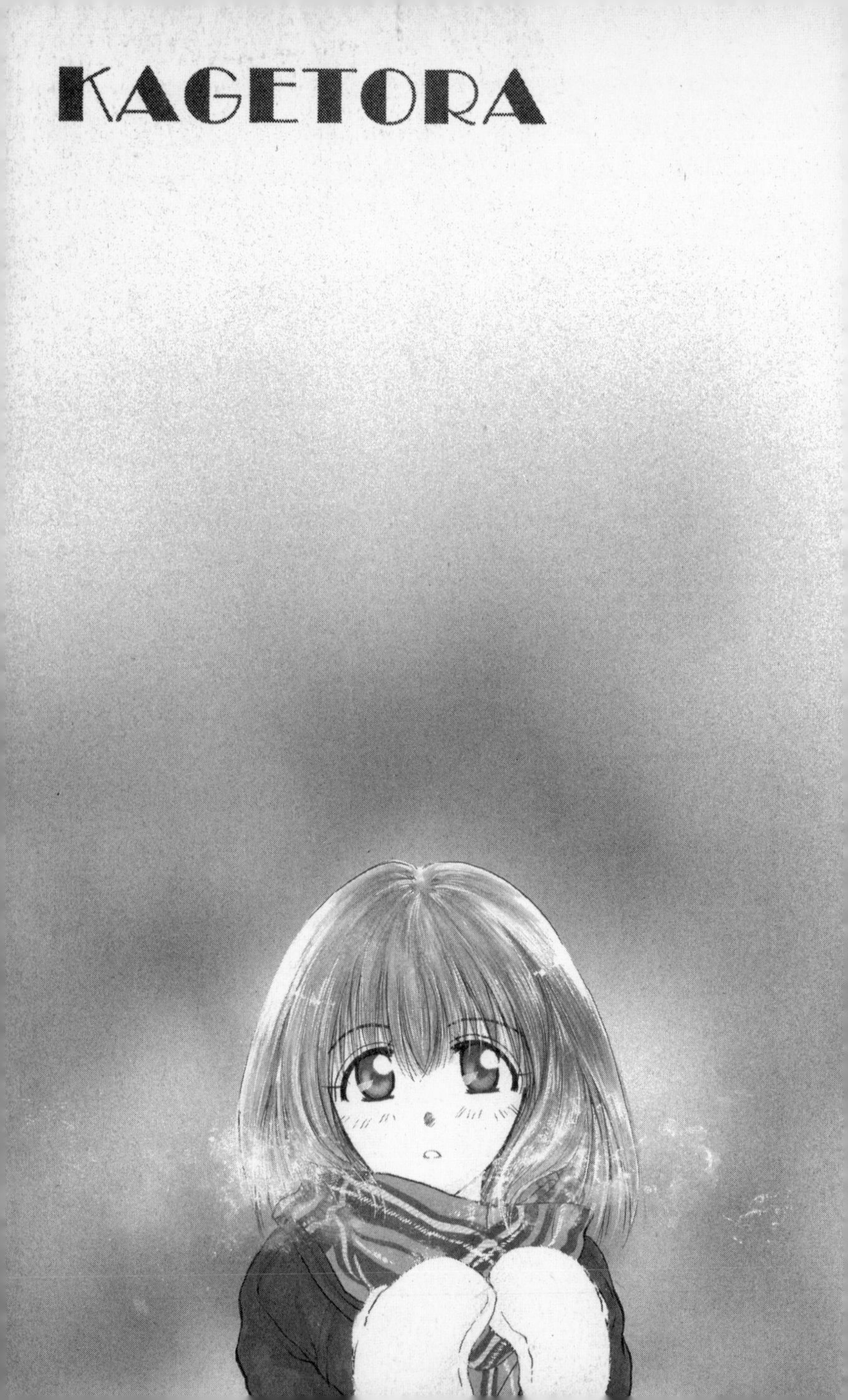
KAGETORA

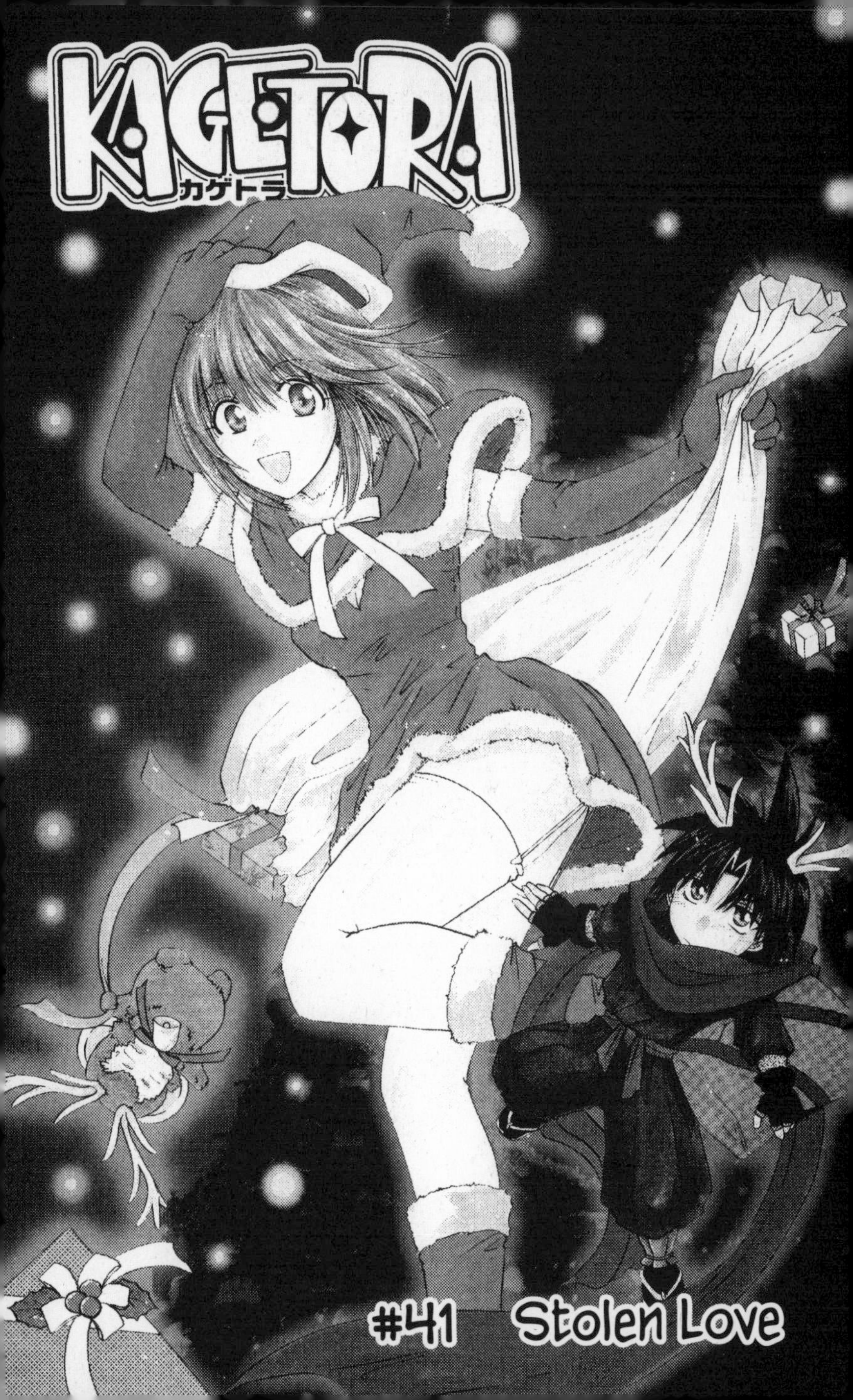
KAGETORA
カゲトラ
#41 Stolen Love

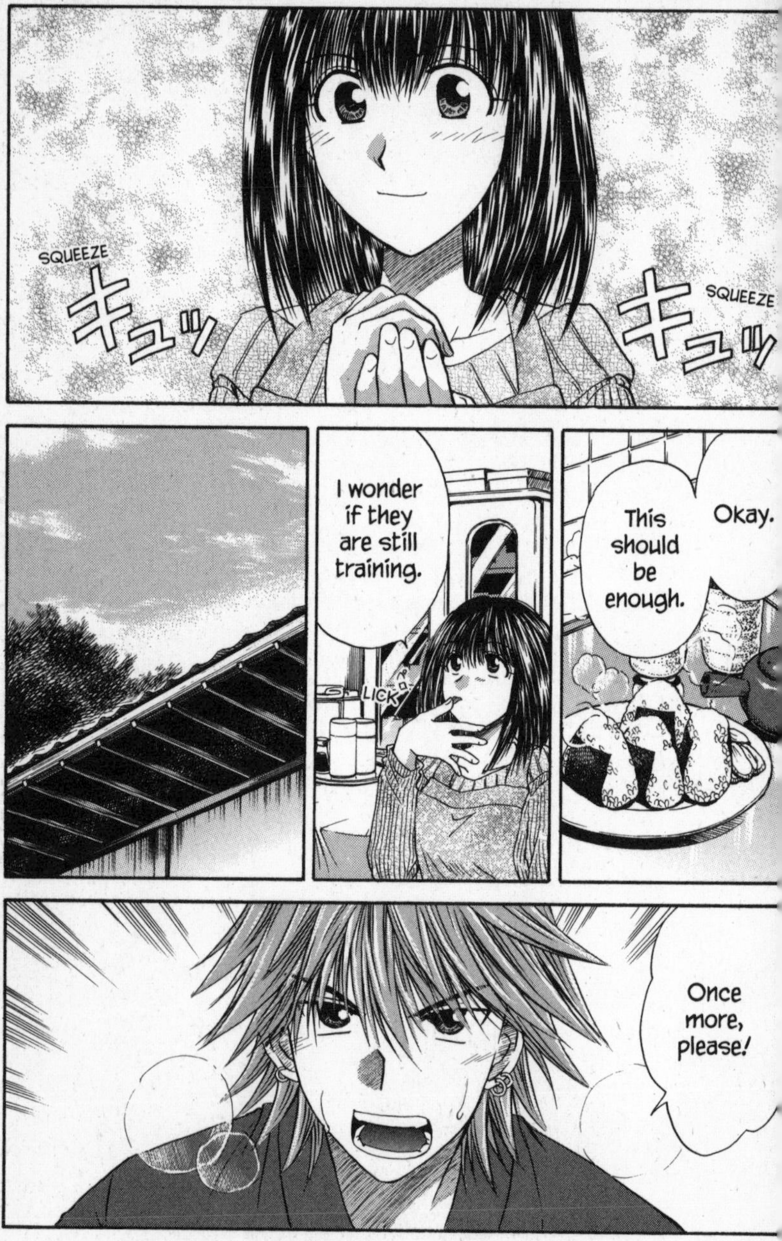
SQUEEZE
キュッ
SQUEEZE
キュッ
Okay.
This should be enough.
I wonder if they are still training.
LICK
Once more, please!

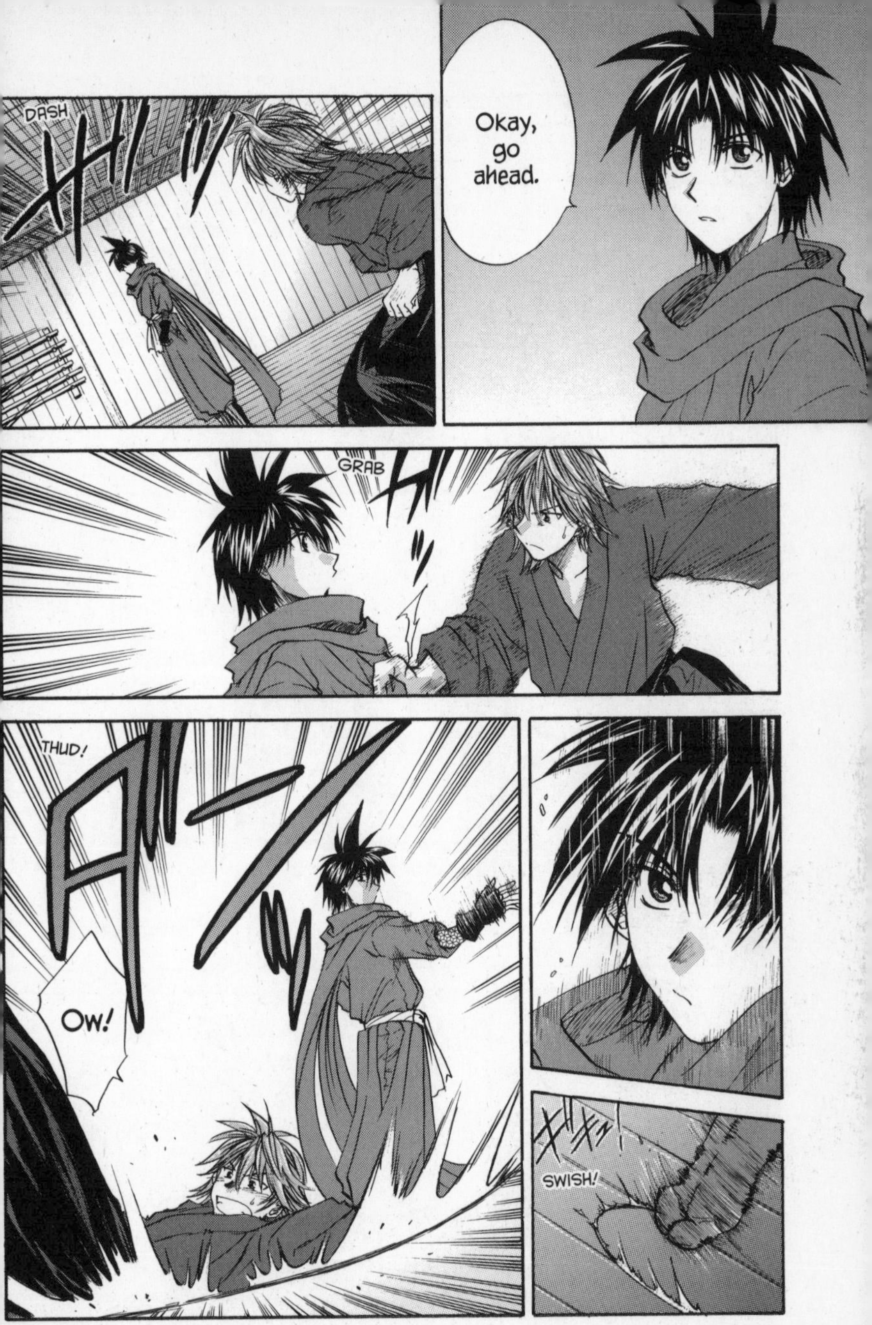
Okay, go ahead.
DASH
GRAB
THUD!
OW!
SWISH!

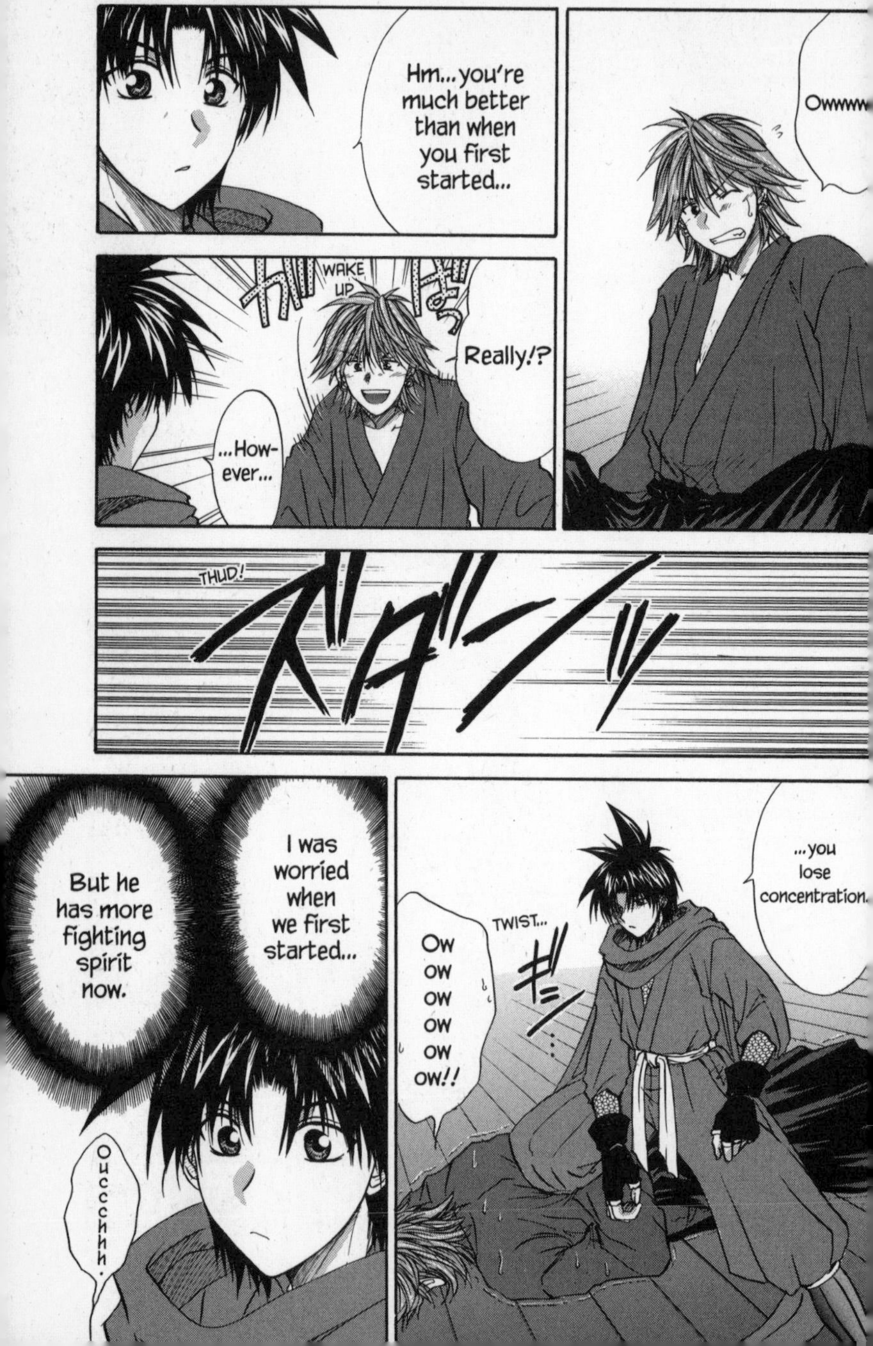
Owwww
Hm...you're much better than when you first started...
WAKE UP
Really!?
...How-ever...
THUD!
...you lose concentration.
TWIST...
Ow ow ow ow ow ow!!
I was worried when we first started...
But he has more fighting spirit now.
Ouccchhh.

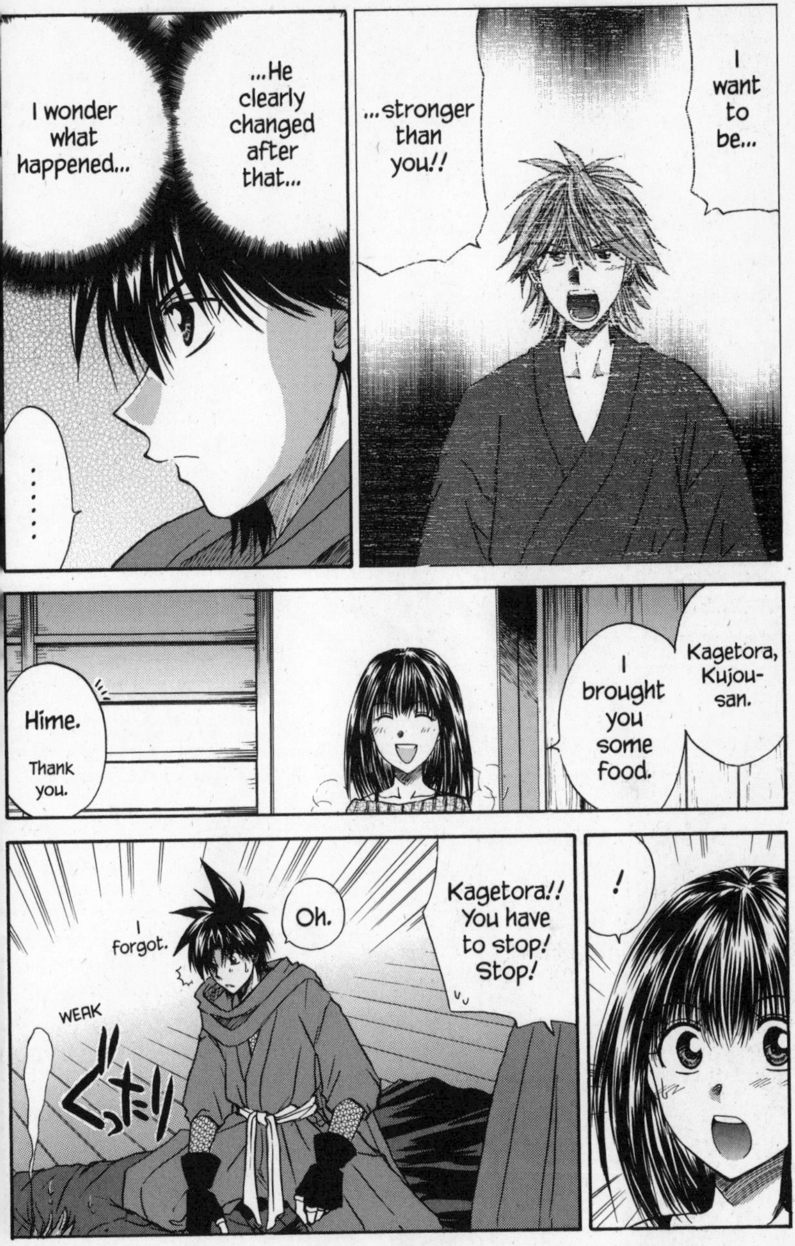
I want to be...
...stronger than you!!
...He clearly changed after that...
I wonder what happened...
......
Kagetora, Kujou-san.
I brought you some food.
Hime.
Thank you.
!
Kagetora!! You have to stop! Stop!
Oh.
I forgot.
WEAK
ぐったり

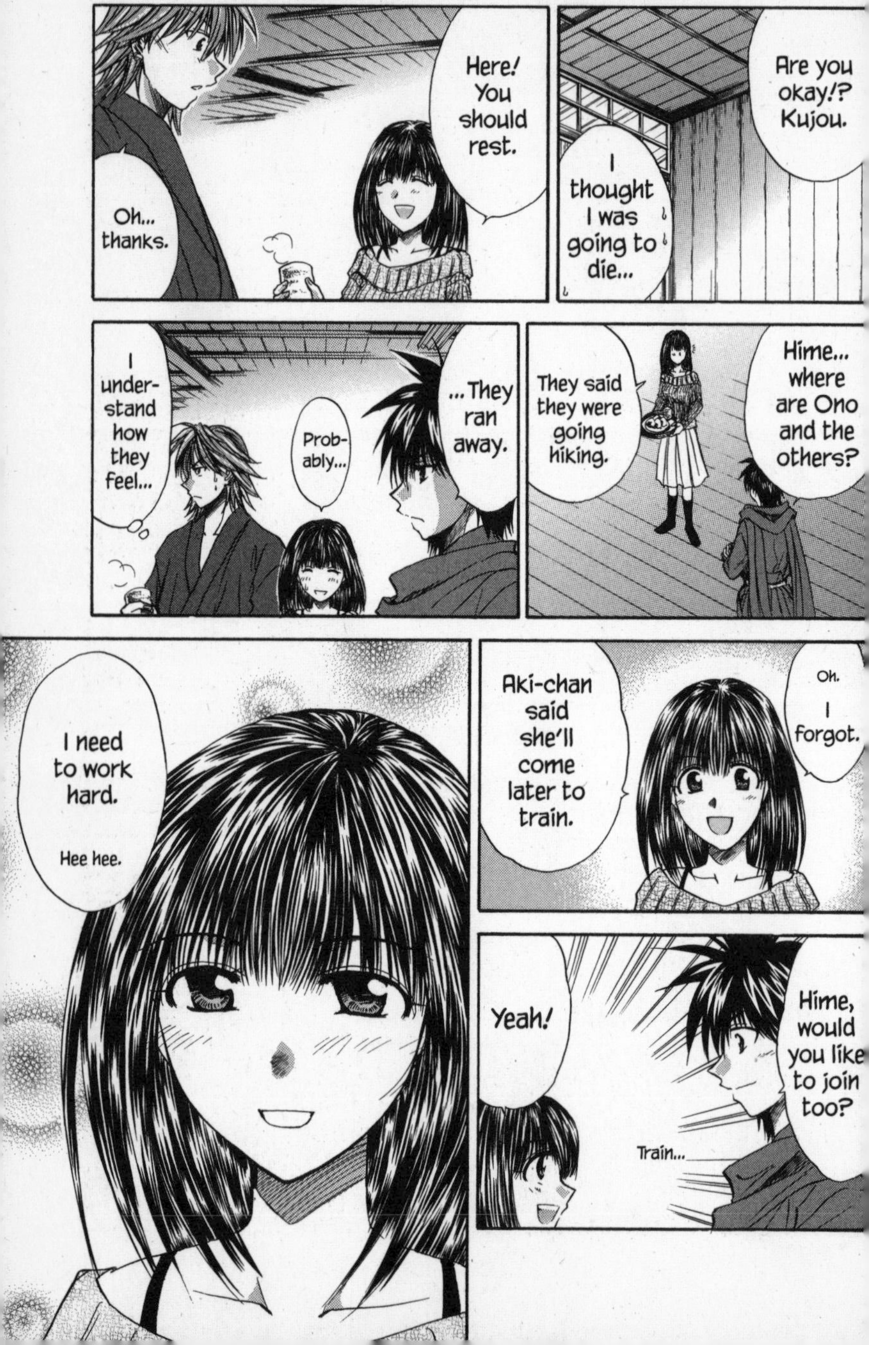
Are you okay!? Kujou.
I thought I was going to die...
Here! You should rest.
Oh... thanks.
Hime... where are Ono and the others?
They said they were going hiking.
...They ran away.
Probably...
I understand how they feel...
Oh.
I forgot.
Aki-chan said she'll come later to train.
Hime, would you like to join too?
Train...
Yeah!
I need to work hard.
Hee hee.

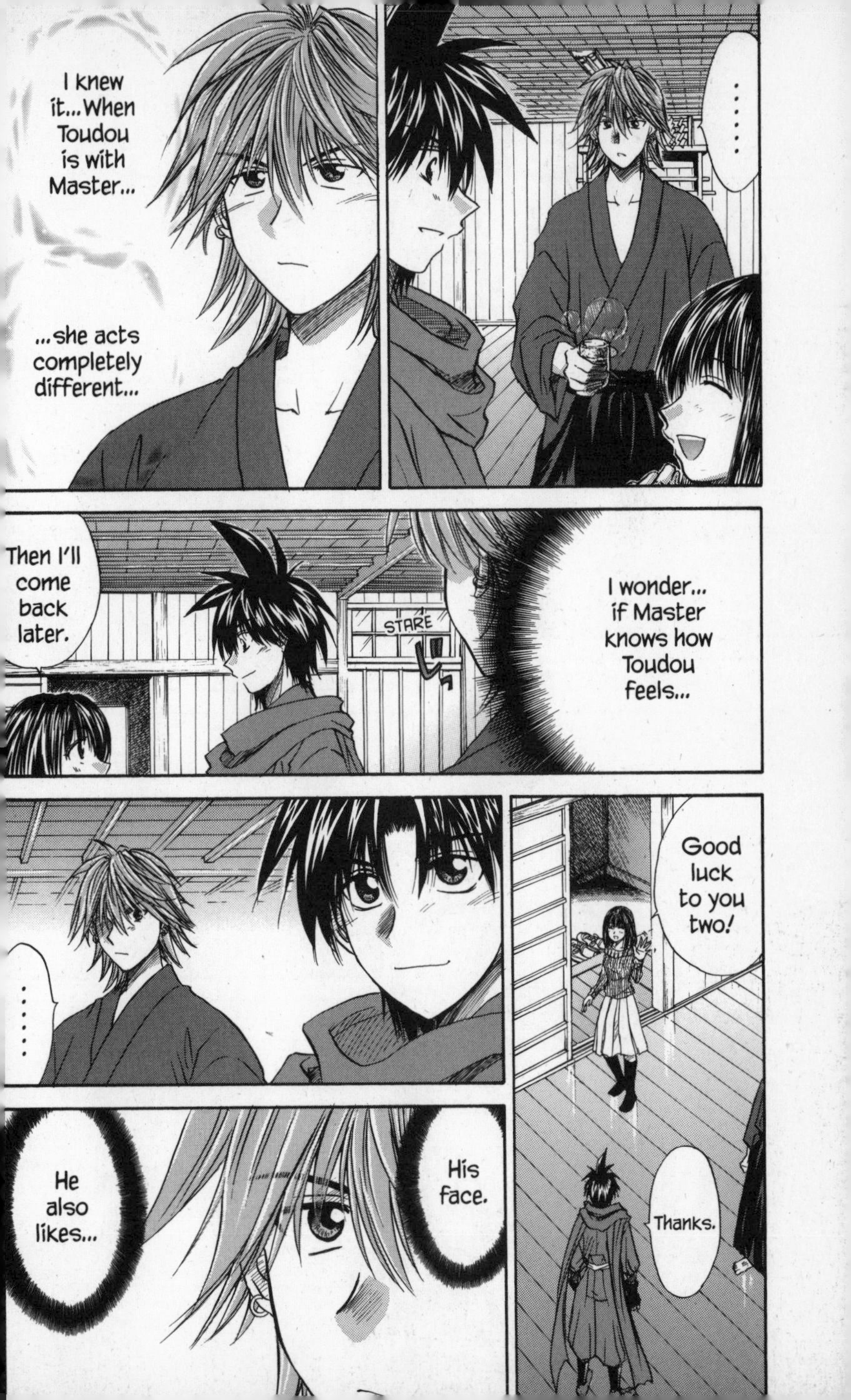

……
I knew it...When Toudou is with Master...
...she acts completely different...
I wonder... if Master knows how Toudou feels...
STARE
Then I'll come back later.
Good luck to you two!
Thanks.
……
His face.
He also likes...

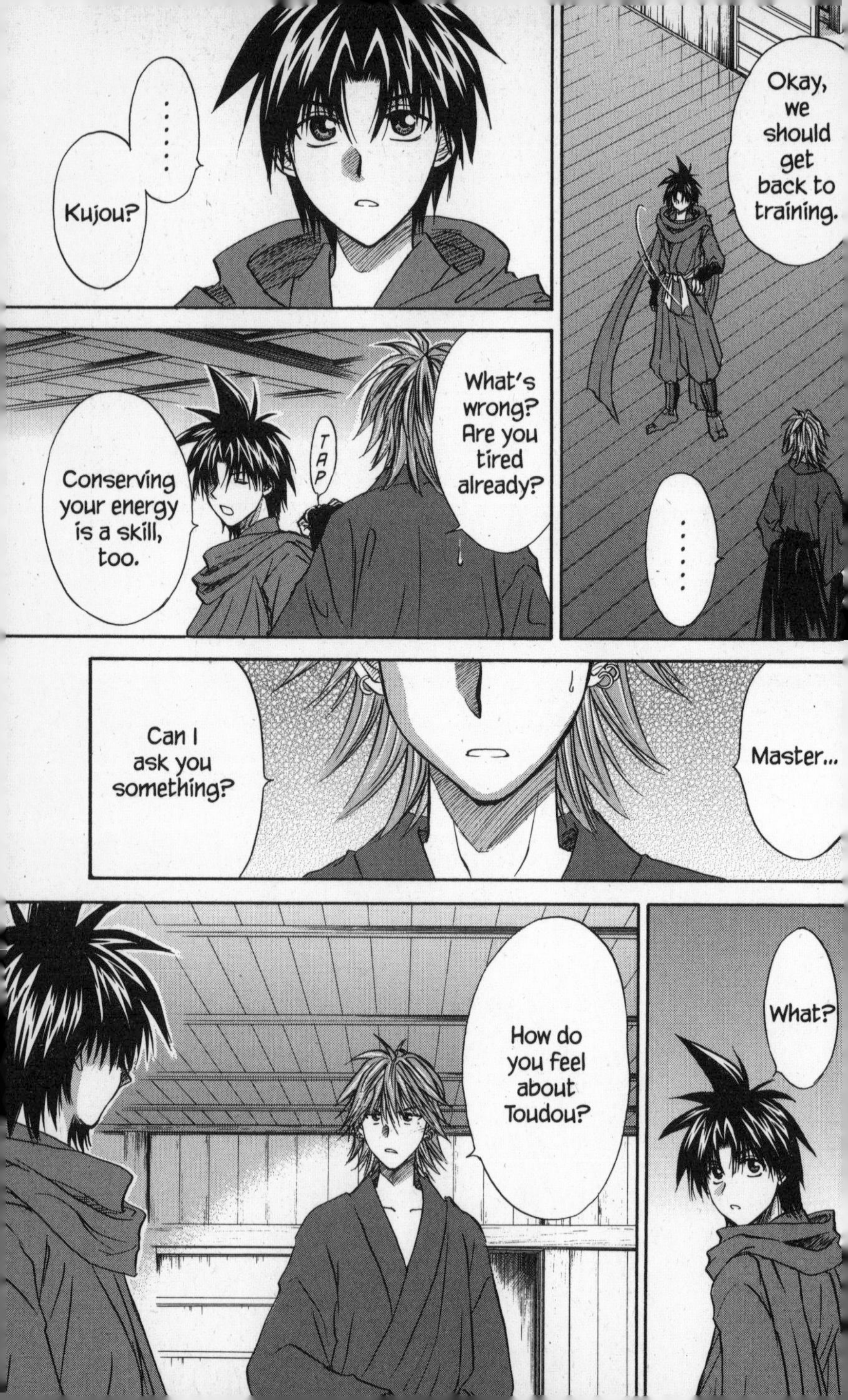
Okay, we should get back to training.
......
......
Kujou?
What's wrong? Are you tired already?
TAP
Conserving your energy is a skill, too.
Master...
Can I ask you something?
What?
How do you feel about Toudou?

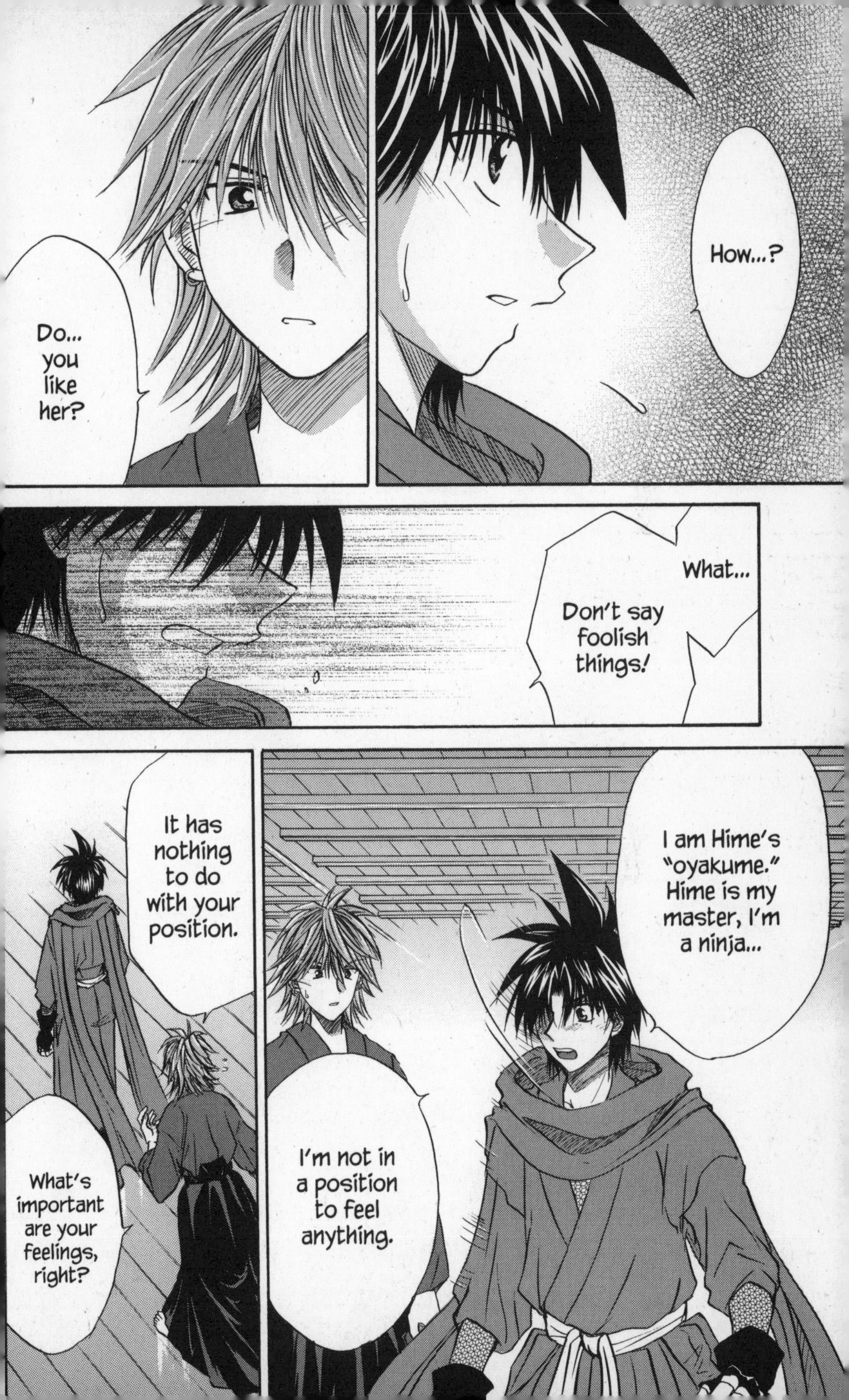
How...?
Do... you like her?
What...
Don't say foolish things!
I am Hime's "oyakume." Hime is my master, I'm a ninja...
I'm not in a position to feel anything.
It has nothing to do with your position.
What's important are your feelings, right?

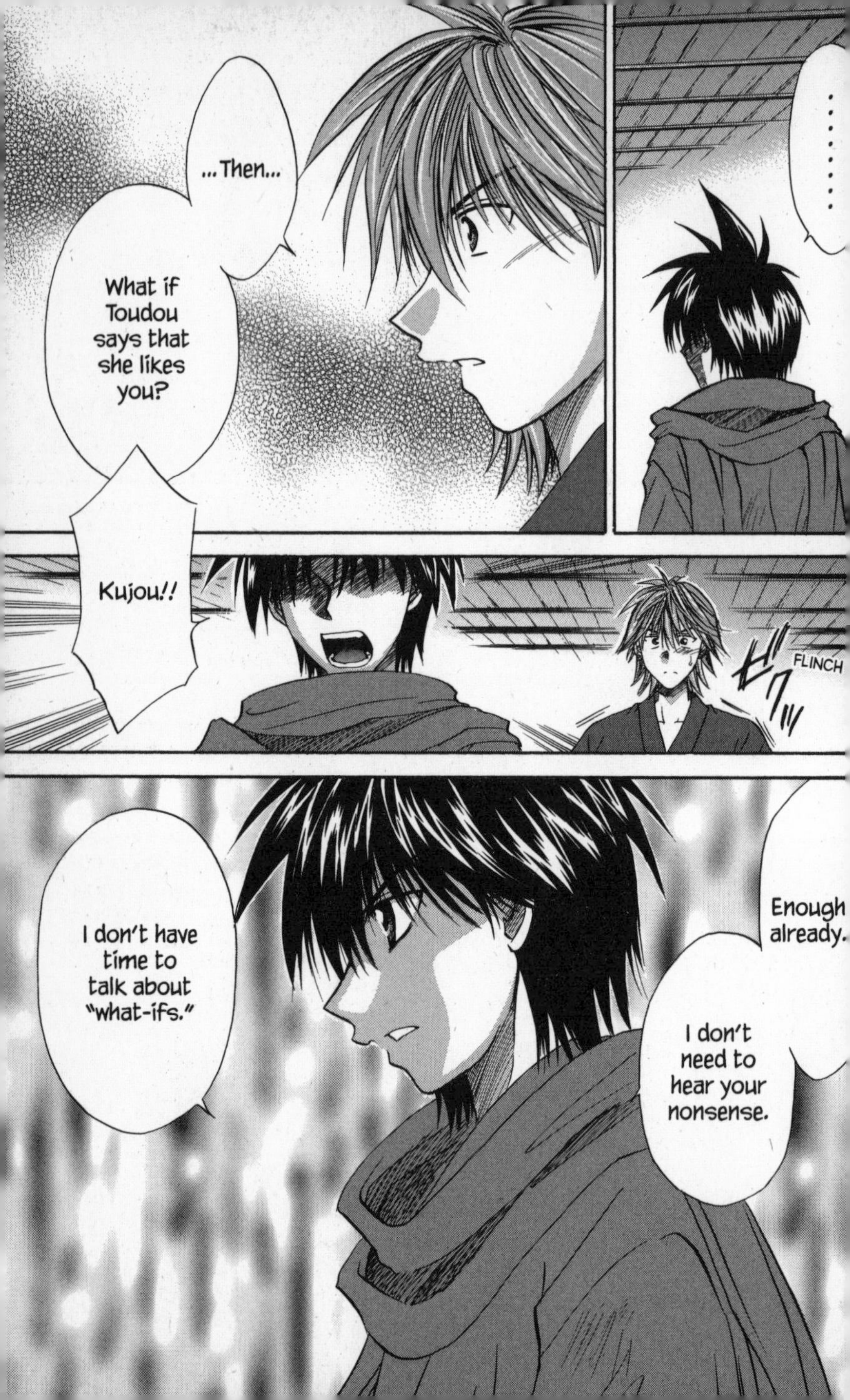
......
...Then...
What if Toudou says that she likes you?
Kujou!!
FLINCH
Enough already.
I don't need to hear your nonsense.
I don't have time to talk about "what-ifs."

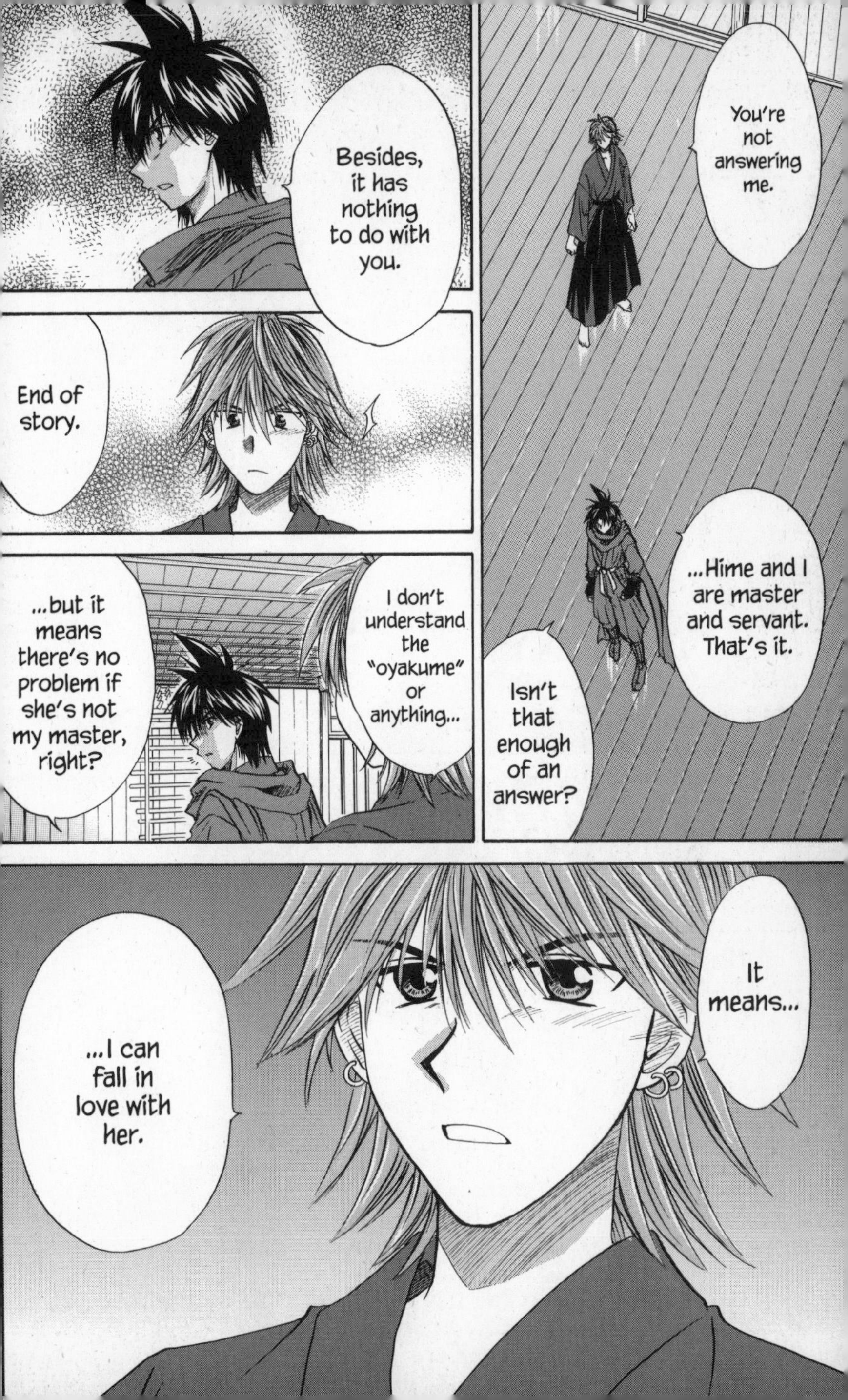
You're not answering me.
...Hime and I are master and servant. That's it.
Isn't that enough of an answer?
Besides, it has nothing to do with you.
End of story.
I don't understand the "oyakume" or anything...
...but it means there's no problem if she's not my master, right?
It means...
...I can fall in love with her.

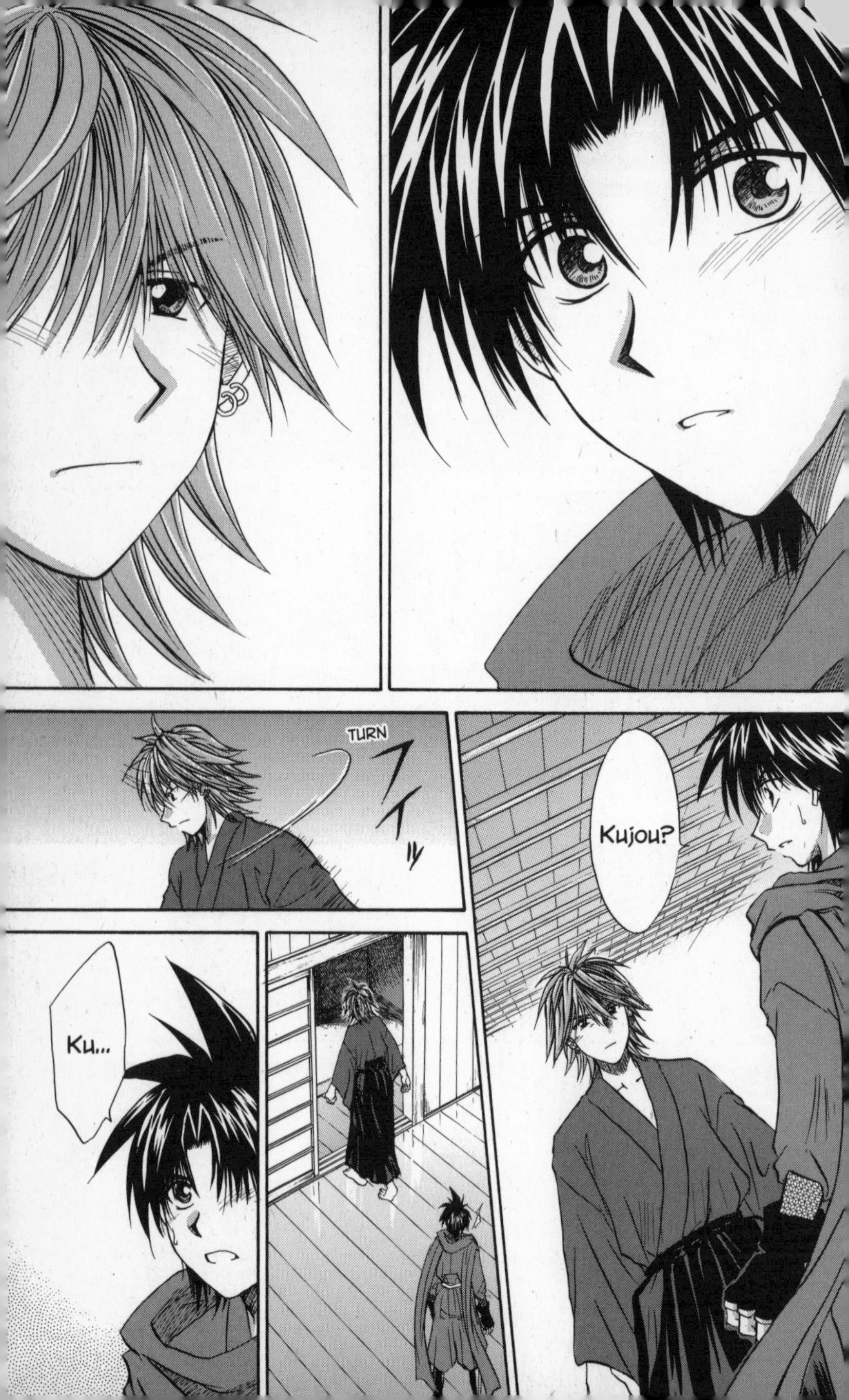
Kujou?
TURN
Ku...

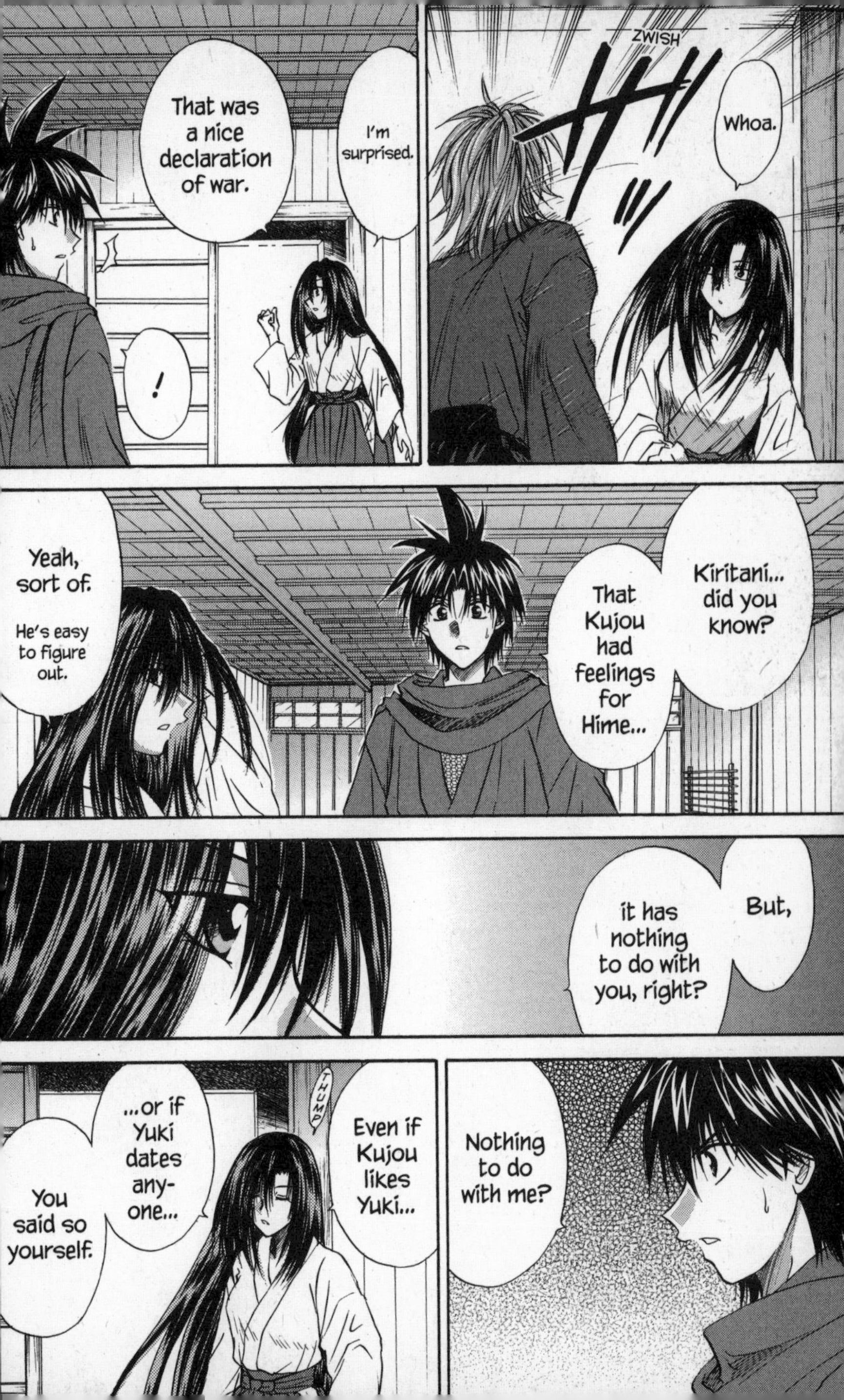
ZWISH
Whoa.
I'm surprised.
That was a nice declaration of war.
!
Kiritani... did you know?
That Kujou had feelings for Hime...
Yeah, sort of.
He's easy to figure out.
But,
it has nothing to do with you, right?
Nothing to do with me?
THUMP
Even if Kujou likes Yuki...
...or if Yuki dates any-one...
You said so yourself.

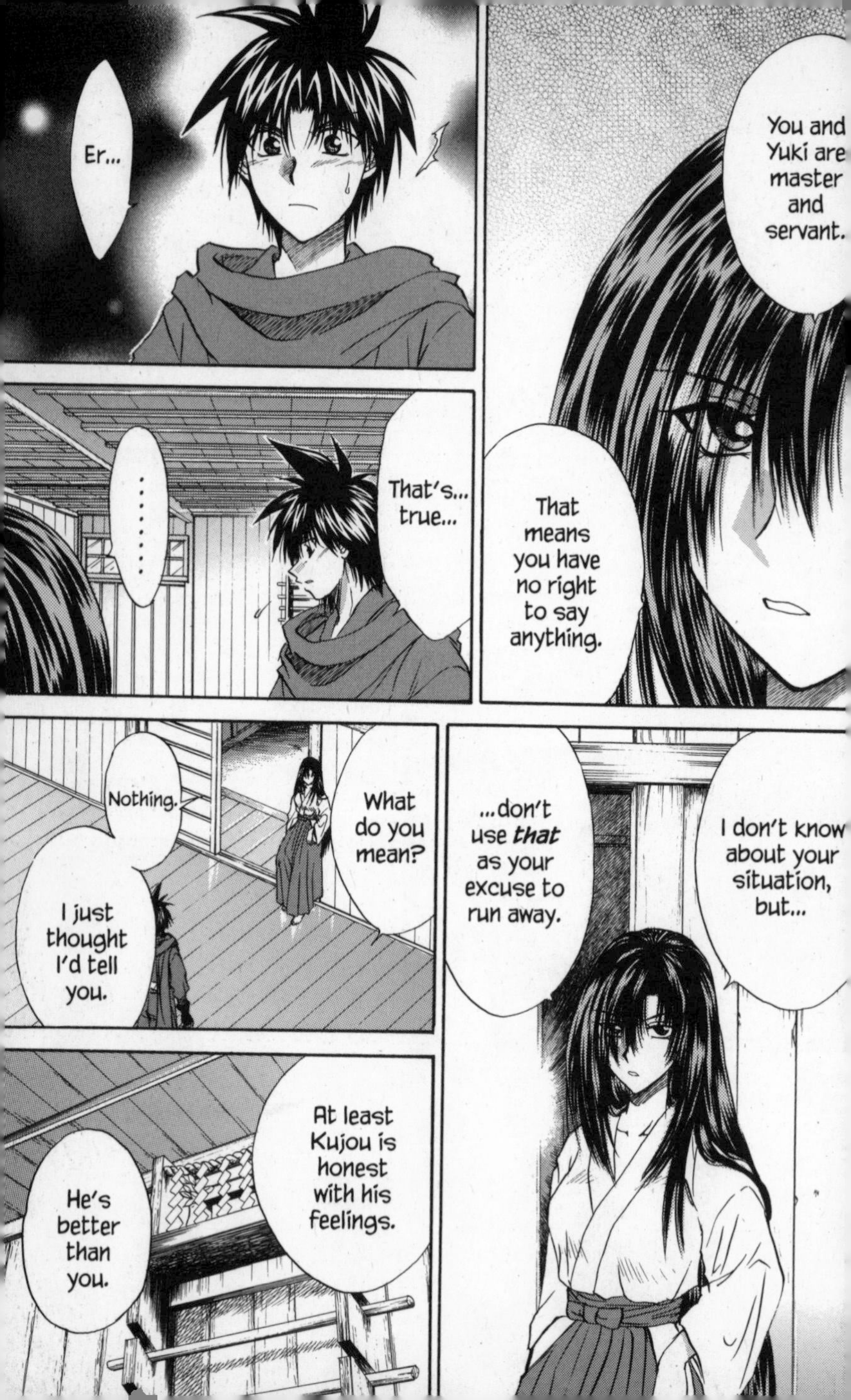
You and Yuki are master and servant.
That means you have no right to say anything.
Er...
That's... true...
......
I don't know about your situation, but...
...don't use *that* as your excuse to run away.
What do you mean?
Nothing.
I just thought I'd tell you.
At least Kujou is honest with his feelings.
He's better than you.

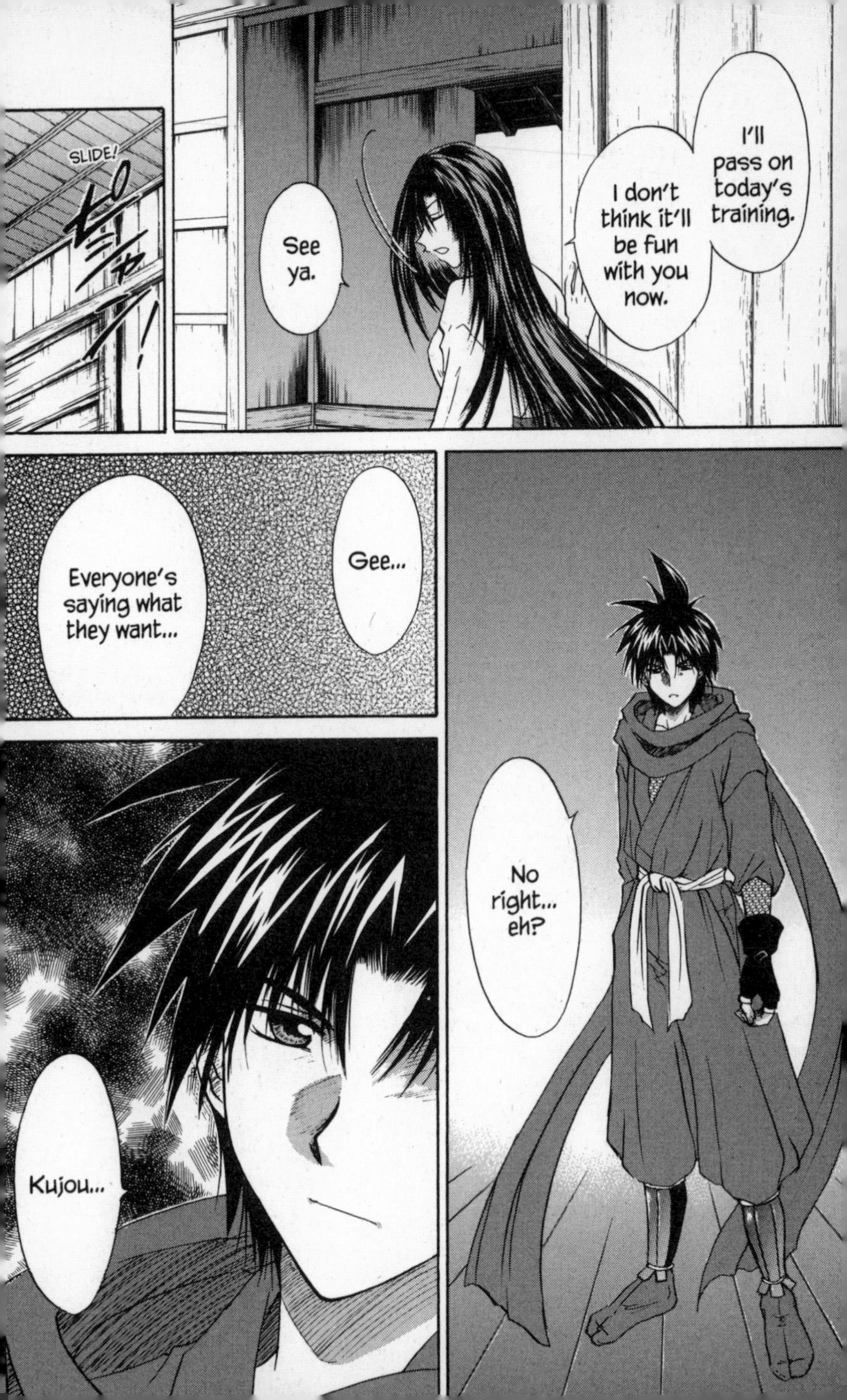
I'll pass on today's training.
I don't think it'll be fun with you now.
See ya.
SLIDE!
No right... eh?
Gee...
Everyone's saying what they want...
Kujou...

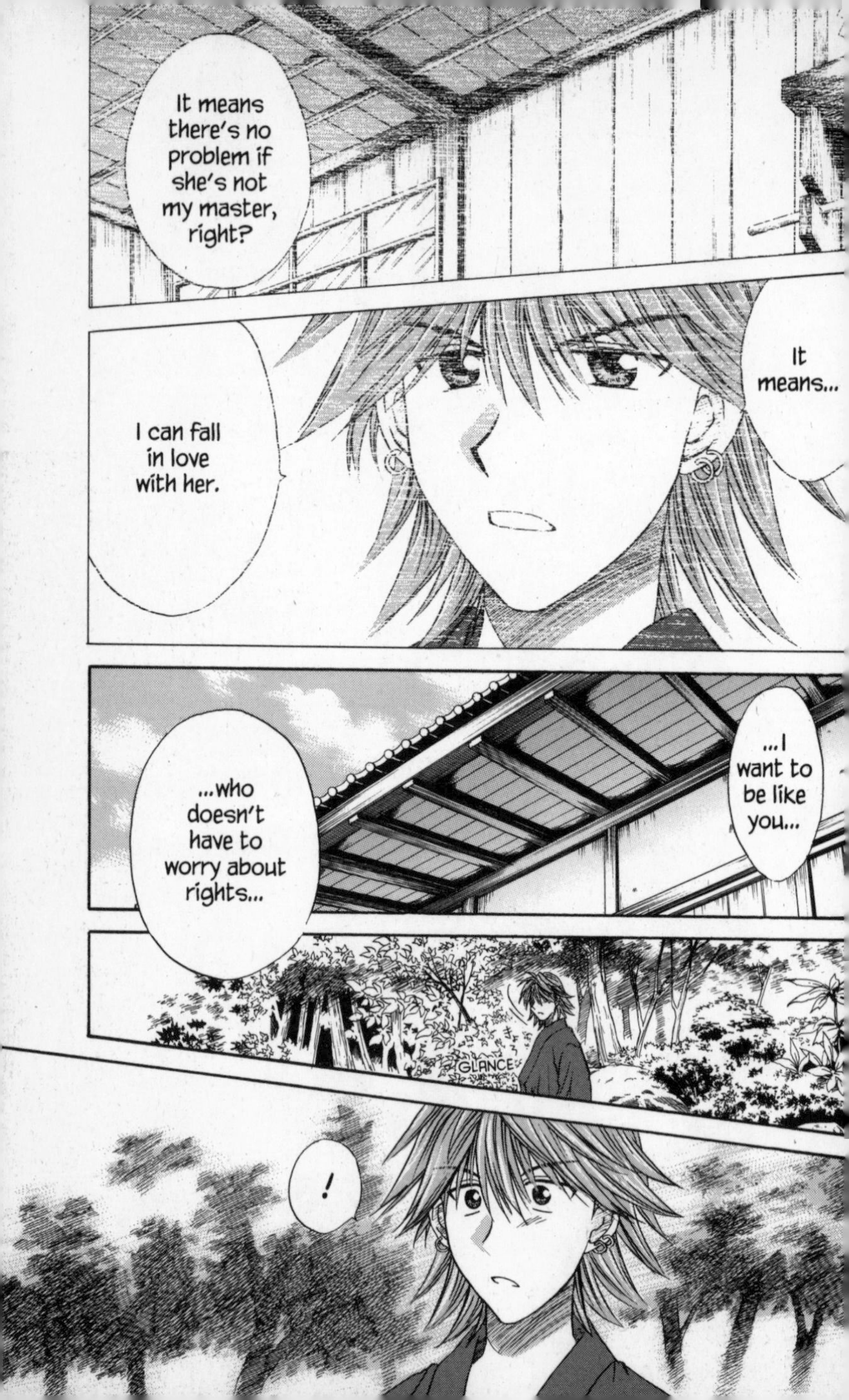
It means there's no problem if she's not my master, right?
It means...
I can fall in love with her.
...I want to be like you...
...who doesn't have to worry about rights...
GLANCE
!

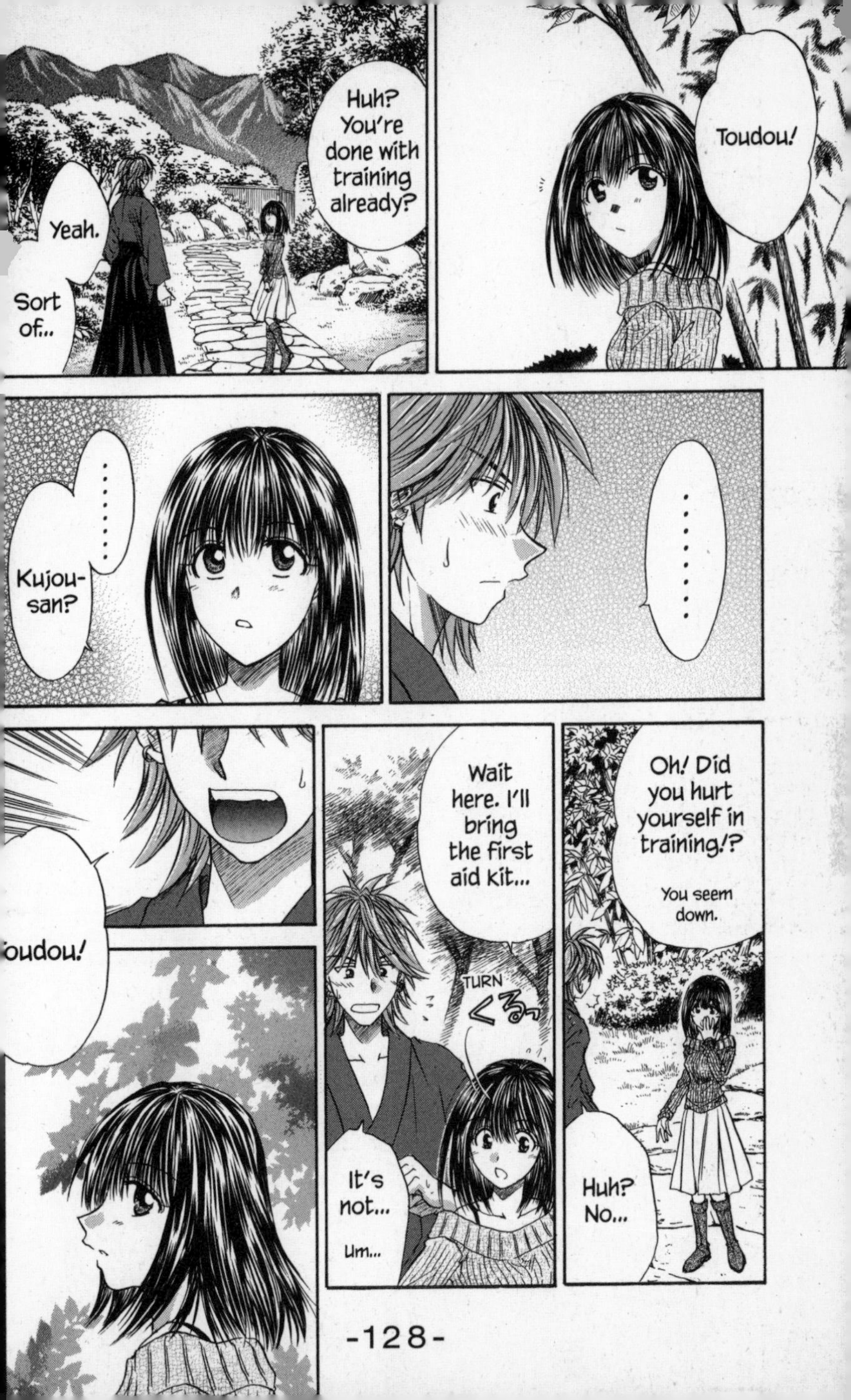
Toudou!
Huh? You're done with training already?
Yeah.
Sort of...
......
......
Kujou-san?
Oh! Did you hurt yourself in training!?
You seem down.
Huh? No...
Wait here. I'll bring the first aid kit...
TURN
くるっ
It's not...
Um...
oudou!

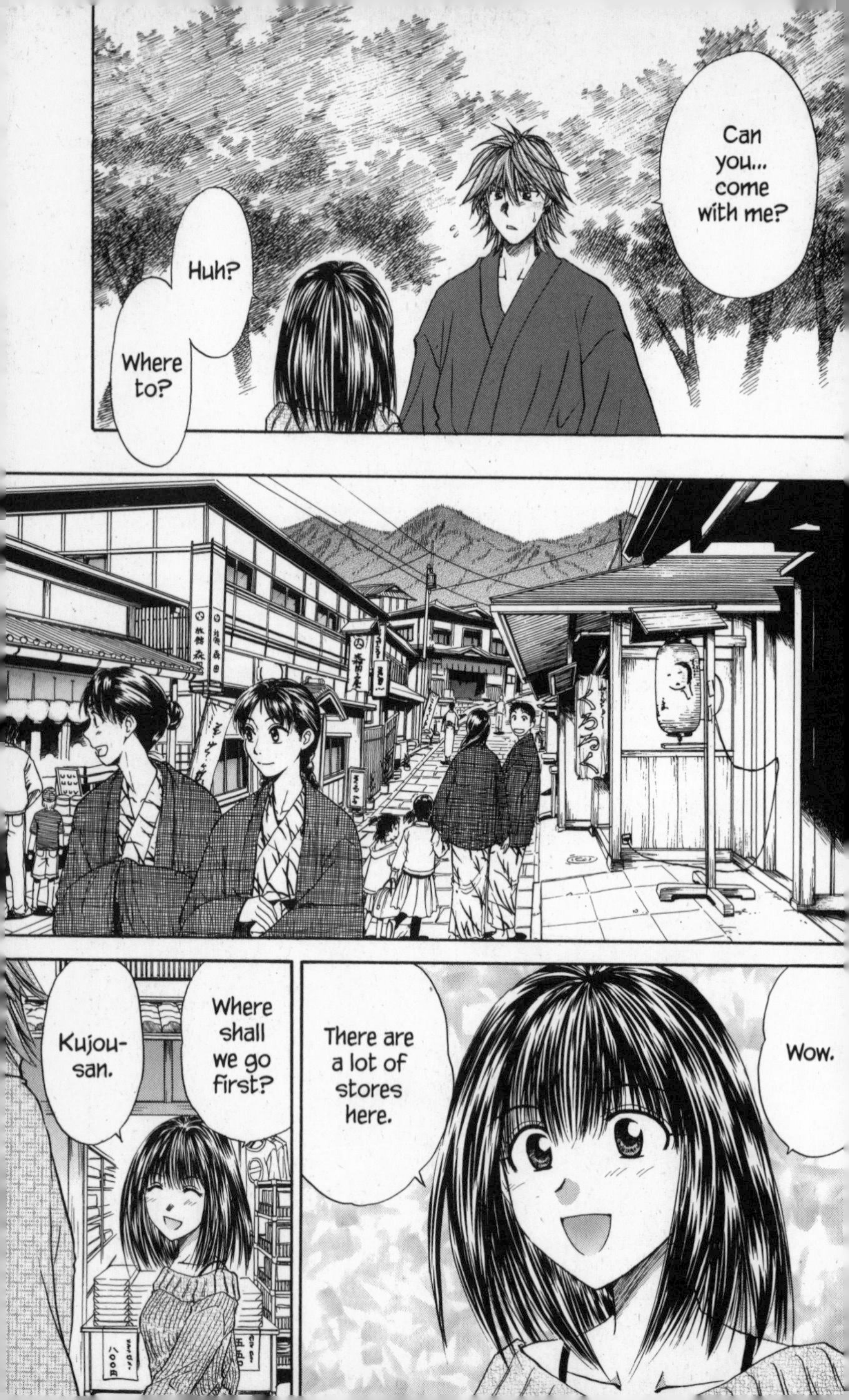
Can you... come with me?
Huh?
Where to?
Wow.
There are a lot of stores here.
Where shall we go first?
Kujou-san.

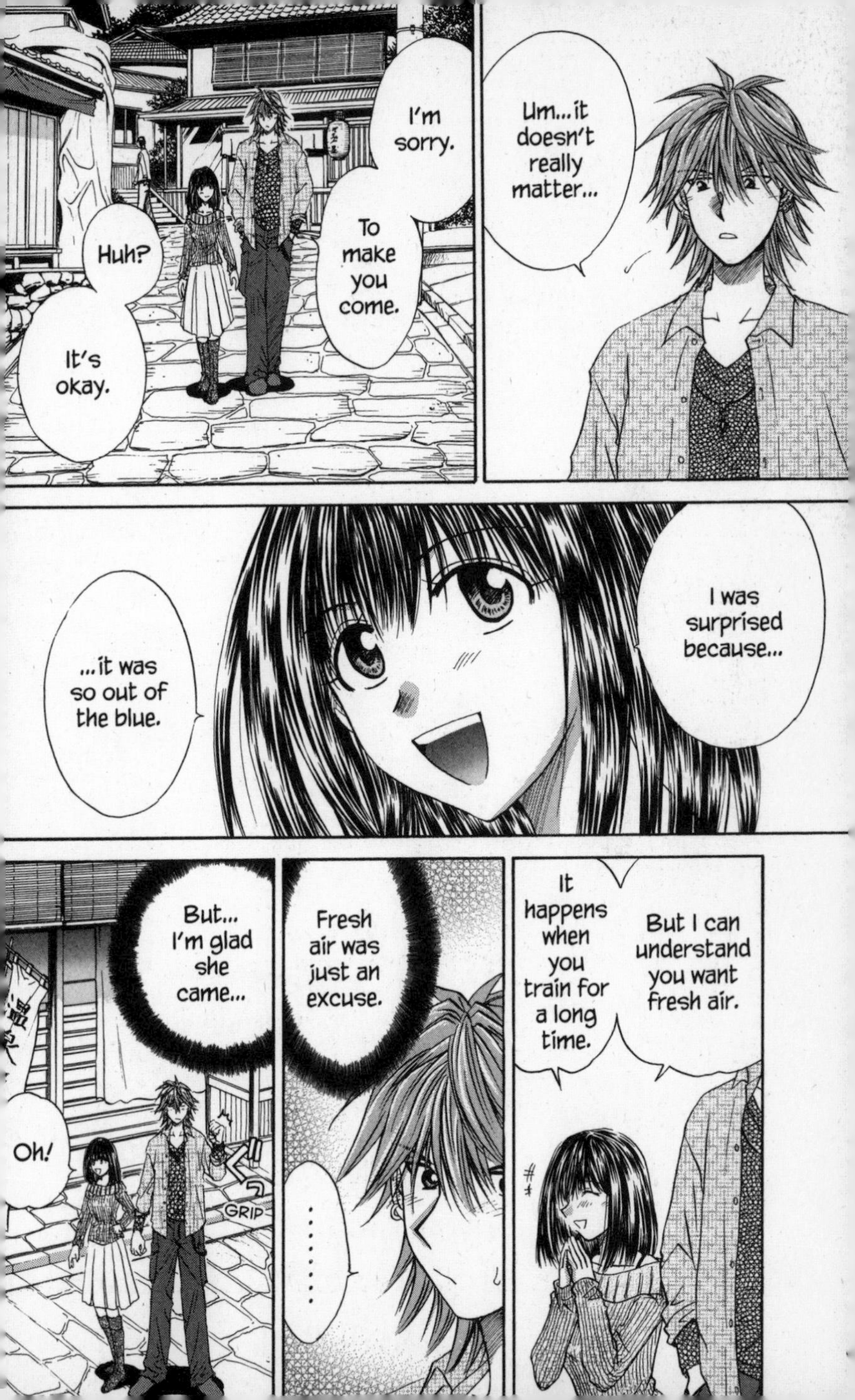
Um...it doesn't really matter...
I'm sorry.
To make you come.
Huh?
It's okay.
I was surprised because...
...it was so out of the blue.
But I can understand you want fresh air.
It happens when you train for a long time.
Fresh air was just an excuse.
......
But... I'm glad she came...
GRIP
Oh!

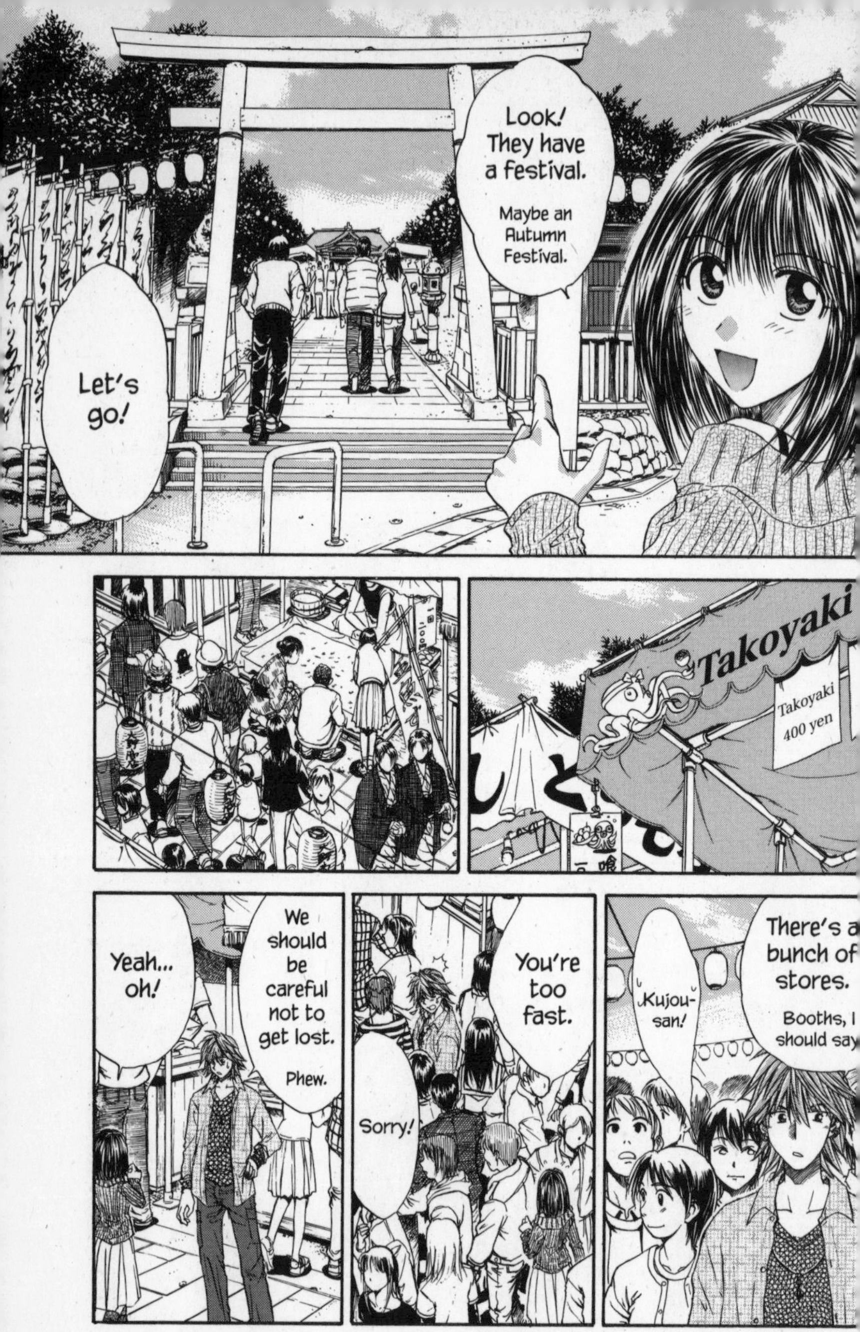
Look! They have a festival.
Maybe an Autumn Festival.
Let's go!
Takoyaki
Takoyaki 400 yen
There's a bunch of stores.
Booths, I should say
Kujou-san!
You're too fast.
Sorry!
We should be careful not to get lost.
Phew.
Yeah... oh!

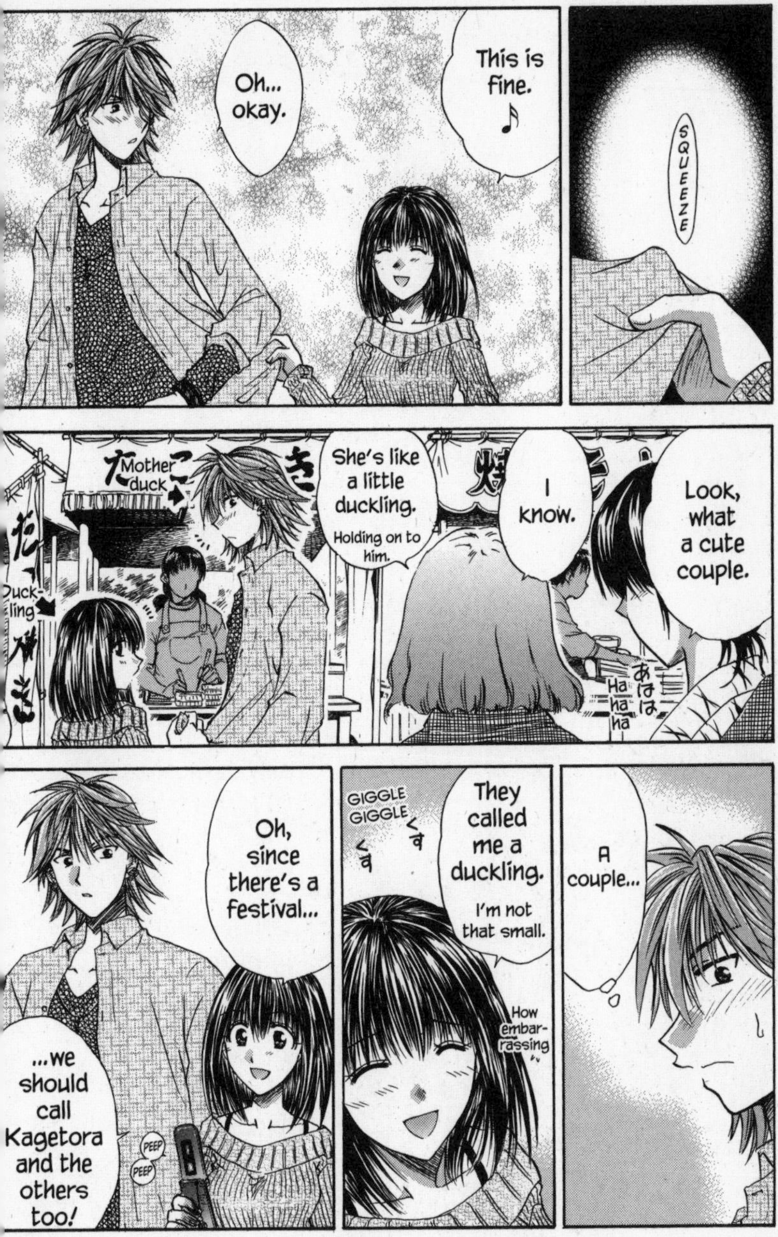
SQUEEZE
This is fine. ♪
Oh... okay.
Look, what a cute couple.
あはは
Ha ha ha
I know.
She's like a little duckling.
Holding on to him.
Mother duck
Duck-ling
A couple...
They called me a duckling.
I'm not that small.
GIGGLE GIGGLE
くすくす
How embarrassing
Oh, since there's a festival...
...we should call Kagetora and the others too!
PEEP
PEEP

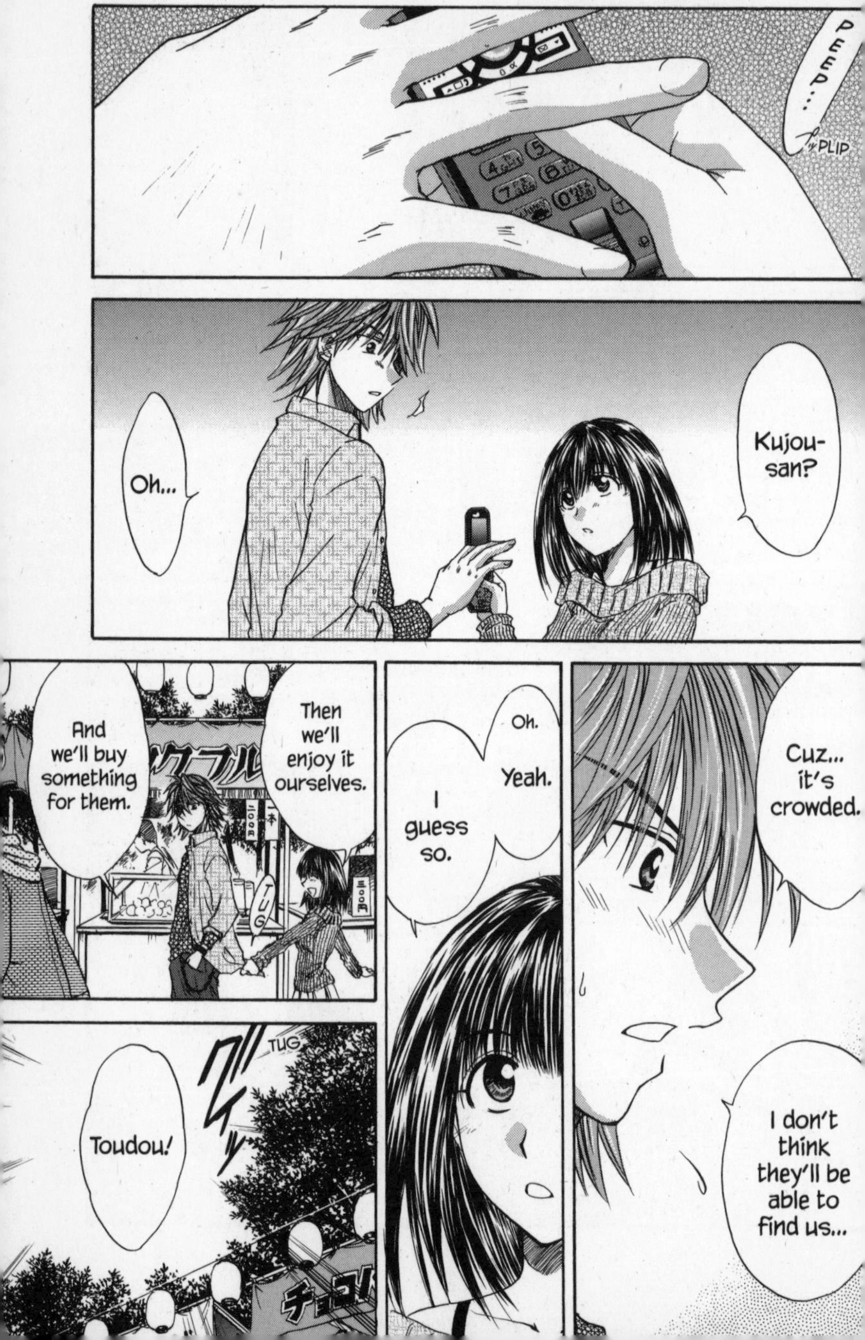
PEEP...
PLIP
Kujou-san?
Oh...
Cuz... it's crowded.
I don't think they'll be able to find us...
Oh.
Yeah.
I guess so.
Then we'll enjoy it ourselves.
And we'll buy something for them.
TUG
TUG
Toudou!

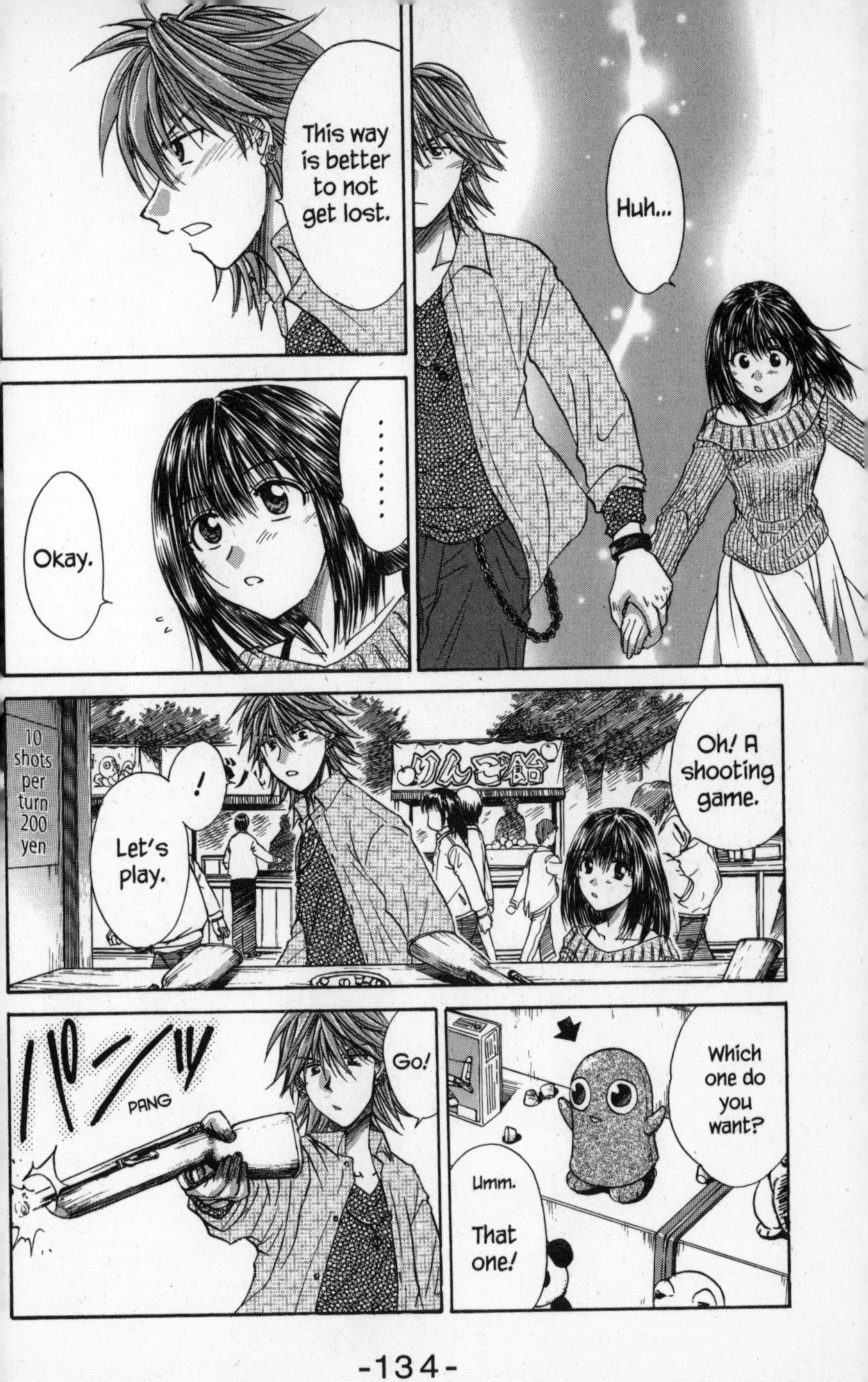
Huh...
This way is better to not get lost.
......
Okay.
Oh! A shooting game.
!
Let's play.
10 shots per turn 200 yen
Which one do you want?
Umm.
That one!
Go!
PANG

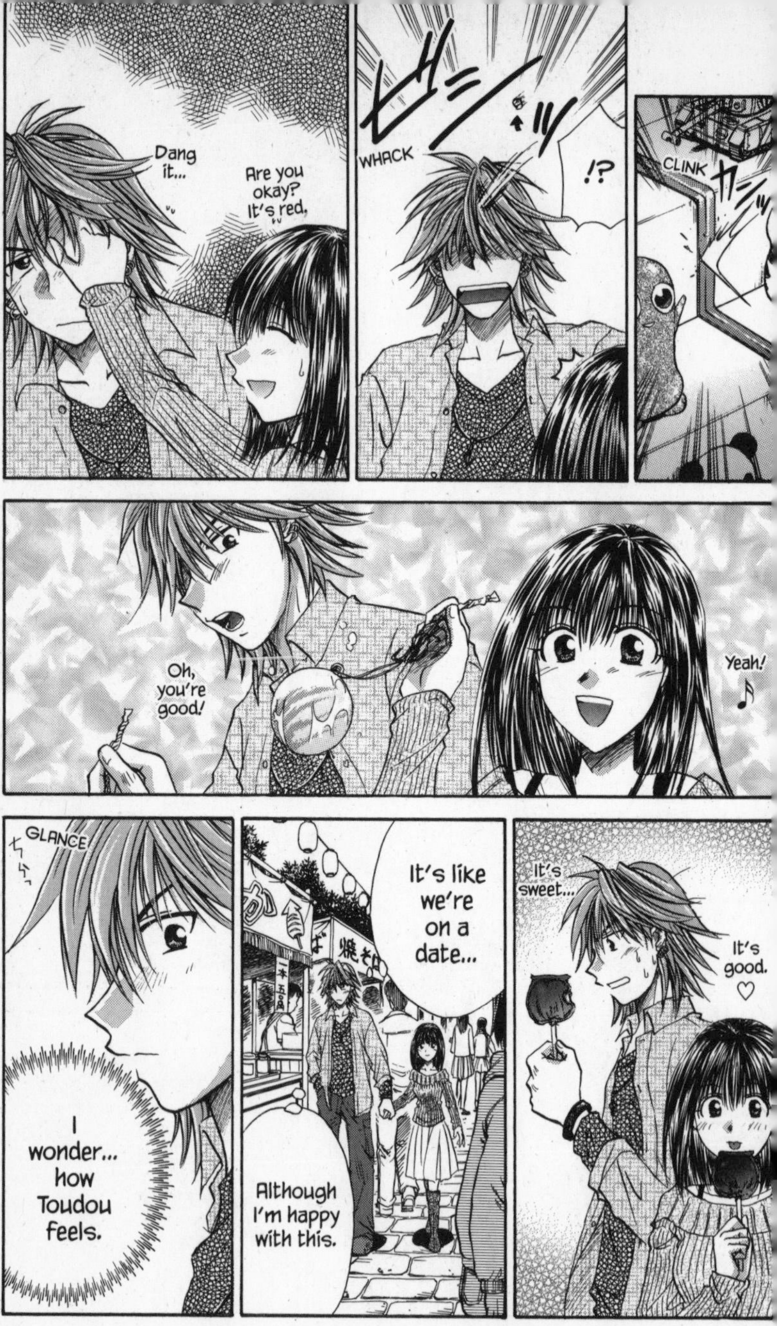
CLINK
WHACK
!?
Dang it...
Are you okay? It's red.
Yeah! ♪
Oh, you're good!
It's sweet...
It's good. ♡
It's like we're on a date...
Although I'm happy with this.
GLANCE
I wonder... how Toudou feels.

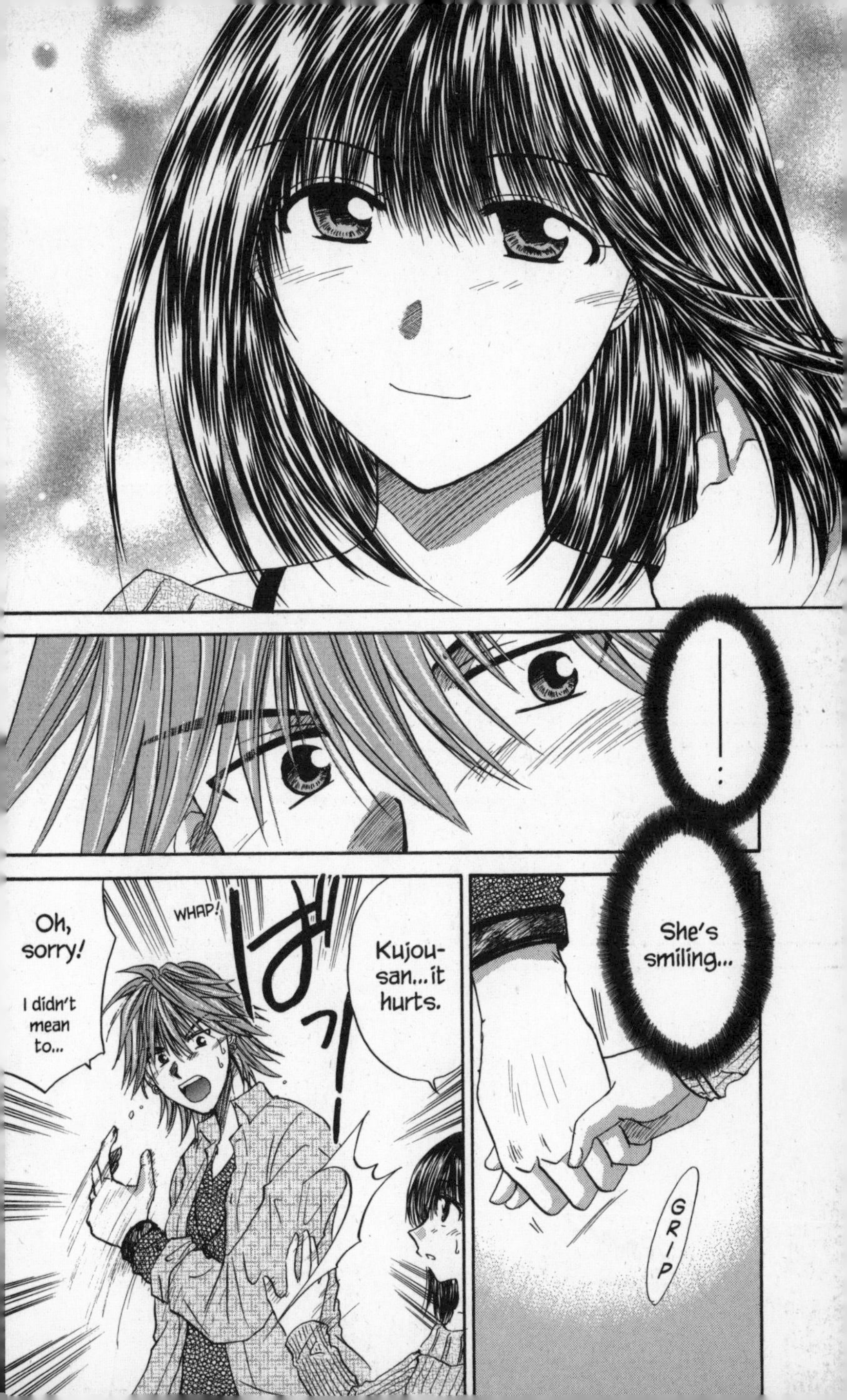
She's smiling...
GRIP
Kujou-san...it hurts.
ばっ
WHAP!
Oh, sorry!
I didn't mean to...

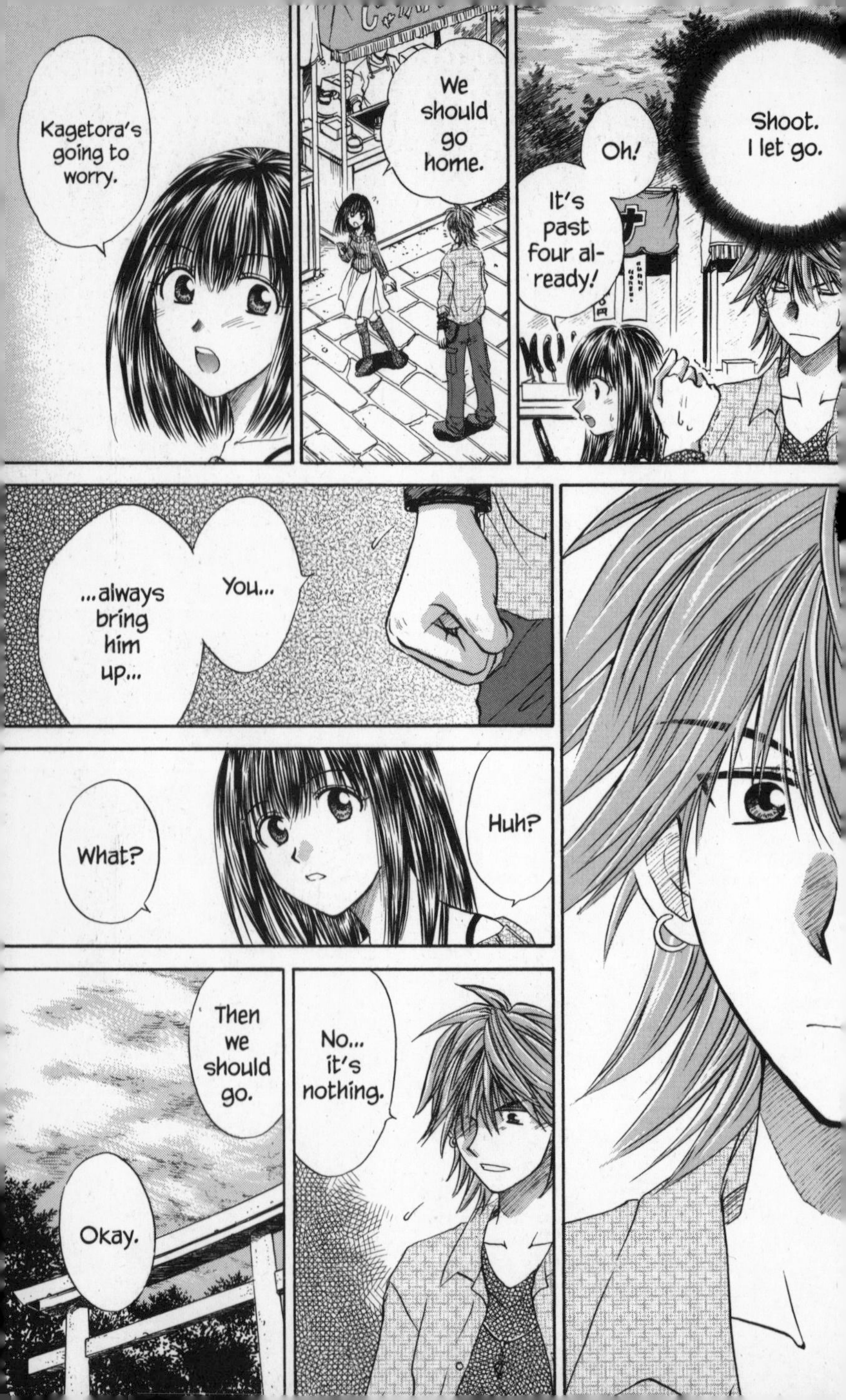
Shoot. I let go.
Oh!
It's past four al-ready!
We should go home.
Kagetora's going to worry.
You...
...always bring him up...
Huh?
What?
No... it's nothing.
Then we should go.
Okay.

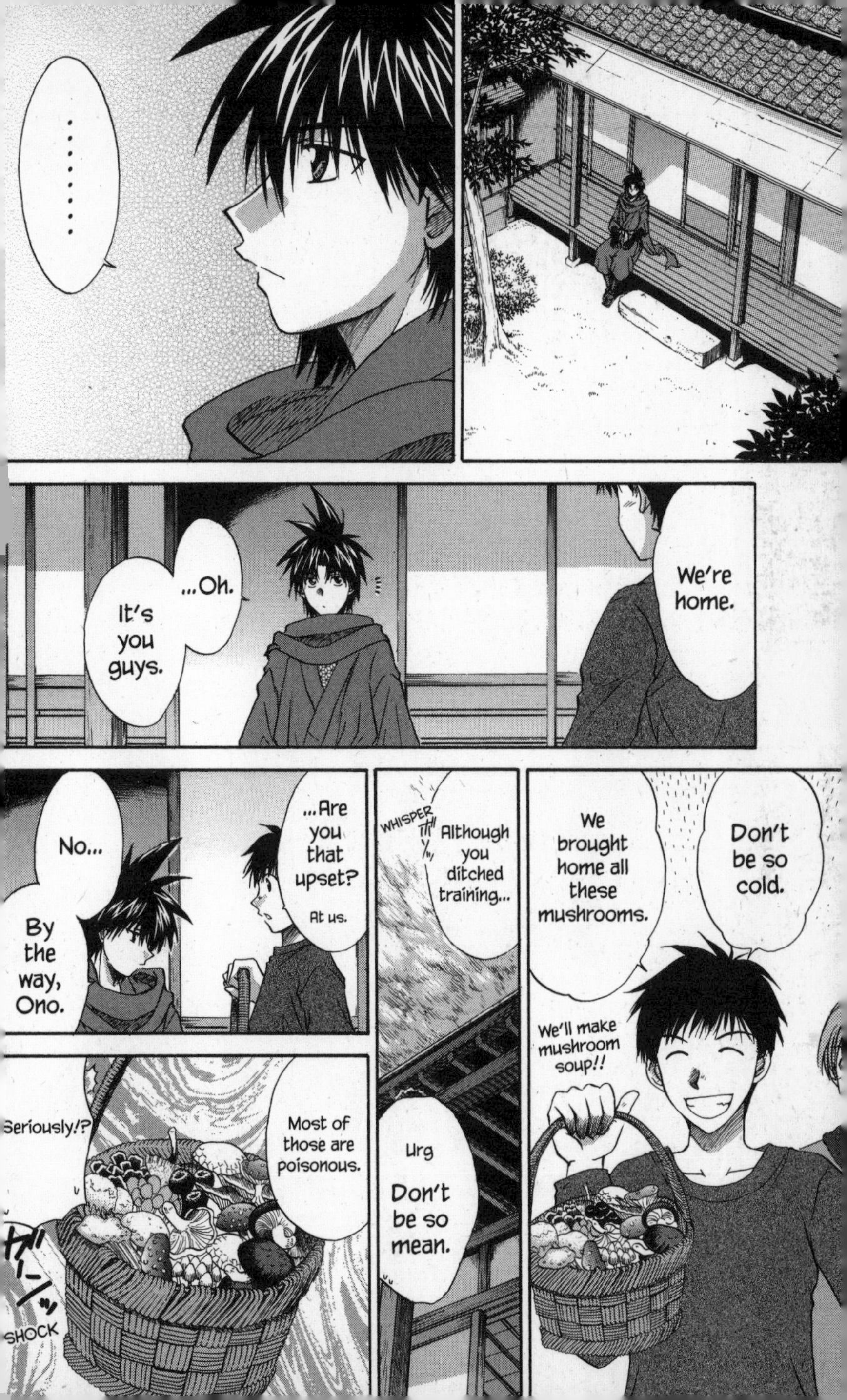
......
We're home.
...Oh.
It's you guys.
Don't be so cold.
We brought home all these mushrooms.
We'll make mushroom soup!!
WHISPER
Although you ditched training...
Urg
Don't be so mean.
...Are you that upset?
At us.
No...
By the way, Ono.
Most of those are poisonous.
Seriously!?
SHOCK

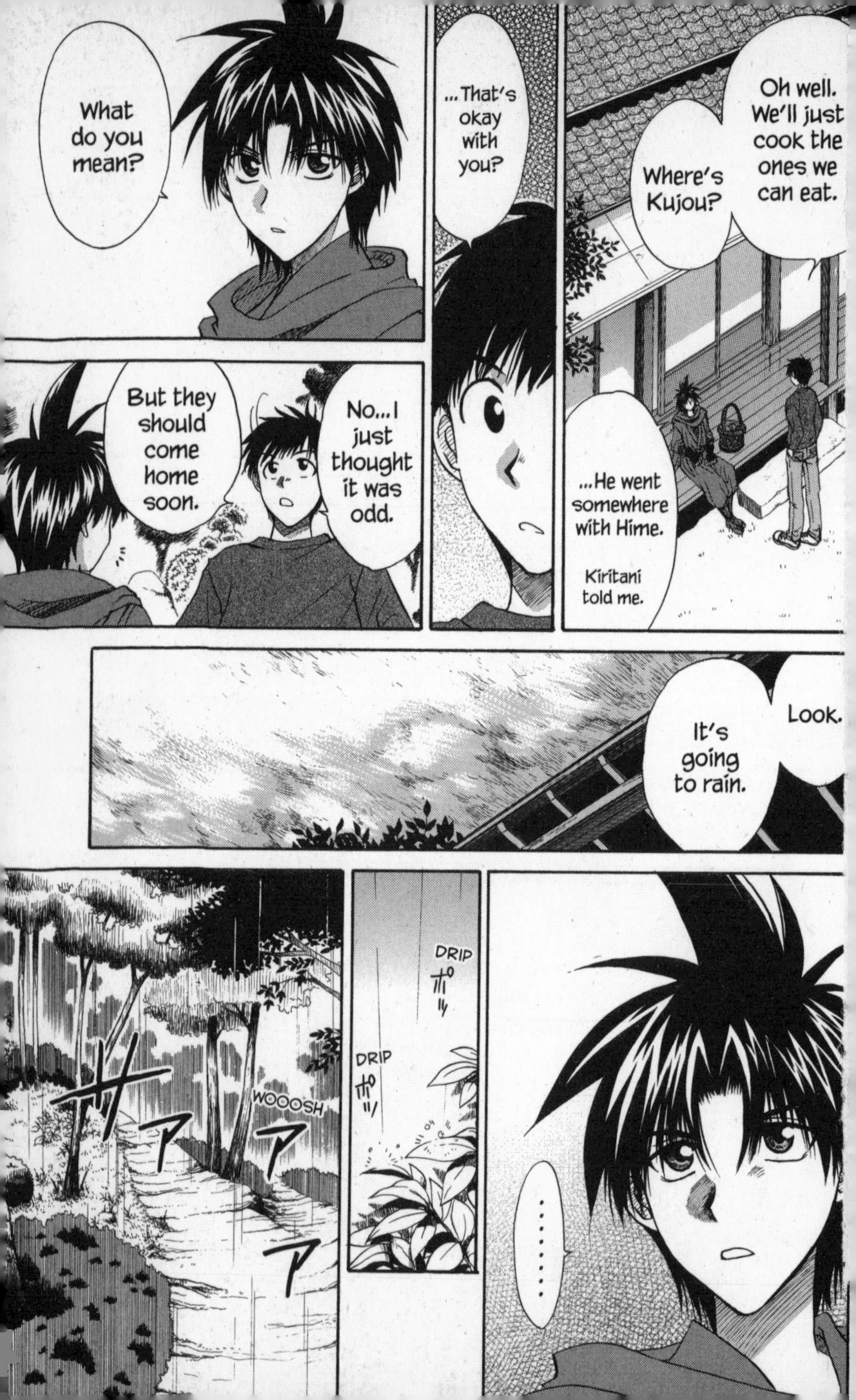
Oh well. We'll just cook the ones we can eat.
Where's Kujou?
...He went somewhere with Hime.
Kiritani told me.
...That's okay with you?
What do you mean?
No...I just thought it was odd.
But they should come home soon.
Look.
It's going to rain.
......
DRIP
DRIP
WOOOSH

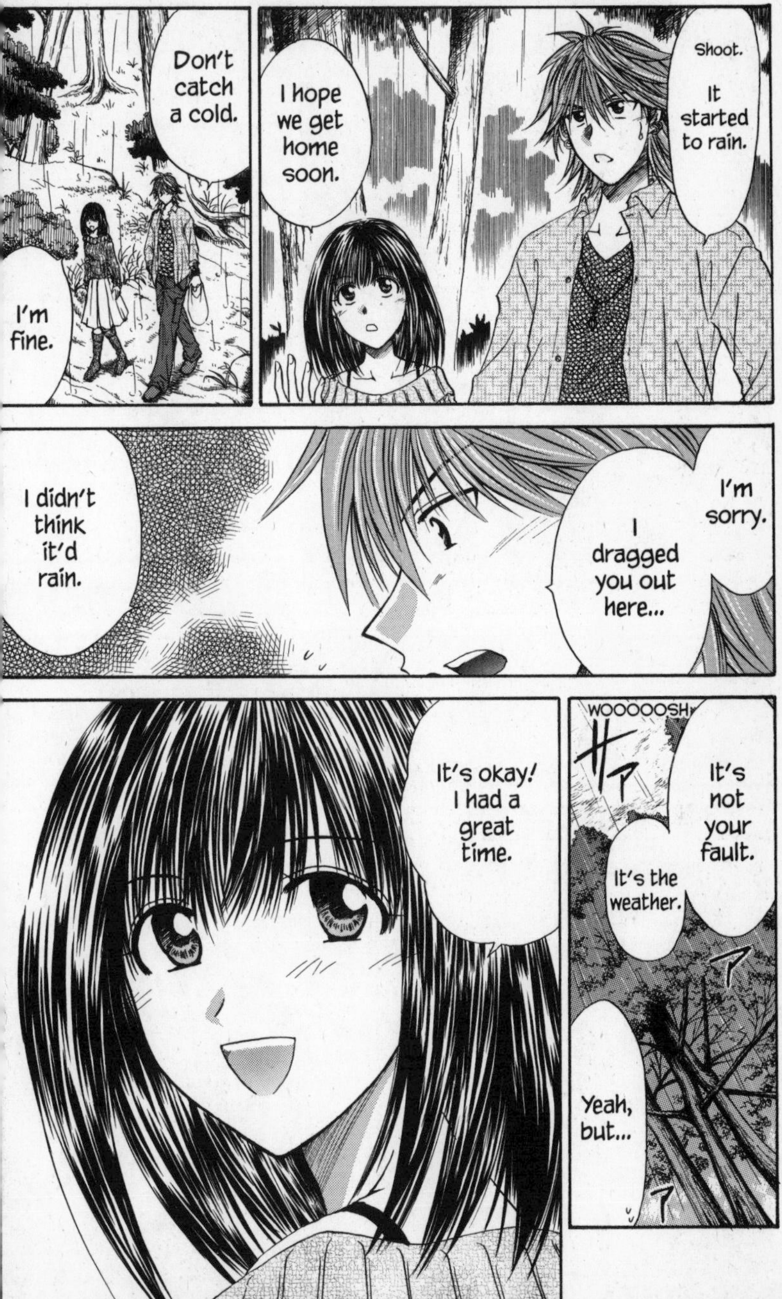

Shoot.
It started to rain.
I hope we get home soon.
Don't catch a cold.
I'm fine.
I'm sorry.
I dragged you out here...
I didn't think it'd rain.
WOOOOOSH
It's not your fault.
It's the weather.
Yeah, but...
It's okay! I had a great time.

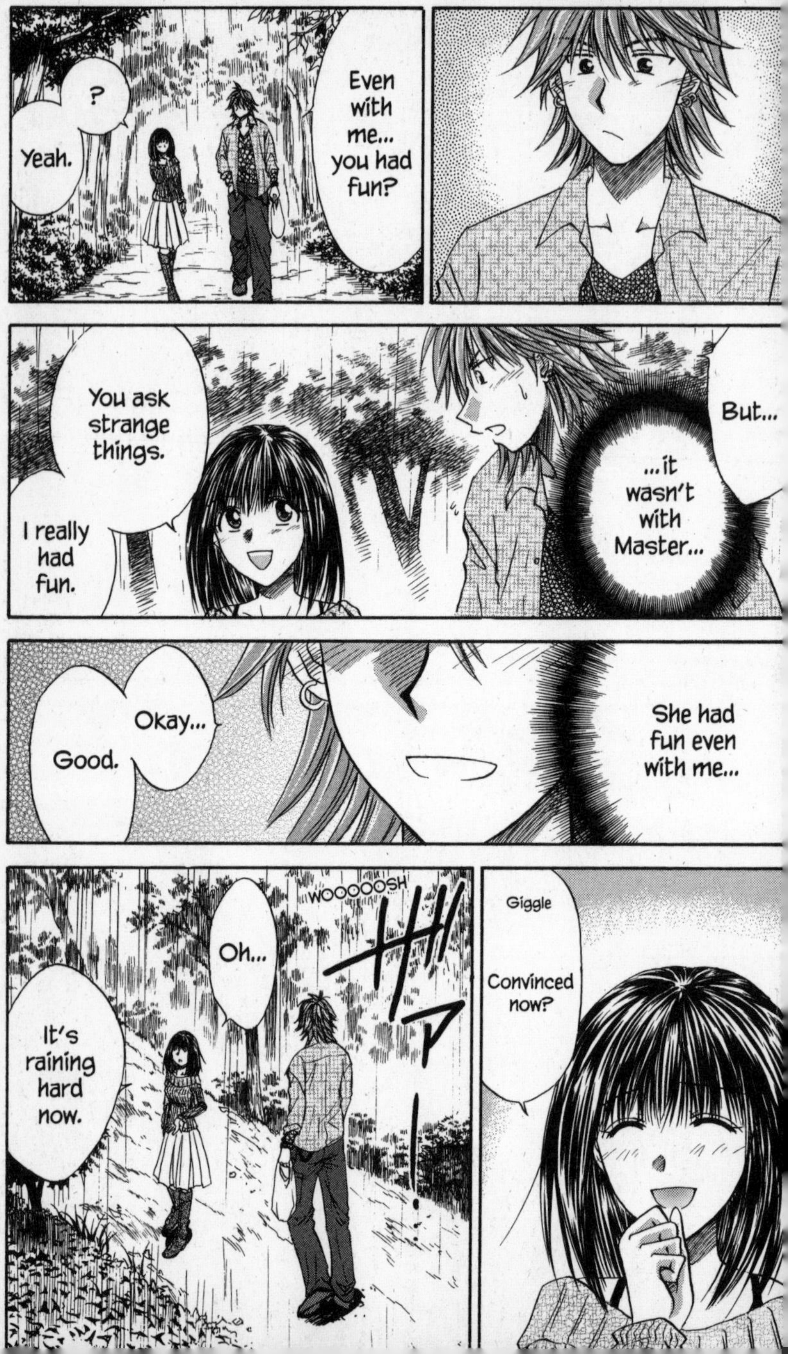
Even with me... you had fun?
?
Yeah.
But...
...it wasn't with Master...
You ask strange things.
I really had fun.
She had fun even with me...
Okay...
Good.
Giggle
Convinced now?
WOOOOOSH
Oh...
It's raining hard now.

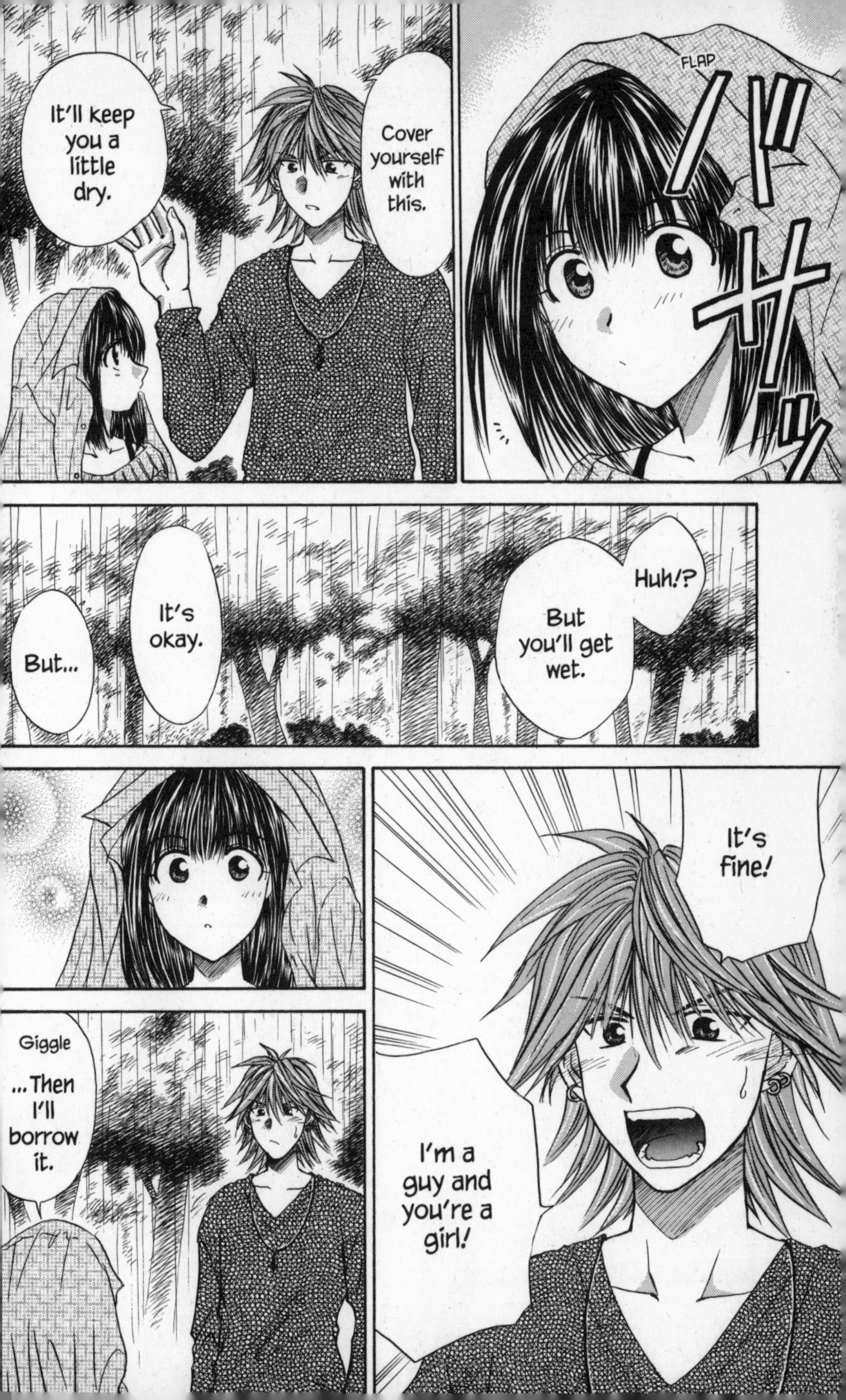
FLAP
Cover yourself with this.
It'll keep you a little dry.
Huh!?
But you'll get wet.
It's okay.
But...
It's fine!
I'm a guy and you're a girl!
Giggle
...Then I'll borrow it.

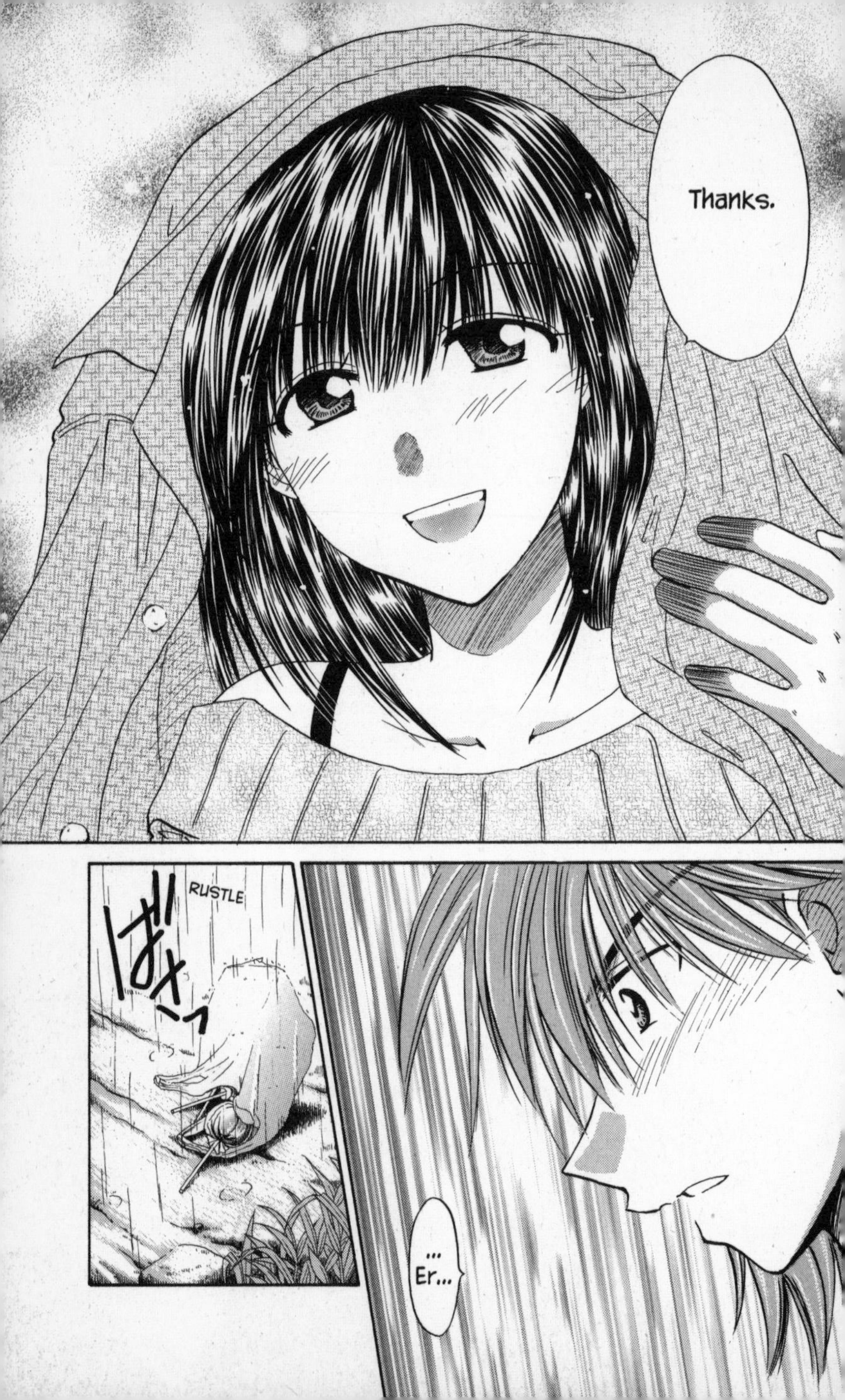
Thanks.
... Er...
RUSTLE
ばさっ

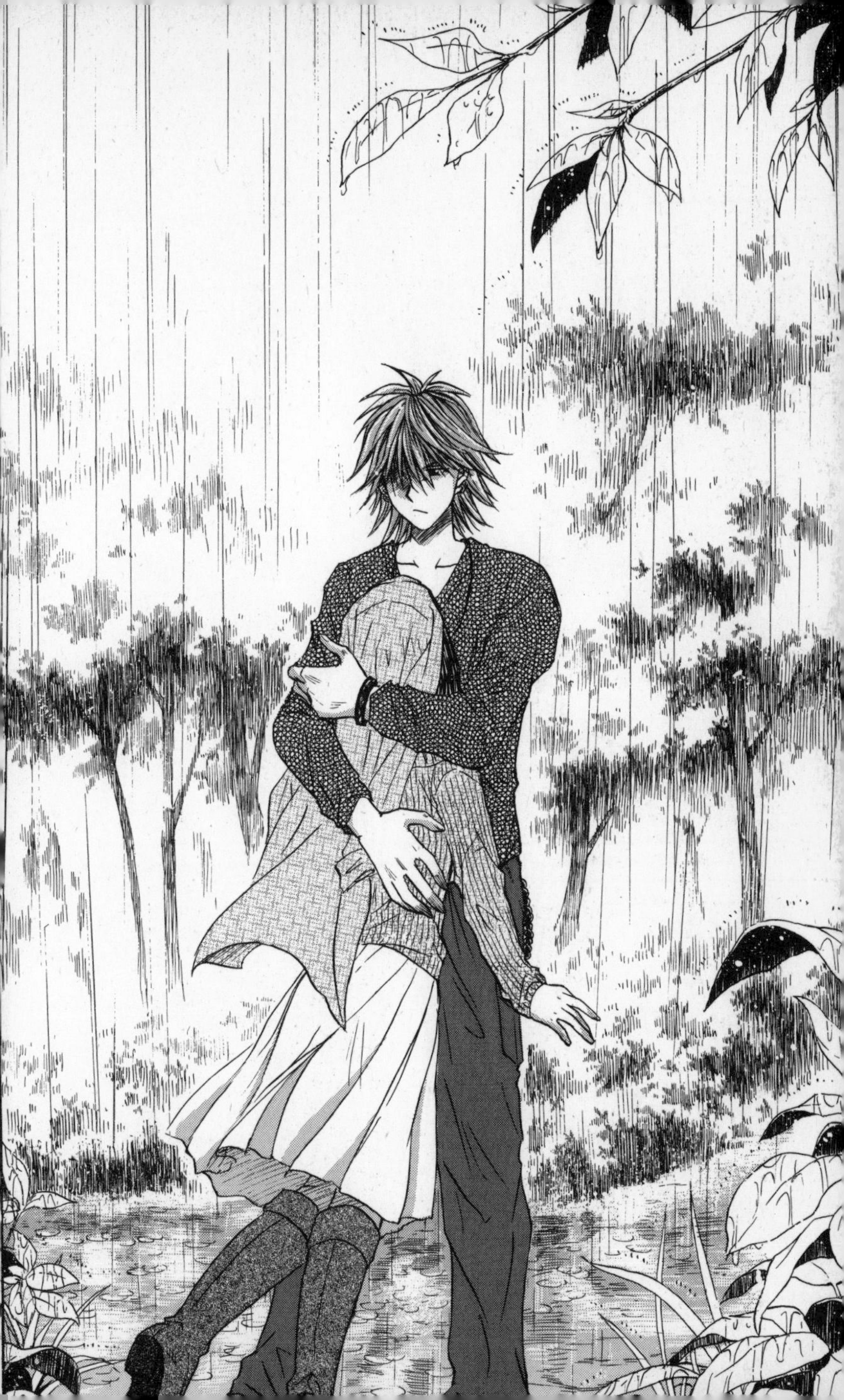

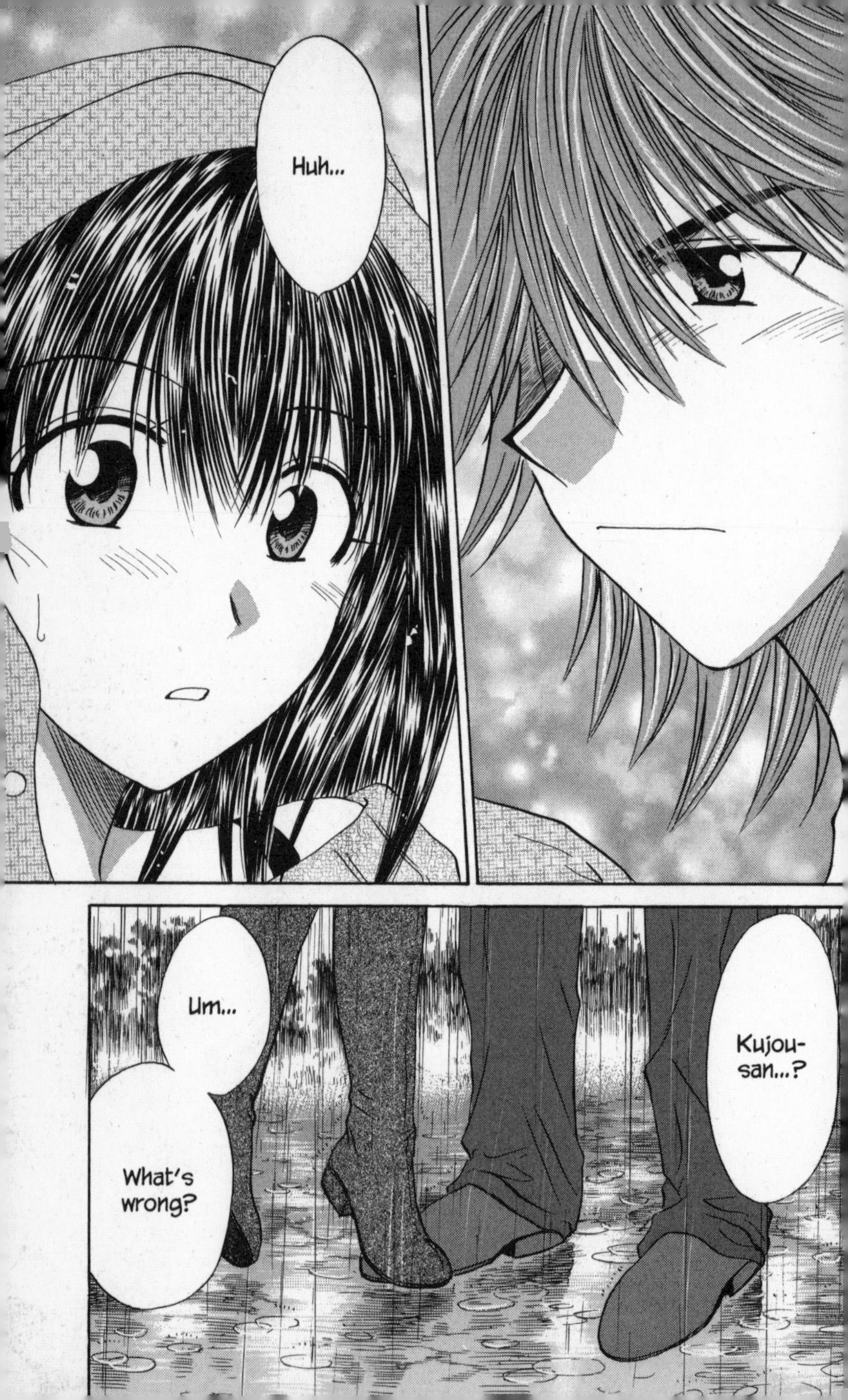
Huh...
Kujou-san...?
Um...
What's wrong?

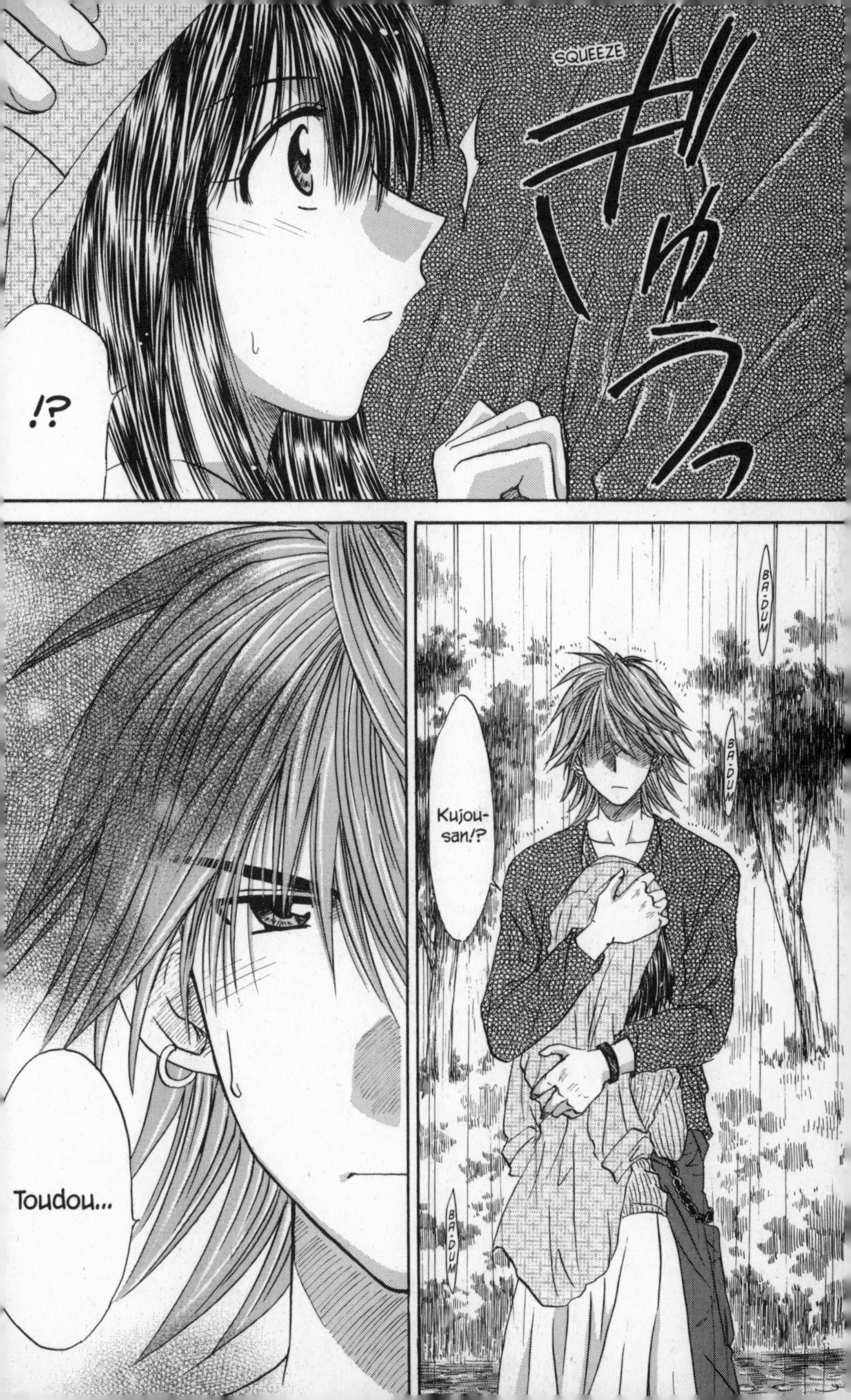
SQUEEZE
ぎゅううっ
!?
BA-DUM
Kujou-san!?
BA-DUM
BA-DUM
Toudou...

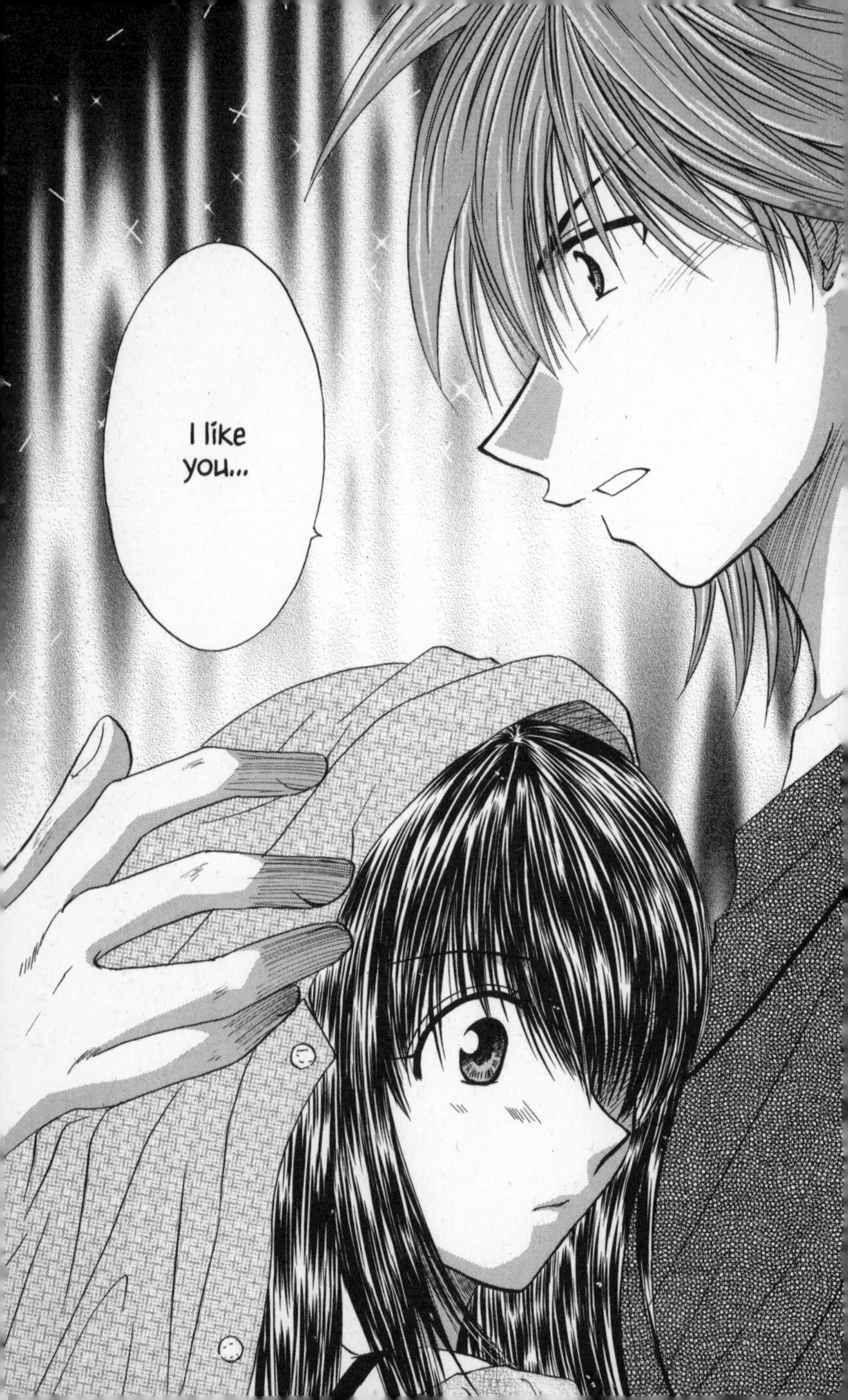
I like you...

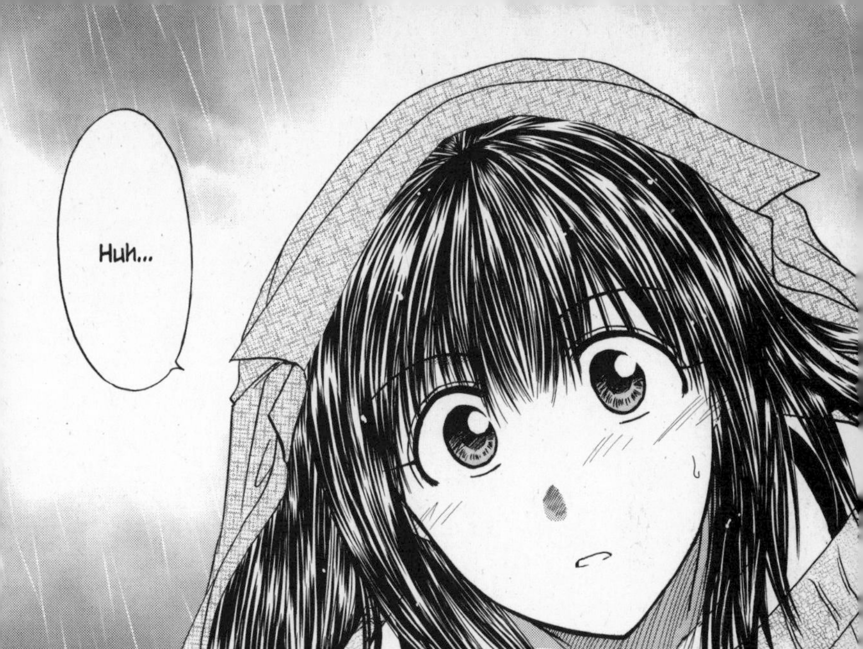
Huh...

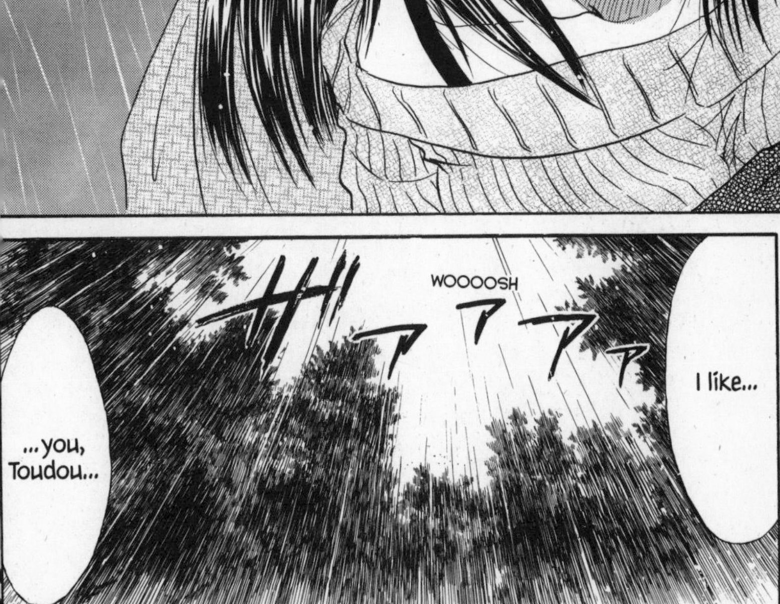
I like...
WOOOOSH
...you, Toudou...

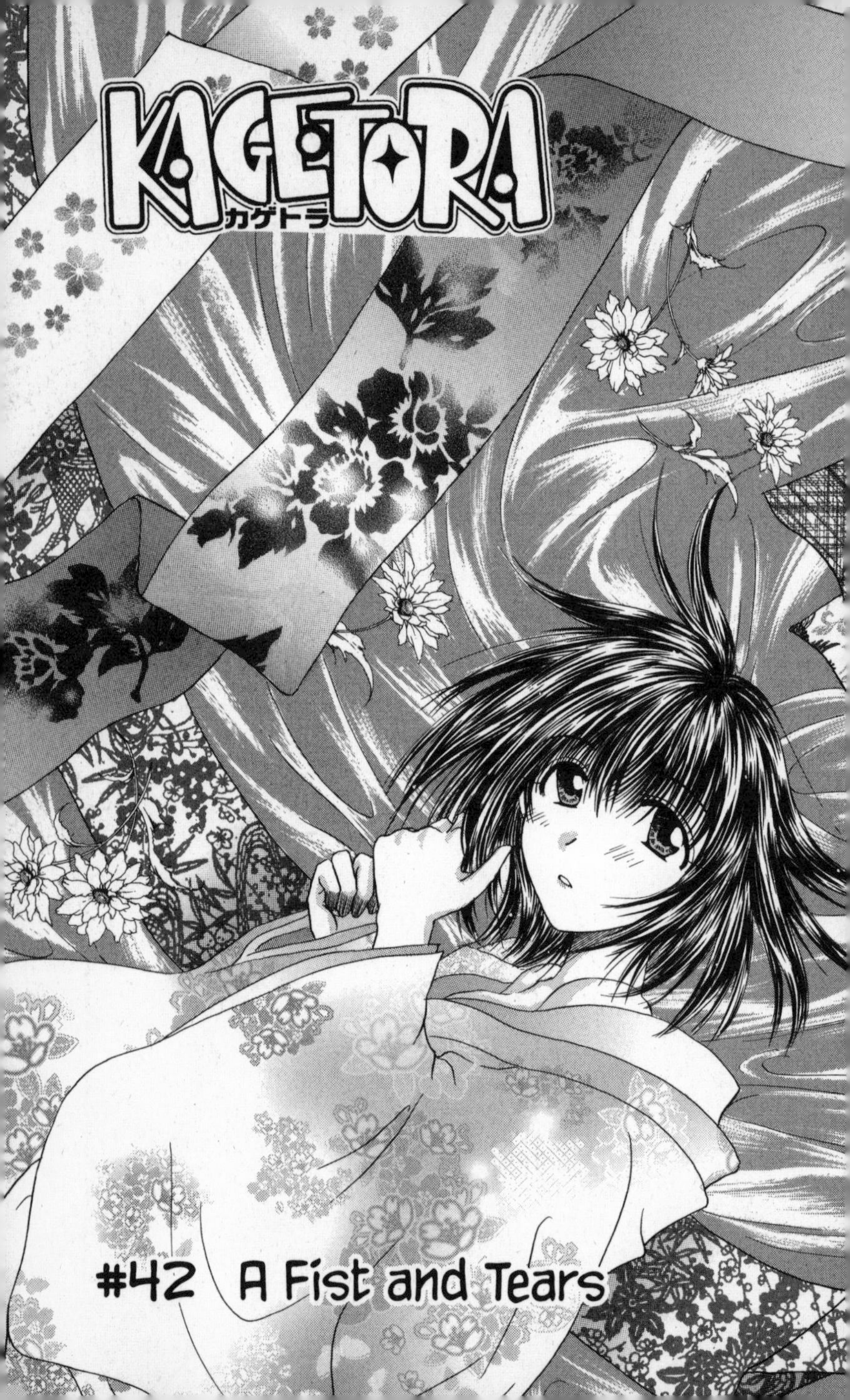
KAGETORA
カゲトラ
#42 A Fist and Tears

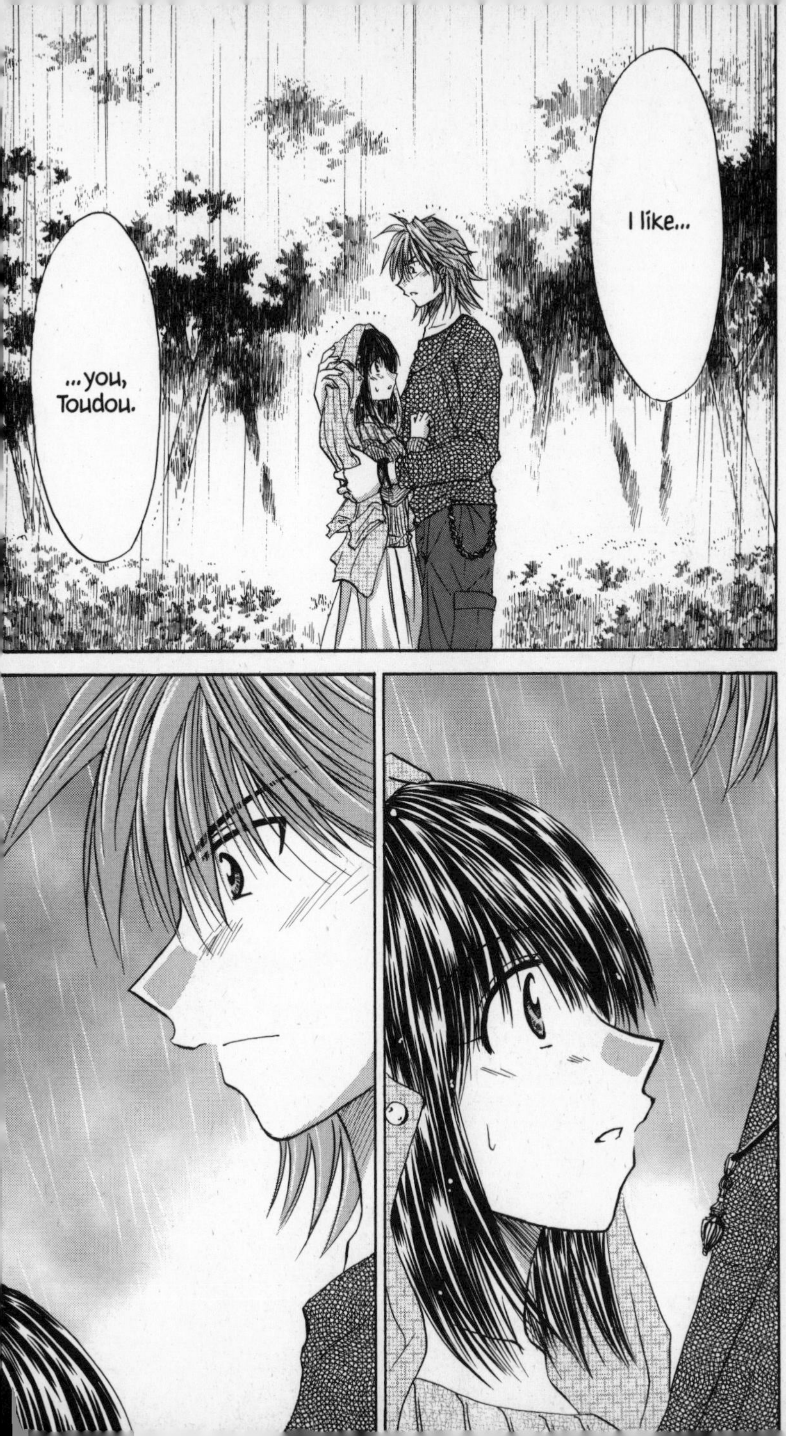
I like...
...you, Toudou.

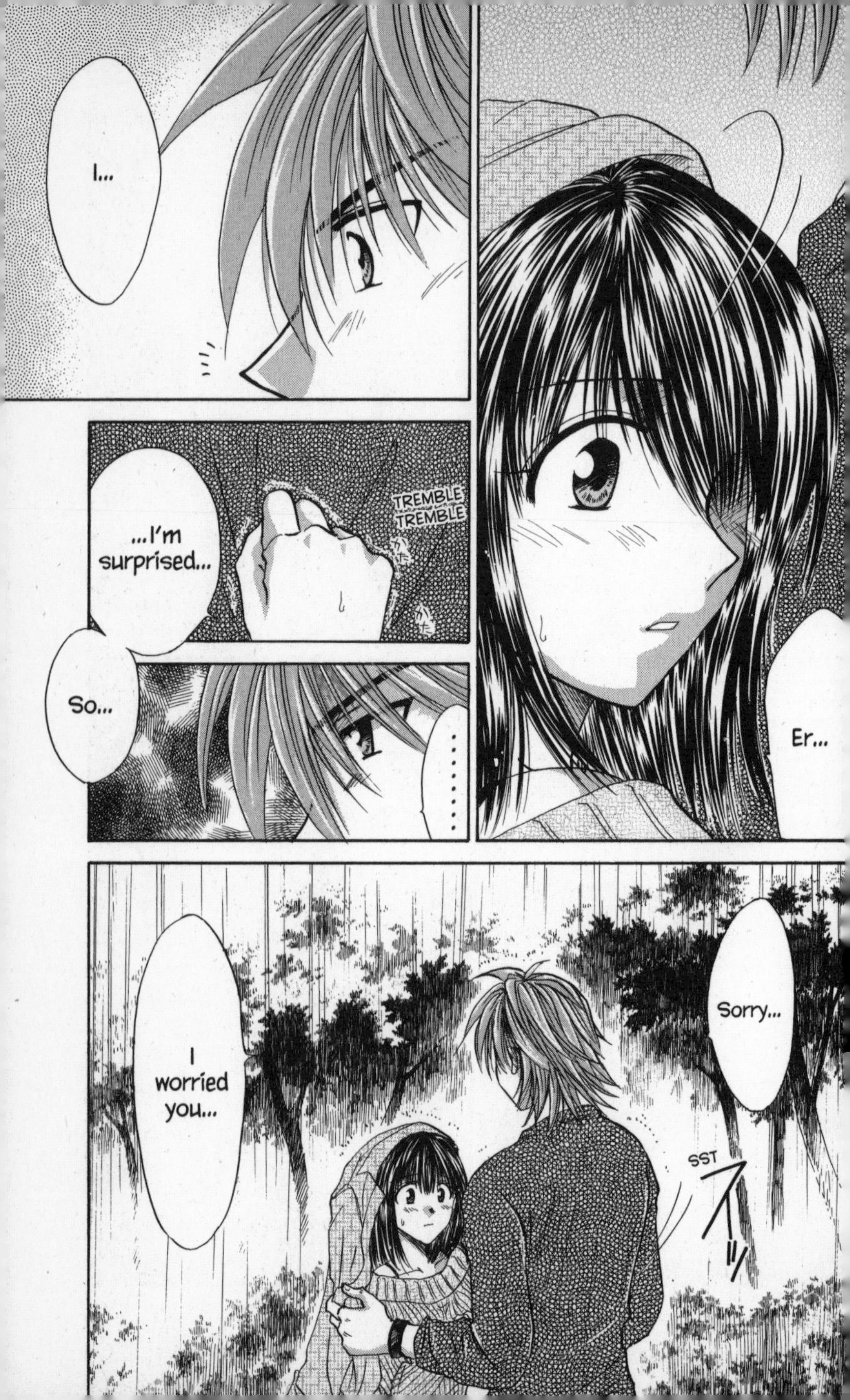
Er...
I...
...I'm surprised...
TREMBLE TREMBLE
So...
......
Sorry...
SST
I worried you...

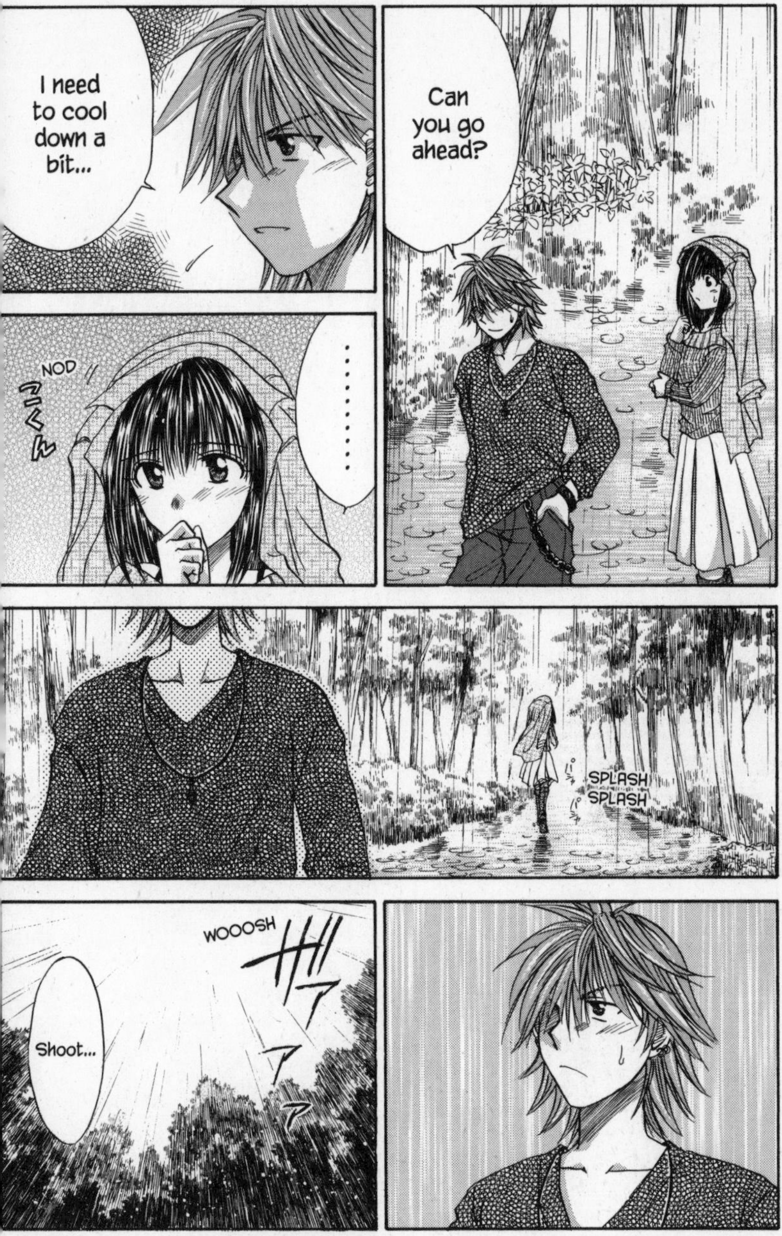
Can you go ahead?
I need to cool down a bit...
NOD
......
SPLASH SPLASH
WOOOSH
Shoot...

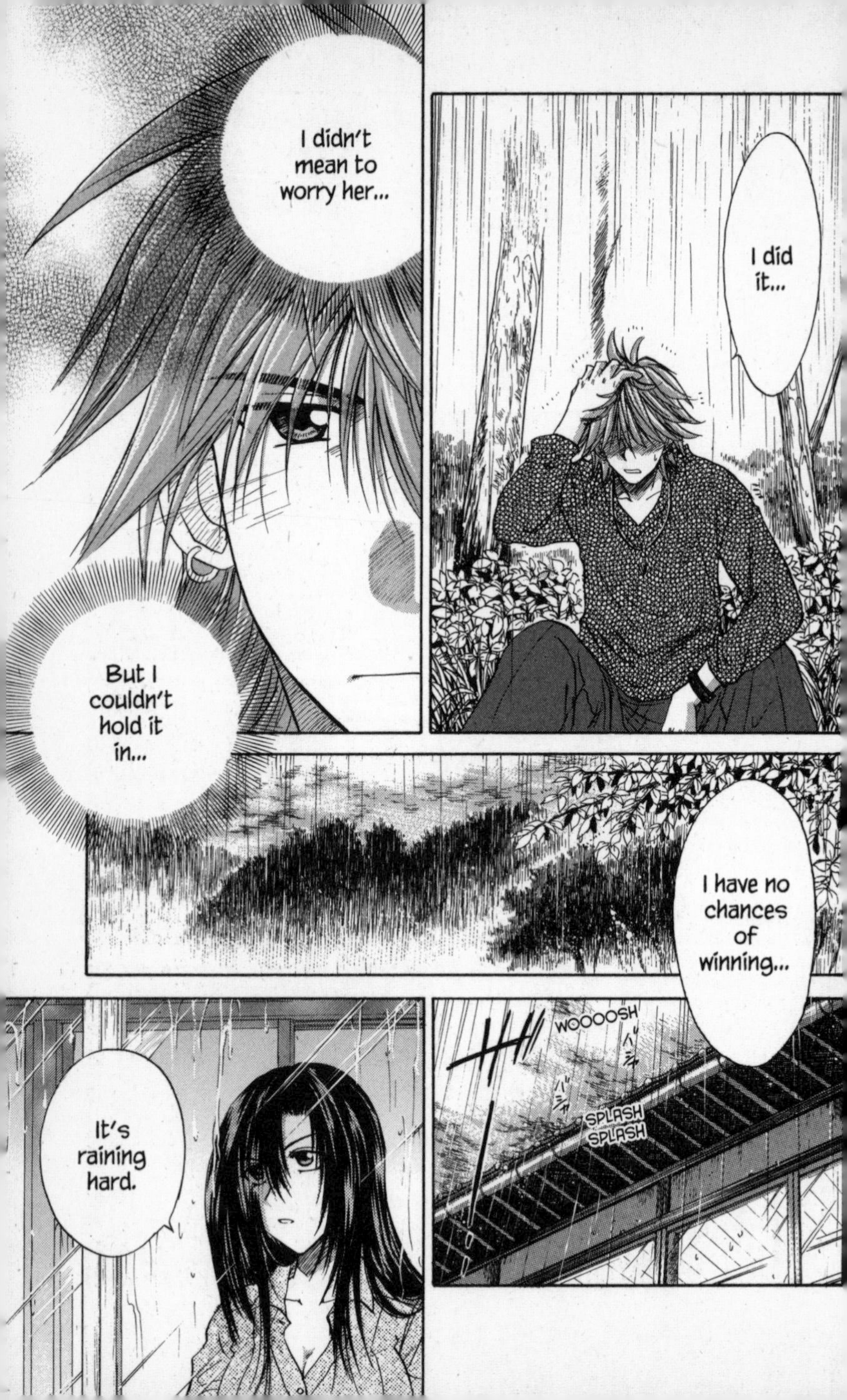
I did it...
I didn't mean to worry her...
But I couldn't hold it in...
I have no chances of winning...
WOOOOSH
SPLASH SPLASH
It's raining hard.

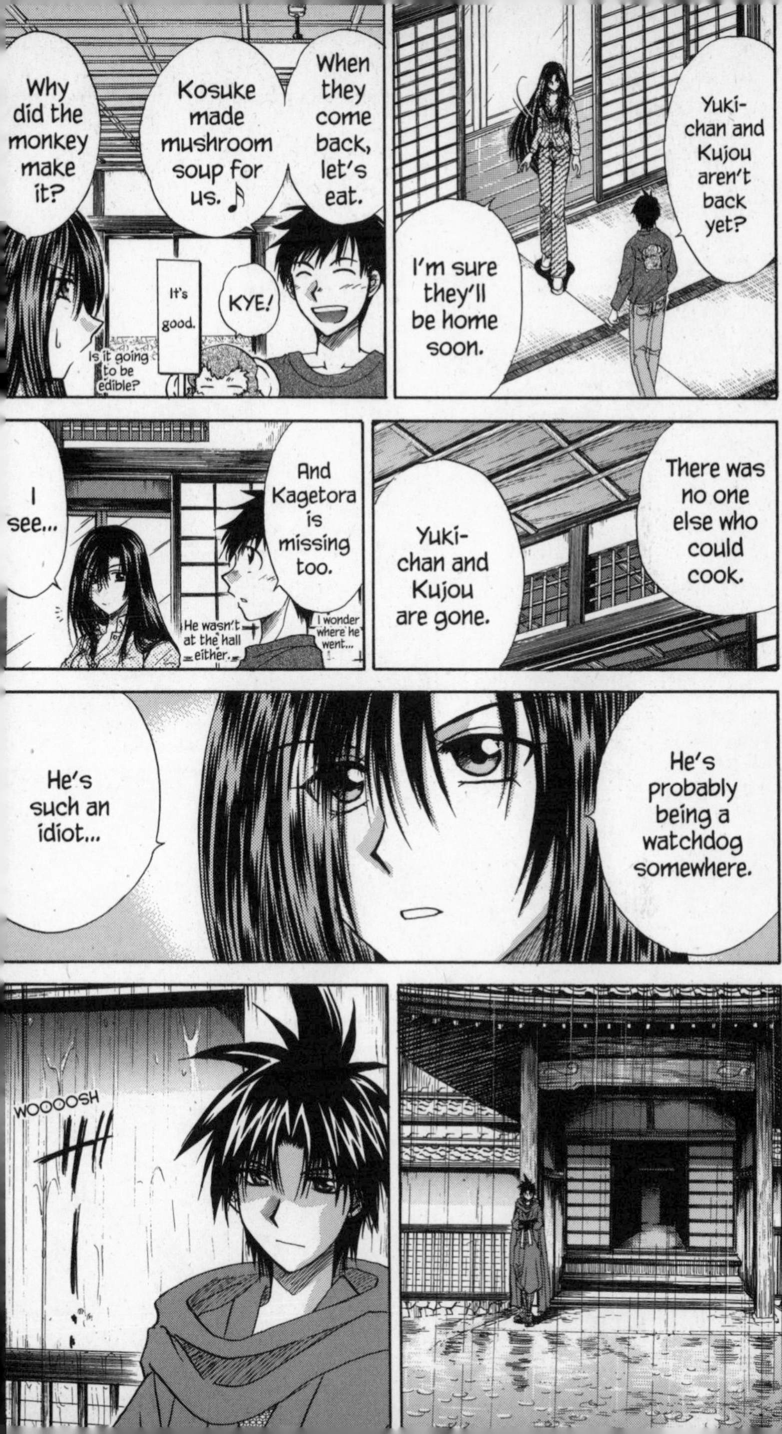
Yuki-chan and Kujou aren't back yet?
I'm sure they'll be home soon.
When they come back, let's eat.
Kosuke made mushroom soup for us. ♪
Why did the monkey make it?
KYE!
It's good.
Is it going to be edible?
There was no one else who could cook.
Yuki-chan and Kujou are gone.
And Kagetora is missing too.
I wonder where he went...
He wasn't at the hall either.
I see...
He's probably being a watchdog somewhere.
He's such an idiot...
WOOOOSH

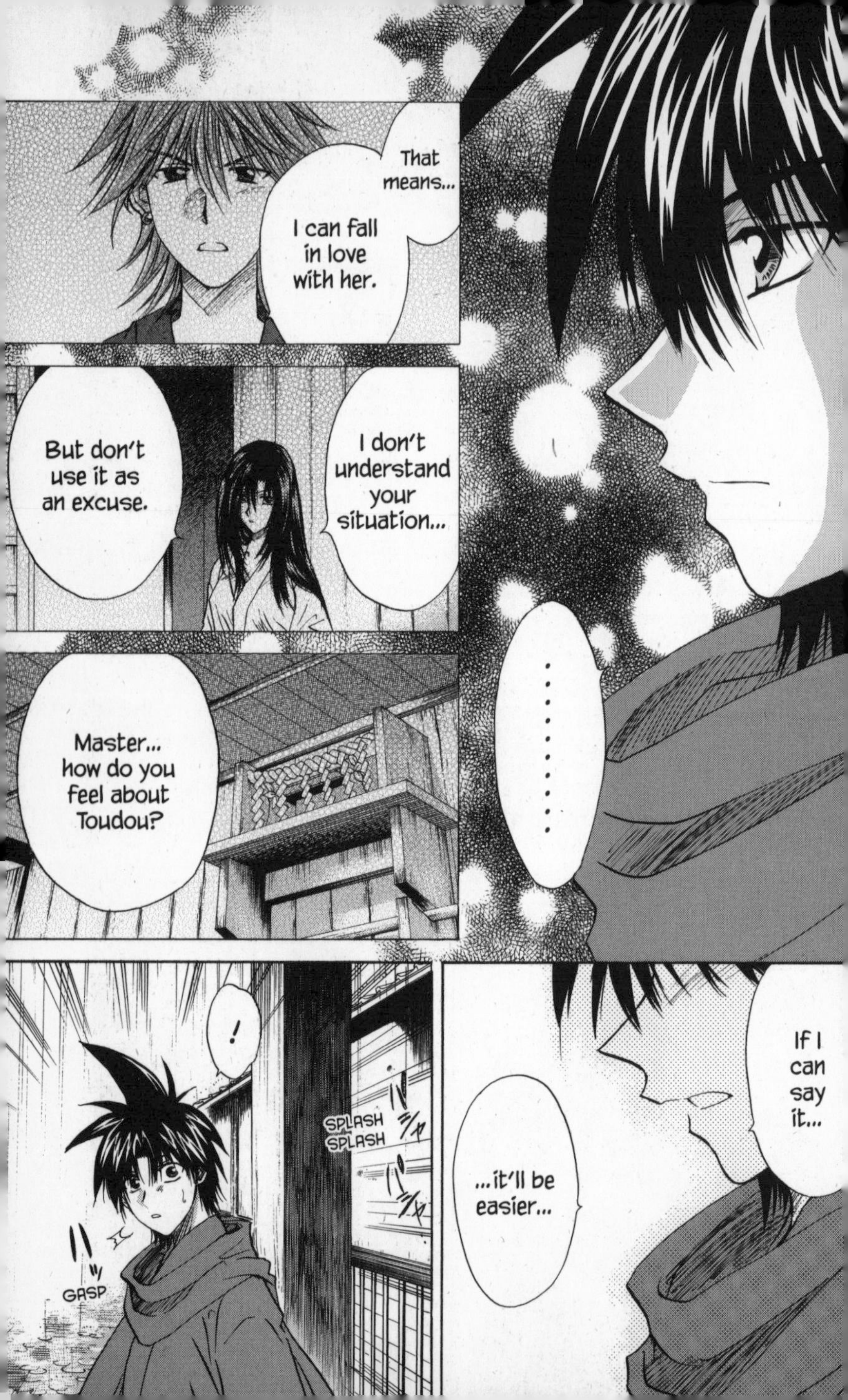
......
That means...
I can fall in love with her.
I don't understand your situation...
But don't use it as an excuse.
Master... how do you feel about Toudou?
If I can say it...
...it'll be easier...
!
SPLASH SPLASH
GASP

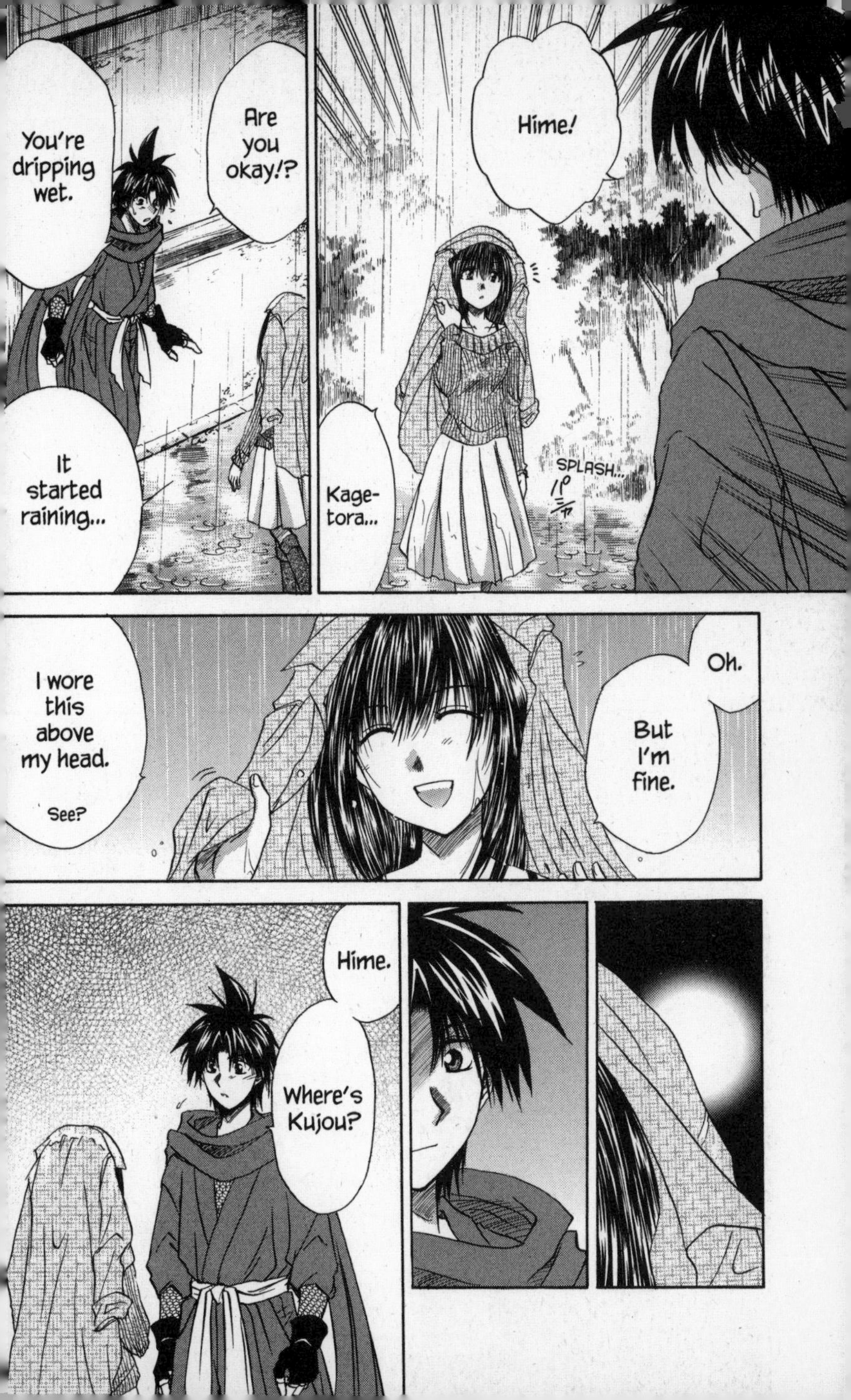
Hime!
Kage-tora...
SPLASH...
Are you okay!?
You're dripping wet.
It started raining...
Oh.
But I'm fine.
I wore this above my head.
See?
Hime.
Where's Kujou?

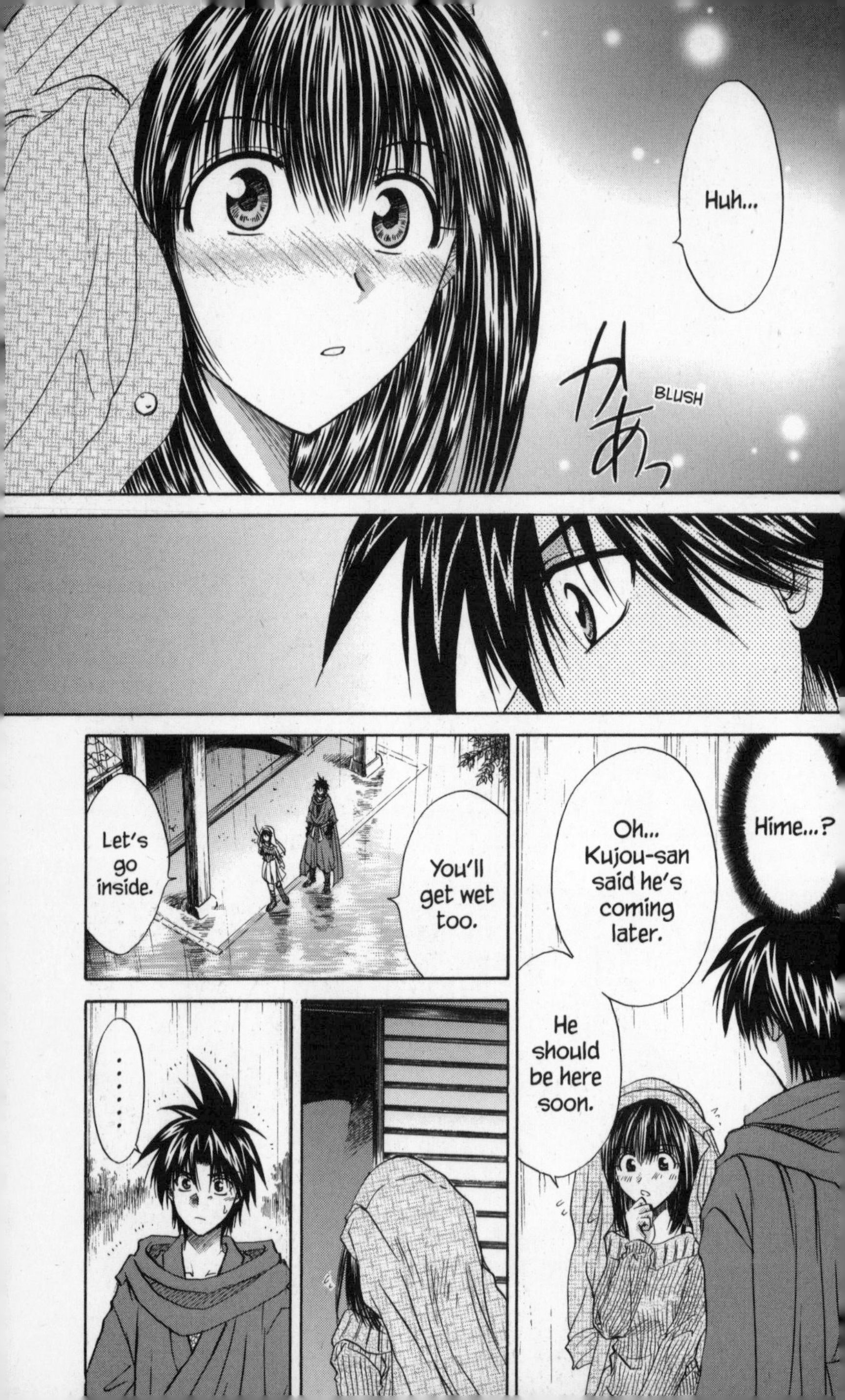

Huh...
かあっ
BLUSH
Hime...?
Oh... Kujou-san said he's coming later.
He should be here soon.
You'll get wet too.
Let's go inside.
......

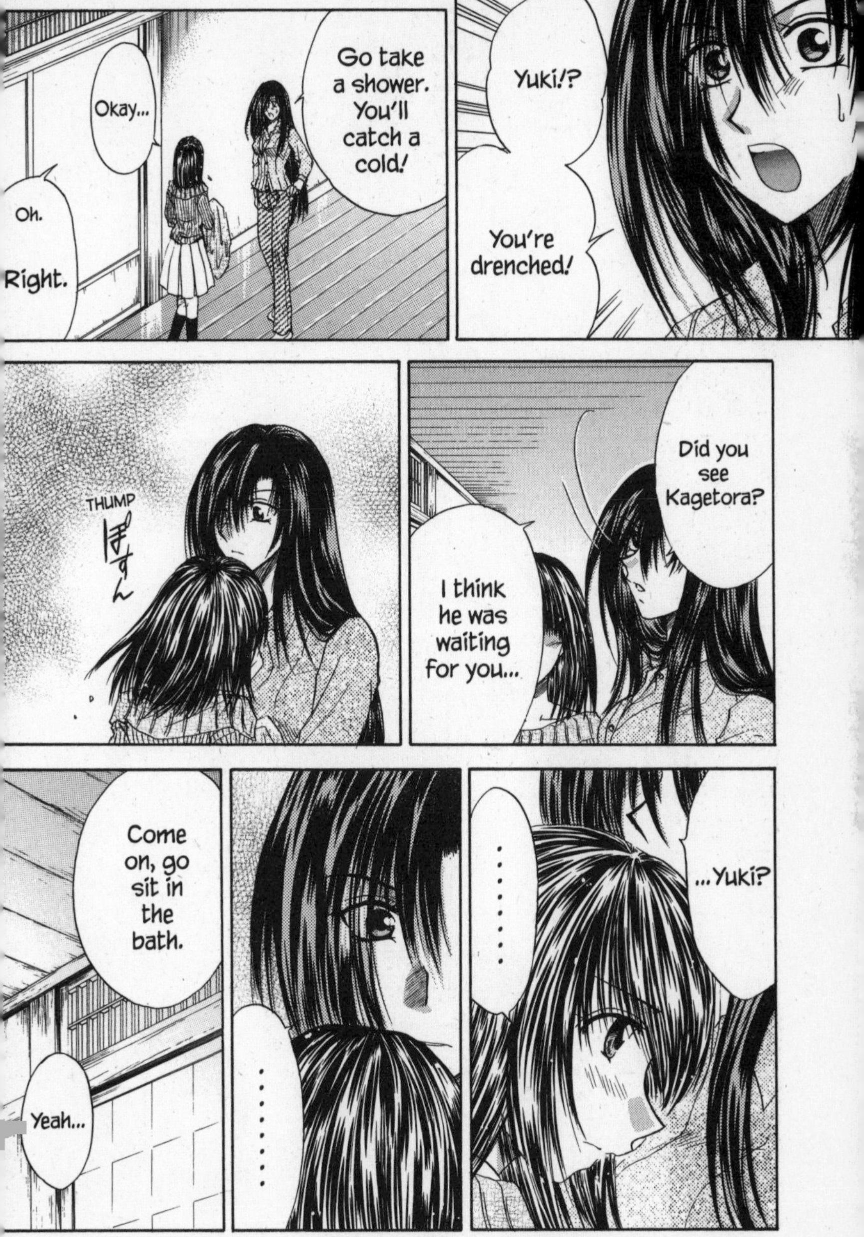
Yuki!?
You're drenched!
Go take a shower. You'll catch a cold!
Okay...
Oh.
Right.
Did you see Kagetora?
I think he was waiting for you...
THUMP
ぽすん
...Yuki?
......
......
Come on, go sit in the bath.
Yeah...

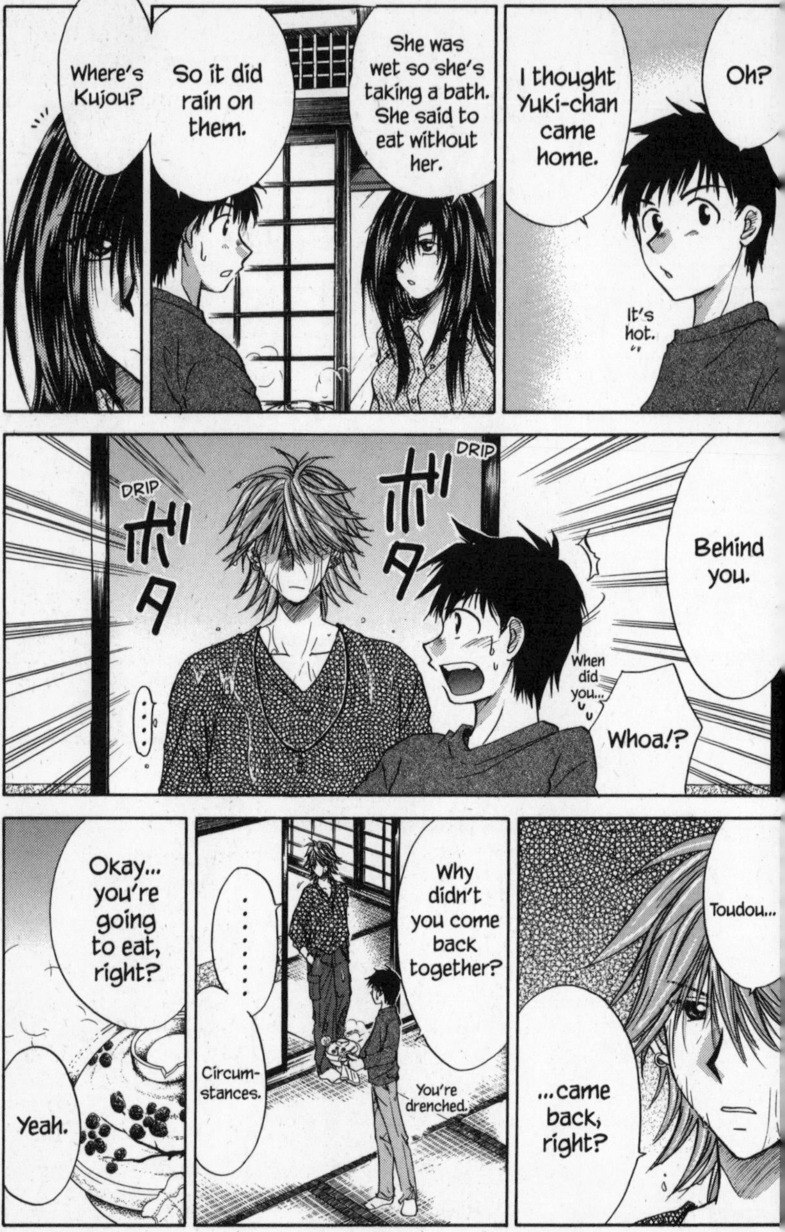
Oh?
I thought Yuki-chan came home.
It's hot.
She was wet so she's taking a bath. She said to eat without her.
So it did rain on them.
Where's Kujou?
Behind you.
Whoa!?
When did you...
DRIP
ボタ
DRIP
ボタ
....
Toudou...
...came back, right?
Why didn't you come back together?
....
Circumstances.
You're drenched.
Okay... you're going to eat, right?
Yeah.

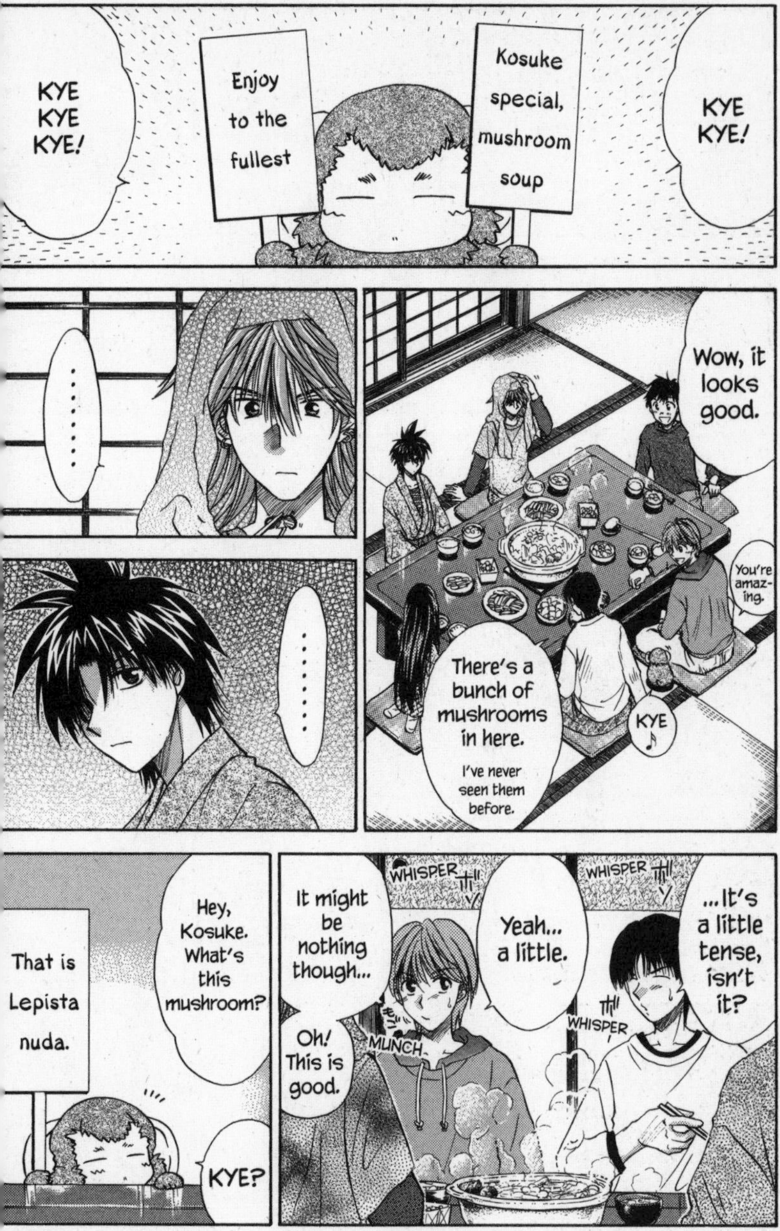

KYE KYE!
Kosuke special, mushroom soup
Enjoy to the fullest
KYE KYE KYE!
Wow, it looks good.
You're amaz-ing.
There's a bunch of mushrooms in here.
I've never seen them before.
KYE ♪
......
......
...It's a little tense, isn't it?
WHISPER
WHISPER
Yeah... a little.
WHISPER
It might be nothing though...
MUNCH
Oh! This is good.
Hey, Kosuke. What's this mushroom?
That is Lepista nuda.
KYE?

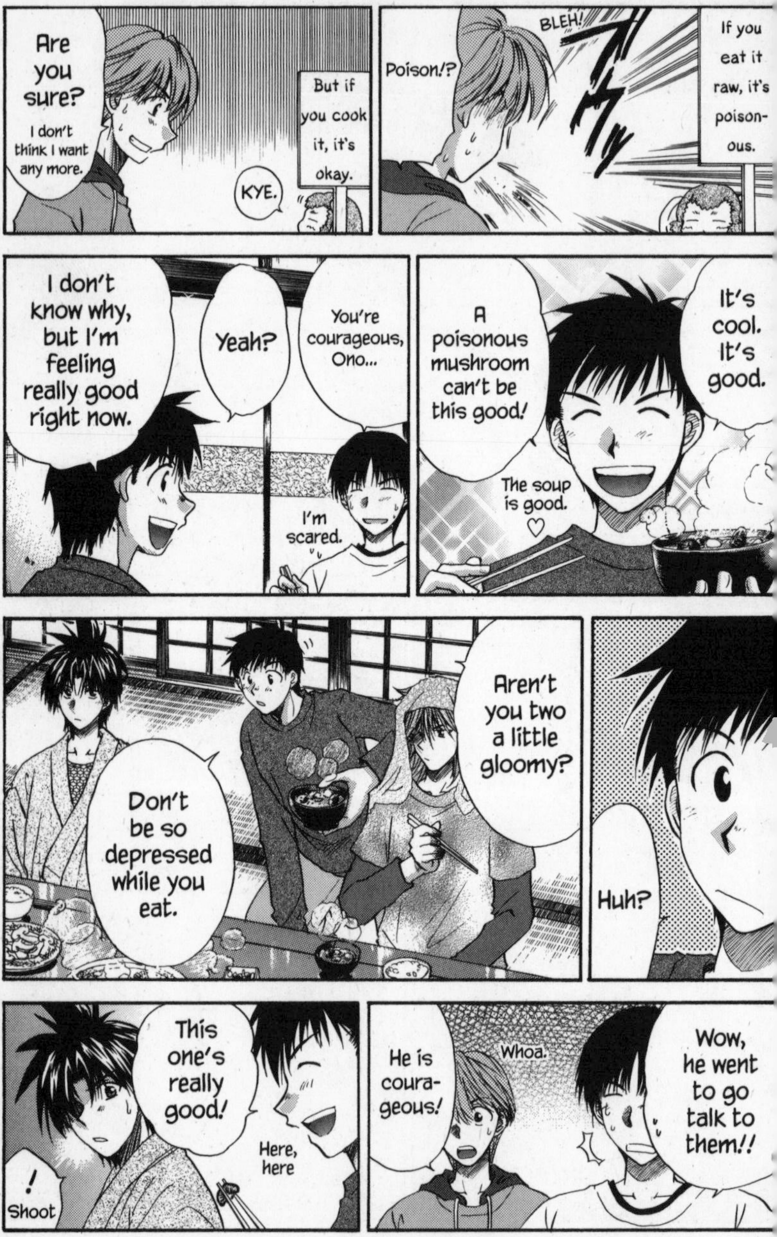
If you eat it raw, it's poison-ous.
BLEH!
Poison!?
But if you cook it, it's okay.
KYE.
Are you sure?
I don't think I want any more.
It's cool. It's good.
A poisonous mushroom can't be this good!
The soup is good. ♡
You're courageous, Ono...
I'm scared.
Yeah?
I don't know why, but I'm feeling really good right now.
Huh?
Aren't you two a little gloomy?
Don't be so depressed while you eat.
Wow, he went to go talk to them!!
Whoa.
He is coura-geous!
This one's really good!
Here, here
!
Shoot

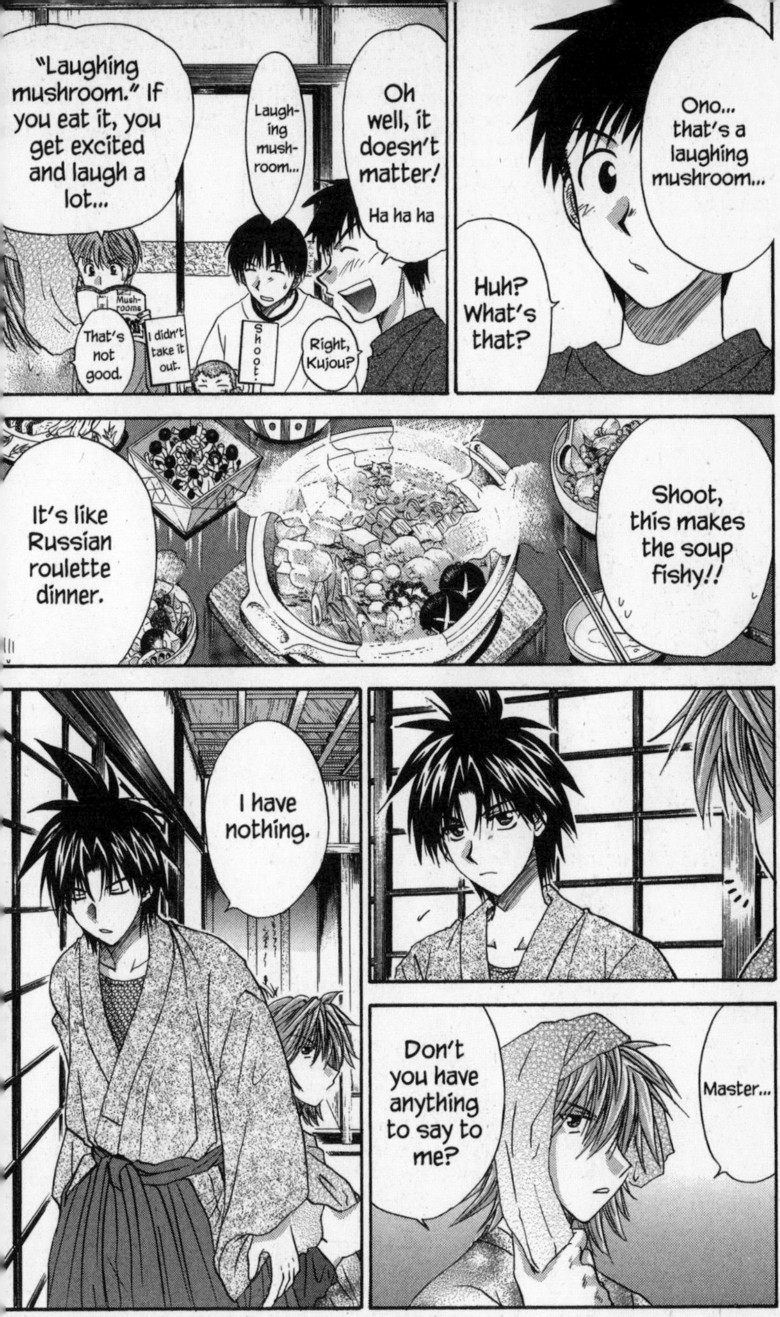
Ono... that's a laughing mushroom...
Huh? What's that?
Oh well, it doesn't matter!
Ha ha ha
Laugh-ing mush-room...
"Laughing mushroom." If you eat it, you get excited and laugh a lot...
Right, Kujou?
Shoot.
I didn't take it out.
That's not good.
Mush-rooms
Shoot, this makes the soup fishy!!
It's like Russian roulette dinner.
Master...
Don't you have anything to say to me?
I have nothing.

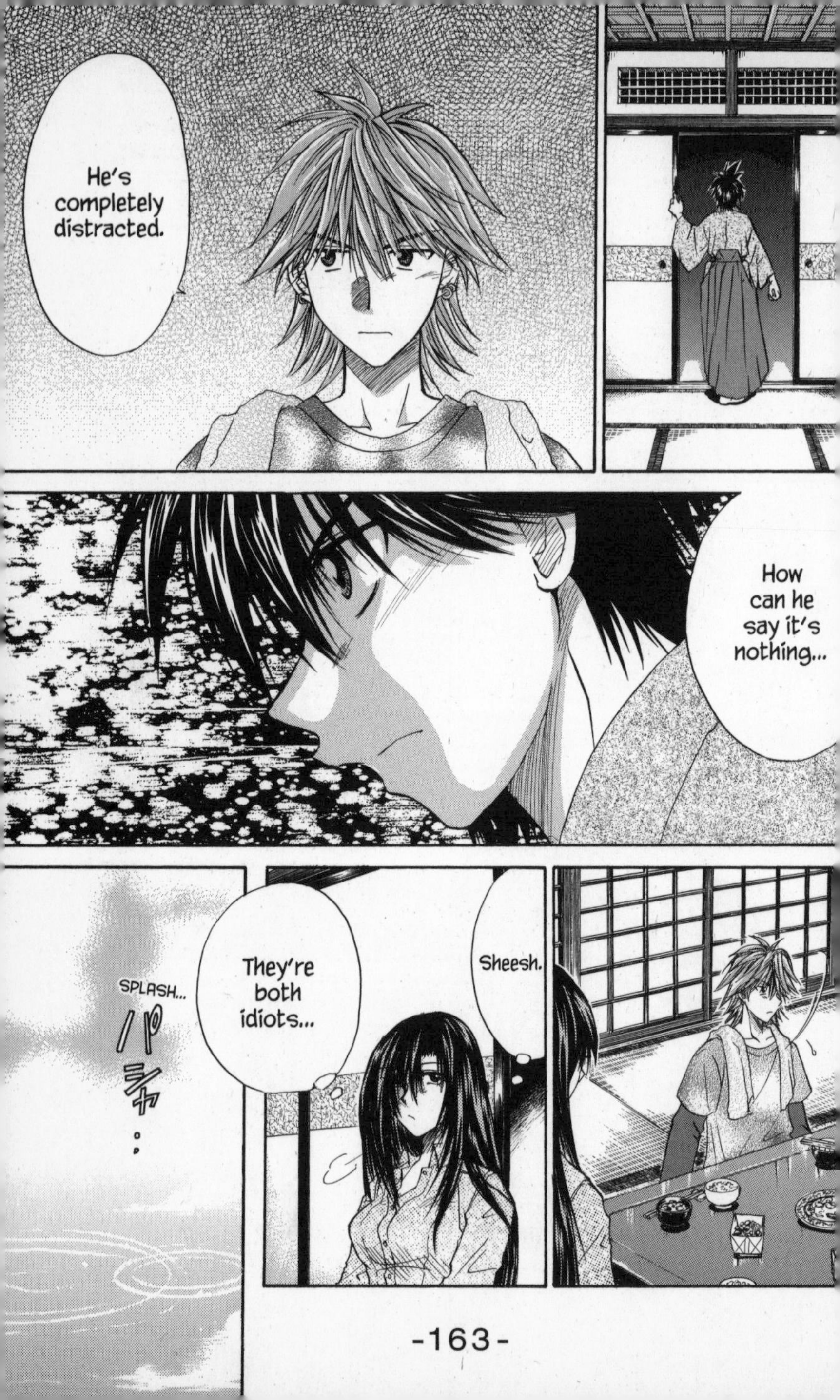
He's completely distracted.
How can he say it's nothing...
Sheesh.
They're both idiots...
SPLASH...
パシャ...

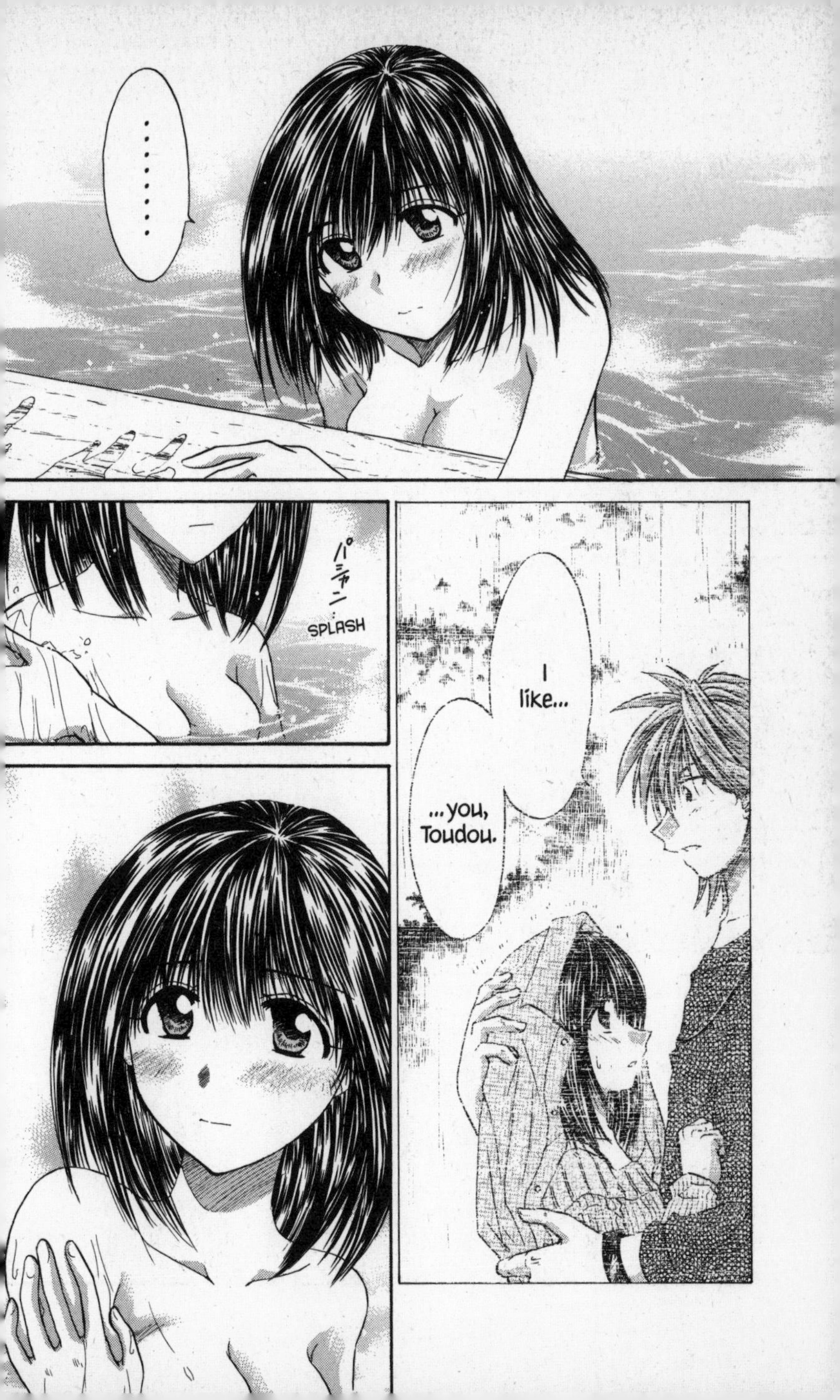

......
パシャン
SPLASH
I like...
...you, Toudou.

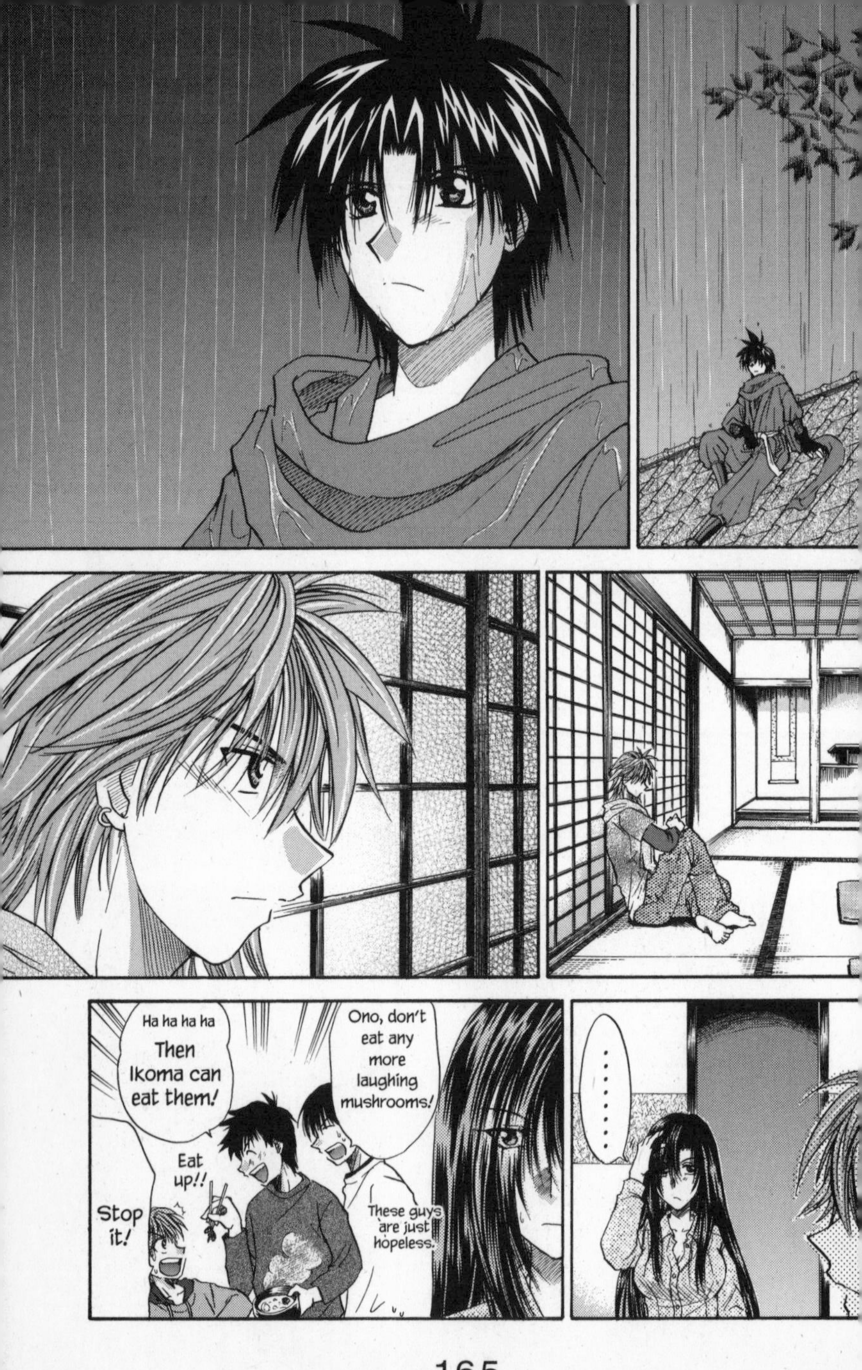
......
Ono, don't eat any more laughing mushrooms!
Ha ha ha ha
Then Ikoma can eat them!
Eat up!!
These guys are just hopeless.
Stop it!

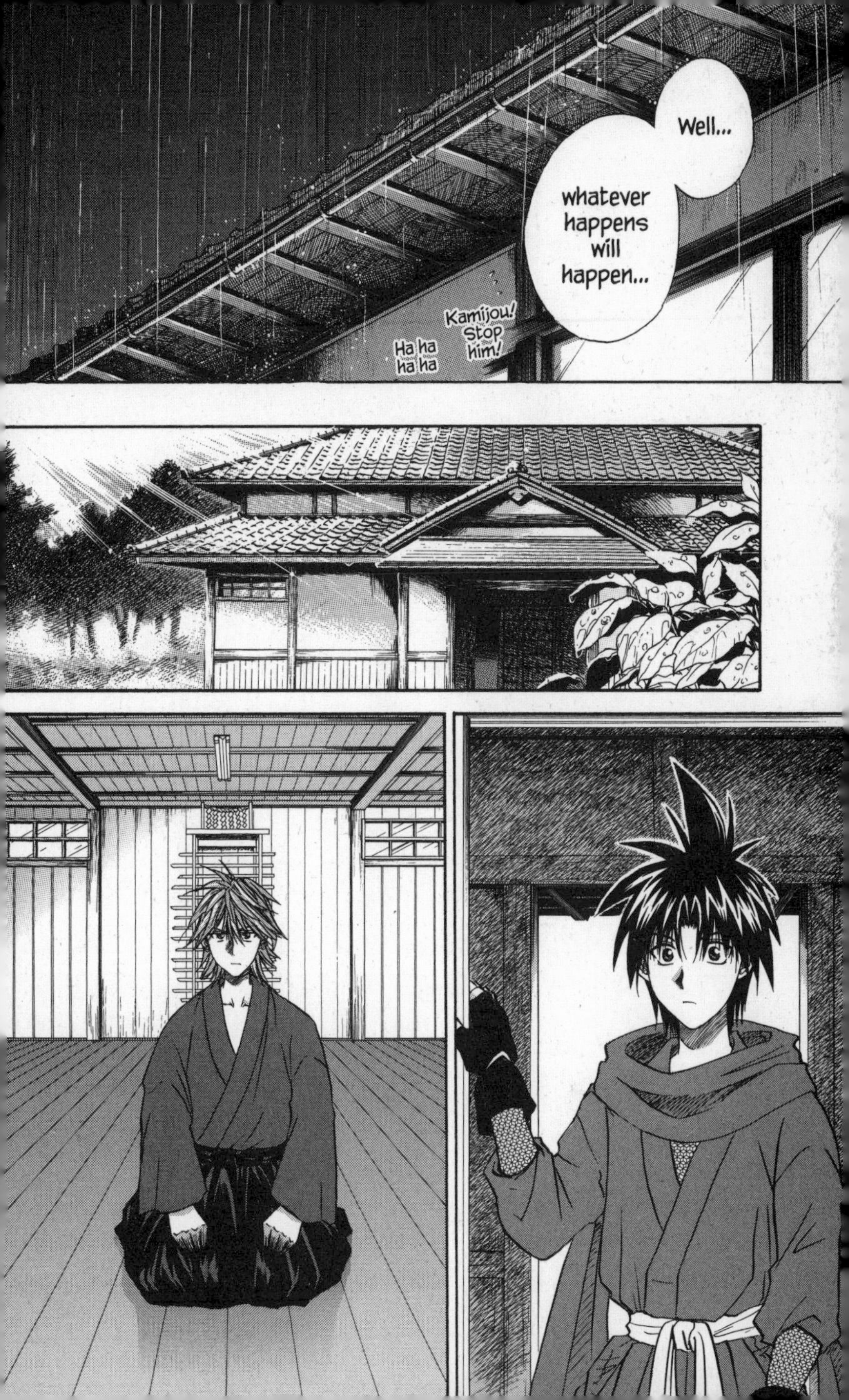
Well...
whatever happens will happen...
Kamijou! Stop him!
Ha ha ha ha

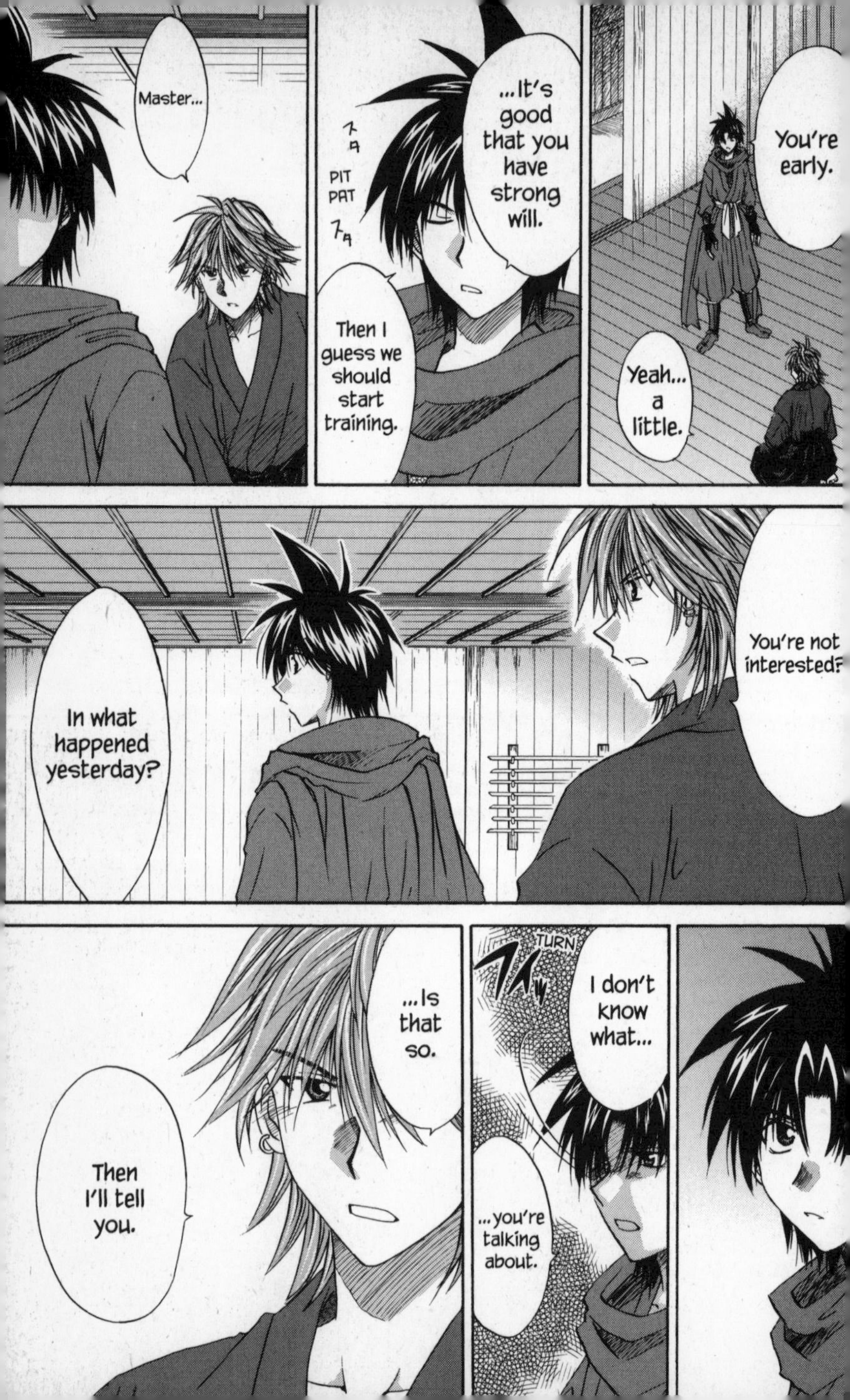
You're early.
Yeah... a little.
...It's good that you have strong will.
PIT PAT
Then I guess we should start training.
Master...
You're not interested?
In what happened yesterday?
TURN
I don't know what...
...you're talking about.
...Is that so.
Then I'll tell you.

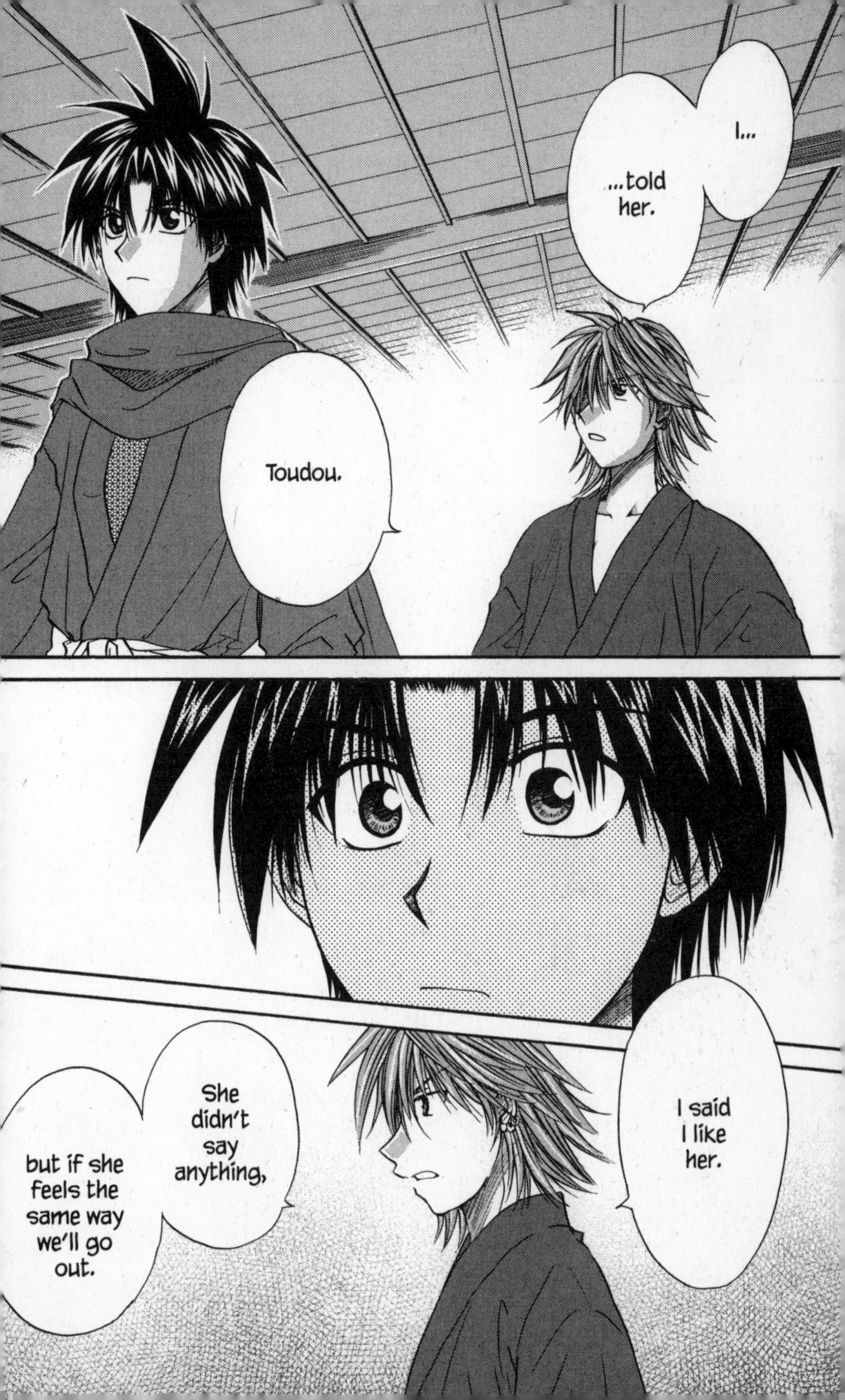
I...
...told her.
Toudou.
I said I like her.
She didn't say anything,
but if she feels the same way we'll go out.

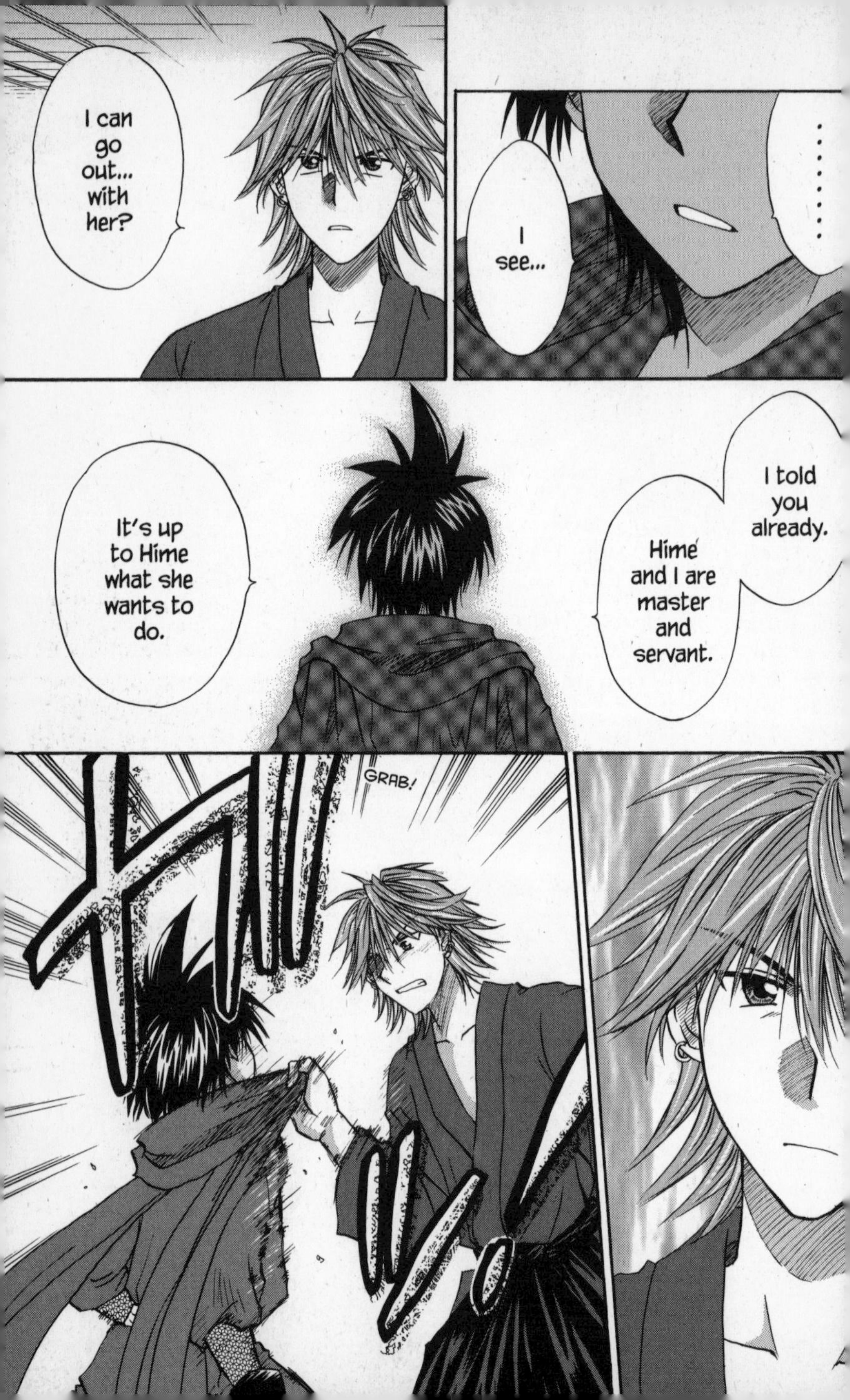
......
I see...
I can go out... with her?
I told you already.
Hime and I are master and servant.
It's up to Hime what she wants to do.
GRAB!

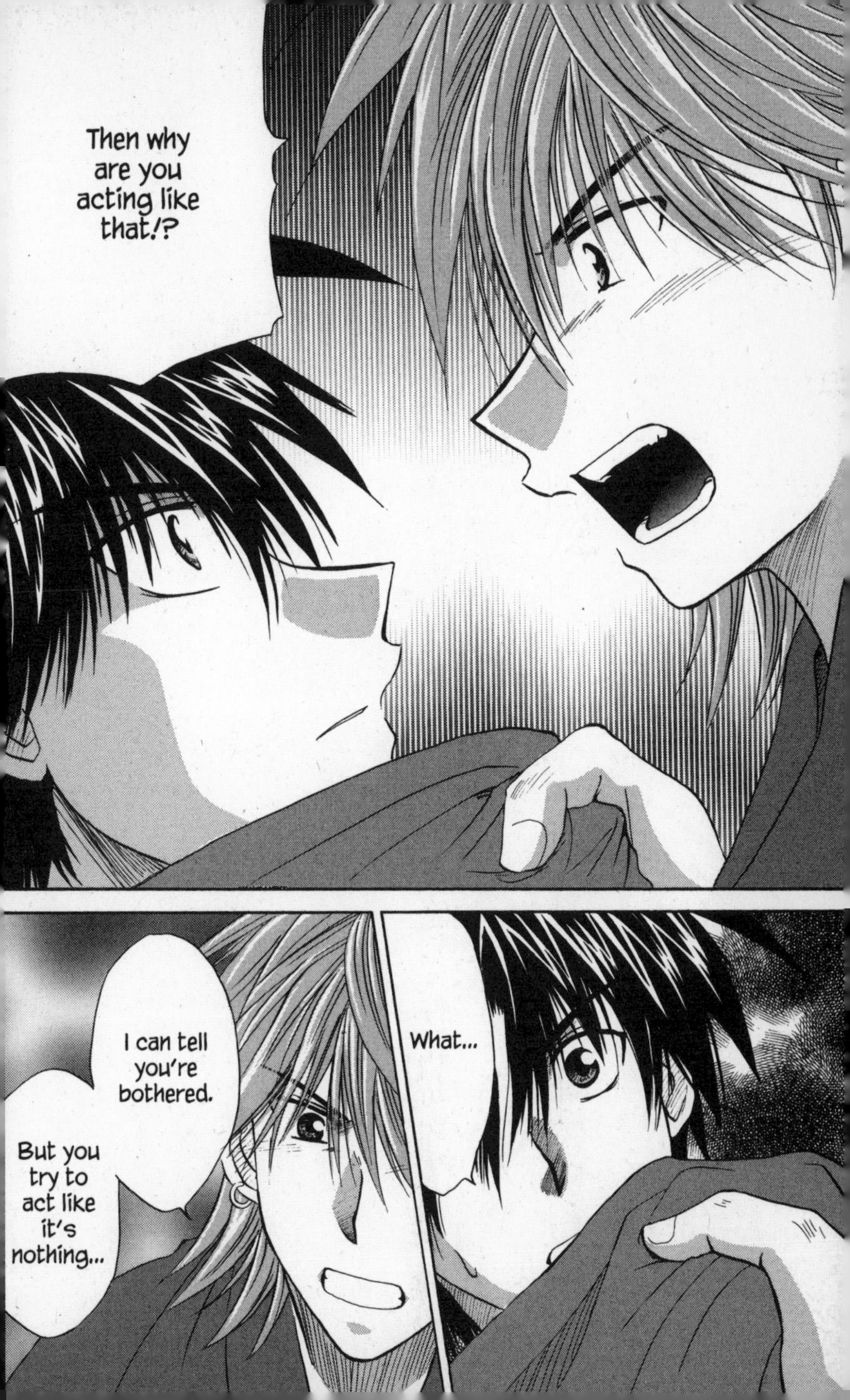
Then why are you acting like that!?
What...
I can tell you're bothered.
But you try to act like it's nothing...

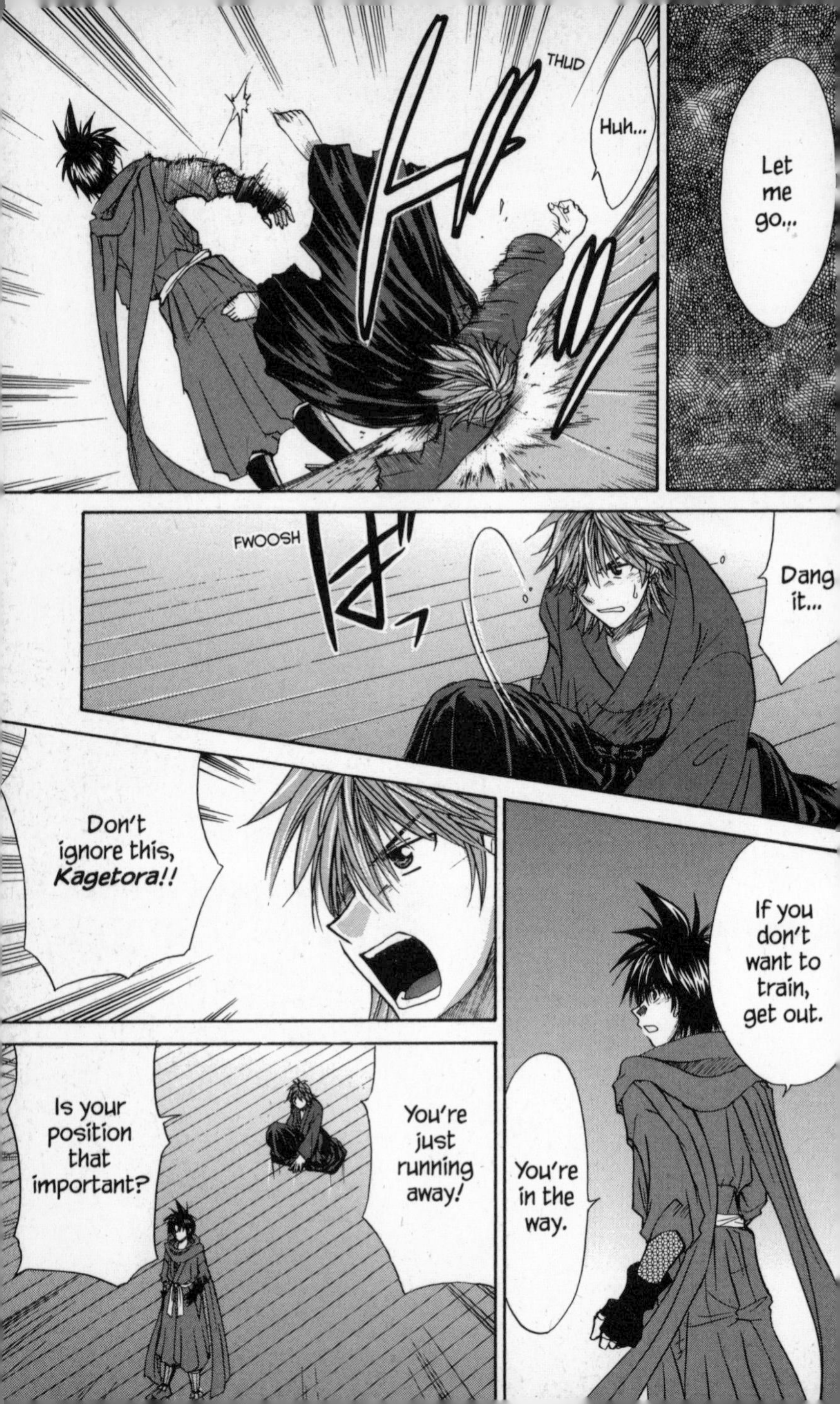

Let me go...
Huh...
THUD
Dang it...
FWOOSH
ばっ
If you don't want to train, get out.
You're in the way.
Don't ignore this, *Kagetora!!*
You're just running away!
Is your position that important?

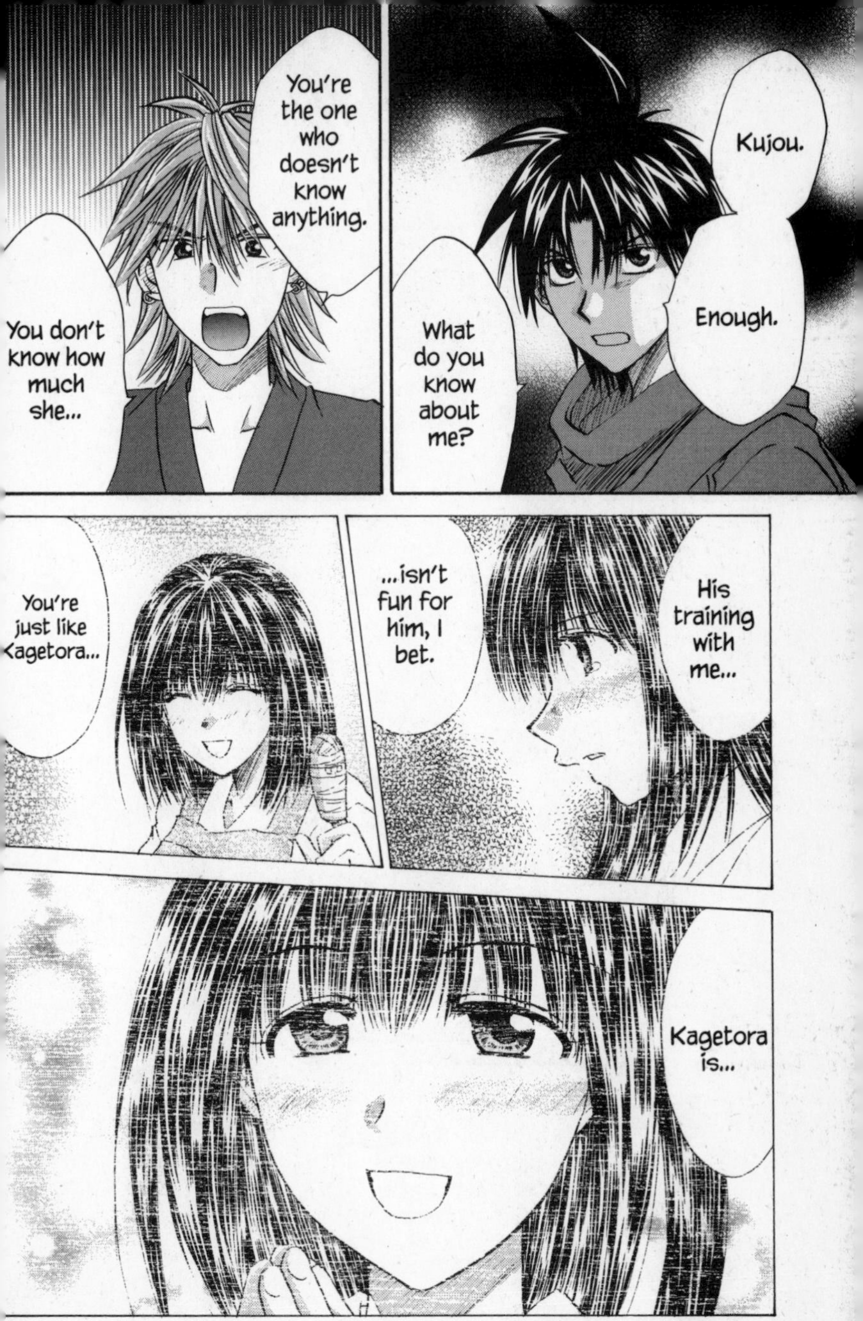
Kujou.
Enough.
What do you know about me?
You're the one who doesn't know anything.
You don't know how much she...
His training with me...
...isn't fun for him, I bet.
You're just like Kagetora...
Kagetora is...

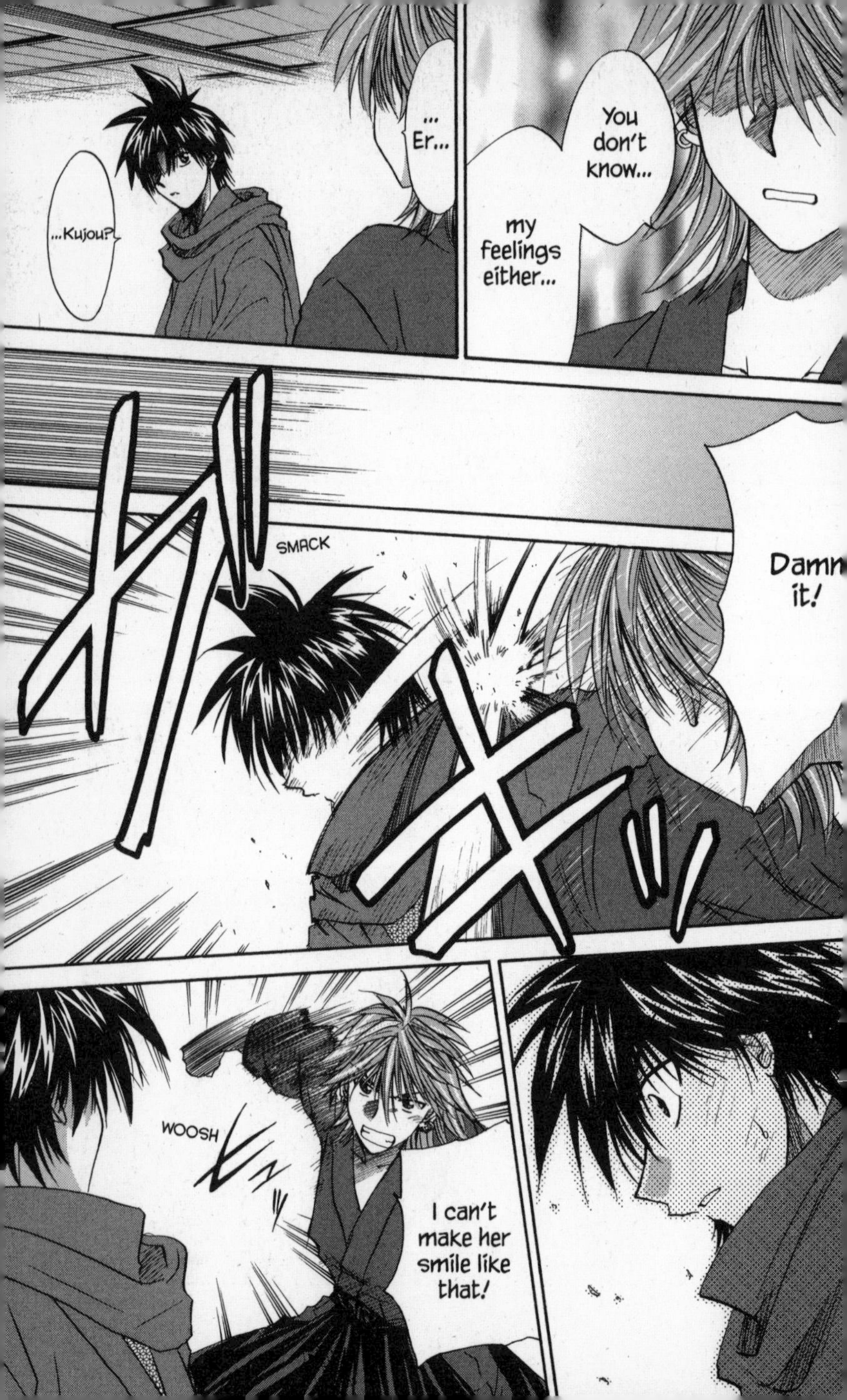
You don't know...
my feelings either...
... Er...
...Kujou?
Damn it!
SMACK
WOOSH
I can't make her smile like that!

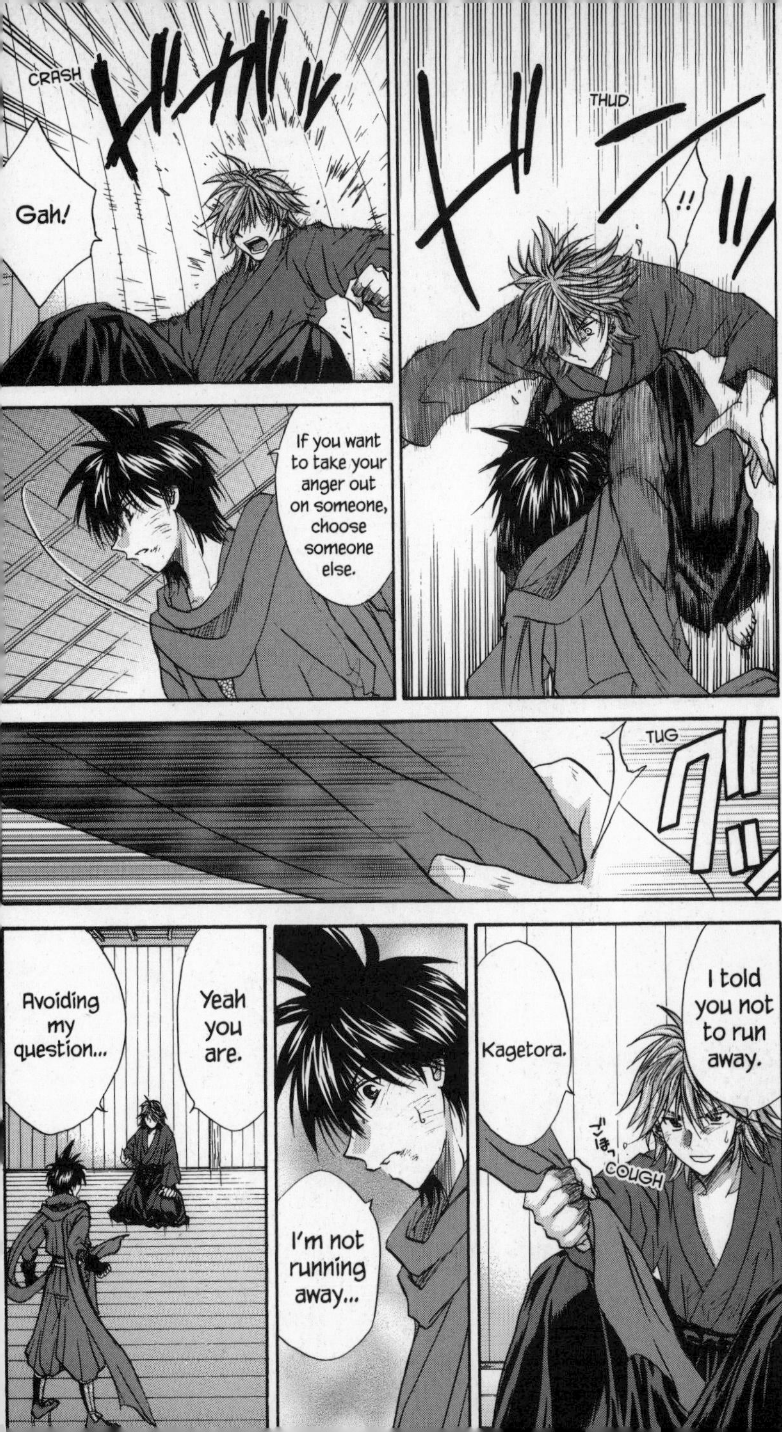
THUD
!!
CRASH
Gah!
If you want to take your anger out on someone, choose someone else.
TUG
I told you not to run away.
COUGH
Kagetora.
I'm not running away...
Yeah you are.
Avoiding my question...

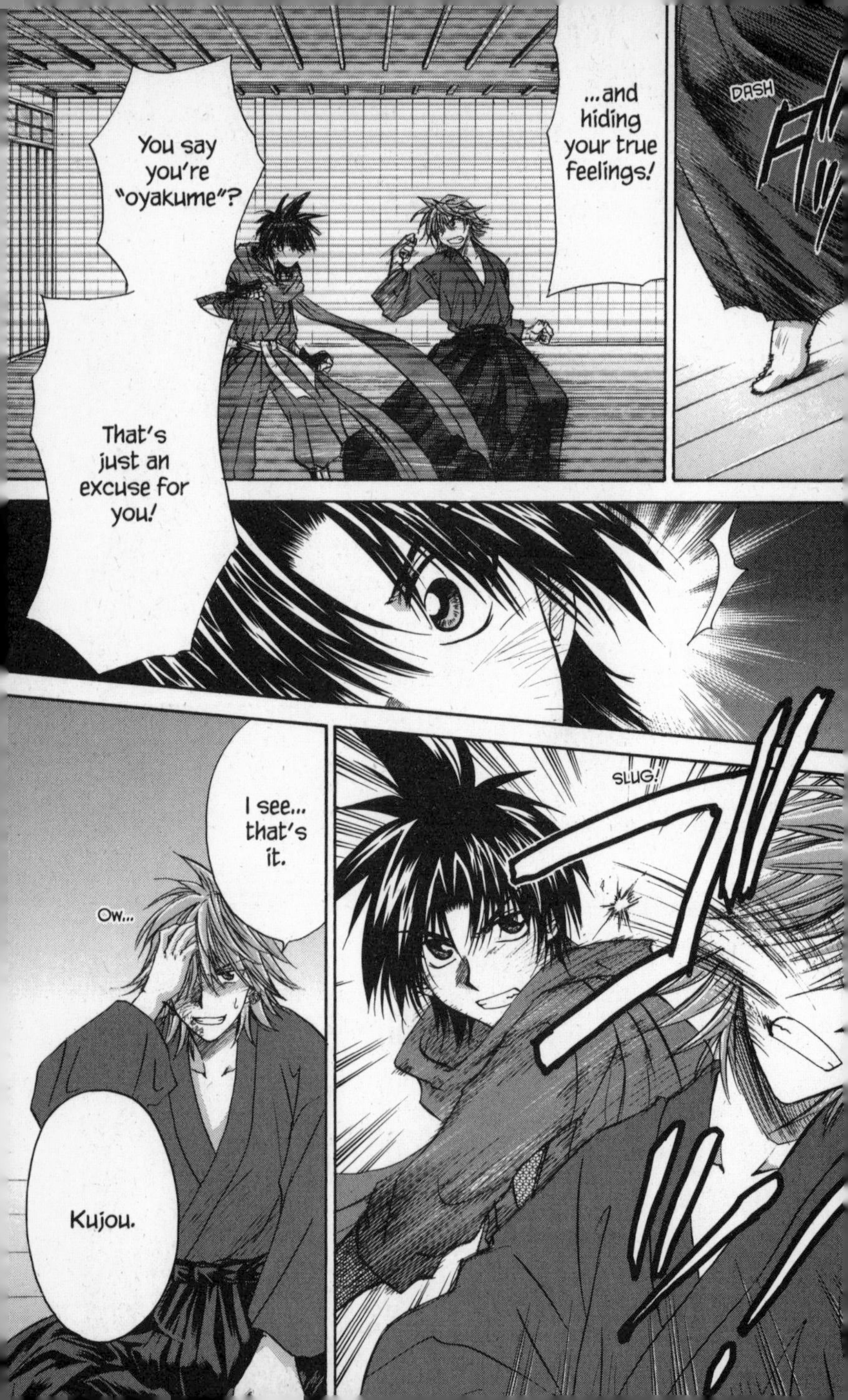
DASH
You say you're "oyakume"?
That's just an excuse for you!
...and hiding your true feelings!
SLUG!
I see... that's it.
Ow...
Kujou.

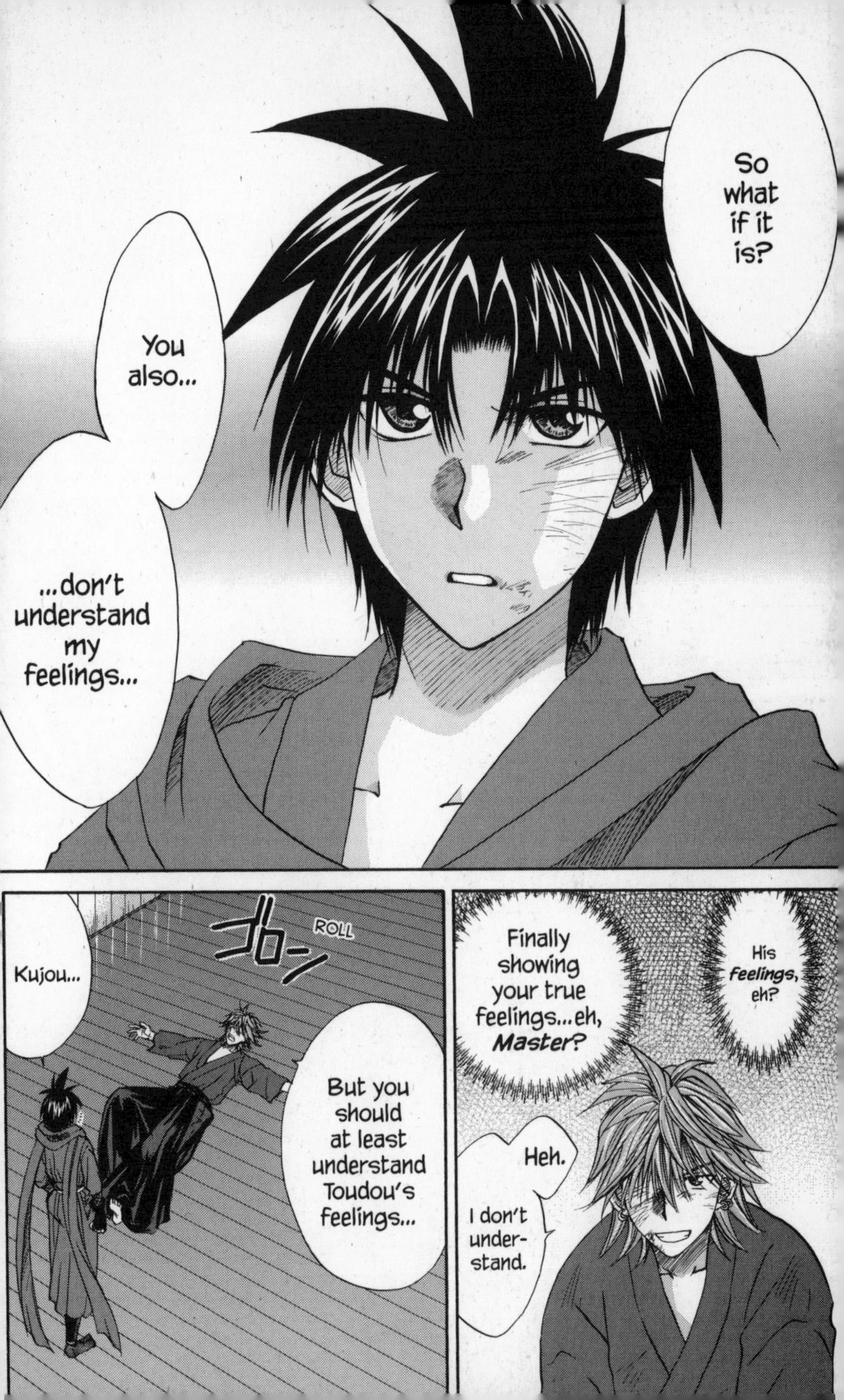

So what if it is?
You also...
...don't understand my feelings...
His *feelings*, eh?
Finally showing your true feelings...eh, ***Master***?
Heh.
I don't under-stand.
ROLL
Kujou...
But you should at least understand Toudou's feelings...

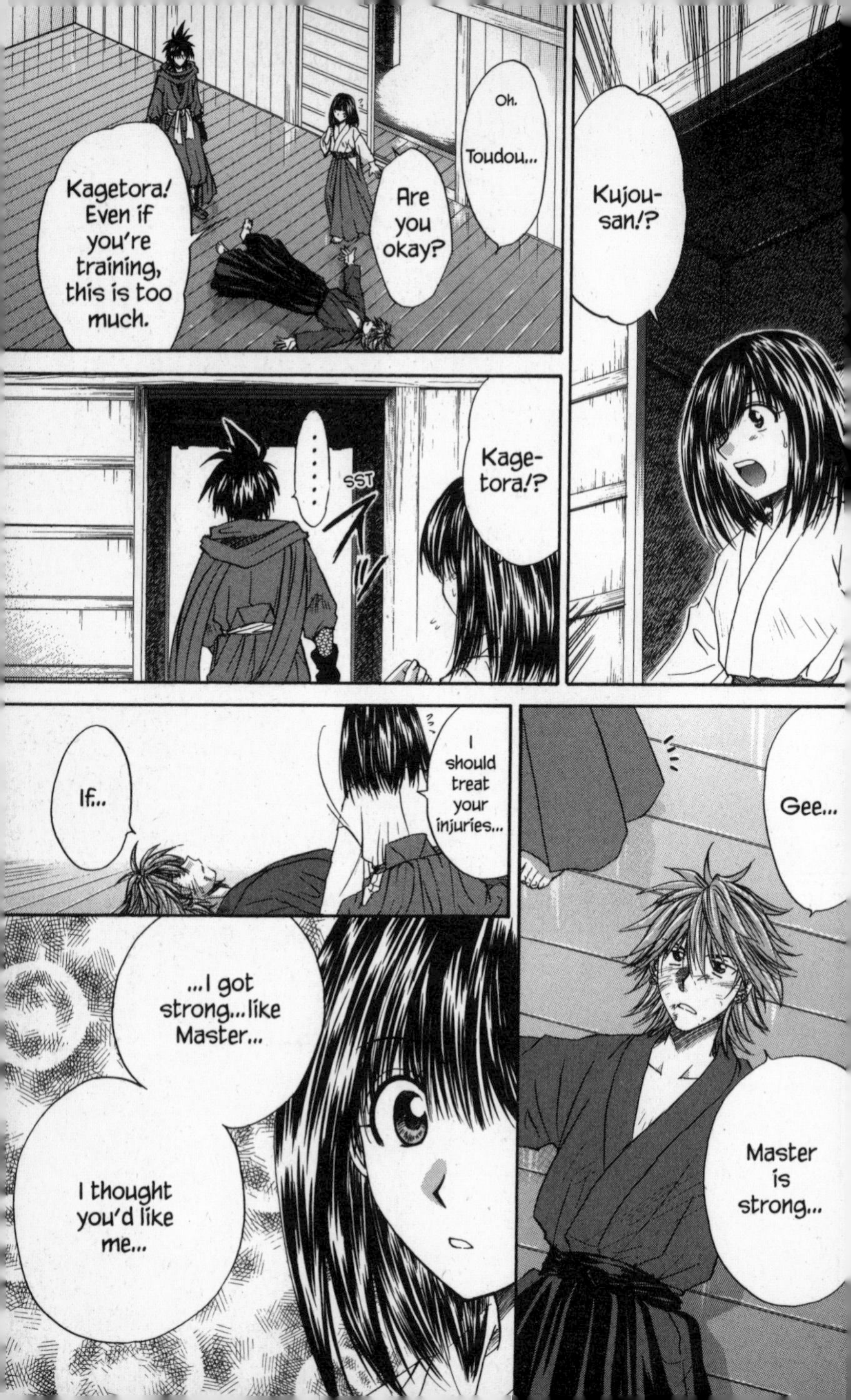

Kujou-san!?
Oh. Toudou...
Are you okay?
Kagetora! Even if you're training, this is too much.
Kage-tora!?
SST
......
Gee...
Master is strong...
I should treat your injuries...
If...
...I got strong...like Master...
I thought you'd like me...

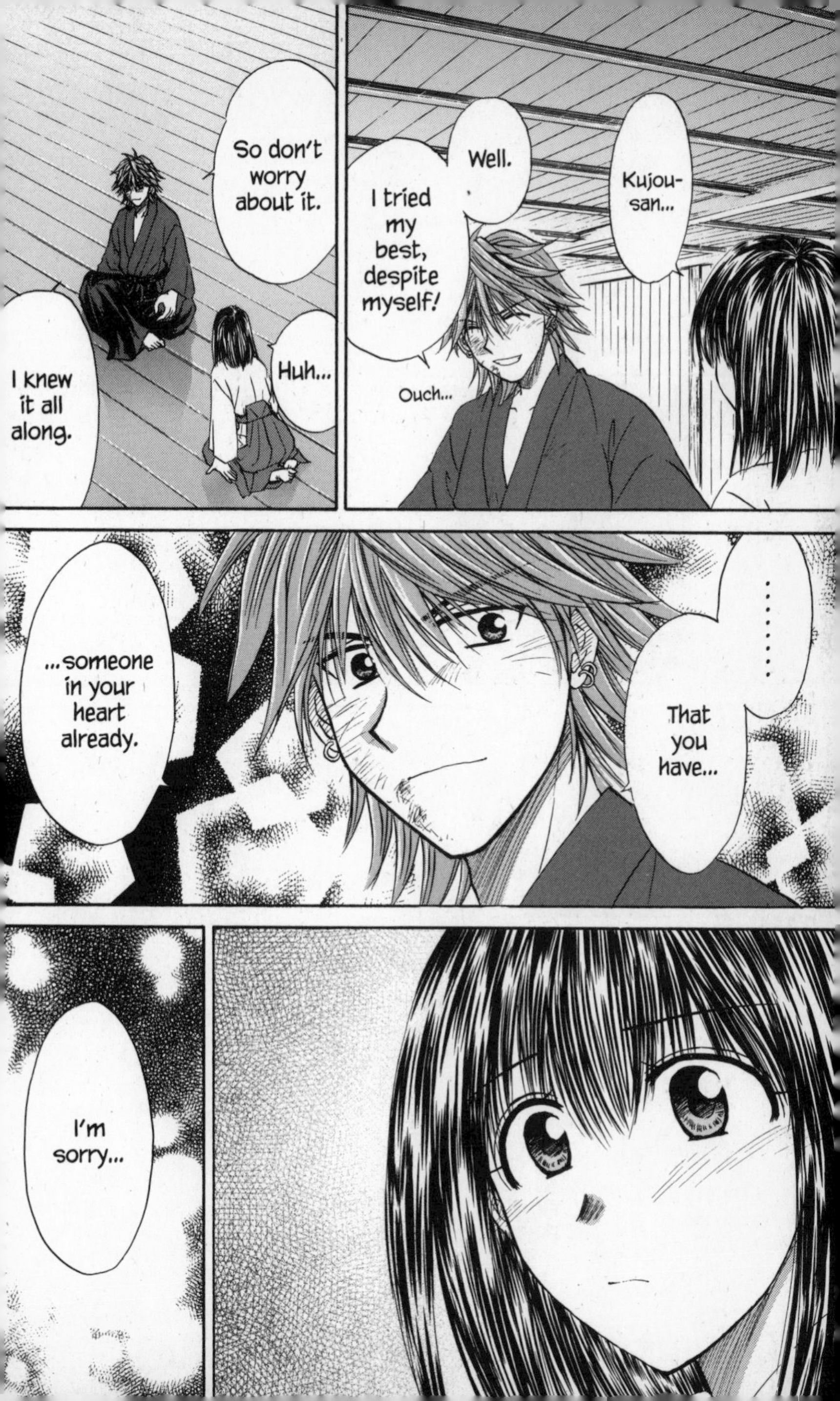
Kujou-san...
Well.
I tried my best, despite myself!
Ouch...
So don't worry about it.
Huh...
I knew it all along.
......
That you have...
...someone in your heart already.
I'm sorry...

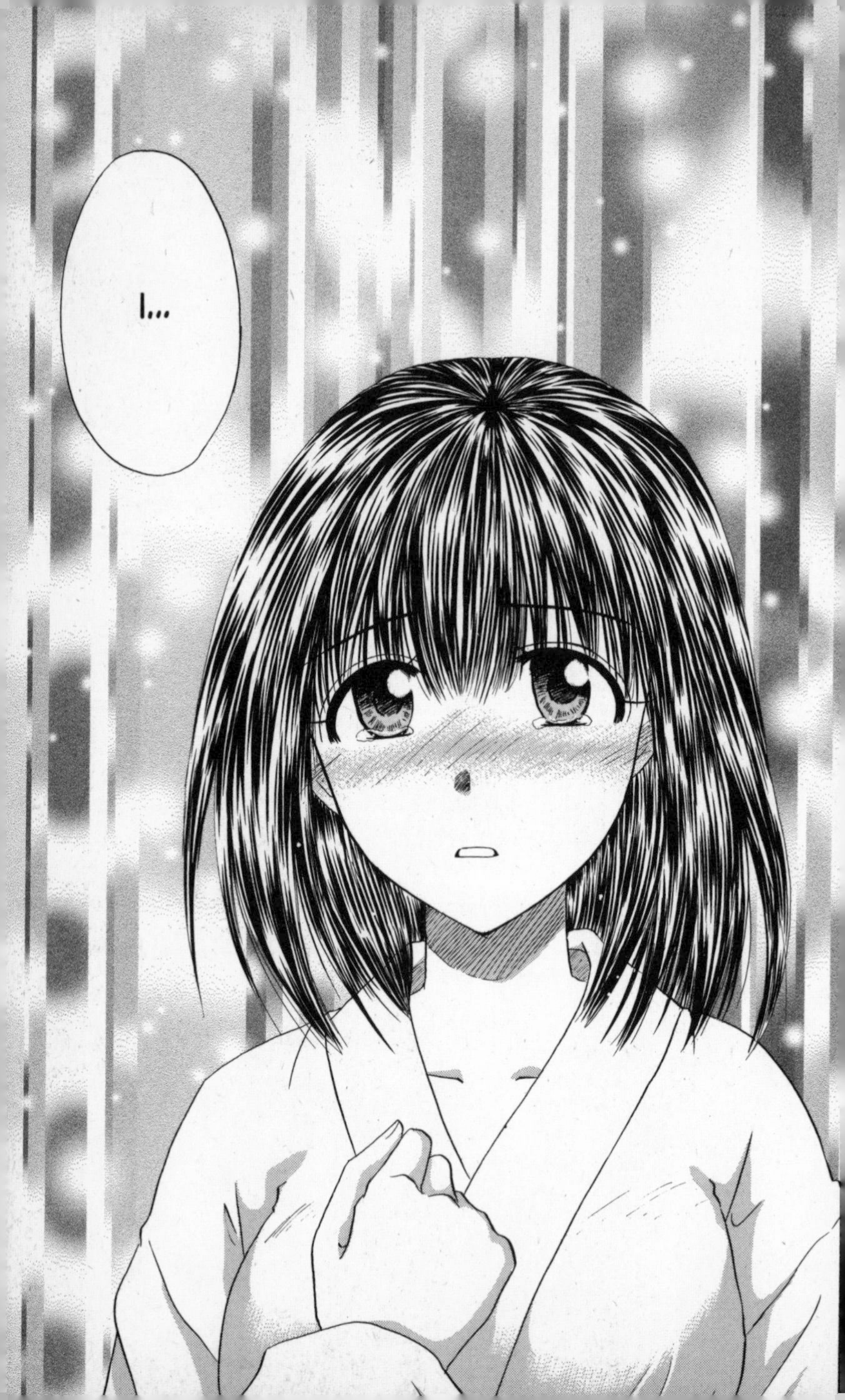
I...

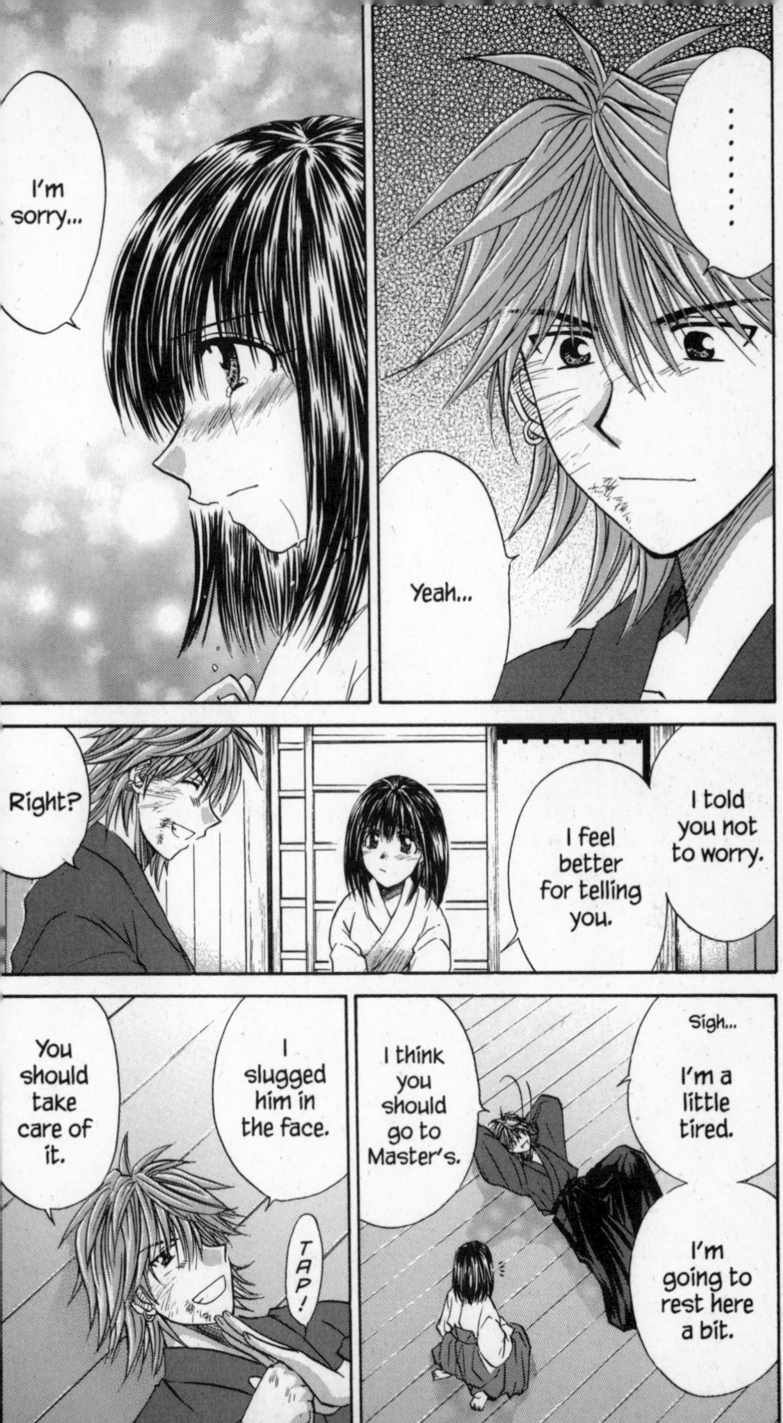
......
Yeah...
I'm sorry...
I told you not to worry.
I feel better for telling you.
Right?
Sigh...
I'm a little tired.
I'm going to rest here a bit.
I think you should go to Master's.
I slugged him in the face.
You should take care of it.
TAP!

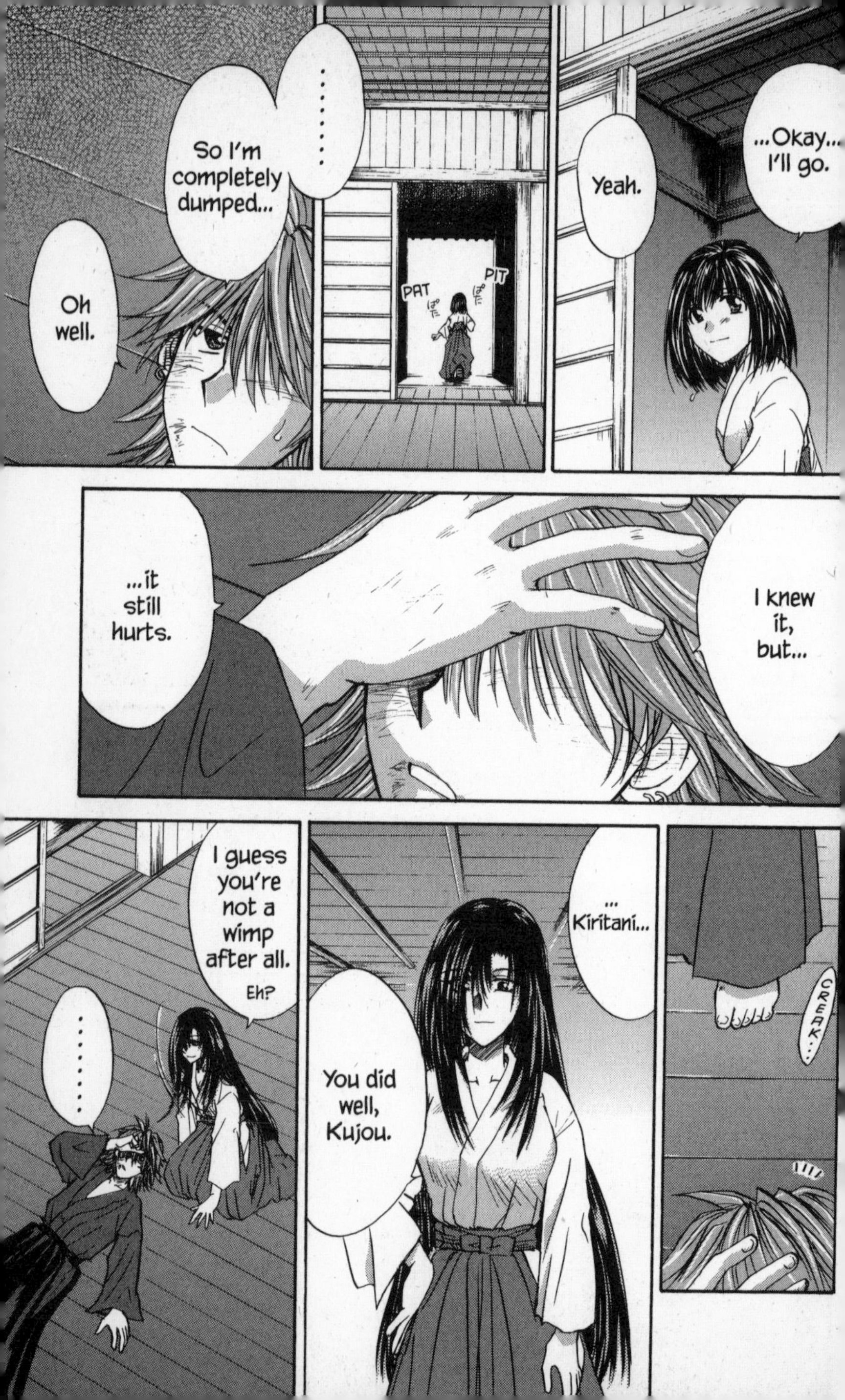
...Okay... I'll go.
Yeah.
PIT
PAT
......
So I'm completely dumped...
Oh well.
I knew it, but...
...it still hurts.
CREAK...
... Kiritani...
You did well, Kujou.
I guess you're not a wimp after all.
Eh?
......

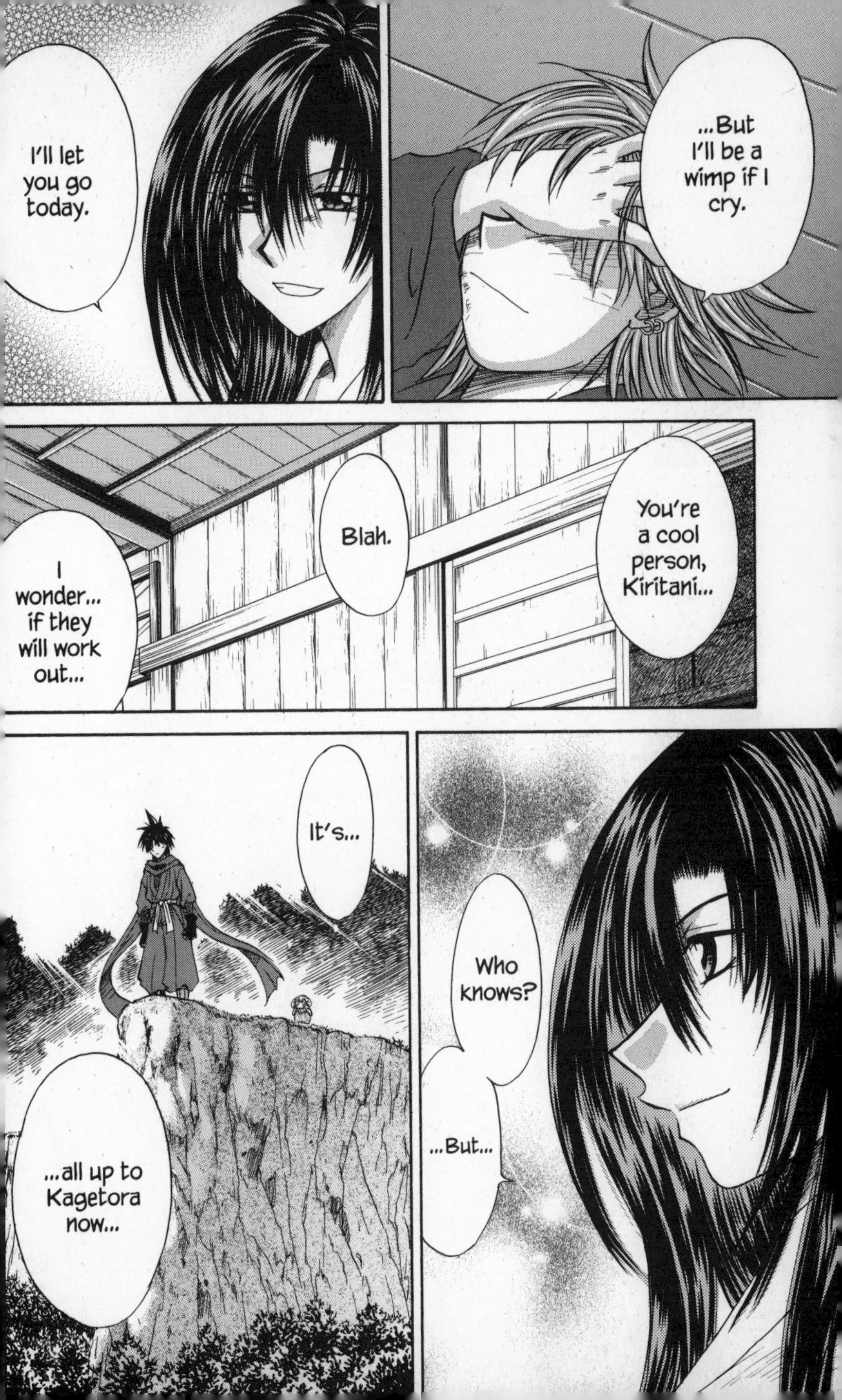
...But I'll be a wimp if I cry.
I'll let you go today.
You're a cool person, Kiritani...
Blah.
I wonder... if they will work out...
Who knows?
...But...
It's...
...all up to Kagetora now...

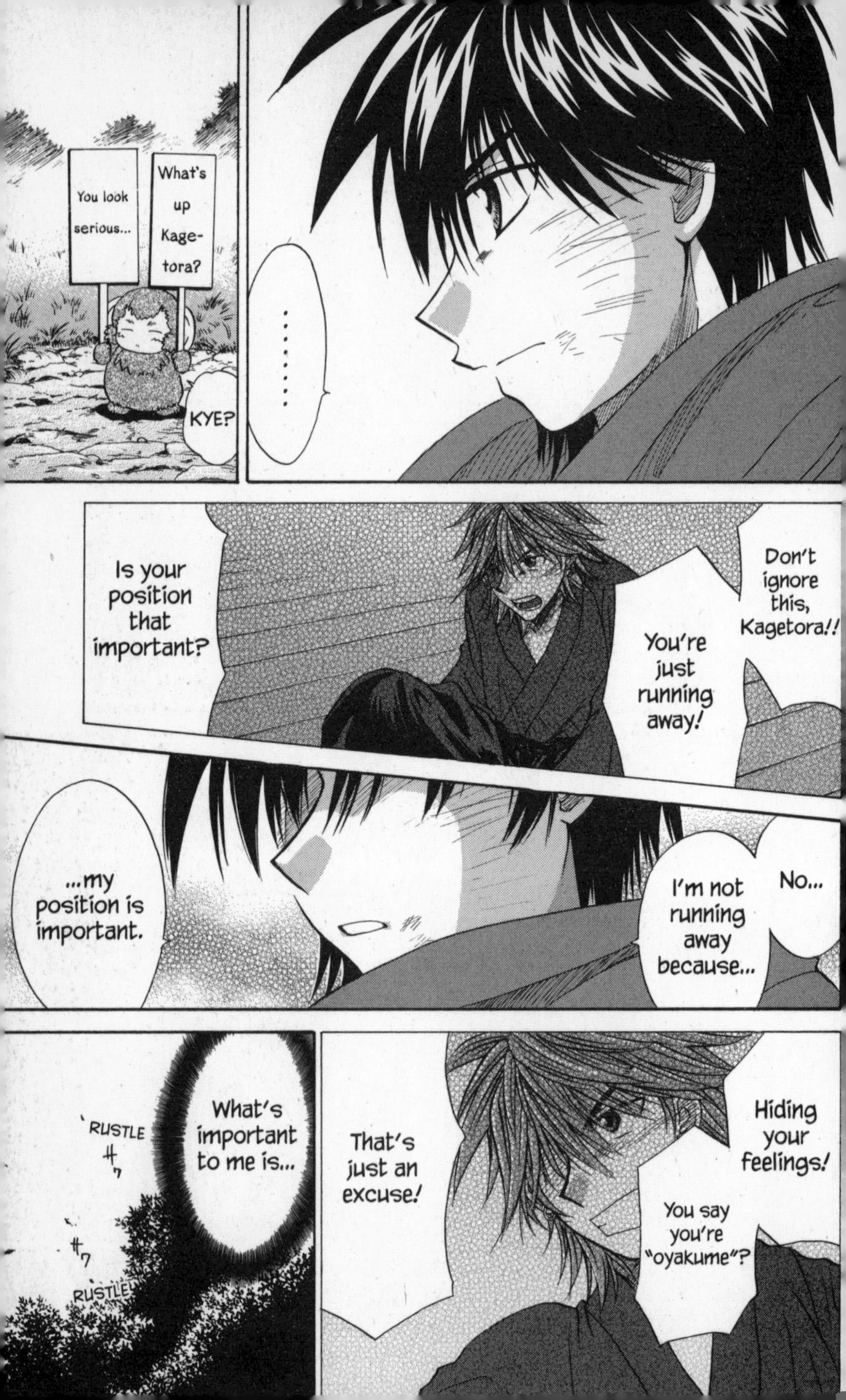
......
What's up Kage-tora?
You look serious...
KYE?
Don't ignore this, Kagetora!!
You're just running away!
Is your position that important?
No...
I'm not running away because...
...my position is important.
Hiding your feelings!
You say you're "oyakume"?
That's just an excuse!
What's important to me is...
RUSTLE
RUSTLE

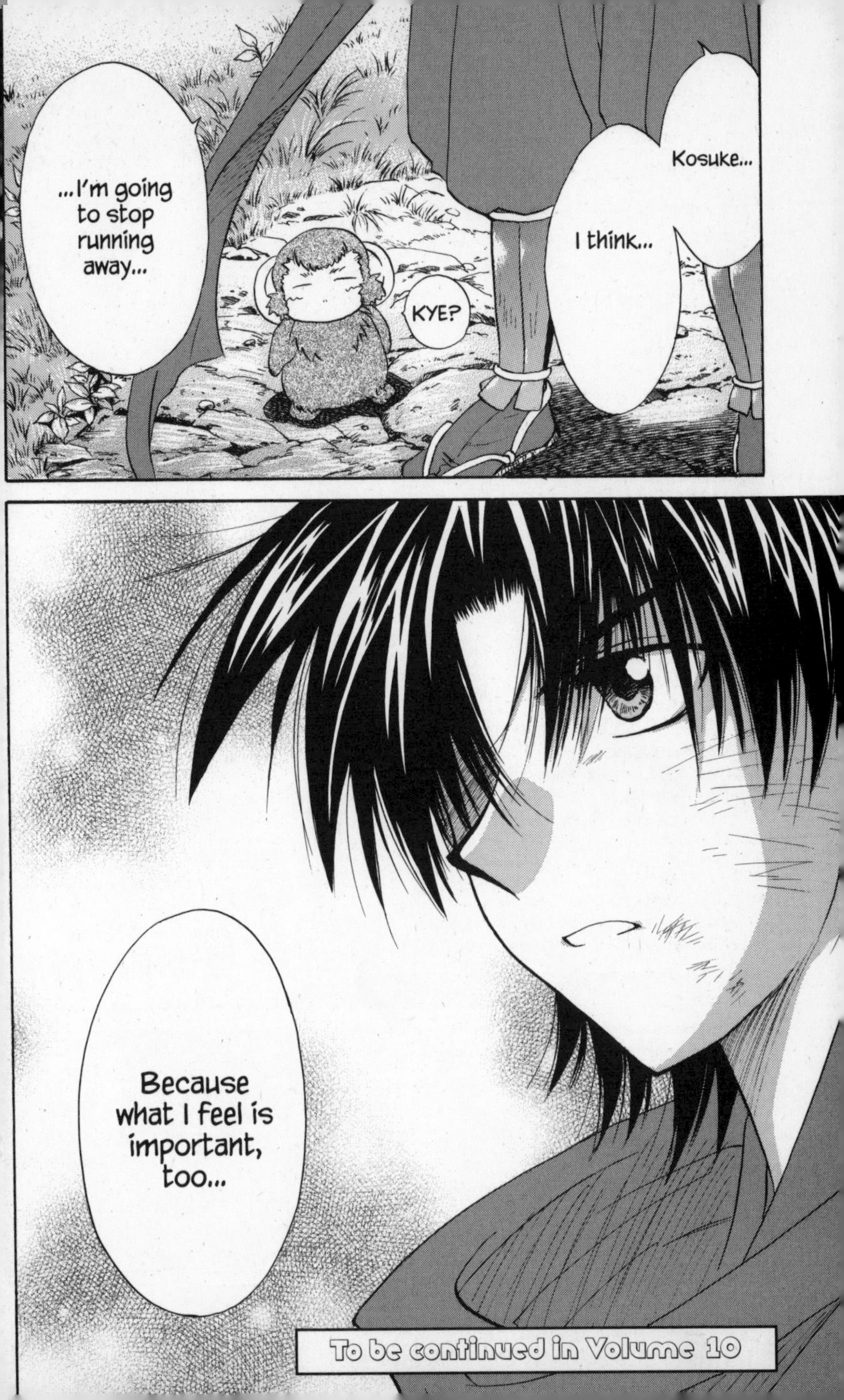

Kosuke...
I think...
KYE?
...I'm going to stop running away...
Because what I feel is important, too...
To be continued in Volume 10

This is Segami. Volume 9 is finally out. That happened fast…Anyway, I'm working hard on volume 10, so please stay with me…Since the readers are the reason a manga can be released. (laugh)

Bonus Page

About Ninjas part 9

I'm still attending that "art of the ninja" class… There are times I cannot make it because of work, but I guess even if I'm absent a lot, they won't kick me out. (laugh)

I'm attending with fellow manga artist Masanari Yuzuka, but I'm not as good as he is…

I hope to at least not get in the way when we train together.

About Traveling

I've been going to research stuff. Usually it is a two-day, one-night trip and very rushed, but even still I have a lot of fun when I go to places I've never been. ♪

I guess I've been having good luck with hot springs. There are many times when there are hot springs available at the inns I stay in…It's very relaxing. Hot springs are nice…

About Weapons

I…I'm buying more 💧💧 When I see some, I just impulse buy them. It's the same gift shop I wrote about in volume 8. (laugh)

I got the okay from the store manager, so I will introduce the store here ↓

It's Sankaido in Kamakura. It's located near the big Buddha. (Mr. Store Manager, thank you for always welcoming me in.)

There are normal souvenirs, so please stop by when you visit Kamakura. It's very fun. (laugh)

KUJOU

Thank you

Thank you for all your letters! I know it's way late, but I am writing back. So please look out for it… 💧💧

Really, it's what keeps me going! Thank you everyone!! Let's work hard together!!

Shooting in the Foot Part 1

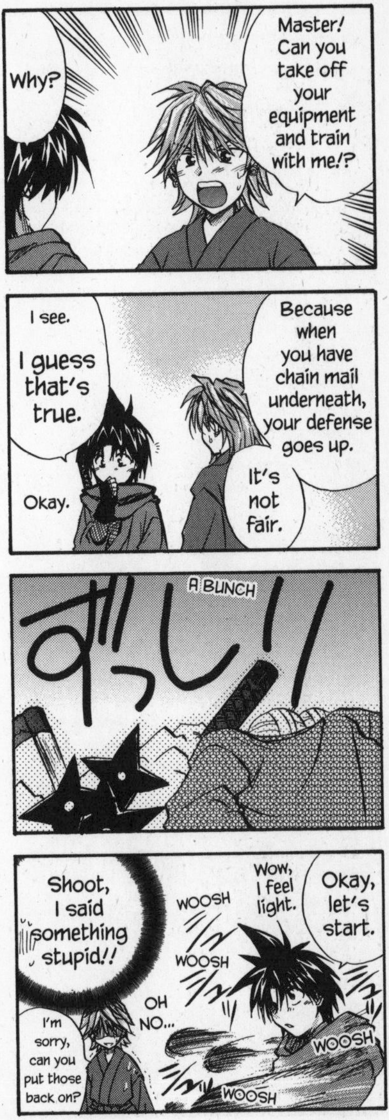
Master! Can you take off your equipment and train with me!?
Why?
Because when you have chain mail underneath, your defense goes up.
I see.
I guess that's true.
It's not fair.
Okay.
A BUNCH
ずっし!!
Okay, let's start.
Wow, I feel light.
WOOSH
Shoot, I said something stupid!!
WOOSH
OH NO...
WOOSH
I'm sorry, can you put those back on?
WOOSH

Shooting in the Foot Part 2

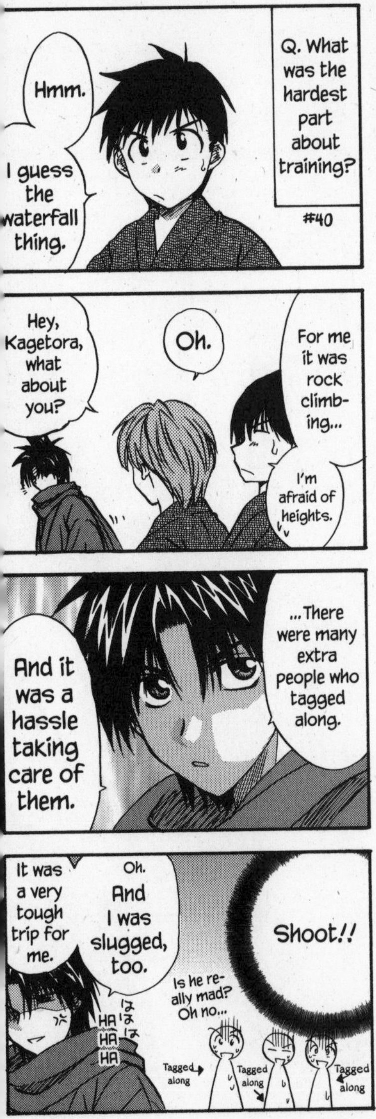
Q. What was the hardest part about training?
#40
Hmm.
I guess the waterfall thing.
For me it was rock climb-ing...
Oh.
Hey, Kagetora, what about you?
I'm afraid of heights.
...There were many extra people who tagged along.
And it was a hassle taking care of them.
Shoot!!
Oh. And I was slugged, too.
It was a very tough trip for me.
ははは
HA HA HA
Is he re-ally mad? Oh no...
Tagged along
Tagged along
Tagged along

Shooting in the Foot Part 3

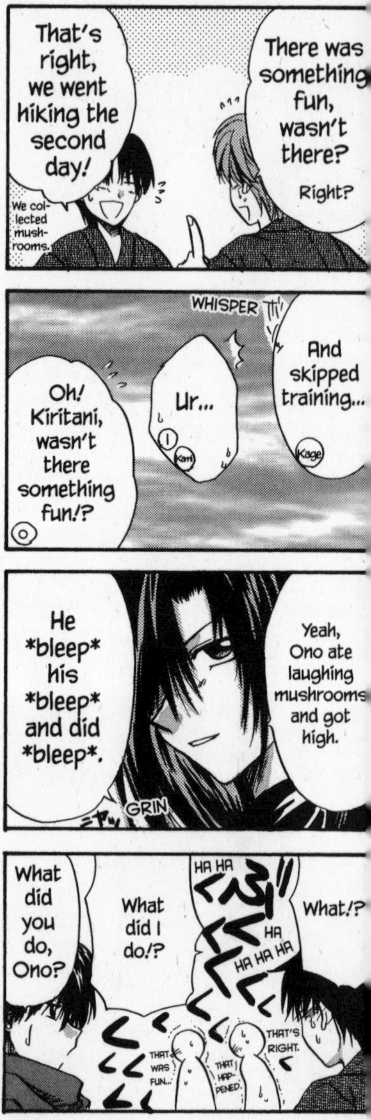
There was something fun, wasn't there?
Right?
That's right, we went hiking the second day!
We collected mushrooms.
WHISPER
And skipped training...
Ur...
Oh! Kiritani, wasn't there something fun!?
Yeah, Ono ate laughing mushrooms and got high.
He *bleep* his *bleep* and did *bleep*.
GRIN
What!?
HA HA
HA
HA HA HA
THAT'S RIGHT.
THAT HAPPENED.
THAT WAS FUN...
What did I do!?
What did you do, Ono?

Pity

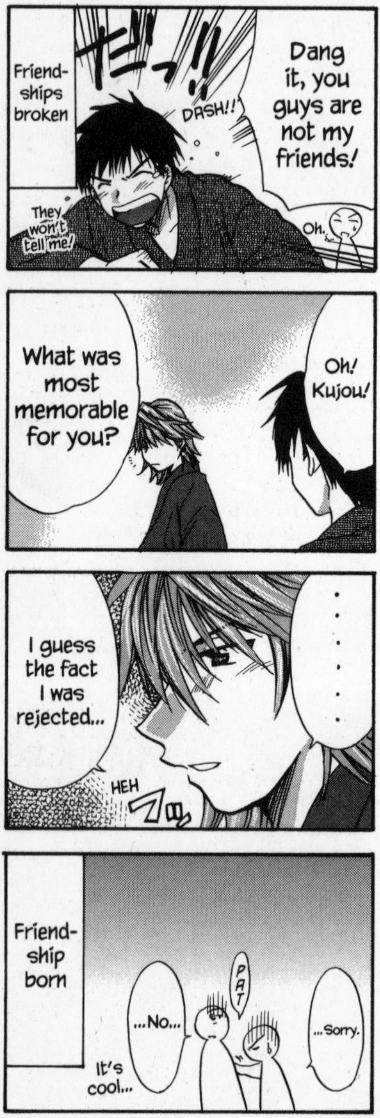
Dang it, you guys are not my friends!
DASH!!
Friendships broken
They won't tell me!
Oh.
Oh! Kujou!
What was most memorable for you?
......
I guess the fact I was rejected...
HEH
...Sorry.
PAT
...No...
It's cool...
Friendship born

I Would Like to Hibernate

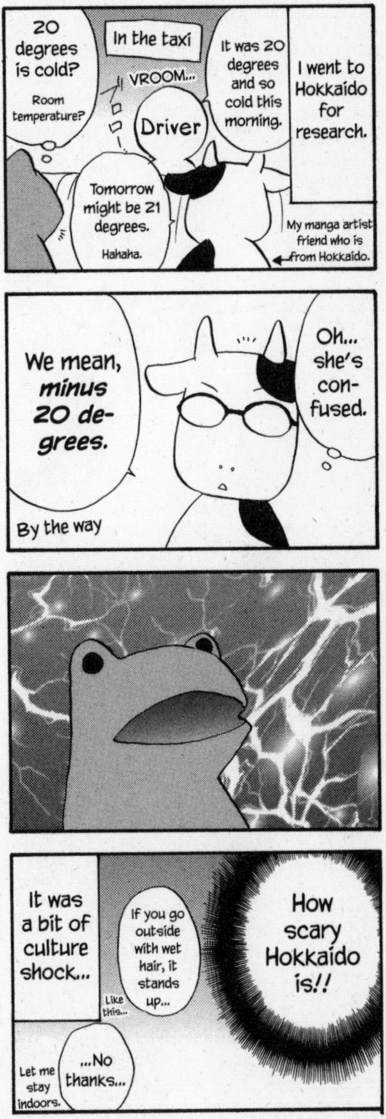
I went to Hokkaido for research.
It was 20 degrees and so cold this morning.
In the taxi
20 degrees is cold?
VROOM...
Driver
Room temperature?
Tomorrow might be 21 degrees.
Hahaha.
My manga artist friend who is from Hokkaido.
Oh... she's confused.
We mean, *minus 20 degrees.*
By the way
How scary Hokkaido is!!
If you go outside with wet hair, it stands up...
It was a bit of culture shock...
Like this...
...No thanks...
Let me stay indoors.

Mysterious Land

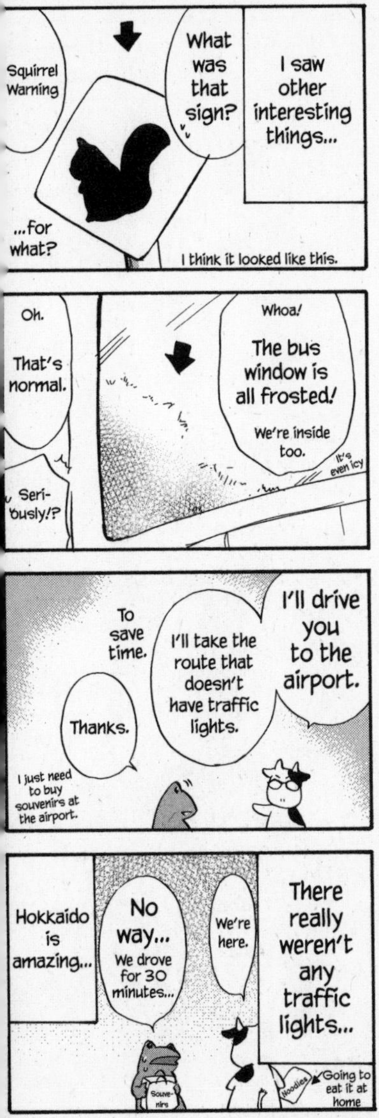
I saw other interesting things...
What was that sign?
Squirrel Warning
...for what?
I think it looked like this.
Whoa!
The bus window is all frosted!
We're inside too.
It's even icy
Oh.
That's normal.
Seri-ously!?
I'll drive you to the airport.
I'll take the route that doesn't have traffic lights.
To save time.
Thanks.
I just need to buy souvenirs at the airport.
There really weren't any traffic lights...
We're here.
No way...
We drove for 30 minutes...
Hokkaido is amazing...
Going to eat it at home
Noodles
Souve-nirs

Special Thanks!

Assistants: Tanaka-kun Oshima-chan

Editor: Mr. Morita

Comics Editor: Houdo-san

Helpers: Hiromu Arakawa-san, Nono-san, Aiya Ball-san, Yoko Ayase-san

And all my readers ♡

1-panel manga

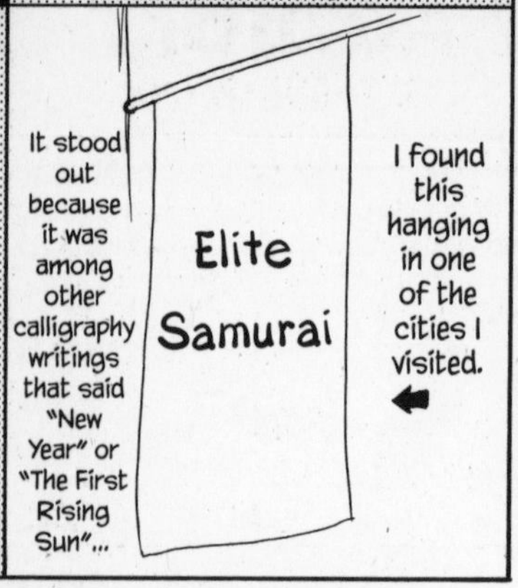

I found this hanging in one of the cities I visited.
Elite Samurai
It stood out because it was among other calligraphy writings that said "New Year" or "The First Rising Sun"...

By the way, on the back of this was the name "Xxxx Sugimura." I actually like the sense of humor of this kid. (laugh) In fact, I love it...

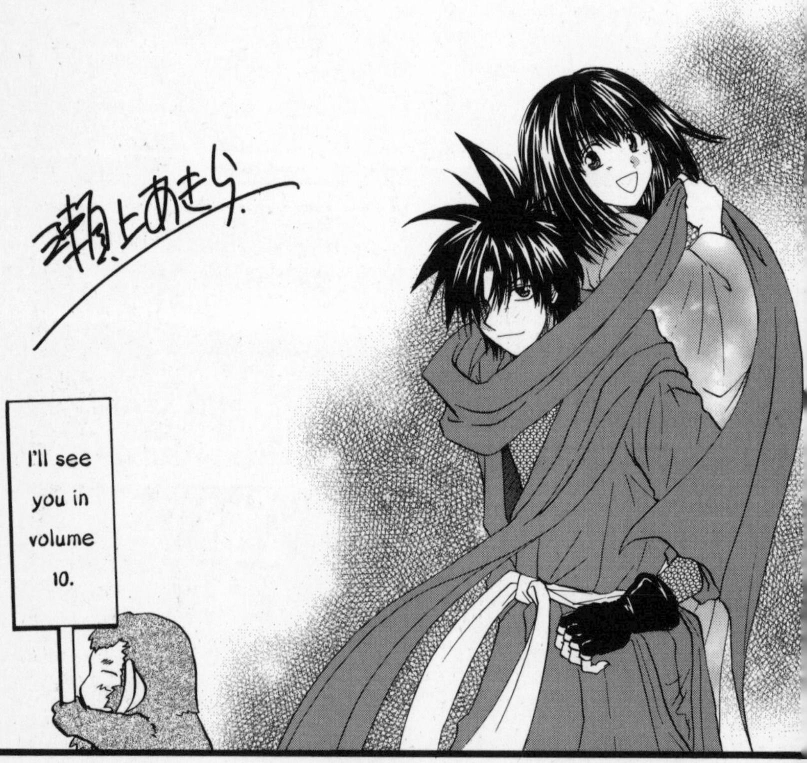

瀬上あきら
I'll see you in volume 10.

About the Author

Akira Segami's first manga was published by Shogakukan in 1996. He went on to do a few other small projects, including two short stories entitled "Kagetora" in 2001 and 2002. The character proved to be popular with fans, so Segami began his first ongoing series, Kagetora, with Kodansha in 2003. The series continues to run today.

Translation Notes

Japanese is a tricky language for most Westerners, and translation is often more art than science. For your edification and reading pleasure, here are notes on some of the places where we could have gone in a different direction with our translation of the work, or where a Japanese cultural reference is used.

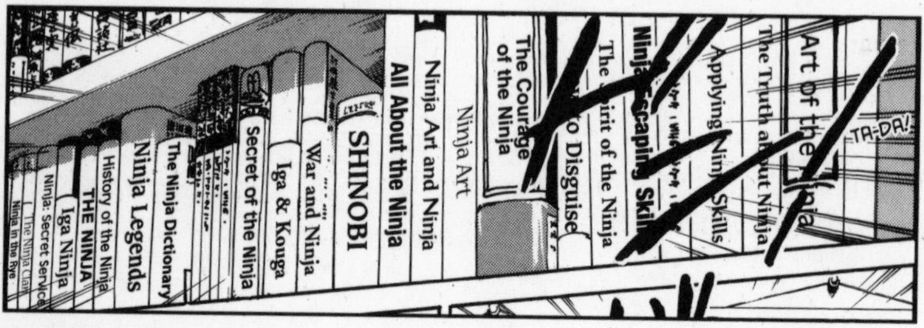

TA-DA!
The Courage of the Ninja
Ninja Art
Ninja Art and Ninja
All About the Ninja
SHINOBI
War and Ninja
Iga & Kouga
Secret of the Ninja
The Ninja Dictionary
Ninja Legends
History of the Ninja
THE NINJA
Iga Ninja
Ninja: Secret Service
The Ninja Clan
Ninja in the Rye

***Shinobi*, page 11**

Shinobi is another way of saying ninja. The kanji for "ninja" is a combination of the kanji for "shinobi" and "person." The term "shinobi" means "secret" or "hide."

Iga, page 11

Iga is a place in the Mie prefecture, in the Western region of Japan. The Iga-style ninja is one of the two famous ninja styles in Japan. (The other famous style is known as Kouga). In modern Japan, Iga has become a place for ninja tourism where tourists can enjoy ninja shows and the museum.

Kouga, page 11

Kouga is a ninja style in Japan. Kouga ninjas were especially known for their skills in medicine use. As part of a historic site, the Kouga Ninja Mansion is still left intact, with trap holes, turning doors, and underground tunnels as well as tools from the old days.

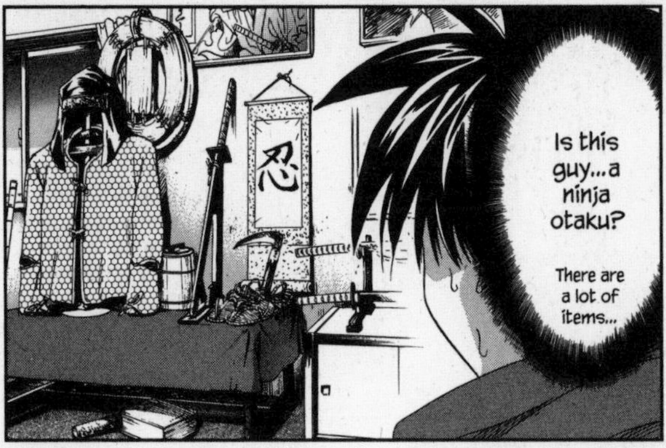
Is this guy...a ninja otaku?
There are a lot of items...

Otaku, page 12

Otaku is a Japanese word for "hard-core fan." Usually in the United States, anime fans refer to themselves as an *otaku,* but the word can be applied to science fiction fans, video game fans, idol fans, etc. Originating from the word *"otaku"* meaning "you" in second person, it is said to have first been used by an essayist named Akio Nakamori around 1980.

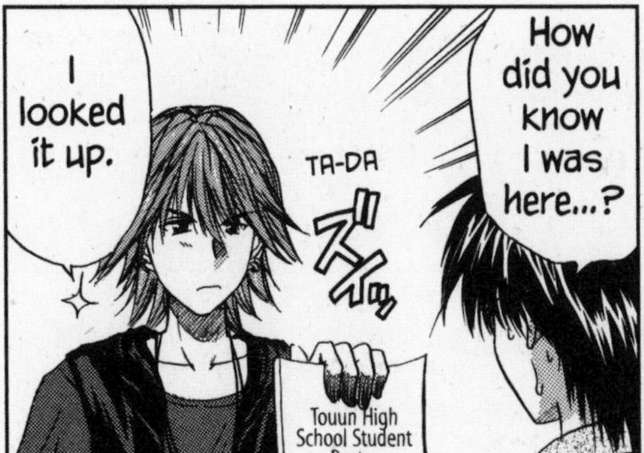
How did you know I was here...?
TA-DA
I looked it up.
Touun High School Student Roster

Student Roster, page 15

Schools in Japan have the student roster available to anyone who would like to see it. The roster has the house address, phone number, grade, and class of every student.

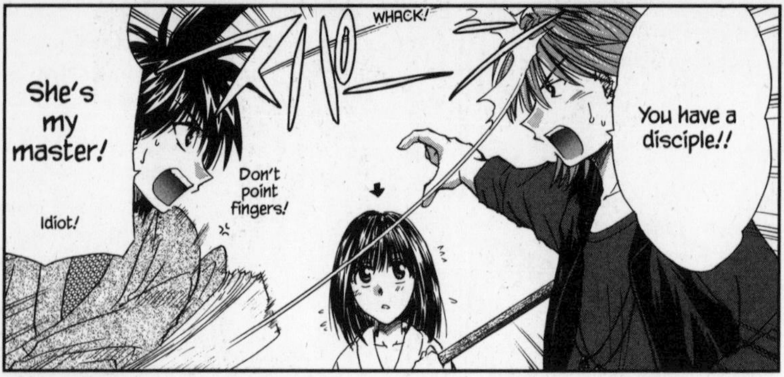
You have a disciple!!
WHACK!
Don't point fingers!
She's my master!
Idiot!

Folded Paper Fan, page 16

Kagetora is using a folded paper fan to hit Kujou. The fan is called *harisen* in Japanese, and is used commonly in manga and anime. It comes from an idea used in Japanese comedy where the comedians hit each other with a folded up *harisen*. It is good for a show because it makes a loud noise with little damage to the victim.

***Naginata*, page 24**

A *naginata* is a long-handled sword. It looks like a spear with a short sword at the tip of it. In modern Japan, it is usually a martial art for women.

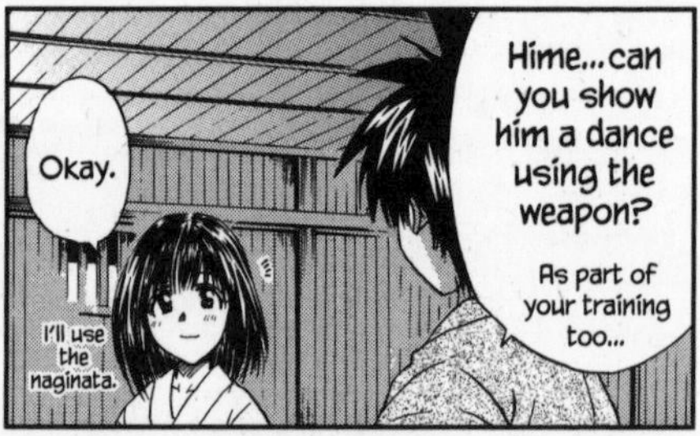
Hime...can you show him a dance using the weapon?
As part of your training too...
Okay.
I'll use the naginata.

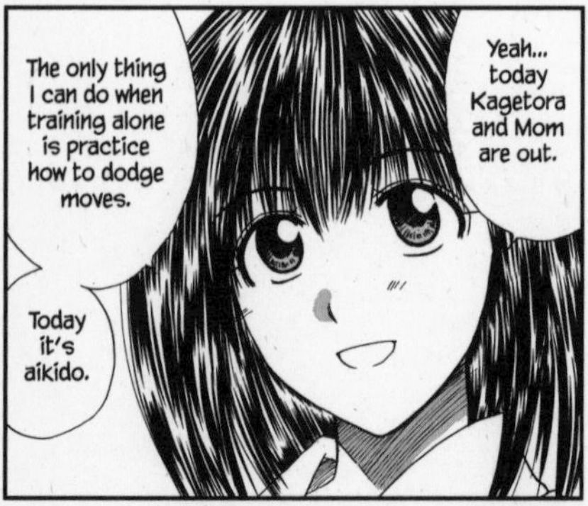
Yeah... today Kagetora and Mom are out.
The only thing I can do when training alone is practice how to dodge moves.
Today it's aikido.

Aikido, page 51

Aikido is a Japanese martial art in which artists use the attacker's force and redirect it against them.

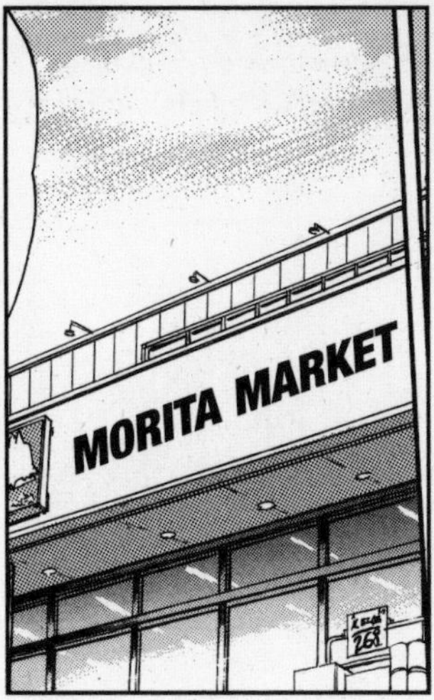
MORITA MARKET

Morita, page 65
If you look at the bonus pages at the end of the Kagetora volumes, you'll notice that Morita is the name of the author's editor.

***Takoyaki*, page 131**
Takoyaki is a grilled ball with a piece of octopus in the middle. It is made on a grill shaped in half circles. You whisk some flour, water, and egg together and pour it onto the hot grill. You then put a piece of octopus and some cut-up green onion in the middle and grill the mixture for a bit. The hardest part is flipping over the pancake to make a ball. You use a *takoyaki* pick, which is similar to an ice pick but thinner.

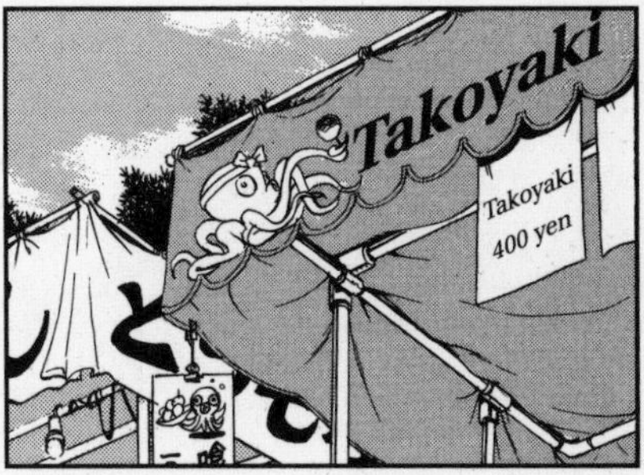
Takoyaki
Takoyaki
400 yen

Big Buddha, page 185
Kamakura has a Big Buddha that is one of the famous Big Buddhas in Japan. The other most famous Big Buddha is in Nara prefecture.

Hiromu Arakawa, page 189
Hiromu Arakawa is the manga artist of the famed *Fullmetal Alchemist*. Since Arakawa's hometown is in Hokkaido and the family operates a farm, Arakawa is depicted as a cow.

Calligraphy, page 189
It's part of New Year's tradition to write something in calligraphy on New Year's Day. To match the holiday, people would usually write something like "New Year." Most people don't do it at home anymore, but kids tend to do it at school or community gatherings.

Preview of Kagetora, volume 10

We're pleased to present you a preview from Kagetora, volume 10. Please check our website (www.delreymanga.com) to see when this volume will be available.

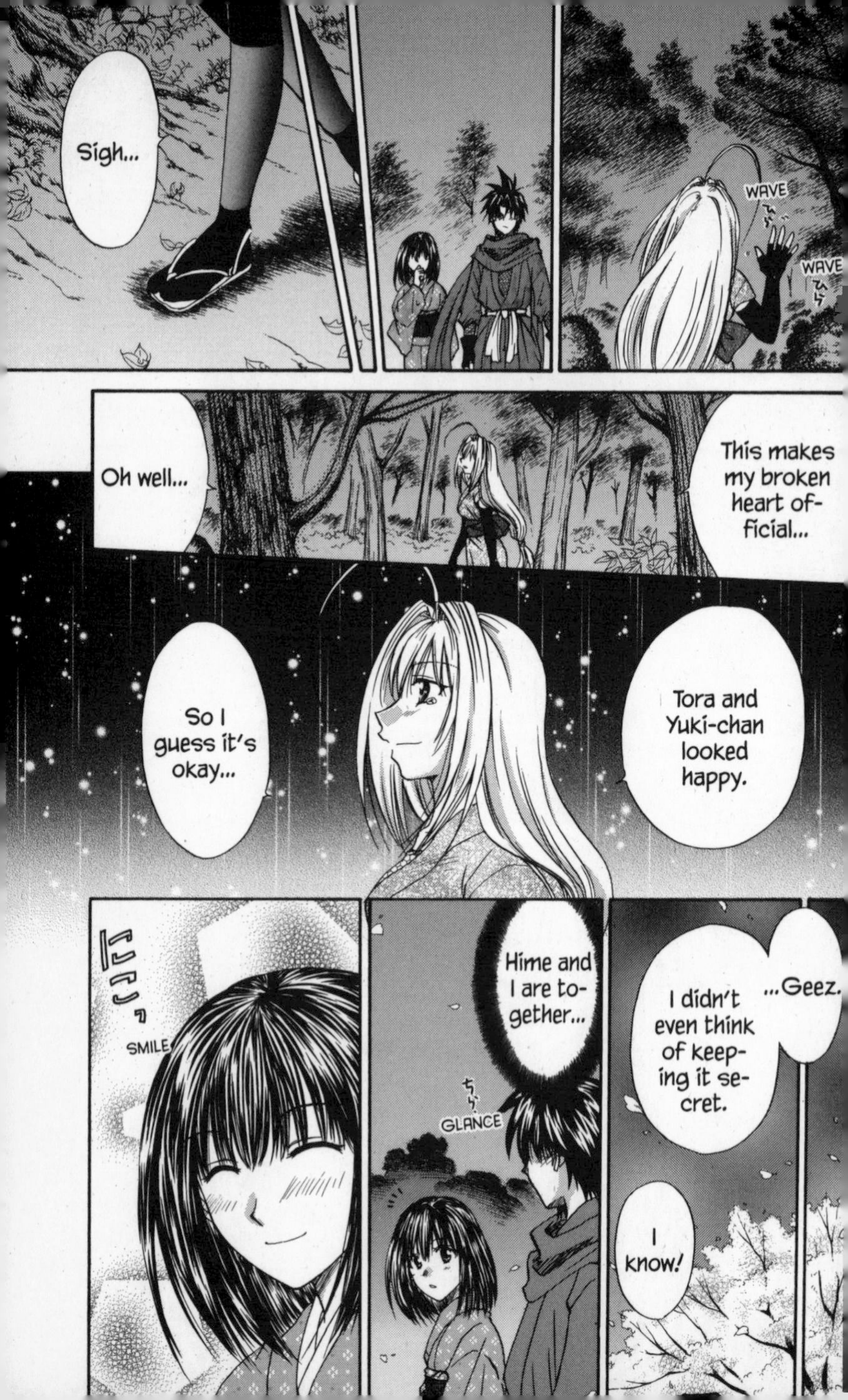
WAVE
WAVE
Sigh...
This makes my broken heart of-ficial...
Oh well...
Tora and Yuki-chan looked happy.
So I guess it's okay...
...Geez.
I didn't even think of keep-ing it se-cret.
I know!
Hime and I are to-gether...
GLANCE
SMILE

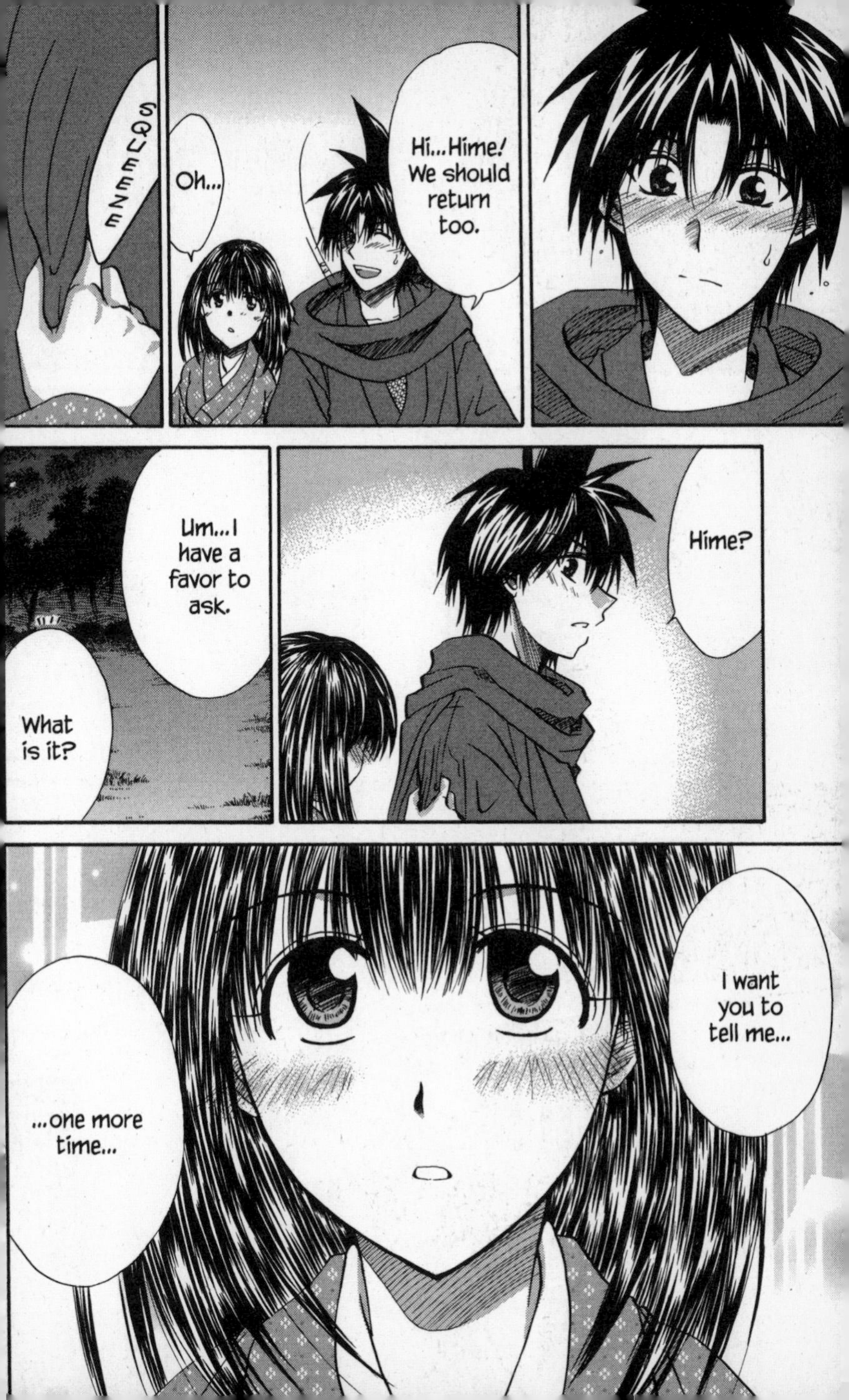

Hi...Hime! We should return too.
Oh...
SQUEEZE
Hime?
Um...I have a favor to ask.
What is it?
I want you to tell me...
...one more time...

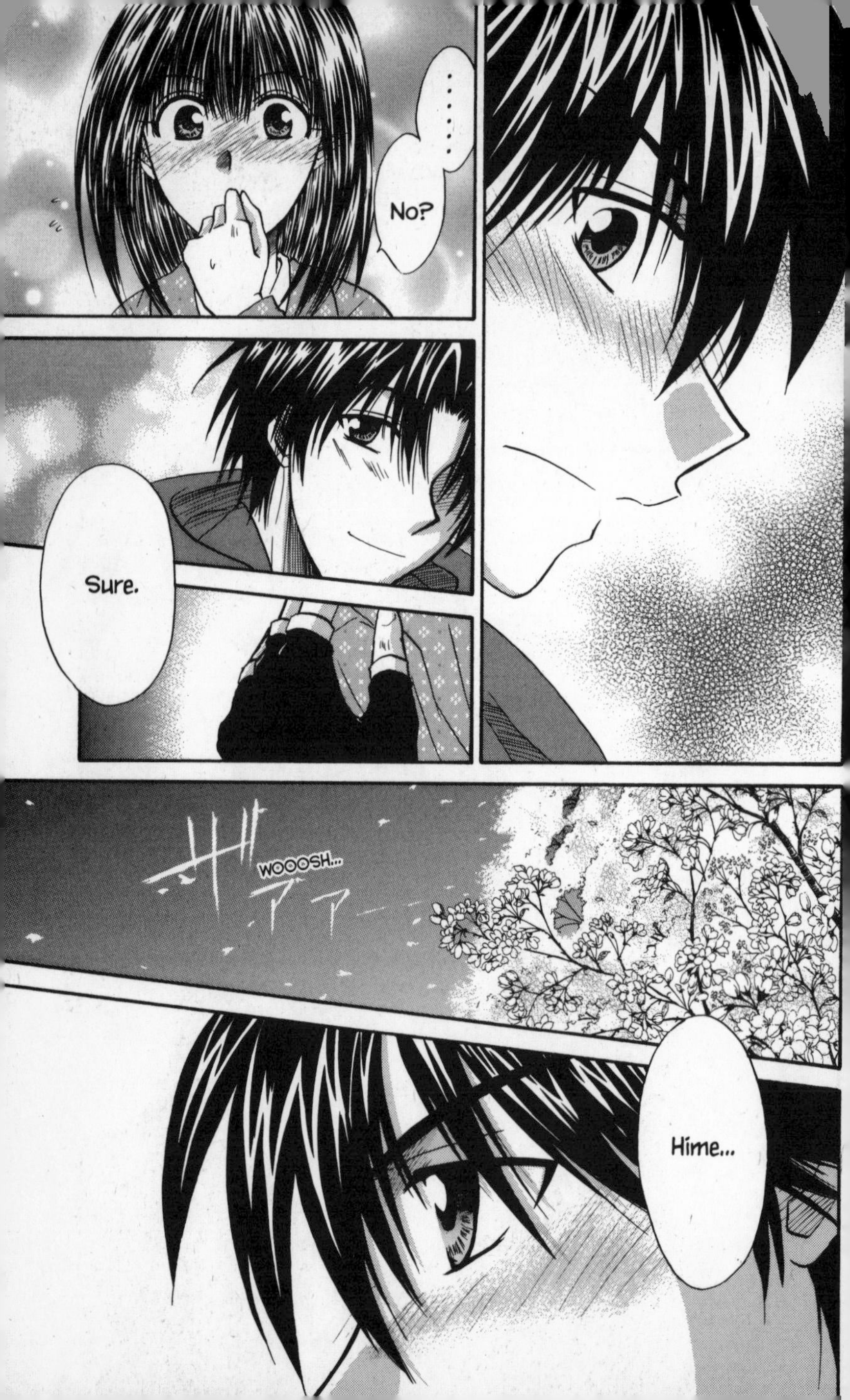
......
No?
Sure.
ザァア
WOOOSH...
Hime...

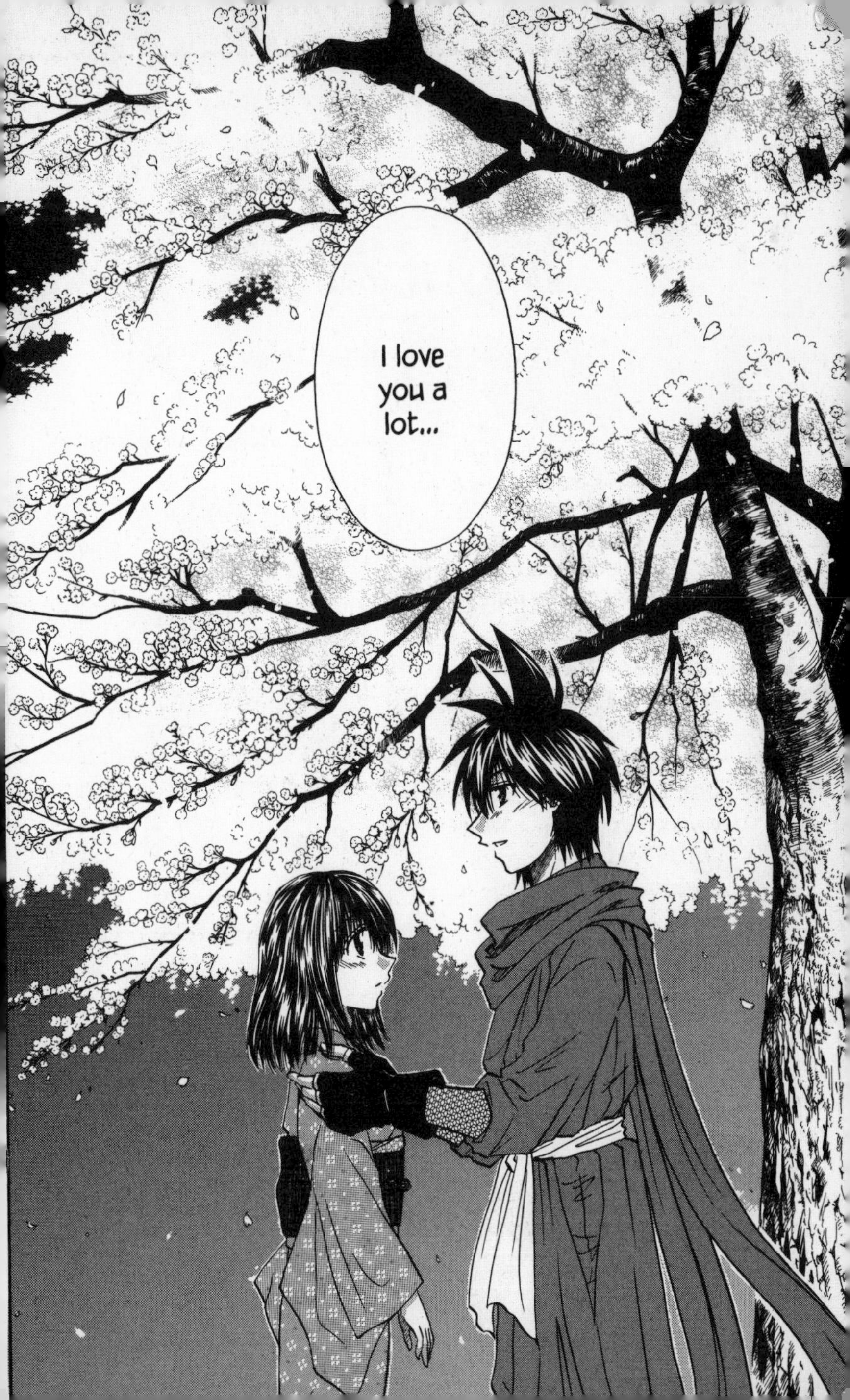
I love you a lot...

DRAGON EYE

BY KAIRI FUJIYAMA

HUMANITY'S SECRET WEAPON

Dracules—bloodthirsty, infectious monsters—have hunted human beings to the brink of extinction. Only the elite warriors of the VIUS Squad stand as humanity's last best hope.

Young Leila Mikami is one of the squad's most promising recruits, but she's not only training to battle the Dracules, she's determined to find the magical Dragon Eye, a weapon that will make her the most powerful warrior in the world.

Special extras in each volume! Read them all!

TOMARE!

[STOP!]

You are going the wrong way!

Manga is a completely different
type of reading experience.

To start at the *beginning*, go to the *end*!

That's right! Authentic manga is read the traditional Japanese
way—from right to left. Exactly the *opposite* of how American
books are read. It's easy to follow: Just go to the other end of
the book, and read each page—and each panel—from right side
to left side, starting at the top right. Now you're experiencing
manga as it was meant to be.